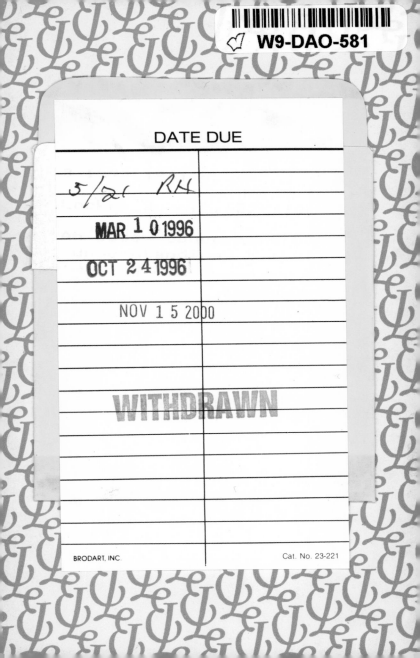

EVERYMAN'S LIBRARY

984

PHILOSOPHY

Everyman, I will go with thee, and be thy guide,
In thy most need to go by thy side

JOHN LOCKE, born 1632. Entered Christ Church, Oxford in 1652, where he received his M.A. in 1658. At Christ Church he was elected Student in 1658, Lecturer in Greek in 1660, Lecturer in Rhetoric in 1662, and Censor of Moral Philosophy, 1664. Physician and Secretary to Anthony Ashley Cooper (later Earl of Shaftesbury), 1667-81. Elected Fellow of the Royal Society, 1668. Secretary to the Lords Proprietors of Carolina, 1668-75. Secretary to the Council of Trade and Plantations, 1673-75. Deprived of his appointment to Christ Church by royal decree, 1684. Voluntary exile in Holland, 1683-89. Commissioner on the Board of Trade, 1696-1700. Died, 1704.

JOHN LOCKE

AN ESSAY CONCERNING
HUMAN UNDERSTANDING

IN TWO VOLUMES · VOLUME TWO

EDITED WITH
AN INTRODUCTION BY
JOHN W. YOLTON
*Professor of Philosophy in
the University of Maryland*

LONDON   J. M. DENT & SONS LTD
NEW YORK   E. P. DUTTON & CO INC

Set by Page & Thomas Ltd · Chesham
and
Printed in Great Britain
by the
Aldine Press · Letchworth · Herts
for
J. M. DENT & SONS LTD
Aldine House · Bedford Street · London
Abridged edition 1947
Complete two-volume edition 1961

CONTENTS

VOLUME TWO

BOOK III

OF WORDS

Analytical Contents   1

CHAPTER

   I. Of words or language in general   9

  II. Of the signification of words   11

 III. Of general terms   15

 IV. Of the names of simple ideas   26

   V. Of the names of mixed modes and relations   33

 VI. Of the names of substances   42

 VII. Of particles   72

VIII. Of abstract and concrete terms   74

 IX. Of the imperfection of words   76

   X. Of the abuse of words   89

 XI. Of the remedies of the foregoing imper-
      fections and abuses   106

BOOK IV

OF KNOWLEDGE AND OPINION

Analytical Contents   121

CHAPTER

   I. Of knowledge in general   133

  II. Of the degrees of our knowledge   138

 III. Of the extent of human knowledge   145

IV.	Of the reality of knowledge	166
V.	Of truth in general	176
VI.	Of universal propositions, their truth and certainty	181
VII.	Of maxims	192
VIII.	Of trifling propositions	208
IX.	Of our knowledge of existence	216
X.	Of our knowledge of the existence of a GOD	217
XI.	Of our knowledge of the existence of other things	228
XII.	Of the improvement of our knowledge	236
XIII.	Some further considerations concerning our knowledge	245
XIV.	Of judgment	247
XV.	Of probability	249
XVI.	Of the degrees of assent	252
XVII.	Of reason	262
XVIII.	Of faith and reason, and their distinct provinces	280
XIX.	Of enthusiasm	288
XX.	Of wrong assent, or error	296
XXI.	Of the division of the sciences	308
Index		311

THE ANALYTICAL CONTENTS

BOOK III

CHAPTER I

OF WORDS OR LANGUAGE IN GENERAL

SECTION
1. Man fitted to form articulate sounds 9
2. To make them signs of ideas 9
3–4. To make general signs 9
5. Words ultimately derived from such as signify sensible ideas 10
6. Distribution 11

CHAPTER II

OF THE SIGNIFICATION OF WORDS

SECTION
1. Words are sensible signs necessary for communication 11
2–3. Words are the sensible signs of his ideas who uses them 12
4. Words often secretly referred, first, to the ideas in other men's minds 13
5. Secondly, to the reality of things 13
6. Words by use readily excite ideas.. 14
7. Words often used without signification 14
8. Their signification perfectly arbitrary 14

CHAPTER III

OF GENERAL TERMS

SECTION
1. The greatest part of words general 15
2. For every particular thing to have a name is impossible 15
3. And useless 16
4. A distinct name for every particular not of great use for improvement of knowledge 16
5. What things have proper names 16
6–8. How general words are made 17

1

9. General natures are nothing but abstract ideas .. 18
10. Why the *genus* is ordinarily made use of in definitions 19
11. General and universal are creatures of the understanding 20
12. Abstract ideas are the essences of the *genera* and *species* 20
13. They are the workmanship of the understanding, but have their foundation in the similitude of things .. 21
14. Each distinct abstract idea is a distinct essence .. 22
15. Real and nominal essence 22
16. Constant connexion between the name and nominal essence 23
17. Supposition, that species are distinguished by their real essences, useless 23
18. Real and nominal essence, the same in simple ideas and modes, different in substances .. 24
19. Essences ingenerable and incorruptible 24
20. Recapitulation 25

CHAPTER IV

OF THE NAMES OF SIMPLE IDEAS

SECTION
1. Names of simple ideas, modes, and substances, have each something peculiar.. 26
2. First, Names of simple ideas and substances intimate real existence 26
3. Secondly, Names of simple ideas and modes signify always both real and nominal essence 26
4. Thirdly, Names of simple ideas undefinable .. 26
5. If all were definable, it would be a process *in infinitum* 27
6. What a definition is 27
7. Simple ideas, why undefinable 27
8–9. Instances motion 27
10. Light.. 28
11. Simple ideas why undefinable, further explained .. 29
12–13. The contrary shown in complex ideas by instances of a statue and rainbow 30
14. The names of complex ideas, when to be made intelligible by words 31
15. Fourthly, Names of simple ideas least doubtful .. 31
16. Fifthly, Simple ideas have few ascents *in linea praedicamentali* 32
17. Sixthly, Names of simple ideas stand for ideas not at all arbitrary 33

CHAPTER V

OF THE NAMES OF MIXED MODES AND RELATIONS

SECTION

1. They stand for abstract ideas, as other general names   33
2. First, The ideas they stand for are made by the understanding   33
3. Secondly, Made arbitrarily and without patterns   33
4. How this is done   34
5. Evidently arbitrary, in that the idea is often before the existence   34
6. Instances: murder, incest, stabbing   35
7. But still subservient to the end of language   36
8. Whereof the intranslatable words of divers languages are a proof   37
9. This shows species to be made for communication   38
10–11. In mixed modes, it is the name that ties the combination together and makes it a species   38
12. For the originals of mixed modes, we look no further than the mind, which also shows them to be the workmanship of the understanding   39
13. Their being made by the understanding without patterns shows the reason why they are so compounded   40
14. Names of mixed modes stand always for their real essences   40
15. Why their names are usually got before their ideas   40
16. Reason of my being so large on this subject   41

CHAPTER VI

OF THE NAMES OF SUBSTANCES

SECTION

1. The common names of substances stand for sorts   42
2. The essence of each sort is the abstract idea   43
3. The nominal and real essence different   43
4–6. Nothing essential to individuals   43
7–8. The nominal essence bounds the species   46
9. Not the real essence which we know not   47
10. Not substantial forms which we know less   48
11. That the nominal essence is that whereby we distinguish species, further evident from spirits   48
12. Whereof there are probably numberless species   49
13. The nominal essence that of the species, proved from water and ice   50

* 984

14–17. Difficulties against a certain number of real essences   51
18–20. Our nominal essences of substances not perfect col-
      lections of properties   51
  21. But such a collection as our names stand for   ..   52
  22. Our abstract ideas are to us the measures of species,
      instance in that of man   53
  23. Species not distinguished by generation   54
  24. Not by substantial forms   54
  25. The specific essences are made by the mind   ..   55
26–27. Therefore very various and uncertain   55
  28. But not so arbitrarily as mixed modes   ..   57
  29. Though very imperfect   58
  30. Which yet serves for common converse   59
  31. Essences of species under the same name, very different   60
  32. The more general our ideas are, the more incomplete
      and partial they are   61
  33. This all accommodated to the end of speech   ..   62
  34. Instance in cassowaries   62
  35. Men make the species, instance gold   63
36–37. Though nature make the similitude   63
  38. Each abstract idea is an essence   64
  39. *Genera* and *species*, in order to naming, instance watch   64
  40. Species of artificial things less confused than natural   66
  41. Artificial things of distinct species   66
  42. Substances alone have proper names   66
  43. Difficulty to treat of words with words   66
44–45. Instance of mixed modes in *kinneah* and *niouph*   67
46–47. Instance of substances in *zahab*   69
  48. Their ideas imperfect and therefore various   ..   70
  49. Therefore to fix their species, a real essence is supposed   70
  50. Which supposition is of no use   70
  51. Conclusion   71

CHAPTER VII

OF PARTICLES

SECTION
  1. Particles connect parts or whole sentences together ..   72
  2. In them consists the art of well speaking   72
3–4. They show what relation the mind gives to its own
    thoughts   72
  5. Instance in *but*   73
  6. This matter but lightly touched here   74

CHAPTER VIII

OF ABSTRACT AND CONCRETE TERMS

SECTION
1. Abstract terms not predicable one of another, and why　74
2. They show the difference of our ideas　..　　..　75

CHAPTER IX

OF THE IMPERFECTION OF WORDS

SECTION
1. Words are used for recording and communicating our thoughts　..　　..　　..　　..　　..　76
2. Any words will serve for recording　..　　..　76
3. Communication by words, civil or philosophical　..　76
4. The imperfection of words is the doubtfulness of their signification　..　　..　　..　　..　　..　77
5. Causes of their imperfection　..　　..　　..　77
6. The names of mixed modes doubtful. First, Because the ideas they stand for are so complex　..　　..　78
7. Secondly, Because they have no standards ..　　..　78
8. Propriety not a sufficient remedy ..　　..　　..　79
9. The way of learning these names contributes also to their doubtfulness　..　　..　　..　80
10. Hence unavoidable obscurity in ancient authors　..　81
11–12. Names of substances referred. First, to real essences that cannot be known　..　　..　　..　81
13–14. Secondly, to co-existing qualities which are known but imperfectly　..　　..　　..　　..　82
15. With this imperfection they may serve for civil, but not well for philosophical use　..　　..　　..　83
16. Instance liquor of nerves　..　　..　　..　84
17. Instance gold　..　　..　　..　　..　　..　85
18. The names of simple ideas, the least doubtful　..　86
19. And next to them simple modes ..　　..　　..　87
20. The most doubtful are the names of very compounded mixed modes and substances　..　　..　　..　87
21. Why this imperfection charged upon words　..　87
22–23. This should teach us moderation, in imposing our own sense of old authors　..　　..　　..　　..　88

CHAPTER X

OF THE ABUSE OF WORDS

SECTION
1. Abuse of words   89
2–3. *First,* Words without any or without clear ideas   ..   89
4. Occasioned by learning names before the ideas they belong to   90
5. *Secondly,* Unsteady application of them   91
6. *Thirdly,* Affected obscurity by wrong application   ..   92
7. Logic and dispute has much contributed to this   ..   92
8. Calling it subtilty   93
9. This learning very little benefits society   93
10. But destroys the instruments of knowledge and communication   94
11. As useful as to confound the sound of the letters   ..   94
12. This art has perplexed religion and justice   95
13. And ought not to pass for learning   95
14. *Fourthly,* Taking them for things   95
15. Instance in matter   96
16. This makes errors lasting   97
17. *Fifthly,* Setting them for what they cannot signify   ..   97
18. V.g. putting them for the real essences of substances ..   98
19. Hence we think every change of our idea in substances not to change the species   99
20. The cause of this abuse, a supposition of nature's working always regularly   99
21. This abuse contains two false suppositions   100
22. *Sixthly,* A supposition that words have a certain and evident signification   101
23. The ends of language. First, to convey our ideas   ..   102
24. Secondly, to do it with quickness..   102
25. Thirdly, therewith to convey the knowledge of things   103
26–31. How men's words fail in all these   103
32. How in substances   104
33. How in modes and relations   104
34. *Seventhly,* Figurative speech also an abuse of language   105

CHAPTER XI

OF THE REMEDIES OF THE FOREGOING IMPERFECTIONS AND ABUSES

SECTION
1. They are worth seeking   106

2. Are not easy 106
3. But yet necessary to philosophy 107
4. Misuse of words, the cause of great errors 107
5. Obstinacy 107
6. And wrangling.. 108
7. Instance bat and bird 108
8. First, Remedy to use no word without an idea .. 109
9. Secondly, To have distinct ideas annexed to them in modes 110
10. And distinct and conformable in substances .. 110
11. Thirdly, Propriety 111
12. Fourthly, To make known their meaning 111
13. And that three ways 112
14. First, in simple ideas by synonymous terms or showing 112
15. Secondly, in mixed modes by definition 112
16. Morality capable of demonstration 113
17. Definitions can make moral discourses clear .. 113
18. And is the only way 114
19. Thirdly, in substances, by showing and defining .. 114
20–21. Ideas of the leading qualities of substances are best got by showing 115
22. The ideas of their powers best by definition .. 116
23. A reflection on the knowledge of spirits 116
24. Ideas also of substances must be conformable to things 116
25. Not easy to be made so 117
26. Fifthly, By constancy in their signification 119
27. When the variation is to be explained 119

BOOK III

OF WORDS

CHAPTER I

OF WORDS OR LANGUAGE IN GENERAL

1.   GOD, having designed man for a sociable creature, made him not only with an inclination and under a necessity to have fellowship with those of his own kind, but furnished him also with language, which was to be the great instrument and common tie of society. *Man*, therefore, had by nature his organs so fashioned as to be *fit to frame articulate sounds*, which we call words.   But this was not enough to produce language; for parrots and several other birds will be taught to make articulate sounds distinct enough, which yet by no means are capable of language.

2.   Besides articulate sounds, therefore, it was further necessary that he should be *able to use these sounds as signs of internal conceptions*, and to make them stand as marks for the *ideas* within his own mind, whereby they might be made known to others, and the thoughts of men's minds be conveyed from one to another.

3.   But neither was this sufficient to make words so useful as they ought to be.   It is not enough for the perfection of language that sounds can be made signs of *ideas*, unless those *signs* can be so made use of as *to comprehend several particular things*: for the multiplication of words would have perplexed their use, had every particular thing need of a distinct name to be signified by.   To remedy this inconvenience, language had yet a further improvement in the use of general terms, whereby one word was made to mark a multitude of particular existences, which advantageous use of sounds was obtained only by the difference of the *ideas* they were made signs of: those names becoming general which are made to stand for general *ideas*, and those remaining particular where the *ideas* they are used for are particular.

4.   Besides these names which stand for *ideas*, there be other
words which men make use of, not to signify any *idea*, but the
want or absence of some *ideas*, simple or complex, or all *ideas*
together: such as are *nihil* in Latin, and in English, *ignorance* and
barrenness. All which negative or privative words cannot be said
properly to belong to or signify no *ideas*, for then they would be
perfectly insignificant sounds; but they relate to positive *ideas*,
and signify their absence.

5.   It may also lead us a little towards the original of all our
notions and knowledge, if we remark how great a dependence
our *words* have on common sensible *ideas*, and how those which
are made use of to stand for actions and notions quite removed
from sense *have their rise from thence, and from obvious sensible* ideas *are transferred to more abstruse significations*, and
made to stand for *ideas* that come not under the cognizance of
our senses: v.g. to *imagine, apprehend, comprehend, adhere, conceive, instil, disgust, disturbance, tranquillity*, etc., are all words
taken from the operations of sensible things, and applied to
certain modes of thinking. *Spirit*, in its primary signification,
is breath; *angel*, a messenger; and I doubt not but, if we could
trace them to their sources, we should find in all languages the
names, which stand for things that fall not under our senses, to
have had their first rise from sensible *ideas*. By which we may
give some kind of guess what kind of notions they were and
whence derived, which filled their minds who were the first
beginners of languages, and how nature, even in the naming of
things, unawares suggested to men the originals and principles
of all their knowledge: whilst, to give names that might make
known to others any operations they felt in themselves, or any
other *ideas* that came not under their senses, they were fain to
borrow words from ordinary known *ideas* of sensation, by that
means to make others the more easily to conceive those operations they experimented in themselves, which made no outward
sensible appearances; and then, when they had got known and
agreed names to signify those internal operations of their own
minds, they were sufficiently furnished to make known by words
all their other *ideas*, since they could consist of nothing but
either of outward sensible perceptions, or of the inward operations of their minds about them: we having, as has been proved,
no *ideas* at all, but what originally come either from sensible
objects without, or what we feel within ourselves, from the

inward workings of our own spirits, of which we are conscious to ourselves within.

6. But to understand better the use and force of language, as subservient to instruction and knowledge, it will be convenient to consider:

First, To what it is that names, in the use of language, are immediately applied.

Secondly, Since all (except proper) names are general, and so stand not particularly for this or that single thing, but for sorts and ranks of things, it will be necessary to consider in the next place what the sorts and kinds or, if you rather like the Latin names, *what the species and genera of things* are, wherein they consist, and how they come to be made. These being (as they ought) well looked into, we shall the better come to find the right use of words, the natural advantages and defects of language, and the remedies that ought to be used, to avoid the inconveniences of obscurity or uncertainty in the signification of words, without which it is impossible to discourse with any clearness or order concerning knowledge, which, being conversant about propositions, and those most commonly universal ones, has greater connexion with words than perhaps is suspected.

These considerations, therefore, shall be the matter of the following chapters.

CHAPTER II

OF THE SIGNIFICATION OF WORDS

1. MAN, though he have great variety of thoughts, and such from which others as well as himself might receive profit and delight, yet they are all within his own breast, invisible and hidden from others, nor can of themselves be made to appear. The comfort and advantage of society not being to be had without communication of thoughts, it was necessary that man should find out some external sensible signs whereby those invisible *ideas*, which his thoughts are made up of, might be made known to others. For this purpose nothing was so fit, either for plenty or quickness, as those articulate sounds which with so

much ease and variety he found himself able to make. Thus we may conceive how *words*, which were by nature so well adapted to that purpose, came to be made use of by men as *the signs of* their *ideas*: not by any natural connexion that there is between particular articulate sounds and certain *ideas*, for then there would be but one language amongst all men; but by a voluntary imposition whereby such a word is made arbitrarily the mark of such an *idea*. The use, then, of words is to be sensible marks of *ideas*, and the *ideas* they stand for are their proper and immediate signification.

2.   The use men have of these marks being either to record their own thoughts for the assistance of their own memory or, as it were, to bring out their *ideas* and lay them before the view of others: *words, in their primary or immediate signification, stand for nothing but the* ideas *in the mind of him that uses them*, how imperfectly soever or carelessly those *ideas* are collected from the things which they are supposed to represent. When a man speaks to another, it is that he may be understood; and the end of speech is that those sounds, as marks, may make known his *ideas* to the hearer. That then which words are the marks of are the *ideas* of the speaker; nor can anyone apply them as marks, immediately, to anything else but the *ideas* that he himself hath, for this would be to make them signs of his own conceptions and yet apply them to other *ideas*, which would be to make them signs and not signs of his *ideas* at the same time, and so in effect to have no signification at all. Words being voluntary signs, they cannot be voluntary signs imposed by him on things he knows not. That would be to make them signs of nothing, sounds without signification. A man cannot make his words the signs either of qualities in things or of conceptions in the mind of another, whereof he has none in his own. Till he has some *ideas* of his own, he cannot suppose them to correspond with the conceptions of another man; nor can he use any signs for them: for thus they would be the signs of he knows not what, which is in truth to be the signs of nothing. But when he represents to himself other men's *ideas* by some of his own, if he consent to give them the same names that other men do, it is still to his own *ideas*: to *ideas* that he has, and not to *ideas* that he has not.

3.   This is so necessary in the use of language that in this respect the knowing and the ignorant, the learned and unlearned

use the *words* they speak (with any meaning) all alike. They, *in every man's mouth, stand for the* ideas *he has,* and which he would express by them. A child having taken notice of nothing in the metal he hears called gold but the bright shining yellow colour, he applies the word gold only to his own *idea* of that colour and nothing else, and therefore calls the same colour in a peacock's tail gold. Another that hath better observed adds to shining yellow great weight, and then the sound gold, when he uses it, stands for a complex *idea* of a shining yellow and very weighty substance. Another adds to those qualities fusibility, and then the word gold to him signifies a body, bright, yellow, fusible, and very heavy. Another adds malleability. Each of these uses equally the word gold, when they have occasion to express the *idea* which they have applied it to; but it is evident that each can apply it only to his own *idea,* nor can he make it stand as a sign of such a complex *idea* as he has not.

4. But though words, as they are used by men, can properly and immediately signify nothing but the *ideas* that are in the mind of the speaker, yet they in their thoughts give them a secret reference to two other things.

First, they suppose their words to be marks of the ideas *in the minds also of other men, with whom they communicate:* for else they should talk in vain and could not be understood, if the sounds they applied to one *idea* were such as by the hearer were applied to another, which is to speak two languages. But in this, men stand not usually to examine whether the *idea* they and those they discourse with have in their minds be the same, but think it enough that they use the word as they imagine in the common acceptation of that language, in which they suppose that the *idea* they make it a sign of is precisely the same to which the understanding men of that country apply that name.

5. *Secondly,* because *men* would not be thought to talk *barely* of their own imaginations, but of things as really they are, therefore they *often suppose their words to stand also for the reality of things.* But this relating more particularly to substances and their names, as perhaps the former does to simple *ideas* and modes, we shall speak of these two different ways of applying words more at large, when we come to treat of the names of mixed modes and substances in particular: though give me leave here to say that it is a perverting the use of words, and brings unavoidable obscurity and confusion into their

signification, whenever we make them stand for anything but those *ideas* we have in our own minds.

6.   Concerning words also it is further to be considered: *First,* That they being immediately the signs of men's *ideas* and, by that means, the instruments whereby men communicate their conceptions and express to one another those thoughts and imaginations they have within their own breasts, *there comes by constant use* to be such *a connexion between certain sounds and the* ideas *they stand for* that the names heard almost as readily excite certain *ideas* as if the objects themselves, which are apt to produce them, did actually affect the senses.   Which is manifestly so in all obvious sensible qualities, and in all substances that frequently and familiarly occur to us.

7.   *Secondly,* That though the proper and immediate signification of words are *ideas* in the mind of the speaker, yet, because by familiar use from our cradles we come to learn certain articulate sounds very perfectly and have them readily on our tongues and always at hand in our memories, but yet are not always careful to examine or settle their significations pefectly, it *often* happens that *men,* even when they would apply themselves to an attentive consideration, do *set their thoughts more on words than things.*   Nay, because words are many of them learned before the *ideas* are known for which they stand: therefore some, not only children but men, speak several words no otherwise than parrots do, only because they have learned them and have been accustomed to those sounds.   But so far as words are of use and signification, so far is there a constant connexion between the sound and the *idea,* and a designation that the one stand for the other: without which application of them, they are nothing but so much insignificant noise.

8.   *Words,* by long and familiar use, as has been said, come to excite in men certain *ideas,* so constantly and readily that they are apt to suppose a natural connexion between them.   But that they *signify* only men's peculiar *ideas,* and that *by a perfectly arbitrary imposition,* is evident in that they often fail to excite in others (even that use the same language) the same *ideas* we take them to be the signs of; and every man has so inviolable a liberty to make words stand for what *ideas* he pleases that no one hath the power to make others have the same *ideas* in their minds that he has, when they use the same words that he does.   And therefore the great *Augustus* himself, in the possession of that power which

ruled the world, acknowledged he could not make a new Latin word, which was as much as to say that he could not arbitrarily appoint what *idea* any sound should be a sign of, in the mouths and common language of his subjects. It is true, common use, by a tacit consent, appropriates certain sounds to certain *ideas* in all languages, which so far limits the signification of that sound that, unless a man applies it to the same *idea*, he does not speak properly. And let me add that, unless a man's words excite the same *ideas* in the hearer which he makes them stand for in speaking, he does not speak intelligibly. But whatever be the consequence of any man's using of words differently, either from their general meaning or the particular sense of the person to whom he addresses them, this is certain: their signification, in his use of them, is limited to his *ideas*, and they can be signs of nothing else.

CHAPTER III

OF GENERAL TERMS

1. ALL things that exist being particulars, it may perhaps be thought reasonable that words, which ought to be conformed to things, should be so too, I mean in their signification, but yet we find the quite contrary. The far *greatest part of words* that make all languages *are general terms*: which has not been the effect of neglect or chance, but of reason and necessity.

2. *First, It is impossible that every particular thing should have a distinct peculiar name.* For, the signification and use of words depending on that connexion which the mind makes between its *ideas* and the sounds it uses as signs of them, it is necessary, in the application of names to things, that the mind should have distinct *ideas* of the things, and retain also the particular name that belongs to every one, with its peculiar appropriation to that *idea*. But it is beyond the power of human capacity to frame and retain distinct *ideas* of all the particular things we meet with: every bird and beast men saw, every tree and plant that affected the senses could not find a place in the most capacious understanding. If it be looked on as an instance of a prodigious memory that some generals have been able to call every soldier

in their army by his proper name, we may easily find a reason why men have never attempted to give names to each sheep in their flock or crow that flies over their heads, much less to call every leaf of plants or grain of sand that came in their way by a peculiar name.

3.   *Secondly*, If it were possible, *it would yet be useless*, because it would not serve to the chief end of language. Men would in vain heap up names of particular things, that would not serve them to communicate their thoughts. Men learn names and use them in talk with others only that they may be understood: which is then only done when, by use or consent, the sound I make by the organs of speech excites, in another man's mind who hears it, the *idea* I apply it to in mine when I speak it. This cannot be done by names applied to particular things, whereof I alone having the *ideas* in my mind, the names of them could not be significant or intelligible to another who was not acquainted with all those very particular things which had fallen under my notice.

4.   *Thirdly*, But yet granting this also feasible (which I think is not), yet *a distinct name for every particular thing would not be of any great use for the improvement of knowledge*, which, though founded in particular things, enlarges itself by general views, to which things reduced into sorts, under general names, are properly subservient. These, with the names belonging to them, come within some compass and do not multiply every moment, beyond what either the mind can contain or use requires. And therefore, in these, men have for the most part stopped, but yet not so as to hinder themselves from distinguishing particular things by appropriated names, where convenience demands it. And therefore in their own species, which they have most to do with and wherein they have often occasion to mention particular persons, they make use of proper names, and there distinct individuals have distinct denominations.

5.   Besides persons, countries also, cities, rivers, mountains, and other the like distinctions of place have usually found peculiar names, and that for the same reason: they being such as men have often an occasion to mark particularly and, as it were, set before others in their discourses with them. And I doubt not but, if we had reason to mention particular horses as often as we have to mention particular men, we should have *proper*

names for the one as familiar as for the other, and *Bucephalus* would be a word as much in use as *Alexander*. And therefore we see that, amongst jockeys, horses have their proper names to be known and distinguished by as commonly as their servants: because amongst them there is often occasion to mention this or that particular horse, when he is out of sight.

6. The next thing to be considered is *how general words come to be made*. For since all things that exist are only particulars, how come we by general terms, or where find we those general natures they are supposed to stand for? Words become general by being made the signs of general *ideas*; and *ideas* become general by separating from them the circumstances of time and place and any other *ideas* that may determine them to this or that particular existence. By this way of abstraction they are made capable of representing more individuals than one: each of which, having in it a conformity to that abstract *idea*, is (as we call it) of that sort.

7. But to deduce this a little more distinctly, it will not perhaps be amiss to trace our notions and names from their beginning and observe by what degrees we proceed and by what steps we enlarge our *ideas* from our first infancy. There is nothing more evident than that the *ideas* of the persons children converse with (to instance in them alone) are, like the persons themselves, only particular. The *ideas* of the nurse and the mother are well framed in their minds and, like pictures of them there, represent only those individuals. The names they first gave to them are confined to these individuals, and the names of *nurse* and *mamma* the child uses determine themselves to those persons. Afterwards, when time and a larger acquaintance have made them observe that there are a great many other things in the world that, in some common agreements of shape and several other qualities, resemble their father and mother and those persons they have been used to, they frame an *idea* which they find those many particulars do partake in, and to that they give, with others, the name *man*, for example. And *thus they come to have a general name*, and a general *idea*. Wherein they make nothing new, but only leave out of the complex *idea* they had of *Peter* and *James*, *Mary* and *Jane* that which is peculiar to each, and retain only what is common to them all.

8. By the same way that they come by the general name and *idea* of *man*, they easily *advance to more general names* and

notions.   For, observing that several things that differ from
their *idea* of *man* and cannot therefore be comprehended under
that name have yet certain qualities wherein they agree with
man, by retaining only those qualities and uniting them into one
idea, they have again another and more general *idea*, to which,
having given a name, they make a term of a more comprehensive
extension: which new *idea* is made, not by any new addition,
but only as before, by leaving out the shape and some other
properties signified by the name *man*, and retaining only a
body, with life, sense, and spontaneous motion, comprehended
under the name *animal*.

9.   That this is the *way whereby men first formed general*
ideas, *and general names to them*, I think is so evident that there
needs no other proof of it but the considering of a man's self, or
others, and the ordinary proceedings of their minds in knowledge; and he that thinks general natures or notions are anything else but such abstract and partial *ideas* of more complex
ones, taken at first from particular existences, will I fear be at a
loss where to find them.   For let anyone reflect and then tell me
wherein does his *idea* of *man* differ from that of *Peter* and *Paul*,
or his *idea* of *horse* from that of *Bucephalus*, but in the leaving
out something that is peculiar to each individual, and retaining
so much of those particular complex *ideas* of several particular
existences as they are found to agree in.   Of the complex *ideas*
signified by the names *man* and *horse*, leaving out but those
particulars wherein they differ, and retaining only those wherein
they agree, and of those making a new distinct complex *idea*, and
giving the name *animal* to it, one has a more general term that
comprehends with man several other creatures.   Leave out of
the *idea* of *animal* sense and spontaneous motion, and the remaining complex *idea*, made up of the remaining simple ones of
body, life, and nourishment, becomes a more general one, under
the more comprehensive term, *vivens*.   And not to dwell longer
upon this particular, so evident in itself, by the same way the
mind proceeds to *body*, *substance*, and at last to *being*, *thing*, and
such universal terms which stand for any of our *ideas* whatsoever.   To conclude: this whole *mystery* of *genera* and *species*,
which make such a noise in the schools and are with justice so
little regarded out of them, is nothing else but abstract *ideas*,
more or less comprehensive, with names annexed to them.   In all
which, this is constant and unvariable: that every more general

term stands for such an *idea* as is but a part of any of those contained under it.

10. This may show us the reason *why, in the defining of words,* which is nothing but declaring their signification, *we make use of the genus,* or next general word that comprehends it. Which is not out of necessity, but only to save the labour of enumerating the several simple *ideas* which the next general word or *genus* stands for, or, perhaps, sometimes the shame of not being able to do it. But though defining by *genus* and *differentia* (I crave leave to use these terms of art, though originally Latin, since they most properly suit those notions they are applied to) I say, though defining by the *genus* be the shortest way, yet I think it may be doubted whether it be the best. This I am sure, it is not the only, and so not absolutely necessary. For, definition being nothing but making another understand by words what *idea* the term defined stands for, a definition is best made by enumerating those simple *ideas* that are combined in the signification of the term defined; and if, instead of such an enumeration, men have accustomed themselves to use the next general term, it has not been out of necessity or for greater clearness, but for quickness and dispatch sake. For I think that, to one who desired to know what *idea* the word *man* stood for, if it should be said that *man* was a solid extended substance, having life, sense, spontaneous motion, and the faculty of reasoning, I doubt not but the meaning of the term *man* would be as well understood, and the *idea* it stands for be at least as clearly made known, as when it is defined to be a *rational animal*; which, by the several definitions of *animal*, *vivens*, and *corpus*, resolves itself into those enumerated *ideas*. I have, in explaining the term *man*, followed here the ordinary definition of the schools, which, though perhaps not the most exact, yet serves well enough to my present purpose. And one may, in this instance, see what gave occasion to the rule that a definition must consist of *genus* and *differentia*; and it suffices to show us the little necessity there is of such a rule, or advantage in the strict observing of it. For definitions, as has been said, being only the explaining of one word by several others so that the meaning or *idea* it stands for may be certainly known, languages are not always so made according to the rules of logic that every term can have its signification exactly and clearly expressed by two others. Experience sufficiently satisfies us to the contrary, or else those who have made

this rule have done ill, that they have given us so few definitions conformable to it. But of definitions, more in the next chapter.

11.   To return to general words: it is plain, by what has been said, that *general* and *universal* belong not to the real existence of things, but *are the inventions* and *creatures of the understanding*, made by it for its own use, *and concern only signs*, whether words or *ideas*. Words are general, as has been said, when used for signs of general *ideas*, and so are applicable indifferently to many particular things; and *ideas* are general when they are set up as the representatives of many particular things: but universality belongs not to things themselves, which are all of them particular in their existence, even those words and *ideas* which in their signification are general.   When therefore we quit particulars, the generals that rest are only creatures of our own making: their general nature being nothing but the capacity they are put into, by the understanding, of signifying or representing many particulars.   For the signification they have is nothing but a relation that, by the mind of man, is added to them.

12.   The next thing therefore to be considered is *what kind of signification it is that general words have*.   For, as it is evident that they do not signify barely one particular thing, for then they would not be general terms but proper names, so on the other side it is as evident they do not signify a plurality, for man and men would then signify the same, and the distinction of numbers (as grammarians call them) would be superfluous and useless.   That then which general words signify is a *sort* of things, and each of them does that by being a sign of an abstract *idea* in the mind; to which *idea*, as things existing are found to agree, so they come to be ranked under that name or, which is all one, be of that sort.   Whereby it is evident that the *essences* of the *sorts or* (if the Latin word pleases better) *species* of things are nothing else but these abstract *ideas*.   For, the having the essence of any species being that which makes any thing to be of that species, and the conformity to the *idea* to which the name is annexed being that which gives a right to that name, the having the essence and the having that conformity must needs be the same thing, since to be of any species and to have a right to the name of that species is all one.   As for example, to be a *man* or of the species *man* and to have right to the name *man* is the same thing.   Again, to be a *man* or of the same species *man* and have the essence of a *man* is the same thing.   Now, since nothing

can be a *man* or have a right to the name *man* but what has a conformity to the abstract *idea* the name *man* stand for, nor
anything be a man or have a right to the species *man* but what
has the essence of that species, it follows that the abstract *idea*
for which the name stands and the essence of the species is one
and the same. From whence it is easy to observe that the
essences of the sorts of things and, consequently, the sorting of
things is the workmanship of the understanding that abstracts
and makes those general *ideas*.

13. I would not here be thought to forget, much less to deny,
that nature, in the production of things, makes several of them
alike: there is nothing more obvious, especially in the races of
animals, and all things propagated by seed. But yet I think we
may say the *sorting* of them under names *is the workmanship of
the understanding, taking occasion, from the similitude* it observes amongst them, to make abstract general *ideas*, and set
them up in the mind, with names annexed to them, as patterns or
forms (for in that sense the word form has a very proper signification), to which, as particular things existing are found to agree,
so they come to be of that species, have that denomination, or are
put into that *classis*. For when we say: this is a *man*, that a *horse*;
this *justice*, that *cruelty*; this a *watch*, that a *jack*, what do we
else but rank things under different specific names as agreeing
to those abstract *ideas* of which we have made those names the
signs? And what are the essences of those species, set out and
marked by names, but those abstract ideas in the mind, which
are, as it were, the bonds between particular things that exist
and the names they are to be ranked under? And when general
names have any connexion with particular beings, these abstract
ideas are the *medium* that unites them: so that the essences of
species, as distinguished and denominated by us, neither are
nor can be anything but those precise abstract *ideas* we have in
our minds. And therefore the supposed real essences of substances, if different from our abstract *ideas*, cannot be the
essences of the species we rank things into. For two species may
be one, as rationally as two different essences be the essence of
one species; and I demand, What are the alterations which may
or may not be made in a *horse* or *lead*, without making either of
them to be of another species? In determining the species of
things by our abstract *ideas*, this is easy to resolve; but if anyone will regulate himself herein by supposed real essences, he

will, I suppose, be at a loss, and he will never be able to know when any thing precisely ceases to be of the species of a *horse* or *lead*.
14.   Nor will anyone wonder that I say these *essences* or abstract *ideas* (which are the measures of name and the boundaries of species) are *the workmanship of the understanding*, who considers that at least the complex ones are often, in several men, different collections of simple *ideas*, and therefore that is *covetousness* to one man which is not so to another.   Nay, even in substances, where their abstract *ideas* seem to be taken from the things themselves, they are not constantly the same; no, not in that species which is most familiar to us and with which we have the most intimate acquaintance, it having been more than once doubted whether the *foetus* born of a woman were a *man*, even so far as that it hath been debated whether it were or were not to be nourished and baptized: which it could not be if the abstract *idea* or essence to which the name man belonged were of nature's making, and were not the uncertain and various collection of simple *ideas* which the understanding puts together, and then abstracting it, affixed a name to it.   So that in truth *every distinct abstract* idea *is a distinct essence*, and the names that stand for such distinct *ideas* are the names of things essentially different.   Thus a circle is as essentially different from an oval as a sheep from a goat, and rain is as essentially different from snow as water from earth, that abstract *idea* which is the essence of one being impossible to be communicated to the other.   And thus any two abstract *ideas* that in any part vary one from another, with two distinct names annexed to them, constitute two distinct sorts or, if you please, *species*, as essentially different as any two the most remote or opposite in the world.
15.   But since the *essences* of things are thought by some (and not without reason) to be wholly unknown, it may not be amiss to consider the *several significations of the word essence*.

First, Essence may be taken for the being of anything whereby it is what it is.   And thus the real internal, but generally (in substances) unknown, constitution of things, whereon their discoverable qualities depend, may be called their *essence*. This is the proper original signification of the word, as is evident from the formation of it: *essentia*, in its primary notation, signifying properly *being*.   And in this sense it is still used, when we speak of the *essence* of particular things, without giving them any name.

Secondly, The learning and disputes of the Schools having been much busied about *genus* and *species*, the word *essence* has almost lost its primary signification and, instead of the real constitution of things, has been almost wholly applied to the artificial constitution of *genus* and *species*. It is true, there is ordinarily supposed a real constitution of the sorts of things, and it is past doubt there must be some real constitution on which any collection of simple *ideas* co-existing must depend. But, it being evident that things are ranked under names into sorts or *species*, only as they agree to certain abstract *ideas* to which we have annexed those names, the *essence* of each *genus* or sort comes to be nothing but that abstract *idea* which the general or *sortal* (if I may have leave so to call it from *sort*, as I do *general* from *genus*) name stands for. And this we shall find to be that which the word *essence* imports in its most familiar use. These two sorts of *essences*, I suppose, may not unfitly be termed the one the *real*, the other the *nominal essence*.

16. *Between the nominal essence and the name* there is so *near a connexion* that the name of any sort of things cannot be attributed to any particular being but what has this *essence*, whereby it answers that abstract *idea* whereof that name is the sign.

17. Concerning the real essences of corporeal substances (to mention those only) there are, if I mistake not, two opinions. The one is of those who, using the word *essence* for they know not what, suppose a certain number of those essences, according to which all natural things are made and wherein they do exactly every one of them partake, and so become of this or that *species*. The other and more rational opinion is of those who look on all natural things to have a real, but unknown, constitution of their insensible parts, from which flow those sensible qualities which serve us to distinguish them one from another, according as we have occasion to rank them into sorts, under common denominations. The former of these opinions, which supposes these *essences* as a certain number of forms or moulds wherein all natural things that exist are cast and do equally partake, has, I imagine, very much perplexed the knowledge of natural things. The frequent productions of monsters in all the species of animals, and of changelings, and other strange issues of human birth carry with them difficulties not possible to consist with this *hypothesis*, since it is as impossible that two things

partaking exactly of the same real *essence* should have different properties, as that two figures partaking of the same real *essence* of a circle should have different properties. But were there no other reason against it, yet the *supposition of essences that cannot be known* and the making them, nevertheless, to be that which distinguishes the species of things *is* so *wholly useless* and unserviceable to any part of our knowledge that that alone were sufficient to make us lay it by and content ourselves with such *essences* of the sorts or species of things as come within the reach of our knowledge: which, when seriously considered, will be found, as I have said, to be nothing else but those abstract complex *ideas* to which we have annexed distinct general names.

18. *Essences* being thus distinguished into *nominal and real*, we may further observe that, *in* the species of *simple* ideas *and modes*, they *are always the same*, but *in substances always quite different*. Thus, a figure including a space between three lines is the real as well as nominal *essence* of a triangle, it being not only the abstract *idea* to which the general name is annexed, but the very *essentia* or being of the thing itself, that foundation from which all its properties flow, and to which they are all inseparably annexed. But it is far otherwise concerning that parcel of matter which makes the ring on my finger, wherein these two *essences* are apparently different. For it is the real constitution of its insensible parts, on which depend all those properties of colour, weight, fusibility, fixedness, etc., which makes it to be *gold* or gives it a right to that name which is therefore its nominal *essence*, since nothing can be called *gold* but what has a conformity of qualities to that abstract complex *idea* to which that name is annexed. But this distinction of *essences* belonging particularly to substances, we shall, when we come to consider their names, have an occasion to treat of more fully.

19. That such *abstract* ideas, *with names to them*, as we have been speaking of, *are essences* may further appear by what we are told concerning *essences*, viz. that they are all ingenerable and incorruptible. Which cannot be true of the real constitutions of things which begin and perish with them. All things that exist, besides their Author, are all liable to change, especially those things we are acquainted with, and have ranked into bands under distinct names or ensigns. Thus, that which was grass today is

tomorrow the flesh of a sheep, and, within a few days after, becomes part of a man: in all which and the like changes, it is evident their real *essence*, i.e. that constitution whereon the properties of these several things depended, is destroyed and perishes with them. But *essences* being taken for *ideas* established in the mind, with names annexed to them, they are supposed to remain steadily the same, whatever mutations the particular substances are liable to. For whatever becomes of *Alexander* and *Bucephalus*, the *ideas* to which *man* and *horse* are annexed are supposed, nevertheless, to remain in the same; and so the *essences* of those species are preserved whole and undestroyed, whatever changes happen to any or all of the individuals of those *species*. By this means the *essence* of a *species* rests safe and entire without the existence of so much as one individual of that kind. For were there now no circle existing anywhere in the world (as, perhaps, that figure exists not anywhere exactly marked out), yet the *idea* annexed to that name would not cease to be what it is, nor cease to be as a pattern to determine which of the particular figures we meet with have or have not a right to the name *circle*, and so to show which of them, by having that essence, was of that *species*. And though there neither were nor had been in nature such a beast as an *unicorn* nor such a fish as a *mermaid*, yet, supposing those names to stand for complex abstract *ideas* that contained no inconsistency in them, the *essence* of a *mermaid* is as intelligible as that of a *man*, and the *idea* of an *unicorn* as certain, steady, and permanent as that of a horse. From what has been said, it is evident that the doctrine of the immutability of *essences* proves them to be only abstract *ideas*, and is founded on the relation established between them and certain sounds as signs of them, and will always be true as long as the same name can have the same signification.

20.   To conclude, this is that which in short I would say, viz. that all the great business of *genera* and *species* and their *essences* amounts to no more but this: that men, making abstract *ideas* and settling them in their minds with names annexed to them, do thereby enable themselves to consider things and discourse of them, as it were in bundles, for the easier and readier improvement and communication of their knowledge, which would advance but slowly were their words and thoughts confined only to particulars.

CHAPTER IV

OF THE NAMES OF SIMPLE IDEAS

1.   THOUGH all words, as I have shown, signify nothing immediately but the *ideas* in the mind of the speaker, yet upon a
nearer survey we shall find that the *names of simple* ideas, *mixed
modes* (under which I comprise relations too) *and natural substances have each of them something peculiar* and different from
the other. For example:

2.   *First*, The *names of simple* ideas *and substances*, with the
abstract *ideas* in the mind which they immediately signify,
intimate also *some real existence* from which was derived their
original pattern. But the *names of mixed modes terminate in the
idea* that is in the mind and lead not the thoughts any further, as
we shall see more at large in the following chapter.

3.   *Secondly*, The *names of simple* ideas *and modes signify
always the real as well as nominal essence of their species.* But *the
names of natural substances signify* rarely, if ever, anything but
barely the nominal essences of those species, as we shall show in
the chapter that treats of the names of substances in particular.

4.   *Thirdly*, The *names of simple* ideas *are not capable of any
definitions*; the names of all complex *ideas* are. It has not, that I
know, hitherto been taken notice of, by anybody, what words
are and what are not capable of being defined: the want whereof
is (as I am apt to think) not seldom the occasion of great
wrangling and obscurity in men's discourses, whilst some
demand definitions of terms that cannot be defined, and others
think they ought to rest satisfied in an explication made by a
more general word and its restriction (or to speak in terms of art
by a genus and difference), when, even after such definition
made according to rule, those who hear it have often no more a
clear conception of the meaning of the word than they had
before. This at least I think, that the showing what words are
and what are not capable of definitions and wherein consists a
good definition is not wholly besides our present purpose, and
perhaps will afford so much light to the nature of these signs and
our *ideas* as to deserve a more particular consideration.

5. I will not here trouble myself to prove that all terms are not definable from that progress *in infinitum* which it will visibly lead us into, if we should allow that all names could be defined. For if the terms of one definition were still to be defined by another, where at last should we stop? But I shall from the nature of our *ideas* and the signification of our words show *why some names can, and others cannot be defined,* and which they are.

6. I think it is agreed that *a definition is* nothing else but *the showing the meaning of one word by several other not synonymous terms.* The meaning of words being only the *ideas* they are made to stand for by him that uses them, the meaning of any term is then shown or the word is defined when, by other words, the *idea* it is made the sign of and annexed to, in the mind of the speaker, is as it were represented or set before the view of another, and thus its signification ascertained: this is the only use and end of definitions, and therefore the only measure of what is or is not a good definition.

7. This being premised, I say that *the names of simple* ideas, and those only, *are incapable of being defined.* The reason whereof is this, that the several terms of a definition signifying several *ideas*, they can all together by no means represent an *idea* which has no composition at all; and therefore a definition which is properly nothing but the showing the meaning of one word by several others, not signifying each the same thing, can in the names of simple *ideas* have no place.

8. The not observing this difference in our *ideas* and their names has produced that eminent trifling in the Schools, which is so easy to be observed in the definitions they give us of some few of these simple *ideas.* For, as to the greatest part of them, even those masters of definitions were fain to leave them untouched, merely by the impossibility they found in it. What more exquisite *jargon* could the wit of man invent than this definition, *The act of a being in power, as far forth as in power,* which would puzzle any rational man, to whom it was not already known by its famous absurdity, to guess what word it could ever be supposed to be the explication of. If *Tully,* asking a *Dutchman* what *beweging* was, should have received this explication in his own language, that it was *Actus entis in potentia quatenus in potentia,* I ask whether anyone can imagine he could thereby have understood what the word *beweging*

signified or have guessed what *idea* a *Dutchman* ordinarily had in his mind and would signify to another when he used that sound.

9.   Nor have the modern philosophers, who have endeavoured to throw off the *jargon* of the Schools and speak intelligibly, much better succeeded in defining simple *ideas,* whether by explaining their causes or any otherwise.   The *atomists,* who define motion to be a *passage from one place to another,* what do they more than put one synonymous word for another?   For what is *passage* other than *motion*?   And if they were asked what passage was, how would they better define it than by *motion*? For is it not at least as proper and significant to say *passage is a motion from one place to another* as to say *motion is a passage,* etc. This is to translate and not to define, when we change two words of the same signification one for another; which, when one is better understood than the other, may serve to discover what *idea* the unknown stands for, but is very far from a *definition,* unless we will say every English word in the dictionary is the definition of the Latin word it answers, and that motion is a definition of *motus.   Nor will the successive application of the parts of the* superficies *of one body to those of another,* which the *Cartesians* give us, prove a much better definition of motion when well examined.

10.   *The act of perspicuous, as far forth as perspicuous* is another peripatetic definition of a simple *idea,* which, though not more absurd than the former of *motion,* yet betrays its uselessness and insignificancy more plainly, because experience will easily convince anyone that it cannot make the meaning of the word *light* (which it pretends to define) at all understood by a blind man; but the definition of *motion* appears not at first sight so useless, because it escapes this way of trial.   For this simple *idea* entering by the touch as well as sight, it is impossible to show an example of anyone who has no other way to get the *idea* of *motion* but barely by the definition of that name.   Those who tell us that *light* is a great number of little globules, striking briskly on the bottom of the eye, speak more intelligibly than the Schools; but yet these words never so well understood would make the *idea* the word *light* stands for no more known to a man that understands it not before, than if one should tell him that *light* was nothing but a company of little tennis-balls which fairies all day long struck with rackets against some men's foreheads, whilst

they passed by others. For granting this explication of the thing to be true, yet the *idea* of the cause of *light*, if we had it never so exact, would no more give us the *idea* of *light* itself as it is such a particular perception in us than the *idea* of the figure and motion of a sharp piece of steel would give us the *idea* of that pain which it is able to cause in us. For the cause of any sensation and the sensation itself, in all the simple *ideas* of one sense, are two *ideas*, and two *ideas* so different and distant one from another that no two can be more so. And therefore should *Descartes's* globules strike never so long on the *retina* of a man who was blind by a *gutta serena*, he would thereby never have any *idea* of *light* or anything approaching to it, though he understood what little globules were and what striking on another body was never so well. And therefore the *Cartesians* very well distinguish between that light which is the cause of that sensation in us, and the *idea* which is produced in us by it and is that which is properly light.

11. *Simple ideas*, as has been shown, *are only* to be *got by* those *impressions* objects themselves make on our minds, by the proper inlets appointed to each sort. If they are not received this way, all the *words* in the world, *made use of to explain or define any of their names, will never be able to produce in us the* idea *it stands for*. For words, being sounds, can produce in us no other simple *ideas* than of those very sounds, nor excite any in us but by that voluntary connexion which is known to be between them and those simple *ideas* which common use has made them signs of. He that thinks otherwise, let him try if any words can give him the taste of a pineapple and make him have the true *idea* of the relish of that celebrated delicious fruit. So far as he is told it has a resemblance with any tastes whereof he has the *ideas* already in his memory, imprinted there by sensible objects, not strangers to his palate, so far may he approach that resemblance in his mind. But this is not giving us that *idea* by a *definition*, but exciting in us other simple *ideas* by their known names, which will be still very different from the true taste of that fruit itself. In light and colours and all other simple *ideas*, it is the same thing, for the signification of sounds is not natural, but only imposed and arbitrary. And no definition of *light* or *redness* is more fitted or able to produce either of those *ideas* in us than the sound *light* or *red* by itself. For to hope to produce an *idea* of light or colour by a sound, however formed, is to

expect that sounds should be visible or colours audible, and to
make the ears do the office of all the other senses. Which is all
one as to say that we might taste, smell, and see by the ears: a
sort of philosophy worthy only of *Sancho Pança*, who had the
faculty to see *Dulcinea* by hearsay. And therefore he that has
not before received into his mind, by the proper inlet, the simple
idea which any word stands for can never come to know the
signification of that word by any other words or sounds, whatsoever put together according to any rules of definition. The
only way is by applying to his senses the proper object, and so
producing that *idea* in him for which he has learned the name
already. A studious blind man, who had mightily beat his head
about visible objects and made use of the explication of his
books and friends to understand those names of light and colours
which often came in his way, bragged one day that he now understood what *scarlet* signified. Upon which, his friend demanding
what *scarlet* was, the blind man answered it was like the sound
of a trumpet. Just such an understanding of the name of any
other simple *idea* will he have who hopes to get it only from a
definition or other words made use of to explain it.

12. The case is quite otherwise *in complex ideas*; which consisting of several simple ones, it is in the power of words, standing for the several *ideas* that make that composition, to imprint
complex *ideas* in the mind which were never there before, and
so make their names be understood. In such collections of *ideas*
passing under one name, *definition* or the teaching the signification of one word by several others has place and *may make
us understand the names* of things which never came within the
reach of our senses, and frame *ideas* suitable to those in other
men's minds when they use those names, provided that none of
the terms of the definition stand for any such simple *ideas* which
he to whom the explication is made has never yet had in his
thought. Thus the word *statue* may be explained to a blind man
by other words, when *picture* cannot, his senses having given
him the *idea* of figure but not of colours, which therefore words
cannot excite in him. This gained the prize to the painter
against the statuary, each of which contending for the excellency
of his art, and the statuary bragging that his was to be preferred
because it reached further, and even those who had lost their
eyes could yet perceive the excellency of it. The painter agreed
to refer himself to the judgment of a blind man, who being

brought where there was a statue made by the one and a picture
drawn by the other, he was first led to the statue, in which he
traced with his hands all the lineaments of the face and body,
and with great admiration applauded the skill of the workman.
But being led to the picture, and having his hands laid upon it,
was told that now he touched the head and then the forehead,
eyes, nose, etc., as his hand moved over the parts of the picture
on the cloth, without finding any the least distinction: where-
upon he cried out that certainly that must needs be a very
admirable and divine piece of workmanship which could represent to them all those parts where he could neither feel nor
perceive anything.

13.   He that should use the word *rainbow* to one who knew all
those colours but yet had never seen that *phenomenon* would, by
enumerating the figure, largeness, position, and order of the
colours, so well define that word that it might be perfectly
understood.   But yet that *definition*, how exact and perfect
soever, would never make a blind man understand it, because
several of the simple *ideas* that make that complex one being
such as he never received by sensation and experience, no
words are able to excite them in his mind.

14.   Simple *ideas*, as has been shown, can only be got by experience from those objects which are proper to produce in us
those perceptions.   *When*, by this means, we have our minds
stored with them and know the names for them, then *we are in
a condition to define* and by *definition* to understand the names
of complex *ideas* that are made up of them.   But when any
term stands for a simple *idea* that a man has never yet had in
his mind, it is impossible, by any words, to make known its
meaning to him.   When any term stands for an *idea* a man is
acquainted with but is ignorant that that term is the sign of it,
there another name of the same *idea*, which he has been accustomed to, may make him understand its meaning. But in no case
whatsoever is any name of any simple *idea* capable of a
definition.

15.   *Fourthly*, But though the names of *simple ideas* have not
the help of *definition* to determine their signification, yet that
hinders not but that they *are generally less doubtful and uncertain than those of mixed modes and substances*; because, they
standing only for one simple perception, men for the most part
easily and perfectly agree in their signification, and there is little

room for mistake and wrangling about their meaning. He that knows once that whiteness is the name of that colour he has observed in snow or milk will not be apt to misapply that word, as long as he retains that *idea*; which when he has quite lost, he is not apt to mistake the meaning of it but perceives he understands it not. There is neither a multiplicity of simple *ideas* to be put together, which makes the doubtfulness in the names of mixed modes, nor a supposed but an unknown real essence with properties depending thereon, the precise number whereof are also unknown, which makes the difficulty in the names of substances. But on the contrary, in simple *ideas*, the whole signification of the name is known at once and consists not of parts, whereof more or less being put in, the *idea* may be varied and so the signification of its name be obscure or uncertain.

16. *Fifthly*, This further may be observed concerning *simple* ideas and their names: that they *have but few ascents in linea praedicamentali* (as they call it), *from the lowest species to the summum genus*. The reason whereof is that, the lowest species being but one simple *idea*, nothing can be left out of it that, so the difference being taken away, it may agree with some other thing in one *idea* common to them both, which, having one name, is the *genus* of the other two: v.g. there is nothing can be left out of the *idea* of white and red to make them agree in one common appearance, and so have one general name: as *rationality*, being left out of the complex *idea* of *man*, makes it agree with brute in the more general *idea* and name of *animal*. And therefore when, to avoid unpleasant enumerations, men would comprehend both *white* and *red*, and several other such simple *ideas* under one general name, they have been fain to do it by a word which denotes only the way they get into the mind. For when *white*, *red*, and *yellow* are all comprehended under the *genus* or name *colour*, it signifies no more but such *ideas* as are produced in the mind only by the sight and have entrance only through the eyes. And when they would frame yet a more general term to comprehend both *colours* and *sounds* and the like simple *ideas*, they do it by a word that signifies all such as come into the mind only by one sense; and so the general term *quality*, in its ordinary acceptation, comprehends colours, sounds, tastes, smells, and tangible qualities, with distinction from extension, number, motion, pleasure, and pain, which

make impressions on the mind and introduce their *ideas* by more senses than one.

17.   *Sixthly*, The names of simple *ideas*, substances, and mixed modes have also this difference: that those *of mixed modes* stand for *ideas* perfectly *arbitrary*; those *of substances* are not perfectly so but *refer to a pattern, though with some latitude; and those of simple* ideas *are* perfectly taken from the existence of things and are *not arbitrary at all*. Which, what difference it makes in the significations of their names, we shall see in the following chapters.

The names of simple modes differ little from those of simple *ideas*.

Chapter V

OF THE NAMES OF MIXED MODES AND RELATIONS

1.   The names of mixed modes being general, they stand, as has been shown, for sorts or species of things, each of which has its peculiar essence. The essences of these species also, as has been shown, are nothing but the abstract *ideas* in the mind, to which the name is annexed. Thus far the names and essences of mixed modes have nothing but what is common to them with other *ideas*; but if we take a little nearer survey of them, we shall find that they have something peculiar, which perhaps may deserve our attention.

2.   The first particularity I shall observe in them is that the abstract *ideas* or, if you please, the essences of the several species *of mixed modes are made by the understanding*, wherein they differ from those of simple *ideas*; in which sort the mind has no power to make any one, but only receives such as are presented to it by the real existence of things operating upon it.

3.   In the next place, these *essences of the species of mixed modes are* not only *made* by the mind, but made *very arbitrarily*, made with patterns, or reference to any real existence. Wherein they differ from those of substances, which carry with them the supposition of some real being, from which they are taken, and to which they are conformable. But, in its complex *ideas* of mixed modes, the mind takes a liberty not to follow the existence

of things exactly. It unites and retains certain collections, as so many distinct specific *ideas*; whilst others, that as often occur in nature and are as plainly suggested by outward things, pass neglected, without particular names or specifications. Nor does the mind, in these of mixed modes, as in the complex *ideas* of substances, examine them by the real existence of things, or verify them by patterns containing such peculiar compositions in nature. To know whether his *idea* of *adultery* or *incest* be right will a man seek it anywhere amongst things existing? Or is it true because anyone has been witness to such an action? No; but it suffices here that men have put together such a collection into one complex *idea* that makes the *archetype* and specific *idea*, whether ever any such action were committed *in rerum natura* or no.

4. To understand this aright, we must consider *wherein this making of these complex* ideas *consists*; and that is not in the making any new *idea*, but putting together those which the mind had before. Wherein the mind does these three things: first, it chooses a certain number. Secondly, it gives them connexion, and makes them into one *idea*. Thirdly, it ties them together by a name. If we examine how the mind proceeds in these and what liberty it takes in them, we shall easily observe how these essences of the species of mixed modes are the workmanship of the mind and, consequently, that the species themselves are of men's making.

5. Nobody can doubt but that these *ideas* of mixed modes are made by a voluntary collection of *ideas* put together in the mind, independent from any original patterns in nature, who will but reflect that this sort of complex *ideas* may be made, abstracted, and have names given them, and so a species be constituted, before any one individual of that species ever existed. Who can doubt but the *ideas* of *sacrilege* or *adultery* might be framed in the minds of men, and have names given them, and so these species of mixed modes be constituted, before either of them was ever committed; and might be as well discoursed of and reasoned about, and as certain truths discovered of them, whilst yet they had no being but in the understanding, as well as now that they have but too frequently a real existence? Whereby it is plain how much *the sorts of mixed modes are the creatures of the understanding*, where they have a being as subservient to all the ends of real truth and knowledge as when they really exist; and

we cannot doubt but law-makers have often made laws about
species of actions which were only the creatures of their own
understandings, beings that had no other existence but in their
own minds. And I think nobody can deny but that the *resurrection*
was a species of mixed modes in the mind, before it really existed.
6.   To see *how arbitrarily these essences of mixed modes are
made* by the mind, we need but take a view of almost any of
them. A little looking into them will satisfy us that it is the mind
that combines several scattered independent *ideas* into one complex one and, by the common name it gives them, makes them
the essence of a certain species, without regulating itself by any
connexion they have in nature. For what greater connexion in
nature has the *idea* of a man, than the *idea* of a sheep, with killing, that this is made a particular species of action, signified by
the word *murder*, and the other not? Or what union is there in
nature between the *idea* of the relation of a father, with killing,
than that of a son or neighbour, that those are combined into
one complex *idea* and thereby made the essence of the distinct
species *parricide*, whilst the other makes no distinct species at
all? But, though they have made killing a man's father or mother
a distinct species from killing his son or daughter, yet, in some
other cases, son and daughter are taken in too, as well as father
and mother; and they are all equally comprehended in the same
species, as in that of *incest*. Thus the mind in mixed modes
arbitrarily unites into complex *ideas* such as it finds convenient;
whilst others that have altogether as much union in nature are
left loose, and never combined into one *idea*, because they have
no need of one name. It is evident then that the mind, by its
free choice, gives a connexion to a certain number of *ideas*
which in nature have no more union with one another than
others that it leaves out. Why else is the part of the weapon the
beginning of the wound is made with taken notice of, to make
the distinct species called *stabbing*, and the figure and matter of
the weapon left out? I do not say this is done without reason,
as we shall see more by and by; but this I say, that it is done by
the free choice of the mind pursuing its own ends, and that
therefore these species of mixed modes are the workmanship of
the understanding; and there is nothing more evident than that
for the most part, in the framing these *ideas*, the mind searches
not its patterns in nature, nor refers the *ideas* it makes to the
real existence of things, but puts such together as may best

serve its own purposes, without tying itself to a precise imitation of anything that really exists.

7. But, though these complex *ideas* or *essences of mixed modes* depend on the mind and are made by it with great liberty, yet they *are not made at random* and jumbled together without any reason at all. Though these complex *ideas* be not always copied from nature, yet they are always suited to the end for which abstract *ideas* are made; and though they be combinations made of *ideas* that are loose enough, and have as little union in themselves as several others to which the mind never gives a connexion that combines them into one *idea*, yet they are always made for the convenience of communication, which is the chief end of language. The use of language is by short sounds to signify with ease and dispatch general conceptions, wherein not only abundance of particulars may be contained, but also a great variety of independent *ideas* collected into one complex one. In the making therefore of the species of mixed modes, men have had regard only to such combinations as they had occasion to mention one to another. Those they have combined into distinct complex *ideas* and given names to, whilst others that in nature have as near a union are left loose and unregarded. For to go no further than human actions themselves, if they would make distinct abstract *ideas* of all the varieties might be observed in them, the number must be infinite, and the memory confounded with the plenty, as well as overcharged to little purpose. It suffices that men make and name so many complex *ideas* of these mixed modes as they find they have occasion to have names for in the ordinary occurrence of their affairs. If they join to the *idea* of killing the *idea* of father or mother and so make a distinct species from killing a man's son or neighbour, it is because of the different heinousness of the crime; and the distinct punishment is due to the murdering a man's father and mother, different from what ought to be inflicted on the murder of a son or neighbour; and therefore they find it necessary to mention it by a distinct name, which is the end of making that distinct combination. But though the *ideas* of mother and daughter are so differently treated in reference to the *idea* of killing that the one is joined with it to make a distinct abstract *idea* with a name, and so a distinct species, and the other not, yet in respect of carnal knowledge they are both taken in under *incest*, and that still for the same convenience of expressing

under one name and reckoning of one species such unclean mixtures as have a peculiar turpitude beyond others; and this to avoid circumlocutions and tedious descriptions.

8. A moderate skill *in different languages* will easily satisfy one of the truth of this, it being so obvious to observe great store of *words in one* language *which have not any that answer them in another*. Which plainly shows that those of one country, by their customs and manner of life, have found occasion to make several complex *ideas* and give names to them, which others never collected into specific *ideas*. This could not have happened if these species were the steady workmanship of nature, and not collections made and abstracted by the mind, in order to naming, and for the convenience of communication. The terms of our law, which are not empty sounds, will hardly find words that answer them in the Spanish or Italian, no scanty languages; much less, I think, could anyone translate them into the *Caribbee* or *Westoe* tongues; and the *versura* of the *Romans* or *corban* of the *Jews* have no words in other languages to answer them, the reason whereof is plain from what has been said. Nay, if we will look a little more nearly into this matter and exactly compare different languages, we shall find that, though they have words which in translations and dictionaries are supposed to answer one another, yet there is scarce one of ten amongst the names of complex *ideas*, especially of mixed modes, that stands for the same precise *idea* which the word does that in dictionaries it is rendered by. There are no *ideas* more common and less compounded than the measures of time, extension, and weight; and the Latin names, *hora, pes, libra*, are without difficulty rendered by the *English* names, *hour, foot*, and *pound*; but yet there is nothing more evident than that the *ideas* a *Roman* annexed to these Latin names were very far different from those which an *Englishman* expresses by those English ones. And if either of these should make use of the measures that those of the other language designed by their names, he would be quite out in his account. These are two sensible proofs to be doubted; and we shall find this much more so in the names of more abstract and compounded *ideas*, such as are the greatest part of those which make up moral discourses; whose names, when men come curiously to compare with those they are translated into in other languages, they will find very few of them exactly to correspond in the whole extent of their significations.

9.   The reason why I take so particular notice of this is that we may not be mistaken about *genera* and *species* and their *essences*, as if they were things regularly and constantly made by nature and had a real existence in things, when they appear upon a more wary survey to be nothing else but an artifice of the understanding, for the easier signifying such collections of *ideas* as it should often have occasion to communicate by one general term; under which, divers particulars, as far forth as they agreed to that abstract *idea*, might be comprehended.   And if the doubtful signification of the word *species* may make it sound harsh to some that I say that the species of mixed modes are made by the understanding, yet I think it can by nobody be denied that it is the mind makes those abstract complex *ideas* to which specific names are given. And if it be true, as it is, that the mind makes the patterns for sorting and naming of things, I leave it to be considered who makes the boundaries of the sort or *species*, since with me, *species* and *sort* have no other difference than that of a Latin and English *idiom*.

10.   *The near relation* that there is *between species, essences, and* their *general name*, at least in *mixed modes*, will further appear when we consider that it is the name that seems to preserve those *essences* and give them their lasting duration.   For, the connexion between the loose parts of those complex *ideas* being made by the mind, this union, which has no particular foundation in nature, would cease again, were there not something that did, as it were, hold it together and keep the parts from scattering. Though therefore it be the mind that makes the collection, it is the name which is as it were the knot that ties them fast together.   What a vast variety of different *ideas* does the word *triumphus* hold together and deliver to us as one *species*! Had this name been never made or quite lost, we might, no doubt, have had descriptions of what passed in that solemnity; but yet I think that which holds those different parts together in the unity of one complex *idea* is that very word annexed to it: without which, the several parts of that would no more be thought to make one thing than any other show which, having never been made but once, had never been united into one complex *idea*, under one denomination.   How much, therefore, in mixed modes the unity necessary to any essence depends on the mind, and how much the continuation and fixing of that unity depends on the name in common use

annexed to it, I leave to be considered by those who look upon *essences* and *species* as real established things in nature.

11. Suitable to this, we find that *men speaking of mixed modes seldom* imagine *or take any other for species of them but such as are set out by name*: because they being of man's making only, in order to naming, no such *species* are taken notice of or supposed to be unless a *name* be joined to it, as the sign of man's having combined into one *idea* several loose ones, and by that *name* giving a lasting union to the parts which would otherwise cease to have any, as soon as the mind laid by that abstract *idea* and ceased actually to think on it. But when a name is once annexed to it, wherein the parts of that complex *idea* have a settled and permanent union, then is the *essence* as it were established and the *species* looked on as complete. For to what purpose should the memory charge itself with such compositions, unless it were by abstraction to make them general? And to what purpose make them general, unless it were that they might have general *names*, for the convenience of discourse and communication? Thus we see that killing a man with a sword or a hatchet are looked on as no distinct species of action; but if the point of the sword first enter the body, it passes for a distinct *species*, where it has a distinct *name*, as in *England*, in whose language it is called *stabbing*; but in another country where it has not happened to be specified under a peculiar *name*, it passes not for a distinct *species*. But in the *species* of corporeal substances, though it be the mind that makes the nominal essence, yet since those *ideas* which are combined in it are supposed to have an union in nature, whether the mind joins them or no, therefore those are looked on as distinct *species* without any operation of the mind, either abstracting or giving a *name* to that complex *idea*.

12. Conformable also to what has been said concerning the *essences* of the *species* of *mixed modes*, that they are the creatures of the understanding rather than the works of nature: conformable, I say, to this, we find that *their names lead our thoughts to the mind, and no further*. When we speak of *justice* or *gratitude*, we frame to ourselves no imagination of anything existing, which we would conceive, but our thoughts terminate in the abstract *ideas* of those virtues and look not further: as they do when we speak of a *horse*, or *iron*, whose specific *ideas* we consider not as barely in the mind, but as in things themselves,

which afford the original patterns of those *ideas*. But in mixed modes, at least the most considerable parts of them, which are moral beings, we consider the original patterns as being in the mind; and to those we refer for the distinguishing of particular beings under names. And hence I think it is that these *essences* of the *species* of mixed modes are by a more particular name called *notions*, as by a peculiar right, appertaining to the understanding.

13. Hence likewise we may learn *why the complex* ideas *of mixed modes are commonly more compounded and decompounded than those of natural substances*. Because they being the workmanship of the understanding, pursuing only its own ends and the conveniency of expressing in short those *ideas* it would make known to another, it does with great liberty unite often into one abstract *idea* things that in their nature have no coherence, and so under one term bundle together a great variety of compounded and decompounded *ideas*. Thus the name of *procession*, what a great mixture of independent *ideas* of persons, habits, tapers, orders, motions, sounds does it contain in that complex one, which the mind of man has arbitrarily put together, to express by that one name! Whereas the complex *ideas* of the sorts of substances are usually made up of only a small number of simple ones; and in the *species* of animals, these two, viz. shape and voice, commonly make the whole nominal essence.

14. Another thing we may observe from what has been said is that *the names of mixed modes always signify* (when they have any determined signification) *the real essences of their species*. For, these abstract *ideas* being the workmanship of the mind and not referred to the real existence of things, there is no supposition of anything more signified by that name, but barely that complex *idea* the mind itself has formed; which is all it would have expressed by it, and is that on which all the properties of the *species* depend, and from which alone they all flow; and so in these the *real* and *nominal essence* is the same; which, of what concernment it is to the certain knowledge of general truth, we shall see hereafter.

15. This also may show us the reason *why for the most part the names of mixed modes are got before the* ideas *they stand for are perfectly known*. Because there being no *species* of these ordinarily taken notice of but what have names, and those *species*, or

rather their essences, being abstract complex *ideas*, made arbitrarily by the mind, it is convenient, if not necessary, to know the names, before one endeavour to frame these complex *ideas*: unless a man will fill his head with a company of abstract complex *ideas*, which, other having no names for, he has nothing to do with but to lay by and forget again. I confess that in the beginning of languages, it was necessary to have the *idea* before one gave it the name; and so it is still, where making a new complex *idea*, one also by giving it a new name, makes a new word. But this concerns not languages made, which have generally pretty well provided for *ideas* which men have frequent occasion to have and communicate; and in such, I ask whether it be not the ordinary method that children learn the names of mixed modes before they have their *ideas*? What one of a thousand ever frames the abstract *ideas* of *glory* and *ambition*, before he has heard the names of them? In simple *ideas* and substances I grant it is otherwise; which being such *ideas* as have a real existence and union in nature, the *ideas* or names are got one before the other, as it happens.

16. What has been said here of mixed modes is with very little difference applicable also to relations; which, since every man himself may observe, I may spare myself the pains to enlarge on, especially since what I have here said concerning words in this Third Book will possibly be thought by some to be much more than what so slight a subject required. I allow it might be brought into a narrower compass; but I was willing to stay my reader on an argument that appears to me new and a little out of the way (I am sure it is one I thought not of, when I began to write), that by searching it to the bottom and turning it on every side, some part or other might meet with everyone's thoughts and give occasion to the most averse or negligent to reflect on a general miscarriage, which, though of great consequence, is little taken notice of. When it is considered what a pudder is made about *essences*, and how much all sorts of knowledge, discourse, and conversation are pestered and disordered by the careless and confused use and application of words, it will, perhaps, be thought worthwhile thoroughly to lay it open. And I shall be pardoned if I have dwelt long on an argument which I think therefore needs to be inculcated, because the faults men are usually guilty of in this kind are not only the greatest hindrances of true knowledge, but are so well thought

of as to pass for it. Men would often see what a small pittance of reason and truth or possibly none at all is mixed with those huffing opinions they are swelled with, if they would but look beyond fashionable sounds and observe what *ideas* are or are not comprehended under those words with which they are so armed at all points and with which they so confidently lay about them. I shall imagine I have done some service to truth, peace, and learning if, by any enlargement on this subject, I can make men reflect on their own use of language and give them reason to suspect that, since it is frequent for others, it may also be possible for them to have sometimes very good and approved words in their mouths and writings, with very uncertain, little, or no signification. And therefore it is not unreasonable for them to be wary herein themselves and not to be unwilling to have them examined by others. With this design, therefore, I shall go on with what I have further to say concerning this matter.

Chapter VI

OF THE NAMES OF SUBSTANCES

1. THE *common names of substances*, as well as other general terms, *stand for sorts*: which is nothing else but the being made signs of such complex *ideas* wherein several particular substances do or might agree, by virtue of which they are capable of being comprehended in one common conception and be signified by one name. I say do or might agree: for, though there be but one sun existing in the world, yet the *idea* of it being abstracted so that more substances (if there were several) might each agree in it, it is as much a sort as if there were as many suns as there are stars. They want not their reasons who think there are, and that each fixed star would answer the *idea* the name *sun* stands for to one who were placed in a due distance; which, by the way, may show us how much the sorts or, if you please, *genera* and *species* of things (for those Latin terms signify to me no more than the English word *sort*) depend on such collections of *ideas* as men have made, and not on the real nature of things: since it is not impossible but that, in propriety of speech, that might be a sun to one which is a star to another.

2. The measure and boundary of each sort or *species*, whereby it is constituted that particular sort and distinguished from others, is that we call its *essence*, which *is* nothing but that *abstract* idea *to which the name is annexed*; so that everything contained in that *idea* is essential to that sort. This, though it be all the *essence* of natural substances that we know or by which we distinguish them into sorts, yet I call it by a peculiar name, the *nominal essence*, to distinguish it from that real constitution of substances upon which depends this *nominal essence* and all the properties of that sort; which, therefore, as has been said, may be called the *real essence*: v.g. the *nominal essence* of *gold* is that complex *idea* the word *gold* stands for, let it be for instance a body yellow, of a certain weight, malleable, fusible, and fixed. But the *real essence* is the constitution of the insensible parts of that body on which those qualities and all the other properties of *gold* depend. How far these two are different, though they are both called *essence*, is obvious at first sight to discover.

3. For, though perhaps voluntary motion, with sense and reason, joined to a body of a certain shape be the complex *idea* to which I and others annex the name *man* and so be the *nominal essence* of the *species* so called, yet nobody will say that that complex *idea* is the *real essence* and source of all those operations which are to be found in any individual of that sort. The foundation of all those qualities which are the ingredients of our complex *idea* is something quite different; and had we such a knowledge of that constitution of *man* from which his faculties of moving, sensation, and reasoning, and other powers flow and on which his so regular shape depends, as it is possible angels have and it is certain his Maker has, we should have a quite other *idea* of his *essence* than what now is contained in our definition of that *species*, be it what it will. And our *idea* of any individual *man* would be as far different from what it now is, as is his who knows all the springs and wheels and other contrivances within of the famous clock at *Strasbourg* from that which a gazing countryman has of it, who barely sees the motion of the hand and hears the clock strike and observes only some of the outward appearances.

4. That *essence*, in the ordinary use of the word, relates to *sorts*, and that it is considered in particular beings no further than as they are ranked into *sorts* appears from hence: that, take but away the abstract *ideas* by which we sort individuals and rank

them under common names, and then the thought of anything *essential* to any of them instantly vanishes: we have no notion of the one without the other, which plainly shows their relation. It is necessary for me to be as I am, GOD and nature has made me so; but there is nothing I have is essential to me. An accident or disease may very much alter my colour or shape; a fever or fall may take away my reason or memory, or both; and an apoplexy leave neither sense, nor understanding, no, nor life. Other creatures of my shape may be made with more and better, or fewer and worse faculties than I have; and others may have reason and sense in a shape and body very different from mine. None of these are essential to the one or the other, or to any individual whatsoever, till the mind refers it to some sort or *species* of things; and then presently, according to the abstract *idea* of that sort, something is found *essential*. Let anyone examine his own thoughts and he will find that, as soon as he supposes or speaks of *essential*, the consideration of some *species* or the complex *idea* signified by some general name comes into his mind: and it is in reference to that that this or that quality is said to be essential. So that, if it be asked whether it be *essential* to me or any other particular corporeal being to have reason, I say no, no more than it is *essential* to this white thing I write on to have words in it. But if that particular being be to be counted of the sort *man* and to have the name *man* given it, then reason is *essential* to it, supposing reason to be a part of the complex *idea* the name *man* stands for, as it is *essential* to this thing I write on to contain words, if I will give it the name *treatise* and rank it under that *species*. So that *essential and not essential relate only to our abstract ideas and the names annexed to them*; which amounts to no more but this: that whatever particular thing has not in it those qualities which are contained in the abstract *idea* which any general term stands for cannot be ranked under that *species* nor be called by that name, since that abstract *idea* is the very *essence* of that *species*. 5. Thus if the *idea* of *body*, with some people, be bare extension or space, then solidity is not *essential* to body. If others make the *idea* to which they give the name *body* to be solidity and extension, then solidity is essential to *body*. That therefore and *that alone is* considered as *essential which makes a part of the complex* idea *the name of a sort stands for*, without which no particular thing can be reckoned of that sort nor be entitled to that name. Should there be found a parcel of matter that had all the other qualities that are in *iron*, but wanted obedience to the loadstone and would neither be drawn by it nor receive direction from it, would anyone question whether it wanted anything *essential*? It would be absurd to ask whether a thing really existing wanted anything *essential* to it. Or could it be demanded whether this made an *essential* or *specific* difference or no, since we have no other measure of *essential* or *specific* but our abstract *ideas*? And to talk of specific differences in nature, without reference to general *ideas* in names, is to talk unintelligibly. For I would ask anyone: What is sufficient to make an *essential* difference in nature between any two particular beings, without any regard had to some abstract *idea*, which is looked upon as the essence and standard of a *species*? All such patterns and standards being quite laid aside, particular beings, considered barely in themselves, will be found to have all their qualities equally *essential*; and everything in each individual will be *essential* to it or, which is more, nothing at all. For, though it may be reasonable to ask whether obeying the magnet be *essential* to *iron*, yet I think it is very improper and insignificant to ask whether it be *essential* to the particular parcel of matter I cut my pen with, without considering it under the name *iron* or as being of a certain *species*. And if, as has been said, our abstract *ideas*, which have names annexed to them, are the boundaries of *species*, nothing can be *essential* but what is contained in those *ideas*.

6. It is true, I have often mentioned a *real essence*, distinct in substances from those abstract *ideas* of them, which I call their *nominal essence*. By this *real essence*, I mean that real constitution of anything, which is the foundation of all those properties that are combined in and are constantly found to co-exist with the *nominal essence*, that particular constitution which everything has within itself, without any relation to anything without it. But *essence*, even in this sense, *relates to a sort*, and supposes a *species*. For, being that real constitution on which the properties depend, it necessarily supposes a sort of things, properties belonging only to *species*, and not to individuals: v.g. supposing the nominal essence of *gold* to be body of such a peculiar colour and weight, with malleability and fusibility, the real essence is that constitution of the parts of matter on which these qualities and their union depend, and is also the foundation of

its solubility in *aqua regia*, and other properties accompanying that complex *idea*. Here are *essences* and *properties*, but all upon supposition of a sort or general abstract *idea*, which is considered as immutable; but there is no individual parcel of matter to which any of these qualities are so annexed as to be *essential* to it or inseparable from it. That which is *essential* belongs to it as a condition whereby it is of this or that sort; but take away the consideration of its being ranked under the name of some abstract *idea*, and then there is nothing necessary to it, nothing inseparable from it. Indeed, as to the *real essences* of substances, we only suppose their being, without precisely knowing what they are; but that which annexes them still to the *species* is the nominal essence, of which they are the supposed foundation and cause.

7. The next thing to be considered is by which of those essences it is that *substances are determined into* sorts or *species*; and that, it is evident, is *by the nominal essence*. For it is that alone that the name, which is the mark of the sort, signifies. It is impossible therefore that anything should determine the sorts of things which we rank under general names but that *idea* which that name is designed as a mark for; which is that, as has been shown, which we call the *nominal essence*. Why do we say, this is a *horse* and that a *mule*, this is an *animal*, that an *herb*? How comes any particular thing to be of this or that *sort* but because it has that nominal essence or, which is all one, agrees to that abstract *idea* that name is annexed to? And I desire anyone but to reflect on his own thoughts when he hears or speaks any of those or other names of substances, to know what sort of *essences* they stand for.

8. And that the *species of things to us are nothing but the ranking them under distinct names, according to the complex* ideas *in us*, and not according to precise, distinct, real *essences* in them, is plain from hence: that we find many of the individuals that are ranked into one sort, called by one common name, and so received as being of one *species*, have yet qualities depending on their real constitutions, as far different one from another as from others from which they are accounted to differ *specifically*. This, as it is easy to be observed by all who have to do with natural bodies, so chemists especially are often, by sad experience, convinced of it, when they, sometimes in vain, seek for the same qualities in one parcel of sulphur, antimony, or vitriol which

they have found in others. For, though they are bodies of the same *species*, having the same nominal *essence*, under the same name, yet do they often, upon severe ways of examination, betray qualities so different one from another as to frustrate the expectation and labour of very wary chemists. But if things were distinguished into *species*, according to their real essences, it would be as impossible to find different properties in any two individual substances of the same *species* as it is to find different properties in two circles, or two equilateral triangles. That is properly the *essence* to us which determines every particular to this or that *classis* or, which is the same thing, to this or that general name; and what can that be else but that abstract *idea* to which that name is annexed, and so has, in truth, a reference, not so much to the being of particular things, as to their general denominations?

9. Nor indeed *can we* rank and *sort things*, and consequently (which is the end of sorting) denominate them *by their real essences*, because we know them not. Our faculties carry us no further towards the knowledge and distinction of substances than a collection of those sensible *ideas* which we observe in them; which, however made with the greatest diligence and exactness we are capable of, yet is more remote from the true internal constitution from which those qualities flow than, as I said, a countryman's *idea* is from the inward contrivance of that famous clock at *Strasbourg*, whereof he only sees the outward figure and motions. There is not so contemptible a plant or animal that does not confound the most enlarged understanding. Though the familiar use of things about us take off our wonder, yet it cures not our ignorance. When we come to examine the stones we tread on or the iron we daily handle, we presently find we know not their make, and can give no reason of the different qualities we find in them. It is evident the internal constitution, whereon their properties depend, is unknown to us. For to go no further than the grossest and most obvious we can imagine amongst them, what is that texture of parts, that real *essence*, that makes lead and antimony fusible, wood and stones not? What makes lead and iron malleable, antimony and stones not? And yet how infinitely these come short of the fine contrivances and inconceivable *real essences* of plants or animals, everyone knows. The workmanship of the all-wise and powerful God in the great fabric of the universe and every part thereof further

exceeds the capacity and comprehension of the most inquisitive
and intelligent man than the best contrivance of the most ingenious man doth the conceptions of the most ignorant of
rational creatures. Therefore we in vain pretend to range things
into sorts and dispose them into certain classes under names, by
their *real essences* that are so far from our discovery or comprehension. A blind man may as soon sort things by their colours,
and he that has lost his smell as well distinguish a lily and a rose
by their odours as by those internal constitutions which he knows
not. He that thinks he can distinguish sheep and goats by their
real essences that are unknown to him may be pleased to try his
skill in those *species* called *cassowary* and *querechinchio*, and by
their internal real essences determine the boundaries of those
species, without knowing the complex *idea* of sensible qualities
that each of those names stand for in the countries where those
animals are to be found.

10. Those, therefore, who have been taught that the several
species of substances had their distinct internal *substantial forms*,
and that it was those *forms* which made the distinction of substances into their true *species* and *genera*, were led yet further out
of the way by having their minds set upon fruitless inquiries
after *substantial forms* wholly unintelligible and whereof we
have scarce so much as any obscure or confused conception in
general.

11. That our *ranking* and distinguishing natural *substances into
species consists in the nominal essences* the mind makes, and not
in the real essences to be found in the things themselves, is
further evident from our *ideas* of *spirits*. For the mind getting,
only by reflecting on its own operations, those simple *ideas*
which it attributes to *spirits*, it hath or can have no other notion
of *spirit* but by attributing all those operations it finds in itself
to a sort of beings, without consideration of matter. And even
the most advanced notion we have of God is but attributing the
same simple *ideas* which we have got from reflection on what we
find in ourselves, and which we conceive to have more perfection
in them than would be in their absence: attributing, I say, those
simple *ideas* to him in an unlimited degree. Thus, having got
from reflecting on ourselves the *idea* of existence, knowledge,
power, and pleasure, each of which we find it better to have than
to want, and the more we have of each the better: joining all
these together, with infinity to each of them, we have the complex

idea of an eternal, omniscient, omnipotent, infinitely wise and happy Being. And though we are told that there are different *species of angels*, yet we know not how to frame distinct specific *ideas* of them: not out of any conceit that the existence of more *species* than one of *spirits* is impossible, but because, having no more simple *ideas* (nor being able to frame more) applicable to such beings, but only those few taken from ourselves and from the actions of our own minds in thinking and being delighted and moving several parts of our bodies, we can no otherwise distinguish in our conceptions the several *species of spirits* one from another but by attributing those operations and powers we find in ourselves to them in a higher or lower degree; and so have no very distinct specific *ideas* of *spirits* except only of GOD, to whom we attribute both duration and all those other *ideas* with infinity, to the other *spirits* with limitation. Nor as I humbly conceive do we, between GOD and them in our *ideas*, put any difference by any number of simple *ideas* which we have of one and not of the other, but only that of infinity. All the particular *ideas* of existence, knowledge, will, power, and motion, etc., being *ideas* derived from the operations of our minds, we attribute all of them to all sorts of *spirits*, with the difference only of degrees, to the utmost we can imagine, even infinity, when we would frame as well as we can an *idea* of the first Being; who yet, it is certain, is infinitely more remote in the real excellency of his nature from the highest and perfectest of all created beings than the greatest man, nay, purest seraphim, is from the most contemptible part of matter; and consequently must infinitely exceed what our narrow understandings can conceive of him.

12. It is not impossible to conceive, nor repugnant to reason, that there may be many *species of spirits*, as much separated and diversified one from another by distinct properties whereof we have no *ideas*, as the *species* of sensible things are distinguished one from another by qualities which we know and observe in them. That there should be more *species* of intelligent creatures above us than there are of sensible and material below us is probable to me from hence: that in all the visible corporeal world we see no chasms or gaps. All quite down from us the descent is by easy steps and a continued series of things, that in each remove differ very little one from the other. There are fishes that have wings and are not strangers to the airy region;

and there are some birds that are inhabitants of the water, whose blood is cold as fishes', and their flesh so like in taste that the scrupulous are allowed them on fish-days. There are animals so near of kin both to birds and beasts that they are in the middle between both, amphibious animals link the terrestrial and aquatic together: seals live at land and at sea, and porpoises have the warm blood and entrails of a hog, not to mention what is confidently reported of mermaids or sea-men. There are some brutes that seem to have as much knowledge and reason as some that are called men; and the animal and vegetable kingdoms are so nearly joined that, if you will take the lowest of one and the highest of the other, there will scarce be perceived any great difference between them; and so on, till we come to the lowest and most inorganical parts of matter, we shall find everywhere that the several *species* are linked together and differ but in almost insensible degrees. And when we consider the infinite power and wisdom of the Maker, we have reason to think that it is suitable to the magnificent harmony of the universe and the great design and infinite goodness of the Architect that the *species* of creatures should also, by gentle degrees, ascend upward from us toward his infinite perfection, as we see they gradually descend from us downwards; which if it be probable, we have reason then to be persuaded that there are far more *species* of creatures above us than there are beneath: we being, in degrees of perfection, much more remote from the infinite being of GOD than we are from the lowest state of being and that which approaches nearest to nothing. And yet of all those distinct *species*, for the reasons above said, we have no clear distinct *ideas*.

13.   But to return to the *species* of corporeal substances. If I should ask anyone whether *ice* and *water* were two distinct *species* of things, I doubt not but I should be answered in the affirmative; and it cannot be denied but he that says they are two distinct *species* is in the right. But if an *Englishman* bred in *Jamaica*, who perhaps had never seen nor heard of *ice*, coming into *England* in the winter, find the water he put in his basin at night in a great part frozen in the morning and, not knowing any peculiar name it had, should call it hardened water, I ask whether this would be a new *species* to him, different from water? And I think it would be answered here: It would not be to him a new *species*, no more than congealed jelly, when it is cold, is a

distinct *species* from the same jelly fluid and warm; or than liquid gold in the furnace is a distinct *species* from hard gold in the hands of a workman. And if this be so, it is plain that our *distinct species are nothing but distinct complex* ideas, *with distinct names annexed to them.* It is true, every substance that exists has its peculiar constitution, whereon depend those sensible qualities and powers we observe in it. But the ranking of things into *species*, which is nothing but sorting them under several titles, is done by us according to the *ideas* that we have of them: which, though sufficient to distinguish them by names so that we may be able to discourse of them when we have them not present before us, yet if we suppose it to be done by their real internal constitutions, and that things existing are distinguished by nature into species by real essences, according as we distinguish them into *species* by names, we shall be liable to great mistakes.

14. To distinguish substantial beings into *species*, according to the usual supposition that there are certain precise *essences* or *forms* of things whereby all the individuals existing are by nature distinguished into *species*, these things are necessary:

15. *First*, To be assured that nature, in the production of things, always designs them to partake of certain regulated established *essences*, which are to be the models of all things to be produced. This, in that crude sense it is usually proposed, would need some better explication before it can fully be assented to.

16. *Secondly*, It would be necessary to know whether nature always attains that *essence* it designs in the production of things. The irregular and monstrous births, that in divers sorts of animals have been observed, will always give us reason to doubt of one or both of these.

17. *Thirdly*, It ought to be determined whether those we call *monsters* be really a distinct *species*, according to the scholastic notion of the word *species*, since it is certain that everything that exists has its particular constitution; and yet we find that some of these monstrous productions have few or none of those qualities which are supposed to result from and accompany the *essence* of that *species* from whence they derive their originals, and to which, by their descent, they seem to belong.

18. *Fourthly*, The *real essences* of those things which we distinguish into *species*, and as so distinguished we name, ought to be known: i.e. we ought to have *ideas* of them. But since we are

ignorant in these four points, *the supposed real essences of things
stand us not in stead for the distinguishing substances into species.*
19.   *Fifthly,* The only imaginable help in this case would be
that, having framed perfect complex *ideas* of the *properties* of
things flowing from their different real essences, we should
thereby distinguish them into *species.* But neither can this be
done; for, being ignorant of the real essence itself, it is impossible to know all those properties that flow from it and are so
annexed to it that, any one of them being away, we may certainly conclude that that essence is not there, and so the thing is
not of that *species.* We can never know what are the precise
number of properties depending on the real essence of *gold*; any
one of which failing, the real essence of gold, and consequently
gold, would not be there, unless we knew the real essence of
gold itself, and by that determined that *species.* By the word
gold here, I must be understood to design a particular piece of
matter: v.g. the last guinea that was coined. For if it should
stand here in its ordinary signification for that complex *idea*
which I or anyone else calls gold, i.e. for the nominal essence of
gold, it would be *jargon*: so hard is it to show the various meaning and imperfection of words when we have nothing else but
words to do it by.
20.   By all which it is clear that our *distinguishing substances
into species* by names *is not* at all *founded on their real essences*;
nor can we pretend to range and determine them exactly into
species according to internal essential differences.
21.   But since, as has been remarked, we have need of general
words, though we know not the real essences of things, all we can
do is to collect such a number of simple *ideas* as, by examination,
we find to be united together in things existing, and thereof to
make one complex *idea.* Which, though it be not the real essence
of any substance that exists, is yet *the specific essence* to which
our name belongs, and is convertible with it; by which we may at
least try the truth of these nominal essences. For example: there
be those that say that the essence of *body* is *extension*; if it be
so, we can never mistake in putting the essence of anything for
the thing itself. Let us then in discourse put *extension* for *body*;
and when we would say that body moves, let us say that extension moves, and see how it will look. He that should say that one
extension by impulse moves another extension would, by the
bare expression, sufficiently show the absurdity of such a

notion. The *essence* of anything, in respect of us, is the whole complex *idea* comprehended and marked by that name; and in substances, besides the several distinct simple *ideas* that make them up, the confused one of substance or of an unknown support and cause of their union is always a part; and therefore the essence of body is not bare extension, but an extended solid thing; and so to say an extended solid thing moves or impels another is all one, and as intelligible, as to say *body* moves or impels. Likewise, to say that a rational animal is capable of conversation is all one as to say a *man*. But no one will say that rationality is capable of conversation, because it makes not the whole essence to which we give the name man.

22. There are creatures in the world that have shapes like ours, but are hairy and want language and reason. There are naturals amongst us that have perfectly our shape, but want reason, and some of them language too. There are creatures, as it is said (*sit fides penes auctorem*, but there appears no contradiction that there should be such) that, with language and reason, and a shape in other things agreeing with ours, have hairy tails; others where the males have no beards, and others where the females have. If it be asked whether these be all *men* or no, all of human *species*, it is plain the question refers only to the nominal essence: for those of them to whom the definition of the word *man* or the complex *idea* signified by that name agrees are *men*, and the other not. But if the inquiry be made concerning the supposed real essence, and whether the internal constitution and frame of these several creatures be specifically different, it is wholly impossible for us to answer, no part of that going into our specific *idea*: only we have reason to think that, where the faculties or outward frame so much differs, the internal constitution is not exactly the same. But what difference in the internal real constitution makes a specific difference it is in vain to inquire, whilst *our measures of species* be, as they *are*, *only our abstract ideas*, which we know, and not that internal constitution which makes no part of them. Shall the difference of hair only on the skin be a mark of a different internal specific constitution between a changeling and a drill, when they agree in shape and want of reason and speech? And shall not the want of reason and speech be a sign to us of different real constitutions and *species* between a changeling and a reasonable man? And so of the rest, if we pretend that the distinction of *species* or sorts is fixedly

established by the real frame and secret constitutions of things.

23. Nor let anyone say that the power of propagation, in animals by the mixture of male and female and in plants by seeds, keeps the supposed *real species* distinct and entire. For, granting this to be true, it would help us in the distinction of the *species* of things no further than the tribes of animals and vegetables. What must we do for the rest? But in those too it is not sufficient: for if history lie not, women have conceived by drills; and what real *species*, by that measure, such a production will be in nature will be a new question: and we have reason to think this not impossible, since mules and jumarts, the one from the mixture of an ass and a mare, the other from the mixture of a bull and a mare, are so frequent in the world. I once saw a creature that was the issue of a cat and a rat, and had the plain marks of both about it, wherein nature appeared to have followed the pattern of neither sort alone, but to have jumbled them both together. To which he that shall add the monstrous productions that are so frequently to be met with in nature will find it hard, even in the race of animals, to determine by the pedigree of what *species* every animal's issue is, and be at a loss about the real essence, which he thinks certainly conveyed by generation and has alone a right to the specific name. But further, if the *species* of animals and plants are to be distinguished only by propagation, must I go to the *Indies* to see the sire and dam of the one and the plant from which the seed was gathered that produced the other, to know whether this be a tiger or that tea?

24. Upon the whole matter, it is evident that it is their own collections of sensible qualities that men make the essences of their several sorts of substances, and that their real internal structures are not considered by the greatest part of men in the sorting them. Much less were any *substantial forms* ever thought on by any but those who have in this one part of the world learned the language of the schools; and yet those ignorant men, who pretend not any insight into the real essences nor trouble themselves about substantial forms but are content with knowing things one from another by their sensible qualities, are often better acquainted with their differences, can more nicely distinguish them from their uses, and better know what they may expect from each than those learned quick-sighted

men who look so deep into them and talk so confidently of something more hidden and essential.

25. But supposing that the *real essences* of substances were discoverable by those that would severely apply themselves to that inquiry, yet we could not reasonably think that the *ranking of things under general names was regulated by* those internal real constitutions, or anything else but *their obvious appearances*, since languages in all countries have been established long before sciences. So that they have not been philosophers, or logicians, or such who have troubled themselves about *forms* and *essences*, that have made the general names that are in use amongst the several nations of men; but those more or less comprehensive terms have for the most part, in all languages, received their birth and signification from ignorant and illiterate people, who sorted and denominated things by those sensible qualities they found in them, thereby to signify them when absent to others, whether they had an occasion to mention a sort or a particular thing.

26. Since then it is evident that we sort and name substances by their *nominal* and not by their real *essences*, the next thing to be considered is how and by whom these *essences* come to be made. As to the latter, it is evident they *are made by the mind*, and not by nature: for were they nature's workmanship, they could not be so various and different in several men as experience tells us they are. For if we will examine it, we shall not find the nominal essence of any one *species* of substances in all men the same: no, not of that which of all others we are the most intimately acquainted with. It could not possibly be that the abstract *idea* to which the name *man* is given should be different in several men, if it were of nature's making, and that to one it should be *animal rationale*, and to another *animal implume bipes latis unguibus*. He that annexes the name *man* to a complex *idea*, made up of sense and spontaneous motion, joined to a body of such a shape, has thereby one essence of the *species man*; and he that, upon further examination, adds rationality has another essence of the *species* he calls *man*: by which means the same individual will be a true *man* to the one which is not so to the other. I think there is scarce anyone will allow this upright figure, so well known, to be the essential difference of the *species man*; and yet how far men determine of the sorts of animals, rather by their shape than descent, is very visible, since

it has been more than once debated whether several human *foetus* should be preserved or received to baptism or no, only because of the difference of their outward configuration from the ordinary make of children, without knowing whether they were not as capable of reason as infants cast in another mould; some whereof, though of an approved shape, are never capable of as much appearance of reason all their lives as is to be found in an ape or an elephant, and never give any signs of being acted by a rational soul.   Whereby it is evident that the outward figure, which only was found wanting, and not the faculty of reason, which nobody could know would be wanting in its due season, was made essential to the human *species*.   The learned divine and lawyer must, on such occasions, renounce his sacred definition of *animal rationale* and substitute some other essence of the human *species*. Monsieur *Ménage* furnishes us with an example worth the taking notice of on this occasion.   *When the Abbot of St. Martin,* says he, *was born, he had so little of the figure of a man that it bespake him rather a monster.   It was for some time under deliberation whether he should be baptized or no.   However, he was baptized and declared a man provisionally* (till time should show what he would prove).   *Nature had moulded him so untowardly that he was called all his life the Abbot Malotru,* i.e. ill-shaped.   *He was of* Caen.[1]   This child we see was very near being excluded out of the *species* of *man*, barely by his shape. He escaped very narrowly as he was; and, it is certain, a figure a little more oddly turned had cast him, and he had been executed as a thing not to be allowed to pass for a man. And yet there can be no reason given why, if the lineaments of his face had been a little altered, a rational soul could not have been lodged in him; why a visage somewhat longer, or a nose flatter, or a wider mouth could not have consisted, as well as the rest of his ill figure, with such a soul, such parts as made him, disfigured as he was, capable to be a dignitary in the church.

27.   Wherein, then, would I gladly know, consist the precise and *unmovable boundaries of* that *species*?   It is plain, if we examine, there is *no* such thing *made by nature* and established by her amongst men.   The real essence of that or any other sort of substances, it is evident, we know not; and therefore are so undetermined in our nominal essences, which we make ourselves, that, if several men were to be asked concerning some

[1]*Ménagiana.* 2. éd. 1694. t. i, p. 278.

oddly-shaped *foetus*, as soon as born, whether it were a *man* or no, it is past doubt one should meet with different answers. Which could not happen if the nominal essences, whereby we limit and distinguish the *species* of substances, were not made by man with some liberty, but were exactly copied from precise boundaries set by nature, whereby it distinguished all substances into certain *species*. Who would undertake to resolve what *species* that monster was of which is mentioned by *Licetus*,[1] with a man's head and hog's body? Or those other which to the bodies of men had the heads of beasts, as dogs, horses, etc. If any of these creatures had lived and could have spoke, it would have increased the difficulty. Had the upper part to the middle been of human shape, and all below swine, had it been murder to destroy it? Or must the bishop have been consulted whether it were man enough to be admitted to the font or no? As I have been told, it happened in *France* some years since, in somewhat a like case. So uncertain are the boundaries of *species* of animals to us, who have no other measures than the complex *ideas* of our own collecting, and so far are we from certainly knowing what a *man* is, though perhaps it will be judged great ignorance to make any doubt about it. And yet I think I may say that the certain boundaries of that *species* are so far from being determined, and the precise number of simple *ideas*, which make the nominal essence, so far from being settled and perfectly known, that very material doubts may still arise about it; and I imagine none of the definitions of the word *man* which we yet have, nor descriptions of that sort of animal are so perfect and exact as to satisfy a considerate inquisitive person, much less to obtain a general consent and to be that which men would everywhere stick by in the decision of cases and determining of life and death, baptism or no baptism, in productions that might happen.

28. But though these *nominal essences of substances* are made by the mind, they are *not* yet *made so arbitrarily as those of mixed modes*. To the making of any nominal essence it is necessary, *first*, that the *ideas* whereof it consists have such an union as to make but one *idea*, how compounded soever. *Secondly*, that the particular *ideas* so united be exactly the same, neither more nor less. For if two abstract complex *ideas* differ either in number or sorts of their component parts, they

[1] Liceto, F. *De monstrorum caussis* . . . 1616. lib. i, c. 3.

make two different, and not one and the same essence. In the first of these, the mind, in making its complex *ideas* of substances, only follows nature and puts none together which are not supposed to have an union in nature. Nobody joins the voice of a sheep with the shape of a horse, nor the colour of lead with the weight and fixedness of gold, to be the complex *ideas* of any real substances, unless he has a mind to fill his head with *chimeras* and his discourse with unintelligible words. Men, observing certain qualities always joined and existing together, therein copied nature, and of *ideas* so united made their complex ones of substances. For though men may make what complex *ideas* they please and give what names to them they will, yet if they will be understood when they speak of things really existing, they must in some degree conform their *ideas* to the things they would speak of; or else men's language will be like that of *Babel*, and every man's words, being intelligible only to himself, would no longer serve to conversation and the ordinary affairs of life, if the ideas they stand for be not some way answering the common appearances and agreement of substances as they really exist.

29.   *Secondly*, Though the mind of man, *in making* its *complex ideas of substances*, never puts any together that do not really, or are not supposed to, co-exist, and so it truly borrows that union from nature: yet *the number* it combines *depends upon the various care, industry, or fancy of him that makes it.* Men generally content themselves with some few sensible obvious qualities, and often, if not always, leave out others as material and as firmly united as those that they take. Of sensible substances there are two sorts: one of organized bodies, which are propagated by seed; and in these the shape is that which to us is the leading quality and most characteristical part that determines the *species*; and therefore in vegetables and animals, an extended solid substance of such a certain figure usually serves the turn. For however some men seem to prize their definition of *animal rationale*, yet, should there a creature be found that had language and reason but partaked not of the usual shape of a man, I believe it would hardly pass for a *man*, how much soever it were *animal rationale*. And if *Balaam's* ass had, all his life, discoursed as rationally as he did once with his master, I doubt yet whether anyone would have thought him worthy the name *man* or allowed him to be of the same *species* with

himself. As in vegetables and animals it is the shape, so in most other bodies not propagated by seed it is the colour we most fix on and are most led by. Thus, where we find the colour of gold, we are apt to imagine all the other qualities comprehended in our complex *idea* to be there also; and we commonly take these two obvious qualities, viz. shape and colour, for so presumptive *ideas* of several *species* that in a good picture we readily say, this is a lion, and that a rose; this is a gold, and that a silver goblet, only by the different figures and colours represented to the eye by the pencil.

30. But though this serves well enough for gross and confused conceptions and inaccurate ways of talking and thinking, yet *men are far enough from having agreed on the precise number of simple* ideas *or* qualities *belonging to any sort of things, signified by its name.* Nor is it a wonder, since it requires much time, pains and skill, strict inquiry, and long examination to find out what and how many those simple *ideas* are which are constantly and inseparably united in nature and are always to be found together in the same subject. Most men, wanting either time, inclination, or industry enough for this, even to some tolerable degree, content themselves with some few obvious and outward appearances of things, thereby readily to distinguish and sort them for the common affairs of life; and so, without further examination, give them names, or take up the names already in use. Which, though in common conversation they pass well enough for the signs of some few obvious qualities co-existing, are yet far enough from comprehending, in a settled signification, a precise number of simple *ideas*, much less all those which are united in nature. He that shall consider, after so much stir about *genus* and *species* and such a deal of talk of specific differences, how few words we have yet settled definitions of may, with reason, imagine that those *forms* which there hath been so much noise made about are only *chimeras*, which give us no light into the specific natures of things. And he that shall consider how far the names of substances are from having significations wherein all who use them do agree will have reason to conclude that, though the nominal essences of substances are all supposed to be copied from nature, yet they are all, or most of them, very imperfect: since the composition of those complex *ideas* are, in several men, very different; and therefore that these boundaries of *species* are as men, and not as nature, makes them, if at least there are in nature any such prefixed bounds. It is true that

many particular substances are so made by nature that they have agreement and likeness one with another, and so afford a foundation of being ranked into sorts. But the sorting of things by us or the making of determinate *species* being in order to naming and comprehending them under general terms, I cannot see how it can be properly said that nature sets the boundaries of the *species* of things; or, if it be so, our boundaries of *species* are not exactly conformable to those in nature. For we, having need of general names for present use, stay not for a perfect discovery of all those qualities which would best show us their most material differences and agreements; but we ourselves divide them by certain obvious appearances into *species*, that we may the easier, under general names, communicate our thoughts about them. For having no other knowledge of any substance but of the simple *ideas* that are united in it, and observing several particular things to agree with others in several of those simple *ideas*, we make that collection our specific *idea* and give it a general name, that in recording our own thoughts and in our discourse with others we may in one short word design all the individuals that agree in that complex *idea*, without enumerating the simple *ideas* that make it up, and so not waste our time and breath in tedious descriptions; which we see they are fain to do who would discourse of any new sort of things they have not yet a name for.

31.   But, however these *species* of substances pass well enough in ordinary conversation, it is plain that this complex *idea* wherein they observe several individuals to agree is, by different men, made very differently: by some more and others less accurately. In some, this complex *idea* contains a greater, and in others a smaller number of qualities, and so is apparently such as the mind makes it. The yellow shining colour makes *gold* to children; others add weight, malleableness and fusibility; and others yet other qualities which they find joined with that yellow colour, as constantly as its weight and fusibility: for, in all these and the like qualities, one has as good a right to be put into the complex *idea* of that substance, wherein they are all joined, as another. And therefore *different men*, leaving out or putting in several simple *ideas* which others do not, according to their various examination, skill, or observation of that subject, *have different essences of gold*, which must therefore be of their own and not of nature's making.

32.   If the *number of simple* ideas *that make the nominal essence*
of the lowest *species* or first sorting of individuals *depends on the*
mind of man variously collecting them, it is much more evident
that they do so in the more comprehensive *classis* which, by the
masters of logic, are called *genera*.   These are complex *ideas*
designedly imperfect; and it is visible at first sight that several
of those qualities that are to be found in the things themselves
are purposely left out of *generical ideas*.   For as the mind, to
make general *ideas* comprehending several particulars, leaves
out those of time and place and such other that make them
incommunicable to more than one individual, so to make other
yet more general *ideas* that may comprehend different sorts, it
leaves out those qualities that distinguish them and puts into its
new collection only such *ideas* as are common to several sorts.
The same convenience that made men express several parcels
of yellow matter coming from *Guinea* and *Peru* under one name,
sets them also upon making of one name that may comprehend
both gold and silver and some other bodies of different sorts.
This is done by leaving out those qualities which are peculiar
to each sort and retaining a complex *idea* made up of those that
are common to them all.   To which the name *metal* being annexed, there is a *genus* constituted; the essence whereof, being
that abstract *idea* containing only malleableness and fusibility,
with certain degrees of weight and fixedness wherein some
bodies of several kinds agree, leaves out the colour and other
qualities peculiar to gold and silver and the other sorts comprehended under the name *metal*.   Whereby it is plain that men
follow not exactly the patterns set them by nature, when they
make their general *ideas* of substances, since there is no body to
be found which has barely malleableness and fusibility in it,
without other qualities as inseparable as those.   But men, in
making their general *ideas*, seeking more the convenience of
language and quick dispatch by short and comprehensive signs
than the true and precise nature of things as they exist, have in
the framing their abstract *ideas* chiefly pursued that end which
was to be furnished with store of general and variously comprehensive names.   So that in this whole business of *genera* and
species, the *genus* or more comprehensive is but a partial conception of what is in the *species*, and the *species* but a partial *idea*
of what is to be found in each individual.   If therefore anyone
will think that a *man* and a *horse* and an animal and a plant, etc.,

are distinguished by real essences made by nature, he must
think nature to be very liberal of these real essences, making one
for body, another for an animal, and another for a horse; and all
these essences liberally bestowed upon *Bucephalus*. But if we
would rightly consider what is done in all these *genera* and
species or sorts, we should find that there is no new thing made,
but only more or less comprehensive signs whereby we may be
enabled to express, in a few syllables, great numbers of particular
things as they agree in more or less general conceptions, which
we have framed to that purpose. In all which we may observe
that the more general term is always the name of a less complex
idea, and that each *genus* is but a partial conception of the *species*
comprehended under it. So that if these abstract general *ideas*
be thought to be complete, it can only be in respect of a certain
established relation between them and certain names which are
made use of to signify them, and not in respect of anything
existing as made by nature.

33. *This* is *adjusted to the true end of speech*, which is to be the
easiest and shortest way of communicating our notions. For
thus he that would make and discourse of things as they agreed
in the complex *idea* of extension and solidity, needed but use
the word *body* to denote all such. He that to these would join
others, signified by the words life, sense, and spontaneous
motion, needed but use the word *animal* to signify all which
partaked of those *ideas*; and he that had made a complex *idea* of
a body, with life, sense, and motion, with the faculty of reasoning
and a certain shape joined to it, needed but use the short monosyllable *man* to express all particulars that correspond to that
complex *idea*. This is the proper business of *genus* and *species*;
and this men do without any consideration of *real essences*, or
substantial forms, which come not within the reach of our knowledge when we think of those things, nor within the signification
of our words when we discourse with others.

34. Were I to talk with anyone of a sort of birds I lately saw in
St. *James'* Park: about three- or four-foot high, with a covering
of something between feathers and hair, of a dark brown colour,
without wings, but in the place thereof two or three little
branches coming down like sprigs of Spanish broom, long great
legs, with feet only of three claws and without a tail: I must
make this description of it and so may make others understand
me; but when I am told that the name of it is *cassowary*, I may

then use that word to stand in discourse for all my complex *idea*
mentioned in that description, though by that word, which is
now become a specific name, I know no more of the real
essence or constitution of that sort of animals than I did before,
and knew probably as much of the nature of that *species* of
birds before I learned the name, as many *Englishmen* do of
swans or herons, which are specific names very well known of
sorts of birds common in *England*.

35.   From what has been said, it is evident that *men make sorts
of things*.   For it being different essences alone that make
different *species*, it is plain that they who make those abstract
ideas which are the nominal essences, do thereby make the
species or sort.   Should there be a body found having all the
other qualities of gold except malleableness, it would, no doubt,
be made a question whether it were gold or no, i.e. whether it
were of that *species*.   This could be determined only by that
abstract *idea* to which everyone annexed the name *gold*; so that
it would be true gold to him and belong to that *species*, who
included not malleableness in his nominal essence, signified by
the sound *gold*; and on the other side, it would not be true gold
or of that *species* to him who included malleableness in his
specific *idea*.   And who, I pray, is it that makes these divers
species, even under one and the same name, but men that make
two different abstract *ideas* consisting not exactly of the same
collection of qualities?   Nor is it a mere supposition to imagine
that a body may exist wherein the other obvious qualities of
gold may be without malleableness, since it is certain that gold
itself will be sometimes so eager (as artists call it) that it will as
little endure the hammer as glass itself.   What we have said of
the putting in or leaving out of malleableness, out of the complex *idea* the name *gold* is by anyone annexed to, may be said of
its peculiar weight, fixedness, and several other the like qualities:
for whatsoever is left out or put in, it is still the complex *idea*
to which that name is annexed that makes the *species*: and as
any particular parcel of matter answers that *idea*, so the name of
the sort belongs truly to it and it is of that *species*.   And thus
anything that is true *gold*, perfect *metal*.   All which determination
of the *species*, it is plain, depends on the understanding of man,
making this or that complex *idea*.

36.   This, then, in short, is the case: *nature makes many
particular things, which do agree* one with another in many

sensible qualities, and probably too in their internal frame and constitution; but it is not this real essence that distinguishes them into *species*: it is *men* who, taking occasion from the qualities they find united in them and wherein they observe often several individuals to agree, *range them into sorts, in order to their naming,* for the convenience of comprehensive signs; under which individuals, according to their conformity to this or that abstract *idea,* come to be ranked as under ensigns: so that this is of the blue, that the red regiment; this is a man, that a drill; and in this, I think, consists the whole business of *genus* and *species*.

37.   I do not deny but nature, in the constant production of particular beings, makes them not always new and various, but very much alike and of kin one to another; but I think it nevertheless true that *the boundaries of the species, whereby men sort them, are made by men*: since the essences of the *species,* distinguished by different names, are, as has been proved, of man's making, and seldom adequate to the internal nature of the things they are taken from. So that we may truly say such a manner of sorting of things is the workmanship of men.

38.   One thing I doubt not but will seem very strange in this doctrine, which is that, from what has been said, it will follow that *each abstract* idea *with a name to it makes a distinct species.* But who can help it if truth will have it so? For so it must remain till somebody can show us the *species* of things limited and distinguished by something else, and let us see that general terms signify not our abstract *ideas* but something different from them. I would fain know why a shock and a hound are not as distinct *species* as a spaniel and an elephant. We have no other *idea* of the different essence of an elephant and a spaniel than we have of the different essence of a shock and a hound: all the essential difference whereby we know and distinguish them one from another consisting only in the different collection of simple *ideas* to which we have given those different names.

39.   How much *the making of* species *and* genera *is in order to general names,* and how much general names are necessary, if not to the being, yet at least to the completing of a *species* and making it pass for such, will appear, besides what has been said above concerning ice and water, in a very familiar example. A silent and a striking *watch* are but one *species* to those who have

but one name for them; but he that has the name *watch* for one and *clock* for the other, and distinct complex *ideas* to which those names belong, to him they are different *species*. It will be said, perhaps, that the inward contrivance and constitution is different between these two, which the watchmaker has a clear *idea* of. And yet it is plain they are but one *species* to him when he has but one name for them. For what is sufficient in the inward contrivance to make a new *species*? There are some *watches* that are made with four wheels, others with five: is this a specific difference to the workman? Some have strings and fusees and others none; some have the balance loose, and others regulated by a spiral spring, and others by hog's bristles; are any or all of these enough to make a specific difference to the workman that knows each of these and several other different contrivances in the internal constitutions of *watches*? It is certain each of these hath a real difference from the rest; but whether it be an essential, a specific difference or no, relates only to the complex *idea* to which the name *watch* is given; as long as they all agree in the *idea* which that name stands for, and that name does not as a generical name comprehend different *species* under it, they are not essentially nor specifically different. But if anyone will make minuter divisions from differences that he knows in the internal frame of watches, and to such precise complex *ideas* give names that shall prevail, they will then be new *species* to them who have those *ideas* with names to them and can, by those differences, distinguish watches into these several sorts; and then *watch* will be a generical name. But yet they would be no distinct *species* to men ignorant of clockwork and the inward contrivances of watches, who had no other *idea* but the outward shape and bulk, with the marking of the hours by the hand. For to them, all those other names would be but synonymous terms for the same *idea* and signify no more nor no other thing but a *watch*. Just thus, I think, it is in natural things. Nobody will doubt that the wheels or springs (if I may so say) within are different in a *rational man* and a *changeling*, no more than that there is a difference in the frame between a *drill* and a *changeling*. But whether one or both these differences be essential or specifical is only to be known to us by their agreement or disagreement with the complex *idea* that the name *man* stands for: for by that alone can it be determined whether one or both or neither of those be a man or no.

40. From what has been before said, we may see the reason *why, in the species of artificial things, there is generally less confusion and uncertainty than in natural.* Because an *artificial* thing being a production of man, which the artificer designed and therefore well knows the *idea* of, the name of it is supposed to stand for no other *idea* nor to import any other essence than what is certainly to be known and easy enough to be apprehended. For the *idea* or essence of the several sorts of *artificial* things consisting for the most part in nothing but the determinate figure of sensible parts, and sometimes motion depending thereon, which the artificer fashions in matter, such as he finds for his turn: it is not beyond the reach of our faculties to attain a certain *idea* thereof and so settle the signification of the names whereby the species of *artificial* things are distinguished, with less doubt, obscurity, and equivocation than we can in things natural, whose differences and operations depend upon contrivances beyond the reach of our discoveries.

41. I must be excused here if I think *artificial things are of distinct species* as well as natural, since I find they are as plainly and orderly ranked into sorts by different abstract *ideas*, with general names annexed to them, as distinct one from another as those of natural substances. For why should we not think a watch and pistol as distinct species one from another as a horse and a dog, they being expressed in our minds by distinct *ideas*, and to others by distinct appellations?

42. This is further to be observed concerning *substances*, that they *alone* of all our several sorts of *ideas have* particular or *proper names* whereby one only particular thing is signified. Because in simple *ideas*, modes, and relations, it seldom happens that men have occasion to mention often this or that particular when it is absent. Besides, the greatest part of mixed modes, being actions which perish in their birth, are not capable of a lasting duration, as substances which are the actors and wherein the simple *ideas* that make up the complex *ideas* designed by the name have a lasting union.

43. I must beg pardon of my reader for having dwelt so long upon this subject and perhaps with some obscurity. But I desire it may be considered how *difficult* it is *to lead another by words into the thoughts of things, stripped of those specific differences* we give them; which things, if I name not, I say nothing, and if I do name them, I thereby rank them into some sort or

other and suggest to the mind the usual abstract *idea* of that *species*, and so cross my purpose. For to talk of a *man*, and to lay by at the same time the ordinary signification of the name man, which is our complex *idea* usually annexed to it, and bid the reader consider *man* as he is in himself and as he is really distinguished from others in his internal constitution or real essence, that is, by something he knows not what, looks like trifling; and yet thus one must do who would speak of the supposed real essences and *species* of things as thought to be made by nature, if it be but only to make it understood that there is no such thing signified by the general names which substances are called by. But because it is difficult by known familiar names to do this, give me leave to endeavour by an example to make the different consideration the mind has of specific names and *ideas* a little more clear, and to show how the complex *ideas* of modes are referred sometimes to archetypes in the minds of other intelligent beings or, which is the same, to the signification annexed by others to their received names, and sometimes to no archetypes at all. Give me leave also to show how the mind always refers its *ideas* of substances either to the substances themselves or to the signification of their names, as to the *archetypes*; and also to make plain the nature of *species* or sorting of things as apprehended and made use of by us, and of the essences belonging to those *species*: which is, perhaps, of more moment to discover the extent and certainty of our knowledge than we at first imagine.

44. Let us suppose *Adam* in the state of a grown man, with a good understanding, but in a strange country, with all things new and unknown about him, and no other faculties to attain the knowledge of them but what one of this age has now. He observes *Lamech* more melancholy than usual, and imagines it to be from a suspicion he has of his wife *Adah* (whom he most ardently loved) that she had too much kindness for another man. *Adam* discourses these his thoughts to *Eve*, and desires her to take care that *Adah* commit not folly; and in these discourses with *Eve* he makes use of these two new words, *kinneah* and *niouph*. In time, *Adam's* mistake appears, for he finds *Lamech's* trouble proceeded from having killed a man; but yet the two names, *kinneah* and *niouph*, the one standing for suspicion in a husband of his wife's disloyalty to him, and the other for the act of committing disloyalty, lost not their distinct

significations. It is plain, then, that here were two distinct complex *ideas* of mixed modes with names to them, two distinct species of actions essentially different; I ask wherein consisted the essences of these two distinct species of actions? And it is plain it consisted in a precise combination of simple *ideas*, different in one from the other. I ask whether the complex *idea* in *Adam's* mind, which he called *kinneah*, were adequate or no? And it is plain it was; for, it being a combination of simple *ideas* which he, without any regard to any archetype, without respect to anything as a pattern, voluntarily put together, abstracted, and gave the name *kinneah* to, to express in short to others by that one sound all the simple *ideas* contained and united in that complex one, it must necessarily follow that it was an adequate *idea*. His own choice having made that combination, it had all in it he intended it should, and so could not but be perfect, could not but be adequate, it being referred to no other archetype which it was supposed to represent.

45. These words, *kinneah* and *niouph*, by degrees grew into common use, and then the case was somewhat altered. *Adam's* children had the same faculties, and thereby the same power that he had, to make what complex *ideas* of mixed modes they pleased in their own minds, to abstract them and make what sounds they pleased the signs of them; but the use of names being to make our *ideas* within us known to others, that cannot be done but when the same sign stands for the same *idea* in two who would communicate their thoughts and discourse together. Those therefore of *Adam's* children that found these two words, *kinneah* and *niouph*, in familiar use, could not take them for insignificant sounds, but must needs conclude they stood for something, for certain *ideas*, abstract *ideas*, they being general names, which abstract *ideas* were the essences of the species distinguished by those names. If therefore they would use these words as names of species already established and agreed on, they were obliged to conform the *ideas* in their minds signified by these names to the *ideas* that they stood for in other men's minds, as to their patterns and *archetypes*; and then indeed their *ideas* of these complex modes were liable to be inadequate, as being very apt (especially those that consisted of combinations of many simple *ideas*) not to be exactly conformable to the *ideas* in other men's minds using the same names; though for this, there be usually a remedy at hand, which is to ask the meaning

of any word we understand not of him that uses it: it being as
impossible to know certainly what the words jealousy and
adultery (which I think answer קנאה and נאוף) stand for
in another man's mind with whom I would discourse about
them, as it was impossible, in the beginning of language, to
know what *kinneah* and *niouph* stood for in another man's
mind without explication, they being voluntary signs in every
one.

46. Let us now also consider, after the same manner, the
names of substances in their first application. One of *Adam's*
children, roving in the mountains, lights on a glittering substance which pleases his eye. Home he carries it to *Adam*, who,
upon consideration of it, finds it to be hard, to have a bright
yellow colour, and an exceeding great weight. These perhaps,
at first, are all the qualities he takes notice of in it; and abstracting this complex *idea* consisting of a substance having that
peculiar bright yellowness and a weight very great in proportion
to its bulk, he gives it the name *zahab*, to denominate and mark
all substances that have these sensible qualities in them. It is
evident now that, in this case, *Adam* acts quite differently from
what he did before in forming those *ideas* of mixed modes, to
which he gave the names *kinneah* and *niouph*. For there he put
ideas together only by his own imagination, not taken from the
existence of anything; and to them he gave names to denominate
all things that should happen to agree to those his abstract *ideas*,
without considering whether any such thing did exist or no: the
standard there was of his own making. But in the forming his
idea of this new substance he takes the quite contrary course:
here he has a standard made by nature; and therefore, being to
represent that to himself by the *idea* he has of it, even when it is
absent, he puts in no simple *idea* into his complex one but what
he has the perception of from the thing itself. He takes care
that his *idea* be conformable to this *archetype*, and intends the
name should stand for an *idea* so conformable.

47. This piece of matter, thus denominated *zahab* by *Adam*,
being quite different from any he had seen before, nobody, I
think, will deny to be a distinct species and to have its peculiar
essence, and that the name *zahab* is the mark of the species and
a name belonging to all things partaking in that essence. But
here, it is plain, the essence *Adam* made the name *zahab* stand
for was nothing but a body hard, shining, yellow, and very

heavy. But the inquisitive mind of man, not content with the
knowledge of these, as I may say, superficial qualities, puts
Adam upon further examination of this matter. He therefore
knocks and beats it with flints to see what was discoverable in
the inside; he finds it yield to blows, but not easily separate into
pieces; he finds it will bend without breaking. Is not now
ductility to be added to his former *idea* and made part of the
essence of the species that name *zahab* stands for? Further
trials discover fusibility and fixedness. Are not they also, by the
same reason that any of the others were, to be put into the complex *idea* signified by the name *zahab*? If not, what reason will
there be shown more for the one than the other? If these must,
then all the other properties, which any further trials shall discover in this matter, ought by the same reason to make a part of
the ingredients of the complex *idea* which the name *zahab*
stands for, and so be the essence of the species marked by that
name. Which properties because they are endless, it is plain
that the *idea* made after this fashion by this *archetype* will be
always inadequate.

48. But this is not all: it would also follow that the *names of
substances* would not only have (as in truth they have) but
would also be supposed to *have different significations as used by
different men,* which would very much cumber the use of
language. For if every distinct quality that were discovered in
any matter by anyone were supposed to make a necessary part of
the complex *idea* signified by the common name given it, it
must follow that men must suppose the same word to signify
different things in different men, since they cannot doubt but
different men may have discovered several qualities in substances of the same denomination which others know nothing of.

49. To avoid this therefore, they have *supposed a real essence
belonging to every species,* from which these properties all flow,
and would have their name of the species stand for that. But
they not having any *idea* of that real essence in substances, and
their words signifying nothing but the *ideas* they have, that
which is done by this attempt is only to put the name or sound
in the place and stead of the thing having that real essence,
without knowing what the real essence is; and this is that
which men do when they speak of species of things, as supposing them made by nature and distinguished by real essences.

50. For let us consider: when we affirm that all *gold* is fixed,

either it means that fixedness is a part of the definition, part of the nominal essence the word *gold* stands for; and so this affirmation, *All gold is fixed*, contains nothing but the signification of the term *gold*. Or else it means that fixedness, not being a part of the definition of the word *gold*, is a property of that substance itself: in which case it is plain that the word *gold* stands in the place of a substance having the real essence of a species of things made by nature. In which way of substitution, it has so confused and uncertain a signification that, though this proposition, *Gold is fixed*, be in that sense an affirmation of something real, yet it is a truth will always fail us in its particular application, and so is of no real use nor certainty. For let it be never so true that all *gold*, i.e. all that has the real essence of *gold*, is fixed: what serves this for, whilst we know not in this sense what is or is not *gold*? For if we know not the real essence of gold, it is impossible we should know what parcel of matter has that essence, and so whether it be true *gold* or no.

51. To conclude: What liberty *Adam* had at first to make any complex *ideas* of mixed modes by no other pattern but by his own thoughts, the same have all men ever since had. And the same necessity of conforming his *ideas* of substances to things without him, as to *archetypes* made by nature, that *Adam* was under, if he would not wilfully impose upon himself, the same are all men ever since under, too. The same liberty also that *Adam* had of affixing any new name to any *idea*, the same has anyone still (especially the beginners of languages, if we can imagine any such), but only with this difference: that in places where men in society have already established a language amongst them, the signification of words are very warily and sparingly to be altered. Because men being furnished already with names for their *ideas*, and common use having appropriated known names to certain *ideas*, an affected misapplication of them cannot but be very ridiculous. He that hath new notions will, perhaps, venture sometimes on the coining new terms to express them; but men think it a boldness, and it is uncertain whether common use will ever make them pass for current. But in communication with others, it is necessary that we conform the *ideas* we make the vulgar words of any language stand for to their known proper significations (which I have explained at large already) or else to make known that new signification we apply them to.

CHAPTER VII

OF PARTICLES

1. BESIDES words which are names of *ideas* in the mind, there
are a great many others that are made use of to signify the *connexion* that the mind gives to *ideas or propositions, one with
another*. The mind, in communicating its thought to others,
does not only need signs of the *ideas* it has then before it, but
others also to show or intimate some particular action of its own
at that time relating to those *ideas*. This it does several ways, as
is and *is not* are the general marks of the mind, affirming or
denying. But besides affirmation or negation, without which
there is in words no truth or falsehood, the mind does, in
declaring its sentiments to others, connect not only the parts of
propositions but whole sentences one to another, with their
several relations and dependencies, to make a coherent discourse.

2. The words whereby it signifies what connexion it gives to
the several affirmations and negations that it unites in one
continued reasoning or narration, are generally called *particles*;
and it is in the right use of these that more particularly consists
the clearness and beauty of a good style. To think well, it is
not enough that a man has *ideas* clear and distinct in his thoughts,
nor that he observes the agreement or disagreement of some of
them; but he must think in train and observe the dependence of
his thoughts and reasonings one upon another; and to express
well such methodical and rational thoughts, he must have
words to *show* what *connexion, restriction, distinction, opposition, emphasis*, etc., he gives to each respective *part of his discourse*. To mistake in any of these is to puzzle, instead of in-
forming his hearer; and therefore it is that those words which
are not truly by themselves the names of any *ideas* are of such
constant and indispensable use in language and do much contribute to men's well expressing themselves.

3. This part of grammar has been, perhaps, as much neglected
as some others over-diligently cultivated. It is easy for men to

write one after another of *cases* and *genders*, *moods* and *tenses*, *gerunds* and *supines*. In these and the like there has been great diligence used; and particles themselves, in some languages, have been, with great show of exactness, ranked into their several orders. But though *prepositions* and *conjunctions*, etc., are names well known in grammar, and the particles contained under them carefully ranked into their distinct subdivisions, yet he who would show the right use of particles, and what significancy and force they have, must take a little more pains, enter into his own thoughts, and observe nicely the several postures of his mind in discoursing.

4. Neither is it enough, for the explaining of these words, to render them, as is usually in dictionaries, by words of another tongue which come nearest to their signification; for what is meant by them is commonly as hard to be understood in one as another language. They are all *marks of some action or intimation of the mind*; and therefore to understand them rightly, the several views, postures, stands, turns, limitations, and exceptions, and several other thoughts of the mind, for which we have either none or very deficient names, are diligently to be studied. Of these, there are a great variety, much exceeding the number of particles that most languages have to express them by; and therefore it is not to be wondered that most of these particles have divers and sometimes almost opposite significations. In the Hebrew tongue there is a particle consisting but of one single letter, of which there are reckoned up, as I remember, seventy, I am sure above fifty several significations.

5. 'BUT' is a particle, none more familiar in our language; and he that says it is a discretive conjunction, and that it answers *sed* in Latin or *mais* in French, thinks he has sufficiently explained it. But it seems to me to intimate several relations the mind gives to the several propositions, or parts of them, which it joins by this monosyllable.

First, *BUT to say no more*: here it intimates a stop of the mind, in the course it was going, before it came to the end of it.

Secondly, *I saw BUT two plants*: here it shows that the mind limits the sense to what is expressed, with a negation of all other.

Thirdly, *You pray; BUT it is not that GOD would bring you to the true religion.*

Fourthly, *BUT that he would confirm you in your own.* The

74 Book III, Chapter VIII

first of these *BUTS* intimates a supposition in the mind of
something otherwise than it should be; the latter shows that the
mind makes a direct opposition between that and what goes
before it.

Fifthly, *All animals have sense; BUT a dog is an animal*: here
it signifies little more but that the latter proposition is joined to
the former, as the *minor* of a syllogism.

6. To these, I doubt not, might be added a great many other
significations of this particle, if it were my business to examine
it in its full latitude and consider it in all the places it is to be
found: which, if one should do, I doubt whether, in all those
manners it is made use of, it would deserve the title of *discretive*
which grammarians give to it. But I intend not here a full
explication of this sort of signs. The instances I have given in
this one may give occasion to reflect upon their use and force in
language, and lead us into the contemplation of several actions
of our minds in discoursing, which it has found a way to intimate
to others by these particles, some whereof constantly, and others
in certain constructions, have the sense of a whole sentence contained in them.

CHAPTER VIII

OF ABSTRACT AND CONCRETE TERMS

1. THE ordinary words of language and our common use of
them would have given us light into the nature of our *ideas*, if
they had been but considered with attention. The mind, as has
been shown, has a power to abstract its *ideas*; and so they become
essences, general essences, whereby the sorts of things are distinguished. Now each abstract *idea* being distinct, so that of
any two the one can never be the other, the mind will, by its
intuitive knowledge, perceive their difference; and therefore in
propositions no two whole *ideas* can ever be affirmed one of
another. This we see in the common use of language, which
permits *not any two abstract words, or names of abstract ideas,*
to be *affirmed one of another*. For how near of kin soever they
may seem to be, and how certain soever it is that man is an
animal or rational or white, yet everyone at first hearing perceives the falsehood of these propositions: *Humanity is animality*

or *rationality* or *whiteness*; and this is as evident as any of the most allowed maxims. All our affirmations then are only in concrete, which is the affirming not one abstract *idea* to be another, but one abstract *idea* to be joined to another; which abstract *ideas* in substances may be of any sort, in all the rest are little else but of relations; and in substances the most frequent are of powers: v.g. *A man is white* signifies that the thing that has the essence of a man has also in it the essence of whiteness, which is nothing but a power to produce the *idea* of whiteness in one whose eyes can discover ordinary objects; or *A man is rational* signifies that the same thing, that hath the essence of a man, hath also in it the essence of rationality, i.e. a power of reasoning.

2. This distinction of names shows us also the difference of our *ideas*: for, if we observe them, we shall find that our *simple ideas have all abstract as well as concrete names*, the one whereof is (to speak the language of grammarians) a substantive, the other an adjective: as whiteness, white; sweetness, sweet. The like also holds in our *ideas* of *modes* and relations, as justice, just; equality, equal; only with this difference: that some of the concrete names of relations amongst men chiefly are substantives: as *paternitas, pater*; whereof it were easy to render a reason. But as to our *ideas* of *substances*, we have very few or *no abstract names* at all. For though the Schools have introduced *animalitas, humanitas, corporietas*, and some others, yet they hold no proportion with that infinite number of names of substances, to which they never were ridiculous enough to attempt the coining of abstract ones; and those few that the Schools forged and put into the mouths of their scholars, could never yet get admittance into common use or obtain the licence of public approbation. Which seems to me at least to intimate the confession of all mankind that they have no *ideas* of the real essences of substances, since they have not names for such *ideas*: which no doubt they would have had, had not their consciousness to themselves of their ignorance of them kept them from so idle an attempt. And therefore, though they had *ideas* enough to distinguish gold from a stone and metal from wood, yet they but timorously ventured on such terms as *aurietas* and *saxietas, metallietas* and *lignietas* or the like names, which should pretend to signify the real essences of those substances whereof they knew they had no *ideas*. And indeed it

was only the doctrine of *substantial forms* and the confidence of mistaken pretenders to a knowledge that they had not which first coined and then introduced *animalitas* and *humanitas* and the like; which yet went very little further than their own Schools, and could never get to be current amongst under-standing men. Indeed, *humanitas* was a word familiar amongst the *Romans*, but in a far different sense, and stood not for the abstract essence of any substance, but was the abstract name of a mode, and its concrete *humanus*, not *homo*.

CHAPTER IX

OF THE IMPERFECTION OF WORDS

1.   FROM what has been said in the foregoing chapters, it is easy to perceive what imperfection there is in language and how the very nature of words makes it almost unavoidable for many of them to be doubtful and uncertain in their significations. To examine the perfection or imperfection of words, it is necessary first to consider their use and end: for as they are more or less fitted to attain that, so are they more or less perfect. We have, in the former part of this discourse, often upon occasion men-tioned *a double use of words*.

First, One for the recording of our own thoughts.

Secondly, The other for the communicating of our thoughts to others.

2.   As to the first of these, *for the recording our own thoughts* for the help of our own memories, whereby, as it were, we talk to ourselves, any words will serve the turn. For since sounds are voluntary and indifferent signs of any *ideas*, a man may use what words he pleases to signify his own *ideas* to himself; and there will be no imperfection in them if he constantly use the same sign for the same *idea*, for then he cannot fail of having his meaning understood; wherein consists the right use and per-fection of language.

3.   *Secondly*, as to *communication of words*, that too *has a double use*.

   I. *Civil.*

   II. *Philosophical.*

First, By their *civil use*, I mean such a communication of thoughts and *ideas* by words as may serve for the upholding common conversation and commerce about the ordinary affairs and conveniences of civil life in the societies of men one amongst another.

Secondly, By the *philosophical use* of words, I mean such an use of them as may serve to convey the precise notions of things, and to express in general propositions certain and undoubted truths which the mind may rest upon and be satisfied with in its search after true knowledge. These two uses are very distinct; and a great deal less exactness will serve in the one than in the other, as we shall see in what follows.

4. The chief end of language in communication being to be understood, words serve not well for that end, neither in civil nor philosophical discourse, when any word does not excite in the hearer the same *idea* which it stands for in the mind of the speaker. Now, since sounds have no natural connexion with our *ideas*, but have all their signification from the arbitrary imposition of men, the *doubtfulness* and uncertainty *of their signification*, which *is the imperfection* we here are speaking of, has its cause more in the *ideas* they stand for than in any incapacity there is in one sound more than in another to signify any *idea*, for in that regard they are all equally perfect.

That, then, which makes doubtfulness and uncertainty in the signification of some more than other words, is the difference of *ideas* they stand for.

5. Words having naturally no signification, the *idea* which each stands for must be learned and retained by those who would exchange thoughts and hold intelligible discourse with others in any language. But this is hardest to be done where,

First, The *ideas* they stand for are very complex, and made up of a great number of *ideas* put together.

Secondly, Where the *ideas* they stand for have no certain connexion in nature, and so no settled standard anywhere in nature existing, to rectify and adjust them by.

Thirdly, Where the signification of the word is referred to a standard, which standard is not easy to be known.

Fourthly, Where the signification of the word and the real essence of the thing are not exactly the same.

These are difficulties that attend the signification of several words that are intelligible. Those which are not intelligible at all, such as names standing for any simple *ideas* which another has not organs or faculties to attain, as the names of colours to a blind man or sounds to a deaf man, need not here be mentioned.

In all these cases, we shall find an imperfection in words, which I shall more at large explain in their particular application to our several sorts of *ideas*; for, if we examine them, we shall find that the *names of mixed modes are most liable to doubtfulness and imperfection, for the two first of these reasons, and the names of substances chiefly for the two latter.*

6. *First,* The names of *mixed modes* are, many of them, liable to great uncertainty and obscurity in their signification.

I. *Because of* that *great composition* these complex *ideas* are often made up of. To make words serviceable to the end of communication, it is necessary (as has been said) that they excite in the hearer exactly the same *idea* they stand for in the mind of the speaker. Without this, men fill one another's heads with noise and sounds, but convey not thereby their thoughts, and lay not before one another their *ideas*, which is the end of discourse and language. But when a word stands for a very complex *idea* that is compounded and decompounded, it is not easy for men to form and retain that *idea* so exactly as to make the name in common use stand for the same precise *idea*, without any the least variation. Hence it comes to pass that men's names of very compound *ideas*, such as for the most part are moral words, have seldom in two different men the same precise signification, since one man's complex *idea* seldom agrees with another's, and often differs from his own, from that which he had yesterday or will have tomorrow.

7. II. *Because the names of mixed modes* for the most part *want standards* in nature whereby men may rectify and adjust their significations; therefore they are very various and doubtful. They are assemblages of *ideas* put together at the pleasure of the mind, pursuing its own ends of discourse and suited to its own notions, whereby it designs not to copy anything really existing, but to denominate and rank things as they come to agree with those archetypes or forms it has made. He that first brought the word *sham, wheedle,* or *banter* in use, put together as he thought fit those *ideas* he made it stand for; and as it is with any new names of modes that are now brought into any language, so was it with the old ones when they were first made use of. Names,

therefore, that stand for collections of *ideas* which the mind makes at pleasure must needs be of doubtful signification, when such collections are nowhere to be found constantly united in nature, nor any patterns to be shown whereby men may adjust them. What the word *murder* or *sacrilege*, etc., signifies can never be known from things themselves: there be many of the parts of those complex *ideas* which are not visible in the action itself; the intention of the mind, or the relation of holy things, which make a part of *murder* or *sacrilege*, have no necessary connexion with the outward and visible action of him that commits either; and the pulling the trigger of the gun with which the murder is committed and is all the action that perhaps is visible, has no natural connexion with those other *ideas* that make up the complex one named *murder*. They have their union and combination only from the understanding which unites them under one name; but, uniting them without any rule or pattern, it cannot be but that the signification of the name that stands for such voluntary collections should be often various in the minds of different men, who have scarce any standing rule to regulate themselves and their notions by in such arbitrary *ideas*.

8. It is true, *common use*, that is, the rule of propriety, may be supposed here to afford some aid, to settle the signification of language; and it cannot be denied but that in some measure it does. Common use *regulates the meaning of words* pretty well for common conversation; but, nobody having an authority to establish the precise signification of words, nor determine to what *ideas* anyone shall annex them, common use is not sufficient to adjust them to philosophical discourses: there being scarce any name of any very complex *idea* (to say nothing of others) which, in common use, has not a great latitude and which, keeping within the bounds of propriety, may not be made the sign of far different *ideas*. Besides, the rule and measure of propriety itself being nowhere established, it is often matter of dispute whether this or that way of using a word be propriety of speech or no. From all which it is evident that the names of such kind of very complex *ideas* are naturally liable to this imperfection, to be of doubtful and uncertain signification, and, even in men that have a mind to understand one another, do not always stand for the same *idea* in speaker and hearer. Though the names *glory* and *gratitude* be the same in every man's mouth, through a whole country, yet the complex collective

idea which everyone thinks on or intends by that name is apparently very different in men using the same language.

9.   *The way* also *wherein the names of mixed modes are ordinarily learned does* not a little *contribute to the doubtfulness of their signification*. For, if we will observe how children learn languages, we shall find that, to make them understand what the names of simple *ideas* or substances stand for, people ordinarily show them the thing whereof they would have them have the *idea*, and then repeat to them the name that stands for it: as *white, sweet, milk, sugar, cat, dog*. But as for mixed modes, especially the most material of them, moral words, the sounds are usually learned first; and then, to know what complex *ideas* they stand for, they are either beholden to the explication of others or (which happens for the most part) are left to their own observation and industry; which being little laid out in the search of the true and precise meaning of names, these moral words are in most men's mouths little more than bare sounds; or when they have any, it is for the most part but a very loose, and undetermined, and, consequently, obscure and confused signi-fication.   And even those themselves who have with more attention settled their notions, do yet hardly avoid the incon-venience to have them stand for complex *ideas* different from those which other, even intelligent and studious men make them the signs of.   Where shall one find any either *controversial debate* or *familiar discourse* concerning *honour, faith, grace, religion, church*, etc., wherein it is not easy to observe the different notions men have of them; which is nothing but this: that they are not agreed in the signification of those words nor have in their minds the same complex *ideas* which they make them stand for, and so all the contests that follow thereupon are only about the meaning of a sound.   And hence we see that, in the interpretation of laws, whether divine or human, there is no end: comments beget comments, and explications make new matter for explications; and of limiting, distinguishing, varying the signification of these moral words, there is no end.   These *ideas* of men's making are, by men still having the same power, multiplied *in infinitum*.   Many a man who was pretty well satisfied of the meaning of a text of scripture or clause in the code, at first reading has, by consulting commentators, quite lost the sense of it, and by those elucidations given rise or increase to his doubts, and drawn obscurity upon the place.   I say not this

that I think commentaries needless, but to show how uncertain the names of mixed modes naturally are, even in the mouths of those who had both the intention and the faculty of speaking as clearly as language was capable to express their thoughts.

10. What obscurity this has unavoidably brought upon the writings of men who have lived in remote ages and different countries, it will be needless to take notice: since the numerous volumes of learned men, employing their thoughts that way, are proofs more than enough to show what attention, study, sagacity, and reasoning is required to find out the true meaning *of ancient authors*. But there being no writings we have any great concernment to be very solicitous about the meaning of, but those that contain either truths we are required to believe, or laws we are to obey and draw inconveniences on us when we mistake or transgress, we may be less anxious about the sense of other authors; who writing but their own opinions, we are under no greater necessity to know them than they to know ours. Our good or evil depending not on their decrees, we may safely be ignorant of their notions; and therefore in the reading of them, if they do not use their words with a due clearness and perspicuity, we may lay them aside and, without any injury done them, resolve thus with ourselves,

Si non vis intelligi, debes negligi.

11. If the signification of the names of mixed modes are uncertain, because there be no real standards existing in nature to which those *ideas* are referred and by which they may be adjusted, the *names of substances are of a doubtful signification* for a contrary reason, viz. *because* the *ideas* they stand for are supposed conformable to the reality of things and are *referred to standards* made by nature. In our *ideas* of substances we have not the liberty, as in mixed modes, to frame what combinations we think fit, to be the characteristical notes to rank and denominate things by. In these we must follow nature, suit our complex *ideas* to real existences, and regulate the signification of their names by the things themselves, if we will have our names to be the signs of them and stand for them. Here, it is true, we have patterns to follow, but patterns that will make the signification of their names very uncertain: for names must be of a very unsteady and various meaning, if the *ideas* they stand for be referred to standards without us *that either cannot be known at all or can be known but imperfectly and uncertainly.*

12. The *names of substances have*, as has been shown, a double *reference* in their ordinary use.

First, Sometimes they are made to stand for, and so their signification is supposed to agree to, *the real constitution of things*, from which all their properties flow and in which they all centre. But this real constitution or (as it is apt to be called) essence being utterly unknown to us, any sound that is put to stand for it must be very uncertain in its application; and it will be impossible to know what things are or ought to be called a *horse* or *antimony*, when those words are put for real essences that we have no *ideas* of at all. And therefore in this supposition, the names of substances being referred to standards that cannot be known, their significations can never be adjusted and established by those standards.

13. *Secondly*, The *simple ideas* that are found *to co-exist in substances* being that which their names immediately signify, these, as united in the several sorts of things, *are* the proper *standards* to which their names are referred, and by which their significations may be best rectified. But neither will these *archetypes* so well serve to this purpose as to leave these names without very various and uncertain significations. Because these simple *ideas* that co-exist and are united in the same subject being very numerous, and having all an equal right to go into the complex specific *idea* which the specific name is to stand for, men, though they propose to themselves the very same subject to consider, yet frame very different *ideas* about it; and so the name they use for it unavoidably comes to have, in several men, very different significations. The simple qualities which make up the complex *ideas*, being most of them powers in relation to changes which they are apt to make in or receive from other bodies, are almost infinite. He that shall but observe what a great variety of alterations any one of the baser metals is apt to receive from the different application only of fire and how much a greater number of changes any of them will receive in the hands of a chemist by the application of other bodies, will not think it strange that I count the properties of any sort of bodies not easy to be collected and completely known by the ways of inquiry which our faculties are capable of. They being therefore at least so many that no man can know the precise and definite number, they are differently discovered by different men, according to their various skill, attention, and ways of

handling; who therefore cannot choose but have different *ideas*
of the same substance, and therefore make the signification of
its common name very various and uncertain. For the complex
ideas of substances being made up of such simple ones as are
supposed to co-exist in nature, everyone has a right to put into
his complex *idea* those qualities he has found to be united
together. For, though in the substance *gold* one satisfies himself with colour and weight, yet another thinks solubility in
aqua regia as necessary to be joined with that colour in his *idea* of
gold as anyone does its fusibility: solubility in *aqua regia* being a
quality as constantly joined with its colour and weight, as
fusibility or any others; others put in its ductility or fixedness,
etc., as they have been taught by tradition or experience. Who
of all these has established the right signification of the word
gold? Or who shall be the judge to determine? Each has his
standard in nature, which he appeals to, and with reason thinks
he has the same right to put into his complex *idea*, signified by
the word *gold*, those qualities which upon trial he has found
united; as another, who has not so well examined, has to leave
them out; or a third, who has made other trials, has to put in
others. For the union in nature of these qualities being the true
ground of their union in one complex *idea*, who can say one of
them has more reason to be put in or left out than another?
From whence it will always unavoidably follow that the complex
ideas of substances, in men using the same name for them, will
be very various; and so the significations of those names, very
uncertain.

14. Besides there is scarce any particular thing existing which,
in some of its simple *ideas*, does not communicate with a greater,
and in others with a less, number of particular beings. Who shall
determine in this case which are those that are to make up the
precise collection that is to be signified by the specific name; or
can with any just authority prescribe which obvious or common
qualities are to be left out; or which more secret or more particular are to be put into the signification of the name of any
substance? All *which* together seldom or never fail to *produce*
that various and *doubtful signification in the names of substances*
which causes such uncertainty, disputes, or mistakes, when we
come to a philosophical use of them.

15. It is true as *to civil and common conversation*, the general
names of substances, regulated in their ordinary signification by

some obvious qualities (as by the shape and figure in things of
known seminal propagation, and in other substances for the
most part by colour, joined with some other sensible qualities),
do well enough to design the things men would be understood to
speak of; and so they usually conceive well enough the substances meant by the word *gold* or *apple*, to distinguish the one
from the other. *But in philosphical inquiries and debates*, where
general truths *are* to be established and consequences drawn
from positions laid down, there the precise signification of the
names of substances will be found not only *not* to be *well
established*, but also very hard to be so. For example, he that
shall make malleableness, or a certain degree of fixedness, a part
of his complex *idea* of *gold*, may make propositions concerning
gold and draw consequences from them that will truly and
clearly follow from *gold*, taken in such a signification, but yet
such as another man can never be forced to admit nor be convinced of their truth, who makes not malleableness, or the
same degree of fixedness, part of that complex *idea* that the
name *gold*, in his use of it, stands for.

16. This is a natural and almost unavoidable imperfection in
almost all the names of substances, in all languages whatsoever,
which men will easily find when, once passing from confused or
loose notions, they come to more strict and close inquiries. For
then they will be convinced how doubtful and obscure those
words are in their signification, which in ordinary use appeared
very clear and determined. I was once in a meeting of very
learned and ingenious physicians, where by chance there arose
a question whether any liquor passed through the filaments of
the nerves. The debate having been managed a good while, by
variety of arguments on both sides, I (who had been used to
suspect that the greatest part of disputes were more about the
signification of words than a real difference in the conception of
things) desired that, before they went any further on in this
dispute, they would first examine and establish amongst them
what the word *liquor* signified. They at first were a little sur-
prised at the proposal; and had they been persons less ingenious, they might perhaps have taken it for a very frivolous or
extravagant one, since there was no one there that thought not
himself to understand very perfectly what the word liquor
stood for; which, I think too, none of the most perplexed
names of substances. However, they were pleased to comply

with my motion, and upon examination found that the signification of that word was not so settled and certain as they had all
imagined, but that each of them made it a sign of a different
complex *idea*. This made them perceive that the main of their
dispute was about the signification of that term, and that they
differed very little in their opinions concerning some fluid and
subtle matter passing through the conduits of the nerves, though
it was not so easy to agree whether it was to be called *liquor* or
no: a thing which, when each considered, he thought it not
worth the contending about.

17. How much this is the case in the greatest part of disputes
that men are engaged so hotly in, I shall, perhaps, have an
occasion in another place to take notice. Let us only here
consider a little more exactly the fore-mentioned instance of the
word *gold*, and we shall see how hard it is precisely to determine
its signification. I think all agree to make it stand for a body of a
certain yellow shining colour; which being the *idea* to which
children have annexed that name, the shining yellow part of a
peacock's tail is properly to them gold. Others, finding fusibility
joined with that yellow colour in certain parcels of matter, make
of that combination a complex *idea* to which they give the name
gold, to denote a sort of substances, and so exclude from being
gold all such yellow shining bodies as by fire will be reduced to
ashes, and admit to be of that species or to be comprehended
under that name *gold* only such substances as, having that
shining yellow colour, will by fire be reduced to fusion and not
to ashes. Another by the same reason adds the weight which,
being a quality as straightly joined with that colour as its fusibility, he thinks has the same reason to be joined in its *idea* and
to be signified by its name; and therefore the other, made up of
body, of such a colour and fusibility, to be imperfect; and so on
of all the rest: wherein no one can show a reason why some of
the inseparable qualities that are always united in nature should
be put into the nominal essence and others left out; or why the
word *gold*, signifying that sort of body the ring on his finger is
made of, should determine that sort rather by its colour, weight,
and fusibility, than by its colour, weight, and solubility in
aqua regia, since the dissolving it by that liquor is as inseparable
from it as the fusion by fire, and they are both of them nothing
but the relation which that substance has to two other bodies,
which have a power to operate differently upon it. For by what

right is it that fusibility comes to be a part of the essence signified by the word *gold*, and solubility but a property of it? Or why is its colour part of the essence, and its malleableness but a property? That which I mean is this: that these being all but properties, depending on its real constitution, and nothing but powers either active or passive in reference to other bodies, no one has authority to determine the signification of the word *gold* (as referred to such a body existing in nature) more to one collection of *ideas* to be found in that body than to another: whereby the signification of that name must unavoidably be very uncertain; since, as has been said, several people observe several properties in the same substance; and, I think, I may say nobody, all. And therefore we have but very imperfect descriptions of things, and words have very uncertain significations.

18.   From what has been said, it is easy to observe what has been before remarked, viz. that the *names of simple* ideas *are*, of all others, the *least liable to mistakes*, and that for these reasons. *First*, Because the *ideas* they stand for, being each but one single perception, are much easier got and more clearly retained than the more complex ones, and therefore are not liable to the uncertainty which usually attends those compounded ones of *substances and mixed modes*, in which the precise number of simple *ideas* that make them up are not easily agreed and so readily kept in the mind. And, *secondly*, Because they are never referred to any other essence, but barely that perception they immediately signify: which reference is that which renders the signification of the names of substances naturally so perplexed, and gives occasion to so many disputes. Men that do not perversely use their words or on purpose set themselves to cavil, seldom mistake, in any language which they are acquainted with, the use and signification of the names of simple *ideas*: *white* and *sweet*, *yellow* and *bitter* carry a very obvious meaning with them, which everyone precisely comprehends, or easily perceives he is ignorant of and seeks to be informed. But what precise collection of simple *ideas modesty* or *frugality* stand for in another's use is not so certainly known. And however we are apt to think, we well enough know what is meant by *gold* or *iron*, yet the precise complex *idea* others make them the signs of is not so certain; and I believe it is very seldom that, in speaker and hearer, they stand for exactly the same collection. Which must

needs produce mistakes and disputes, when they are made use of in discourses wherein men have to do with universal propositions, and would settle in their minds universal truths, and consider the consequences that follow from them.

19. By the same rule, the *names of simple modes are, next to those of simple* ideas, *least liable to doubt and uncertainty*, especially those of figure and number, of which men have so clear and distinct *ideas*. Who ever that had a mind to understand them mistook the ordinary meaning of *seven*, or *a triangle*? And in general the least compounded *ideas* in every kind have the least dubious names.

20. Mixed modes, therefore, that are made up but of a few and obvious simple *ideas* have usually names of no very uncertain signification. But the names of *mixed modes* which comprehend a great number of simple *ideas* are commonly of a very doubtful and undetermined meaning, as has been shown. The names of substances, being annexed to *ideas* that are neither the real essences nor exact representations of the patterns they are referred to, are liable yet to greater imperfection and uncertainty, especially when we come to a philosophical use of them.

21. The great disorder that happens in our names of substances proceeding, for the most part, from our want of knowledge and inability to penetrate into their real constitutions, it may probably be wondered *why I charge this as an imperfection* rather *upon our words* than understandings. This exception has so much appearance of justice that I think myself obliged to give a reason why I have followed this method. I must confess, then, that, when I first began this discourse of the understanding, and a good while after, I had not the least thought that any consideration of words was at all necessary to it. But when, having passed over the original and composition of our *ideas*, I began to examine the extent and certainty of our knowledge, I found it had so near a connexion with words that, unless their force and manner of signification were first well observed, there could be very little said clearly and pertinently concerning knowledge, which, being conversant about truth, had constantly to do with propositions. And though it terminated in things, yet it was, for the most part, so much by the intervention of words that they seemed scarce separable from our general knowledge. At least they interpose themselves so much between our understandings and the truth which it would contemplate and apprehend that,

like the *medium* through which visible objects pass, their obscurity and disorder does not seldom cast a mist before our eyes and impose upon our understandings. If we consider, in the fallacies men put upon themselves as well as others and the mistakes in men's disputes and notions, how great a part is owing to words and their uncertain or mistaken significations, we shall have reason to think this no small obstacle in the way to knowledge which, I conclude, we are the more carefully to be warned of, because it has been so far from being taken notice of as an inconvenience that the arts of improving it have been made the business of men's study, and obtained the reputation of learning and subtilty, as we shall see in the following chapter. But I am apt to imagine that, were the imperfections of language as the instrument of knowledge more thoroughly weighed, a great many of the controversies that make such a noise in the world would of themselves cease, and the way to knowledge and perhaps peace, too, lie a great deal opener than it does.

22.   Sure I am that the signification of words in all languages, depending very much on the thoughts, notions, and *ideas* of him that uses them, must unavoidably be of great uncertainty to men of the same language and country. This is so evident in the Greek authors that he that shall peruse their writings will find, in almost every one of them, a distinct language, though the same words.   But when to this natural difficulty in every country, there shall be added different countries, and remote ages wherein the speakers and writers had very different notions, tempers, customs, ornaments, and figures of speech, etc., every one of which influenced the signification of their words then, though to us now they are lost and unknown, *it would become us to be charitable one to another in our interpretations or misunderstandings of* those *ancient writings*; which, though of great concernment to be understood, are liable to the unavoidable difficulties of speech, which (if we except the names of simple *ideas* and some very obvious things) is not capable, without a constant defining the terms, of conveying the sense and intention of the speaker, without any manner of doubt and uncertainty to the hearer.   And in discourses of religion, law, and morality, as they are matters of the highest concernment, so there will be the greatest difficulty.

23.   The volumes of interpreters and commentators on the Old and New Testament are but too manifest proofs of this. Though

everything said in the text be infallibly true, yet the reader may be, nay, cannot choose but be very fallible in the understanding of it. Nor is it to be wondered that the will of GOD, when clothed in words, should be liable to that doubt and uncertainty which unavoidably attends that sort of conveyance, when even his Son, whilst clothed in flesh, was subject to all the frailties and inconveniences of human nature, sin excepted. And we ought to magnify his goodness, that he hath spread before all the world such legible characters of his works and providence, and given all mankind so sufficient a light of reason that they, to whom this written word never came, could not (whenever they set themselves to search) either doubt of the being of a GOD or of the obedience due to him. Since then the precepts of natural religion are plain and very intelligible to all mankind and seldom come to be controverted, and other revealed truths, which are conveyed to us by books and languages, are liable to the common and natural obscurities and difficulties incident to words, methinks it would become us to be more careful and diligent in observing the former, and less magisterial, positive, and imperious in imposing our own sense and interpretations of the latter.

CHAPTER X

OF THE ABUSE OF WORDS

1. BESIDES the imperfection that is naturally in language, and the obscurity and confusion that is so hard to be avoided in the use of words, there are several *wilful faults and neglects* which men are guilty of in this way of communication, whereby they render these signs less clear and distinct in their signification than naturally they need to be.

2. *First*, In this kind, the first and most palpable abuse is the using of words without clear and distinct *ideas*, or, which is worse, signs without anything signified. Of these there are two sorts:

I. One may observe, in all languages, certain words that, if they be examined, will be found, in their first original and their appropriated use, not to stand for any clear and distinct *ideas*. These, for the most part, the several *sects* of philosophy and religion have introduced. For their authors or promoters, either affecting something singular and out of the way of common apprehensions, or to support some strange opinions or cover some weakness of their hypothesis, seldom fail to *coin* new words and such as, when they come to be examined, may justly be called *insignificant terms*. For having either had no determinate collection of *ideas* annexed to them when they were first invented or at least such as, if well examined, will be found inconsistent, it is no wonder if afterwards, in the vulgar use of the same party, they remain empty sounds with little or no signification amongst those who think it enough to have them often in their mouths, as the distinguishing characters of their church or school, without much troubling their heads to examine what are the precise *ideas* they stand for. I shall not need here to heap up instances, everyone's reading and conversation will sufficiently furnish him; or, if he wants to be better stored, the great mint-masters of these kind of terms, I mean the schoolmen and metaphysicians (under which, I think, the disputing natural and moral philosophers of these latter ages may be comprehended) have wherewithal abundantly to content him.

3.   II. Others there be who extend this abuse still further, who take so little care to lay by words which, in their primary notation, have scarce any clear and distinct *ideas* which they are annexed to, that, by an unpardonable negligence, they familiarly *use words* which the propriety of language has affixed to very important *ideas*, *without any distinct meaning* at all. *Wisdom, glory, grace*, etc., are words frequent enough in every man's mouth; but, if a great many of these who use them should be asked what they mean by them, they would be at a stand and not know what to answer: a plain proof that, though they have learned those sounds and have them ready at their tongues' end, yet there are no determined *ideas* laid up in their minds which are to be expressed to others by them.

4.   *Men* having been *accustomed* from their cradles *to learn words* which are easily got and retained *before they knew* or had framed *the complex ideas* to which they were annexed, or which were to be found in the things *they* were thought to *stand* for, they *usually continue to do so* all their lives; and without taking the pains necessary to settle in their minds determined *ideas*,

they use their words for such unsteady and confused notions as they have, contenting themselves with the same words other people use, as if their very sound necessarily carried with it constantly the same meaning. This, though men make a shift with in the ordinary occurrences of life, where they find it necessary to be understood, and therefore they make signs till they are so: yet this insignificancy in their words, when they come to reason concerning either their tenets or interest, manifestly fills their discourse with abundance of empty unintelligible noise and jargon, especially in moral matters, where the words for the most part standing for arbitrary and numerous collections of *ideas* not regularly and permanently united in nature, their bare sounds are often only thought on, or at least very obscure and uncertain notions annexed to them. Men take the words they find in use amongst their neighbours, and that they may not seem ignorant what they stand for, use them confidently without much troubling their heads about a certain fixed meaning, whereby, besides the ease of it, they obtain this advantage: that as in such discourses they seldom are in the right, so they are as seldom to be convinced that they are in the wrong, it being all one to go about to draw those men out of their mistakes, who have no settled notions, as to dispossess a vagrant of his habitation who has no settled abode. This I guess to be so, and everyone may observe in himself and others whether it be or no.

5. *Secondly,* Another great abuse of words is *inconstancy* in the use of them. It is hard to find a discourse written of any subject, especially of controversy, whereon one shall not observe, if he read with attention, the same words (and those commonly the most material in the discourse and upon which the argument turns) used sometimes for one collection of simple *ideas* and sometimes for another, which is a perfect abuse of language. Words being intended for signs of my *ideas* to make them known to others, not by any natural signification but by a voluntary imposition, it is plain cheat and abuse when I make them stand sometimes for one thing and sometimes for another, the wilful doing whereof can be imputed to nothing but great folly or greater dishonesty. And a man in his accounts with another may, with as much fairness, make the characters of numbers stand sometimes for one and sometimes for another collection of tunis: v.g., this character 3 stand sometimes for three, sometimes

for four, and sometimes for eight, as in his discourse or reasoning make the same words stand for different collections of simple *ideas*. If men should do so in their reckonings, I wonder who would have to do with them? One who would speak thus in the affairs and business of the world, and call 8 sometimes seven and sometimes nine, as best served his advantage, would presently have clapped upon him one of the two names men constantly are disgusted with. And yet in arguings and learned contests, the same sort of proceeding passes commonly for wit and learning; but to me it appears a greater dishonesty than the misplacing of counters in the casting up a debt, and the cheat the greater, by how much truth is of greater concernment and value than money.

6.   *Thirdly*, Another abuse of language is an *affected obscurity* by either applying old words to new and unusual significations, or introducing new and ambiguous terms without defining either, or else putting them so together as may confound their ordinary meaning. Though the peripatetic philosophy has been most eminent in this way, yet other sects have not been wholly clear of it. There is scarce any of them that are not cumbered with some difficulties (such is the imperfection of human knowledge), which they have been fain to cover with obscurity of terms and to confound the signification of words which, like a mist before people's eyes, might hinder their weak parts from being discovered. That *body* and *extension*, in common use, stand for two distinct *ideas* is plain to anyone that will but reflect a little. For were their signification precisely the same, it would be proper, and as intelligible, to say the *body of an extension*, as *the extension of a body*; and yet there are those who find it necessary to confound their signification. To this abuse and the mischiefs of confounding the signification of words, logic and the liberal sciences, as they have been handled in the Schools, have given reputation; and the admired art of disputing hath added much to the natural imperfection of languages, whilst it has been made use of and fitted to perplex the signification of words more than to discover the knowledge and truth of things. And he that will look into that sort of learned writings will find the words there much more obscure, uncertain, and undetermined in their meaning than they are in ordinary conversation.

7.   This is unavoidably to be so, where men's parts and learning

are estimated by their skill in *disputing*. And if reputation and reward shall attend these conquests, which depend mostly on the fineness and niceties of words, it is no wonder if the wit of man so employed should perplex, involve, and subtilize the signification of sounds, so as never to want something to say in opposing or defending any question, the victory being adjudged not to him who had truth on his side but the last word in the dispute.

8. This, though a very useless skill and that which I think the direct opposite to the ways of knowledge, hath yet passed hitherto under the laudable and esteemed names of *subtlety* and *acuteness*, and has had the applause of the Schools and encouragement of one part of the learned men of the world. And no wonder, since the philosophers of old (the disputing and wrangling philosophers I mean, such as *Lucian* wittily and with reason taxes) and the schoolmen since, aiming at glory and esteem for their great and universal knowledge, easier a great deal to be pretended to than really acquired, found this a good expedient to cover their ignorance with a curious and inexplicable web of perplexed words and procure to themselves the admiration of others by unintelligible terms, the apter to produce wonder because they could not be understood; whilst it appears in all history that these profound doctors were no wiser nor more useful than their neighbours and brought but small advantage to human life or the societies wherein they lived: unless the coining of new words, where they produced no new things to apply them to, or the perplexing or obscuring the signification of old ones, and so bringing all things into question and dispute, were a thing profitable to the life of man or worthy commendation and reward.

9. For, notwithstanding these learned disputants, these all-knowing doctors, it was to the unscholastic statesman that the governments of the world owed their peace, defence, and liberties; and from the illiterate and contemned mechanic (a name of disgrace) that they received the improvements of useful arts. Nevertheless, this artificial ignorance and *learned gibberish* prevailed mightily in these last ages, by the interest and artifice of those who found no easier way to that pitch of authority and dominion they have attained than by amusing the men of business and ignorant with hard words, or employing the ingenious and idle in intricate disputes about unintelligible terms, and holding them perpetually entangled in that endless

labyrinth. Besides, there is no such way to gain admittance or give defence to strange and absurd doctrines as to guard them round about with legions of obscure, doubtful, and undefined words. Which yet make these retreats more like the dens of robbers or holes of foxes than the fortresses of fair warriors; which if it be hard to get them out of, it is not for the strength that is in them, but the briars and thorns and the obscurity of the thickets they are beset with. For untruth being unacceptable to the mind of man, there is no other defence left for absurdity but obscurity.

10. Thus, learned ignorance and this art of keeping even inquisitive men from true knowledge hath been propagated in the world and hath much perplexed, whilst it pretended to inform, the understanding. For we see that other well-meaning and wise men, whose education and parts had not acquired that *acuteness*, could intelligibly express themselves to one another and, in its plain use, make a benefit of language. But though unlearned men well enough understood the words *white* and *black*, etc., and had constant notions of the *ideas* signified by those words, yet there were philosophers found who had learning and *subtlety* enough to prove that *snow was black*, i.e. to prove that *white* was *black*. Whereby they had the advantage to destroy the instruments and means of discourse, conversation, instruction, and society, whilst with great art and *subtlety* they did no more but perplex and confound the signification of words, and thereby render language less useful than the real defects of it had made it, a gift which the illiterate had not attained to.

11. These learned men did equally instruct men's understandings and profit their lives, as he who should alter the signification of known characters and, by a subtle device of learning far surpassing the capacity of the illiterate, dull, and vulgar, should in his writing show that he could put *A* for *B*, and *D* for *E*, etc., to the no small admiration and benefit of his reader: it being as senseless to put *black*, which is a word agreed on to stand for one sensible *idea*, to put it, I say, for another or the contrary *idea*, i.e. to call *snow black*, as to put this mark *A*, which is a character agreed on to stand for one modification of sound, made by a certain motion of the organs of speech, for *B*, which is agreed on to stand for another modification of sound, made by another certain motion of the organs of speech.

12.   Nor hath this mischief stopped in logical niceties or curious empty speculations: it hath invaded the great concernments of human life and society; obscured and perplexed the material truths of law and divinity; brought confusion, disorder, and uncertainty into the affairs of mankind; and, if not destroyed, yet in great measure rendered useless those two great rules, religion and justice.   What have the greatest part of the comments and disputes upon the laws of GOD and man served for but to make the meaning more doubtful and perplex the sense? What have been the effects of those multiplied curious distinctions and acute niceties but obscurity and uncertainty, leaving the words more unintelligible and the reader more at a loss? How else comes it to pass that princes, speaking or writing to their servants in their ordinary commands, are easily understood; speaking to their people in their laws, are not so?   And, as I remarked before, doth it not often happen that a man of an ordinary capacity very well understands a text or a law that he reads till he consults an expositor or goes to counsel, who, by that time he hath done explaining them, makes the words signify either nothing at all or what he pleases.

13.   Whether any by-interests of these professions have occasioned this, I will not here examine; but I leave it to be considered whether it would not be well for mankind, whose concernment it is to know things as they are and to do what they ought and not to spend their lives in talking about them or tossing words to and fro, whether it would not be well, I say, that the use of words were made plain and direct and that language, which was given us for the improvement of knowledge and bond of society, should not be employed to darken truth and unsettle people's rights, to raise mists and render unintelligible both morality and religion?   Or that at least, if this will happen, it should not be thought learning or knowledge to do so.

14.   *Fourthly*, Another great *abuse of words is the taking them for things*.   This, though it in some degree concerns all names in general, yet more particularly affects those of substances.   To this abuse those men are most subject who most confine their thoughts to any one system and give themselves up into a firm belief of the perfection of any received hypothesis: whereby they come to be persuaded that the terms of that sect are so suited to the nature of things that they perfectly correspond with their

real existence. Who is there, that has been bred up in the peripatetic philosophy, who does not think the ten names, under which are ranked the ten predicaments, to be exactly conformable to the nature of things? Who is there of that school that is not persuaded that *substantial forms, vegetative souls, abhorrence of a vacuum, intentional species,* etc., are something real? These words men have learned from their very entrance upon knowledge and have found their masters and systems lay great stress upon them, and therefore they cannot quit the opinion that they are conformable to nature and are the representations of something that really exists. The *Platonists* have their *soul of the world,* and the *Epicureans* their *endeavour towards motion* in their atoms when at rest. There is scarce any sect in philosophy has not a distinct set of terms that others understand not. But yet this gibberish, which in the weakness of human understanding serves so well to palliate men's ignorance and cover their errors, comes by familiar use amongst those of the same tribe to seem the most important part of language, and of all other the terms the most significant; and should *aerial* and *aetherial vehicles* come once by the prevalency of that doctrine to be generally received anywhere, no doubt those terms would make impressions on men's minds so as to establish them in the persuasion of the reality of such things, as much as *peripatetic forms* and *intentional species* have heretofore done.

15.   How much *names taken for things* are apt to *mislead the understanding,* the attentive reading of philosophical writers would abundantly discover, and that, perhaps, in words little suspected of any such misuse. I shall instance in one only, and that a very familiar one. How many intricate disputes have there been about *matter,* as if there were some such thing really in nature, distinct from *body,* as it is evident the word *matter* stands for an *idea* distinct from the *idea* of body? For if the *ideas* these two terms stood for were precisely the same, they might indifferently in all places be put one for another. But we see that, though it be proper to say, There is *one matter of all bodies,* one cannot say, There is *one body of all matters;* we familiarly say: one *body* is bigger than another, but it sounds harsh (and I think is never used) to say: one *matter* is bigger than another. Whence comes this then? Viz. from hence: that though *matter* and *body* be not really distinct, but wherever there is the one, there is the other, yet *matter* and *body* stand for

two different conceptions, whereof the one is incomplete and but
a part of the other. For *body* stands for a solid extended figured
substance, whereof *matter* is but a partial and more confused
conception, it seeming to me to be used for the substance and
solidity of body without taking in its extension and figure; and
therefore it is that, speaking of *matter*, we speak of it always as
one, because in truth it expressly contains nothing but the *idea*
of a solid substance which is everywhere the same, everywhere
uniform. This being our *idea* of *matter*, we no more conceive or
speak of different *matters* in the world than we do of different
solidities, though we both conceive and speak of different bodies
because extension and figure are capable of variation. But
since solidity cannot exist without extension and figure, the
taking *matter* to be the name of something really existing under
that precision has no doubt produced those obscure and unintelligible discourses and disputes which have filled the heads
and books of philosophers concerning *materia prima*; which
imperfection or abuse, how far it may concern a great many
other general terms, I leave to be considered. This, I think, I
may at least say, that we should have a great many fewer disputes in the world if words were taken for what they are, the
signs of our *ideas* only and not for things themselves. For when
we argue about *matter* or any the like term, we truly argue only
about the *idea* we express by that sound, whether that precise
idea agree to anything really existing in nature or no. And if
men would tell what *ideas* they make their words stand for,
there could not be half that obscurity or wrangling in the search
or support of truth that there is.

16. But whatever inconvenience follows from this mistake of
words, this I am sure: that by constant and familiar use they
charm men into notions far remote from the truth of things. It
would be a hard matter to persuade anyone that the words
which his father, or schoolmaster, the parson of the parish, or
such a reverend doctor used, signified nothing that really
existed in nature: which, perhaps, is *none of the least causes that
men are so hardly drawn to quit their mistakes*, even in opinions
purely philosophical and where they have no other interest but
truth. For the words they have a long time been used to remaining firm in their minds, it is no wonder that the wrong
notions annexed to them should not be removed.

17. *Fifthly*, Another *abuse of words is the setting them in the*

place of things which they do or can by no means signify. We may observe that in the general names of substances, whereof the nominal essences are only known to us, when we put them into propositions and affirm or deny anything about them, we do most commonly tacitly suppose or intend they should stand for the real essence of a certain sort of substances. For, when a man says *gold is malleable,* he means and would insinuate something more than this, that *what I call gold is malleable* (though truly it amounts to no more), but would have this understood, viz. that *gold,* i.e. *what has the real essence of gold, is malleable;* which amounts to thus much, that *malleableness depends on and is inseparable from the real essence of gold.* But a man not knowing wherein that real essence consists, the connexion in his mind of malleableness is not truly with an essence he knows not, but only with the sound gold he puts for it. Thus when we say that *animal rationale* is, and *animal implume bipes latis unguibus* is not a good definition of a man, it is plain we suppose the name *man* in this case to stand for the real essence of a species and would signify that a *rational animal* better described that real essence than *a two-legged animal with broad nails and without feathers.* For else, why might not *Plato* as properly make the word ἄνθρωπος or *man* stand for his complex *idea,* made up of the *ideas* of a body, distinguished from others by a certain shape and other outward appearances, as *Aristotle* make the complex *idea,* to which he gave the name ἄνθρωπος or *man,* of body and the faculty of reasoning joined together, unless the name ἀνθρωπος or *man* were supposed to stand for something else than what it signifies, and to be put in the place of some other thing than the *idea* a man professes he would express by it?

18.   It is true, the names of substances would be much more useful, and propositions made in them much more certain, were the real essences of substances the *ideas* in our minds which those words signified. And it is for want of those real essences that our words convey so little knowledge or certainty in our discourses about them; and therefore the mind, to remove that imperfection as much as it can, makes them, by a secret supposition, to stand for a thing having that real essence, as if thereby it made some nearer approaches to it. For though the word *man* or *gold* signify nothing truly but a complex *idea* of properties, united together in one sort of substances, yet there is scarce anybody in the use of these words but often supposes

each of those names to stand for a thing having the real essence on which those properties depend. Which is so far from diminishing the imperfection of our words that by a plain abuse it adds to it, when we would make them stand for something which, not being in our complex *idea*, the name we use can no ways be the sign of.

19. This shows us the reason why in *mixed modes*, any of the *ideas* that make the composition of the complex one being left out or changed, it is allowed to be another thing, i.e. to be of another species, as is plain in *chance-medley*, *manslaughter*, *murder*, *parricide*, etc. The reason whereof is because the complex *idea* signified by that name is the real as well as nominal essence, and there is no secret reference of that name to any other essence but that. But in *substances* it is not so. For though in that called *gold*, one puts into his complex *idea* whɔt another leaves out, and *vice versa*, yet men do not usually think that therefore the species is changed, because they secretly in their minds refer that name and suppose it annexed to a real immutable essence of a thing existing, on which those properties depend. He that adds to his complex *idea* of *gold* that of fixedness or solubility in *aqua regia*, which he put not in it before, is not thought to have changed the species, but only to have a more perfect *idea* by adding another simple *idea*, which is always in fact joined with those other, of which his former complex *idea* consisted. But this reference of the name to a thing, whereof we have not the *idea*, is so far from helping at all that it only serves the more to involve us in difficulties. For by this tacit reference to the real essence of that species of bodies, the word *gold* (which, by standing for a more or less perfect collection of simple *ideas*, serves to design that sort of body well enough in civil discourse) comes to have no signification at all, being put for somewhat whereof we have no *idea* at all, and so can signify nothing at all when the body itself is away. For however it may be thought all one, yet, if well considered, it will be found a quite different thing to argue about *gold* in name and about a parcel of the body itself, v.g. a piece of *leaf-gold* laid before us, though in discourse we are fain to substitute the name for the thing.

20. That which I think very much disposes men to substitute their names for the real essences of *species* is the supposition before mentioned, that nature works regularly in the production

of things and sets the boundaries to each of those *species* by giving exactly the same real internal constitution to each individual, which we rank under one general name. Whereas anyone who observes their different qualities can hardly doubt that many of the individuals called by the same name are, in their internal constitution, as different one from another as several of those which are ranked under different specific names. *This supposition*, however, *that the same precise internal constitution goes always with the same specific name*, *makes men forward to take* those *names for the representatives* of those real *essences*, though indeed they signify nothing but the complex *ideas* they have in their minds when they use them. So that, if I may so say, signifying one thing and being supposed for or put in the place of another, they cannot but, in such a kind of use, cause a great deal of uncertainty in men's discourses, especially in those who have thoroughly imbibed the doctrine of *substantial forms*, whereby they firmly imagine the several species of things to be determined and distinguished.

21.   But however preposterous and absurd it be to make our names stand for *ideas* we have not, or (which is all one) essences that we know not, it being in effect to make our words the signs of nothing, yet it is evident, to anyone who ever so little reflects on the use men make of their words, that there is nothing more familiar. When a man asks whether this or that thing he sees, let it be a drill or a monstrous *foetus*, be a *man* or no, it is evident the question is not whether that particular thing agree to his complex *idea*, expressed by the name *man*, but whether it has in it the real essence of a species of things which he supposes his name *man* to stand for. In which way of using the names of substances there are these false suppositions contained:

First, that there are certain precise essences according to which nature makes all particular things and by which they are distinguished into *species*. That everything has a real constitution, whereby it is what it is and on which its sensible qualities depend, is past doubt. But I think it has been proved that this makes not the distinction of *species* as we rank them, nor the boundaries of their names.

Secondly, this tacitly also insinuates as if we had *ideas* of these proposed essences. For to what purpose else is it to inquire whether this or that thing have the real essence of the species *man*, if we did not suppose that there were such a specific essence known? Which yet is utterly false; and therefore such application of names, as would make them stand for *ideas* which we have not, must needs cause great disorder in discourses and reasonings about them and be a great inconvenience in our communication by words.

22. *Sixthly*, There remains yet another more general, though perhaps less observed, *abuse of words*; and that is that, men having by a long and familiar use annexed to them certain *ideas*, they are apt *to imagine so near and necessary a connexion between the names and the signification* they use them in that they forwardly suppose one cannot but understand what their meaning is; and therefore one ought to acquiesce in the words delivered, as if it were past doubt that, in the use of those common received sounds, the speaker and hearer had necessarily the same precise *ideas*: whence presuming that, when they have in discourse used any term, they have thereby, as it were, set before others the very thing they talk of. And so likewise taking the words of others as naturally standing for just what they themselves have been accustomed to apply them to, they never trouble themselves to explain their own or understand clearly others' meaning. From whence commonly proceeds noise and wrangling without improvement or information, whilst men take words to be the constant regular marks of agreed notions, which in truth are no more but the voluntary and unsteady signs of their own *ideas*. And yet men think it strange if, in discourse or (where it is often absolutely necessary) in dispute, one sometimes asks the meaning of their terms, though the arguings one may every day observe in conversation make it evident that there are few names of complex *ideas* which any two men use for the same just precise collection. It is hard to name a word which will not be a clear instance of this. *Life* is a term, none more familiar. Anyone almost would take it for an affront to be asked what he meant by it. And yet if it comes in question whether a plant that lies ready formed in the seed have life, whether the embryo in an egg before incubation, or a man in a swoon without sense or motion be alive or no, it is easy to perceive that a clear, distinct, settled *idea* does not always accompany the use of so known a word as that of *life* is. Some gross and confused conceptions men indeed ordinarily have, to which they apply the common words of their language, and such a loose use of their words serves them well enough in their ordinary discourses or affairs.

But this is not sufficient for philosophical inquiries. Knowledge and reasoning require precise determinate *ideas*. And though men will not be so importunately dull as not to understand what others say, without demanding an explication of their terms, nor so troublesomely critical as to correct others in the use of the words they receive from them: yet where truth and knowledge are concerned in the case, I know not what fault it can be to desire the explication of words whose sense seems dubious, or why a man should be ashamed to own his ignorance in what sense another man uses his words, since he has no other way of certainly knowing it but by being informed. This abuse of taking words upon trust has nowhere spread so far, nor with so ill effects, as amongst men of letters. The multiplication and obstinacy of disputes, which has so laid waste the intellectual world, is owing to nothing more than to this ill use of words. For though it be generally believed that there is great diversity of opinions in the volumes and variety of controversies the world is distracted with, yet the most I can find that the contending learned men of different parties do, in their arguings one with another, is that they speak different languages. For I am apt to imagine that, when any of them, quitting terms, think upon things and know what they think, they think all the same, though perhaps what they would have be different.

23. To conclude this consideration of the imperfection and abuse of language: The *ends of language in our discourse with others* being chiefly these three: *first, to make known* one man's thoughts or *ideas* to another. *Secondly*, to do it *with* as much ease and *quickness* as is possible; and, *thirdly*, thereby *to convey* the *knowledge* of things. Language is either abused or deficient, when it fails of any of these three.

First, Words fail in the first of these ends, and lay not open one man's *ideas* to another's view: *first*, when men have names in their mouths without any determinate *ideas* in their minds whereof they are the signs; or *secondly*, when they apply the common received names of any language to *ideas*, to which the common use of that language does not apply them; or *thirdly*, when they apply them very unsteadily, making them stand now for one, and by and by for another *idea*.

24. *Secondly*, Men fail of conveying their thoughts with all the quickness and ease that may be, when they have complex *ideas* without having distinct names for them. This is sometimes

the fault of the language itself, which has not in it a sound yet applied to such a signification; and sometimes the fault of the man who has not yet learned the name for that *idea* he would show another.

25. *Thirdly*, There is no knowledge of things conveyed by men's words, when their *ideas* agree not to the reality of things. Though it be a defect that has its original in our *ideas*, which are not so conformable to the nature of things as attention, study, and application might make them, yet it fails not to extend itself to our words too, when we use them as signs of real beings, which yet never had any reality or existence.

26. *First*, he that hath words of any language without distinct *ideas* in his mind, to which he applies them, does, so far as he uses them in discourse, only make a noise without any sense or signification; and how learned soever he may seem by the use of hard words or learned terms, is not much more advanced thereby in knowledge than he would be in learning, who had nothing in his study but the bare titles of books, without possessing the contents of them. For all such words, however put into discourse according to the right construction of grammatical rules or the harmony of well-turned periods, do yet amount to nothing but bare sounds, and nothing else.

27. *Secondly*, he that has complex *ideas* without particular names for them, would be in no better a case than a bookseller who had in his warehouse volumes that lay there unbound and without titles; which he could therefore make known to others only by showing the loose sheets and communicate them only by tale. This man is hindered in his discourse for want of words to communicate his complex *ideas*, which he is therefore forced to make known by an enumeration of the simple ones that compose them, and so is fain often to use twenty words to express what another man signifies in one.

28. *Thirdly*, he that puts not constantly the same sign for the same *idea*, but uses the same words sometimes in one and sometimes in another signification, ought to pass in the Schools and conversation for as fair a man as he does in the market and exchange who sells several things under the same name.

29. *Fourthly*, he that applies the words of any language to *ideas* different from those to which the common use of that country applies them, however his own understanding may be filled with truth and light, will not by such words be able to

convey much of it to others without defining his terms. For
however the sounds are such as are familiarly known and easily
enter the ears of those who are accustomed to them, yet standing
for other *ideas* than those they usually are annexed to and are
wont to excite in the mind of the hearers, they cannot make
known the thoughts of him who thus uses them.

30.   *Fifthly*, he that hath imagined to himself substances such
as never have been and filled his head with *ideas* which have not
any correspondence with the real nature of things, to which yet
he gives settled and defined names, may fill his discourse and
perhaps another man's head with the fantastical imaginations of
his own brain, but will be very far from advancing thereby one
jot in real and true knowledge.

31.   He that hath names without *ideas*, wants meaning in his
words and speaks only empty sounds.   He that hath complex
ideas without names for them, wants liberty and dispatch in his
expressions and is necessitated to use periphrases.   He that uses
his words loosely and unsteadily will either be not minded or not
understood.   He that applies his names to *ideas* different from
their common use, wants propriety in his language and speaks
gibberish.   And he that hath *ideas* of substances disagreeing
with the real existence of things, so far wants the materials of
true knowledge in his understanding, and hath instead thereof
chimeras.

32.   In our notions concerning substances we are liable to all
the former inconveniences, v.g.: He that uses the word *tarantula*
without having any imagination or *idea* of what it stands for,
pronounces a good word, but so long means nothing at all by it.
(2) He that, in a new-discovered country, shall see several sorts
of animals and vegetables unknown to him before, may have as
true *ideas* of them as of a horse or a stag but can speak of them
only by a description, till he shall either take the names the
natives call them by or give them names himself.   (3) He that
uses the word *body* sometimes for pure extension and sometimes
for extension and solidity together, will talk very fallaciously.
(4) He that gives the name *horse* to that *idea* which common
usage calls *mule*, talks improperly and will not be understood.
(5) He that thinks the name *centaur* stands for some real being,
imposes on himself and mistakes words for things.

33.   In modes and relations generally, we are liable only to the
four first of these inconveniences, viz.:   (1) I may have in my

memory the names of modes, as *gratitude* or *charity*, and yet not
have any precise *ideas* annexed in my thoughts to those names.
(2) I may have *ideas* and not know the names that belong to
them: v.g., I may have the *idea* of a man's drinking till his
colour and humour be altered, till his tongue trips and his eyes
look red and his feet fail him, and yet not know that it is to be
called *drunkenness*. (3) I may have the *ideas* of virtues or vices
and names also, but apply them amiss: v.g., when I apply the
name *frugality* to that *idea* which others call and signify by this
sound, *covetousness*. (4) I may use any of those names with
inconstancy. (5) But in modes and relations I cannot have
ideas disagreeing to the existence of things: for modes being
complex *ideas* made by the mind at pleasure, and relation being
but my way of considering or comparing two things together,
and so also an *idea* of my own making, these *ideas* can scarce be
found to disagree with anything existing, since they are not in
the mind as the copies of things regularly made by nature, nor
as properties inseparably flowing from the internal constitution
or essence of any substance, but, as it were, patterns lodged in
my memory, with names annexed to them to denominate
actions and relations by, as they come to exist. But the mistake
is commonly in my giving a wrong name to my conceptions; and
so, using words on a different sense from other people, I am not
understood but am thought to have wrong *ideas* of them when I
give wrong names to them. Only if I put in my *ideas* of mixed
modes or relations any inconsistent *ideas* together, I fill my
head also with *chimeras*, since such *ideas*, if well examined,
cannot so much as exist in the mind, much less any real being
be ever denominated from them.

34. Since wit and fancy finds easier entertainment in the world
than dry truth and real knowledge, *figurative speeches* and allu-
sion in language will hardly be admitted as *an* imperfection or
abuse of it. I confess, in discourses where we seek rather
pleasure and delight than information and improvement, such
ornaments as are borrowed from them can scarce pass for
faults. But yet, if we would speak of things as they are, we must
allow that all the art of rhetoric, besides order and clearness, all
the artificial and figurative application of words eloquence hath
invented, are for nothing else but to insinuate wrong *ideas*,
move the passions, and thereby mislead the judgment, and so
indeed are perfect cheat; and therefore however laudable or

allowable oratory may render them in harangues and popular addresses, they are certainly, in all discourses that pretend to inform or instruct, wholly to be avoided and, where truth and knowledge are concerned, cannot but be thought a great fault either of the language or person that makes use of them. What and how various they are will be superfluous here to take notice, the books of rhetoric which abound in the world will instruct those who want to be informed; only I cannot but observe how little the preservation and improvement of truth and knowledge is the care and concern of mankind, since the arts of fallacy are endowed and preferred. It is evident how much men love to deceive and be deceived, since rhetoric, that powerful instrument of error and deceit, has its established professors, is publicly taught, and has always been had in great reputation; and I doubt not but it will be thought great boldness, if not brutality, in me to have said thus much against it. *Eloquence*, like the fair sex, has too prevailing beauties in it to suffer itself ever to be spoken against. And it is in vain to find fault with those arts of deceiving wherein men find pleasure to be deceived.

Chapter XI

OF THE REMEDIES OF THE
FOREGOING IMPERFECTIONS AND ABUSES

1. THE natural and improved imperfections of languages we have seen above at large; and speech being the great bond that holds society together, and the common conduit whereby the improvements of knowledge are conveyed from one man and one generation to another, it would well deserve our most serious thoughts to consider what *remedies* are to be found *for these inconveniences* above-mentioned.

2. I am not so vain to think that anyone can pretend to attempt the perfect *reforming* the *languages* of the world, no, not so much as of his own country, without rendering himself ridiculous. To require that men should use their words constantly in the same sense and for none but determined and uniform *ideas*, would be to think that all men should have the same notions and should talk of nothing but what they have clear and distinct *ideas* of.

Which is not to be expected by anyone who hath not vanity enough to imagine he can prevail with men to be very knowing or very silent. And he must be very little skilled in the world who thinks that a voluble tongue shall accompany only a good understanding, or that men's talking much or little shall hold proportion only to their knowledge.

3. But though the market and exchange must be left to their own ways of talking and gossipings not be robbed of their ancient privilege; though the Schools and men of argument would perhaps take it amiss to have anything offered to abate the length or lessen the number of their disputes, yet methinks those *who* pretend *seriously* to *search after* or maintain *truth,* should think themselves obliged to study how they might deliver themselves without obscurity, doubtfulness, or equivocation; to which men's words are naturally liable, if care be not taken.

4. For he that shall well consider the *errors* and obscurity, the mistakes and confusion that is *spread in the world by an ill use of words,* will find some reason to doubt whether language, as it has been employed, has contributed more to the improvement or hindrance of knowledge amongst mankind. How many are there that, when they would think on things, fix their thoughts only on words, especially when they would apply their minds to moral matters? And who then can wonder if the result of such contemplations and reasonings about little more than sounds, whilst the *ideas* they annexed to them are very confused or very unsteady, or perhaps none at all: who can wonder, I say, that such thoughts and reasonings end in nothing but obscurity and mistake, without any clear judgment or knowledge?

5. This inconvenience in an ill use of words men suffer in their own private meditations; but much more manifest are the disorders which follow from it in conversation, discourse, and arguings with others. For language being the great conduit whereby men convey their discoveries, reasonings, and knowledge from one to another, he that makes an ill use of it, though he does not corrupt the fountains of knowledge which are in things themselves, yet he does, as much as in him lies, break or stop the pipes whereby it is distributed to the public use and advantage of mankind. He that uses words without any clear and steady meaning, what does he but lead himself and others into errors? And he that designedly does it ought to be looked

on as an enemy to truth and knowledge. And yet who can wonder that all the sciences and parts of knowledge have been so overcharged with obscure and equivocal terms and insignificant and doubtful expressions, capable to make the most attentive or quick-sighted very little or not at all the more knowing or orthodox, since subtilty, in those who make profession to teach or defend truth, hath passed so much for a virtue: a virtue indeed which, consisting for the most part in nothing but the fallacious and illusory use of *obscure* or *deceitful terms*, is only fit to *make* men more *conceited* in their ignorance and *obstinate* in their errors.

6.   Let us look into the books of controversy of any kind, there we shall see that the effect of obscure, unsteady, or equivocal terms is nothing but noise and wrangling about sounds, without convincing or bettering a man's understanding. For if the *idea* be not agreed on betwixt the speaker and hearer for which the words stand, the argument is not about things but names. As often as such a word whose signification is not ascertained betwixt them comes in use, their understandings have no other object wherein they agree but barely the sound, the things that they think on at that time as expressed by that word being quite different.

7.   Whether a *bat* be a *bird* or no, is not a question whether a *bat* be another thing than indeed it is, or have other qualities than indeed it has, for that would be extremely absurd to doubt of. But the question is (1) either between those that acknow-ledged themselves to have but imperfect *ideas* of one or both of those sorts of things, for which these names are supposed to stand; and then it is a real inquiry concerning the nature of a *bird* or a *bat*, to make their yet imperfect *ideas* of it more com-plete by examining whether all the simple *ideas*, to which com-bined together they both give the name *bird*, be all to be found in a *bat*; but this is a question only of inquirers (not disputers), who neither affirm nor deny, but examine; or (2) it is a question between disputants, whereof the one affirms and the other denies, that a *bat* is a *bird*. And then the question is barely about the signification of one or both these words, in that, they not having both the same complex *ideas* to which they give these two names, one holds and the other denies that these two names may be affirmed one of another. Were they agreed in the signification of these two names, it were impossible they should dispute about them. For they would presently and clearly see

(were that adjusted between them) whether all the simple *ideas* of the more general name *bird* were found in the complex *idea* of a *bat* or no; and so there could be no doubt whether a *bat* were a *bird* or no. And here I desire it may be considered and carefully examined whether the greatest part of the disputes in the world are not merely verbal and about the signification of words; and whether, if the terms they are made in were defined and reduced in their signification (as they must be where they signify anything) to determined collections of the simple *ideas* they do or should stand for, those disputes would not end of themselves and immediately vanish. I leave it then to be considered what the learning of disputation is and how well they are employed for the advantage of themselves or others, whose business is only the vain ostentation of sounds, i.e. those who spend their lives in disputes and controversies. When I shall see any of those combatants strip all his terms of ambiguity and obscurity (which everyone may do in the words he uses himself) I shall think him a champion for knowledge, truth, and peace, and not the slave of vain-glory, ambition, or a party.

8. *To remedy the defects of speech* before-mentioned to some degree and to prevent the inconveniences that follow from them, I imagine the observation of these following rules may be of use, till somebody better able shall judge it worth his while to think more maturely on this matter and oblige the world with his thoughts on it.

First, A man should take care *to use no word without a signification*, no name without an *idea* for which he makes it stand. This rule will not seem altogether needless to anyone who shall take the pains to recollect how often he has met with such words as *instinct*, *sympathy*, and *antipathy*, etc., in the discourse of others, so made use of as he might easily conclude that those that used them had no *ideas* in their minds to which they applied them, but spoke them only as sounds, which usually served instead of reasons on the like occasions. Not but that these words and the like have very proper significations in which they may be used; but there being no natural connexion between any words and any *ideas*, these and any other may be learned by rote and pronounced or writ by men who have no *ideas* in their minds to which they have annexed them, and for which they make them stand; which is necessary they should, if men would speak intelligibly even to themselves alone.

9.   *Secondly*, It is not enough a man *uses* his words *as signs of*
some *ideas*: those *ideas* he annexes them to, if they be *simple*,
must be clear and distinct; if *complex*, must be *determinate*,
i.e. the precise collection of simple *ideas* settled in the mind,
with that sound annexed to it, as the sign of that precise determined collection, and no other. This is very necessary in names
of modes, and especially moral words, which, having no settled
objects in nature from whence their *ideas* are taken as from their
original, are apt to be very confused. *Justice* is a word in every
man's mouth, but most commonly with a very undetermined
loose signification; which will always be so unless a man has in
his mind a distinct comprehension of the component parts that
complex *idea* consists of; and if it be decompounded, must be
able to resolve it still on, till he at last comes to the simple *ideas*
that make it up; and unless this be done, a man makes an ill use
of the word, let it be *justice*, for example, or any other. I do not
say a man needs stand to recollect and make this analysis at
large every time the word *justice* comes in his way; but this at
least is necessary, that he have so examined the signification of
that name, and settled the *idea* of all its parts in his mind, that
he can do it when he pleases. If one, who makes his complex *idea*
of *justice* to be such a treatment of the person or goods of
another as is according to law, hath not a clear and distinct *idea*
what *law is* which makes a part of his complex *idea* of justice, it
is plain his *idea* of justice itself will be confused and imperfect.
This exactness will, perhaps, be judged very troublesome; and
therefore most men will think they may be excused from settling
the complex *ideas* of mixed modes so precisely in their minds.
But yet I must say, till this be done, it must not be wondered
that they have a great deal of obscurity and confusion in their
own minds and a great deal of wrangling in their discourses with
others.
10.   In the names of *substances*, for a right use of them, something more is required than barely *determined ideas*: in these
the names must also be conformable to things as they exist; but of
this I shall have occasion to speak more at large by and by. This
exactness is absolutely necessary in inquiries after philosophical
knowledge and in controversies about truth. And though it
would be well too if it extended itself to common conversation
and the ordinary affairs of life, yet I think that is scarce to be
expected. Vulgar notions suit vulgar discourses; and both,

though confused enough, yet serve pretty well the market and the wake. Merchants and lovers, cooks and tailors have words wherewithal to dispatch their ordinary affairs; and so, I think, might philosophers and disputants too, if they had a mind to understand and to be clearly understood.

11. *Thirdly*, It is not enough that men have *ideas*, determined *ideas*, for which they make these signs stand; but they *must* also take care to *apply their words* as near as may be *to such* ideas *as common use has annexed them to*. For words, especially of languages already framed, being no man's private possession but the common measure of commerce and communication, it is not for anyone at pleasure to change the stamp they are current in, nor alter the *ideas* they are affixed to; or at least, when there is a necessity to do so, he is bound to give notice of it. Men's intentions in speaking are, or at least should be, to be understood; which cannot be without frequent explanations, demands, and other the like incommodious interruptions, where men do not follow common use. Propriety of speech is that which gives our thoughts entrance into other men's minds with the greatest ease and advantage, and therefore deserves some part of our care and study, especially in the names of moral words. The proper signification and use of terms is best to be learned from those who in their writings and discourses appear to have had the clearest notions and applied to them their terms with the exactest choice and fitness. This way of using a man's words according to the propriety of the language, though it have not always the good fortune to be understood, yet most commonly leaves the blame of it on him who is so unskilful in the language he speaks as not to understand it, when made use of as it ought to be.

12. *Fourthly*, But because common use has not so visibly annexed any signification to words as to make men know always certainly what they precisely stand for; and because men in the improvement of their knowledge come to have *ideas* different from the vulgar and ordinary received ones, for which they must either make new words (which men seldom venture to do, for fear of being thought guilty of affectation or novelty) or else must use old ones in a new signification. Therefore after the observation of the foregoing rules, it is sometimes necessary, for the ascertaining the signification of words, to *declare their meaning* where either common use has left it uncertain and loose (as it has in most names of very complex *ideas*) or where the term,

being very material in the discourse and that upon which it chiefly turns, is liable to any doubtfulness or mistake.

13. As the *ideas* men's words stand for are of different sorts, so the way of making known the *ideas* they stand for, when there is occasion, is also different. For though defining be thought the proper *way to make known the proper signification of words*, yet there be some words that will not be defined, as there be others whose precise meaning cannot be made known but by definition, and, perhaps, a third which partake somewhat of both the other, as we shall see in the names of simple *ideas*, modes, and substances.

14. *First*, When a man makes use of the *name* of *any simple* idea, which he perceives is not understood or is in danger to be mistaken, he is obliged, by the laws of ingenuity and the end of speech, to declare his meaning and make known what *idea* he makes it stand for. This, as has been shown, cannot be done by definition; and therefore, when a synonymous word fails to do it, there is but one of these ways left: *First*, Sometimes the *naming the subject wherein that simple* idea *is* to be found will make its name to be understood by those who are acquainted with that subject and know it by that name. So to make a countryman understand what *feuillemorte* colour signifies, it may suffice to tell him it is the colour of withered leaves falling in *autumn*. *Secondly*, But the only sure way of making known the signification of the name of any simple *idea* is *by presenting to his senses that subject which may produce it in his mind* and make him actually have the *idea* that word stands for.

15. *Secondly*, *Mixed modes*, especially those belonging to morality, being most of them such combinations of *ideas* as the mind puts together of its own choice and whereof there are not always standing patterns to be found existing, the signification of their names cannot be made known, as those of simple *ideas*, by any showing, but, in recompense thereof, may be perfectly and exactly *defined*. For they being combinations of several *ideas* that the mind of man has arbitrarily put together, without reference to any archetypes, men may, if they please, exactly know the *ideas* that go to each composition, and so both use these words in a certain and undoubted signification, and perfectly declare, when there is occasion, what they stand for. This, if well considered, would lay great blame on those who make not their discourses about moral things very clear and distinct. For

since the precise signification of the names of mixed modes or, which is all one, the real essence of each species is to be known, they being not of nature's but man's making, it is a great negligence and perverseness to discourse of moral things with uncertainty and obscurity; which is more pardonable in treating of natural substances, where doubtful terms are hardly to be avoided, for a quite contrary reason, as we shall see by and by.

16.   Upon this ground it is that I am bold to think that *morality is capable of demonstration*, as well as mathematics: since the precise real essence of the things moral words stand for may be perfectly known, and so the congruity or incongruity of the things themselves be certainly discovered, in which consists perfect knowledge.   Nor let anyone object that the names of substances are often to be made use of in morality, as well as those of modes, from which will arise obscurity.   For as to substances, when concerned in moral discourses, their divers natures are not so much inquired into as supposed: v.g. when we say that *man is subject to law*, we mean nothing by *man* but a corporeal rational creature; what the real essence or other qualities of that creature are in this case is no way considered.   And therefore, whether a child or changeling be a *man* in a physical sense may amongst the naturalists be as disputable as it will, it concerns not at all the *moral man*, as I may call him, which is this immoveable unchangeable *idea, a corporeal rational being*.   For were there a monkey or any other creature to be found that had the use of reason to such a degree as to be able to understand general signs and to deduce consequences about general *ideas*, he would no doubt be subject to law and, in that sense, be a *man*, how much soever he differed in shape from others of that name.   The names of substances, if they be used in them as they should, can no more disturb moral than they do mathematical discourses: where, if the mathematician speaks of a *cube* or *globe* of *gold*, or any other body, he has his clear settled *idea*, which varies not, though it may by mistake be applied to a particular body to which it belongs not.

17.   This I have here mentioned by the by, to show of what consequence it is for men in their names of mixed modes and, consequently, in all their moral discourses to define their words when there is occasion, since thereby moral knowledge may be brought to so great clearness and certainty.   And it must be great want of ingenuity (to say no worse of it) to refuse to do it,

since a *definition is the only way whereby the precise meaning of moral words can be known*, and yet a way whereby their meaning may be known *certainly* and without leaving any room for any contest about it. And therefore the negligence or perverseness of mankind cannot be excused, if their discourses in morality be not much more clear than those in natural philosophy, since they are about *ideas* in the mind which are none of them false or disproportionate, they having no external beings for *archetypes* which they are referred to and must correspond with. It is far easier for men to frame in their minds an *idea* which shall be the standard to which they will give the name *justice*, with which pattern so made, all actions that agree shall pass under that denomination, than, having seen *Aristides*, to frame an *idea* that shall, in all things, be exactly like him who is as he is, let men make what *idea* they please of him. For the one, they need but know the combination of *ideas* that are put together within in their own minds; for the other, they must inquire into the whole nature and abstruse hidden constitution and various qualities of a thing existing without them.

18.   Another reason that makes the *defining of mixed modes* so necessary, *especially of moral words*, is what I mentioned a little before, viz. that it is *the only way whereby the signification of the most of* them can be known with certainty. For the *ideas* they stand for being for the most part such whose component parts nowhere exist together, but scattered and mingled with others, it is the mind alone that collects them and gives them the union of one *idea*; and it is only by words, enumerating the several simple *ideas* which the mind has united, that we can make known to others what their names stand for: the assistance of the senses in this case not helping us, by the proposal of sensible objects, to show the *ideas* which our names of this kind stand for, as it does often in the names of sensible simple *ideas* and also to some degree in those of substances.

19.   *Thirdly, For the explaining* the signification of *the names of substances*, as they stand for the *ideas* we have of their distinct species, both the fore-mentioned ways, viz. of *showing and defining, are requisite* in many cases to be made use of. For, there being ordinarily in each sort some leading qualities, to which we suppose the other *ideas* which make up our complex *idea* of that species annexed, we forwardly give the specific name to that thing wherein that characteristical mark is found, which we

take to be the most distinguishing *idea* of that species. These leading or characteristical (as I may so call them) *ideas*, in the sorts of animals and vegetables are (as has been before remarked, ch. vi, § 29, and ch. ix, § 15) mostly figure, and in inanimate bodies colour, and in some both together. Now,

20.   These *leading sensible qualities* are those which make *the chief ingredients of our specific ideas*, and consequently the most observable and invariable part in the definitions of our specific names, as attributed to sorts *of substances* coming under our knowledge.   For though the sound *man*, in its own nature, be as apt to signify a complex *idea* made up of animality and rationality, united in the same subject, as to signify any other combination: yet, used as a mark to stand for a sort of creatures we count of our own kind, perhaps the outward shape is as necessary to be taken into our complex *idea*, signified by the word *man*, as any other we find in it; and therefore, why *Plato's animal implume bipes latis unguibus* should not be as good a definition of the name *man*, standing for that sort of creatures, will not be easy to show: for it is the shape, as the leading quality, that seems more to determine that species than a faculty of reasoning, which appears not at first and in some never.   And if this be not allowed to be so, I do not know how they can be excused from murder who kill monstrous births (as we call them) because of an unordinary shape, without knowing whether they have a rational soul or no, which can be no more discerned in a well-formed than ill-shaped infant as soon as born.   And who is it has informed us that a rational soul can inhabit no tenement, unless it has just such a sort of frontispiece or can join itself to and inform no sort of body but one that is just of such an outward structure.

21.   Now *these leading qualities are best made known by showing* and can hardly be made known otherwise.   For the shape of a *horse* or *cassowary* will be but rudely and imperfectly imprinted on the mind by words, the sight of the animals doth it a thousand times better; and the *idea* of the particular colour of *gold* is not to be got by any description of it, but only by the frequent exercise of the eyes about it; as is evident in those who are used to this metal, who will frequently distinguish true from counterfeit, pure from adulterate, by the sight, where others (who have as good eyes but yet by use have not got the precise nice *idea* of that peculiar yellow) shall not perceive any difference.   The like

may be said of those other simple *ideas*, peculiar in their kind to
any substance; for which precise *ideas* there are no peculiar
names. The particular ringing sound there is in *gold*, distinct
from the sound of other bodies, has no particular name annexed
to it, no more than the particular yellow that belongs to that
metal.

22.   But because many of the simple *ideas* that make up our
specific *ideas* of substances are powers, which lie not obvious to
our senses in the things as they ordinarily appear: therefore, *in
the signification of our names of substances, some part of the
signification will be better made known by enumerating those
simple* ideas *than in showing the substance itself.* For he that, to
the yellow shining colour of *gold* got by sight, shall from my
enumerating them have the *ideas* of great ductility, fusibility,
fixedness, and solubility in *aqua regia* will have a perfecter *idea* of
gold than he can have by seeing a piece of *gold* and thereby
imprinting in his mind only its obvious qualities. But if the
formal constitution of this shining, heavy, ductile thing (from
whence all these its properties flow) lay open to our senses, as the
formal constitution or essence of a triangle does, the signification
of the word *gold* might as easily be ascertained as that of *triangle*.

23.   Hence we may take notice how much the foundation of all
our knowledge of corporeal things lies in our senses. For how
spirits, separate from bodies, (whose knowledge and *ideas* of
these things is certainly much more perfect than ours) know
them we have no notion, no *idea* at all. The whole extent of our
knowledge or imagination reaches not beyond our own *ideas*,
limited to our ways of perception. Though yet it be not to be
doubted that spirits of a higher rank than those immersed in
flesh may have as clear *ideas* of the radical constitution of substances as we have of a triangle, and so perceive how all their
properties and operations flow from thence: but the manner
how they come by that knowledge exceeds our conceptions.

24.   But though definitions will serve to explain the names of
substances as they stand for our *ideas*, yet they leave them not
without great imperfection as they stand for things. For our
names of substances being not put barely for our *ideas*, but
being made use of ultimately to represent things, and so are put
in their place, their signification must agree with the truth of
things as well as with men's *ideas*. And therefore in substances,
we are not always to rest in the ordinary complex *idea* commonly

received as the signification of that word, but must go a little further and inquire into the nature and properties of the things themselves, and thereby perfect, as much as we can, our *ideas* of their distinct species, or else learn them from such as are used to that sort of things and are experienced in them. For since it is intended their names should stand for such collections of simple *ideas* as do really exist in things themselves, as well as for the complex *idea* in other men's minds which in their ordinary acceptation they stand for, therefore *to define their names right, natural history is to be inquired into*, and their properties are, with care and examination, to be found out. For it is not enough, for the avoiding inconveniencies in discourses and arguings about natural bodies and substantial things, to have learned, from the propriety of the language, the common but confused or very imperfect *idea* to which each word is applied, and to keep them to that *idea* in our use of them; but we must, by acquainting ourselves with the history of that sort of things, rectify and settle our complex *idea* belonging to each specific name; and in discourse with others (if we find them mistake us) we ought to tell what the complex *idea* is that we make such a name stand for. This is the more necessary to be done by all those who search after knowledge and philosophical verity in that children, being taught words whilst they have but imperfect notions of things, apply them at random and without much thinking and seldom frame determined *ideas* to be signified by them. Which custom (it being easy and serving well enough for the ordinary affairs of life and conversation) they are apt to continue when they are men, and so begin at the wrong end, learning words first and perfectly, but make the notions, to which they apply those words afterwards, very overtly. By this means it comes to pass that men speaking the proper language of their country, i.e. according to grammar-rules of that language, do yet speak very improperly of things themselves and, by their arguing one with another, make but small progress in the discoveries of useful truths and the knowledge of things as they are to be found in themselves, and not in our imaginations; and it matters not much, for the improvement of our knowledge, how they are called.

25. It were therefore to be wished that men, versed in physical inquiries and acquainted with the several sorts of natural bodies, would set down those simple *ideas* wherein they observe the

individuals of each sort constantly to agree. This would remedy a great deal of that confusion which comes from several persons applying the same name to a collection of a smaller or greater number of sensible qualities, proportionably as they have been more or less acquainted with or accurate in examining the qualities of any sort of things which come under one denomination. But a dictionary of this sort, containing, as it were, a natural history, requires too many hands as well as too much time, cost, pains, and sagacity ever to be hoped for; and till that be done, we must content ourselves with such definitions of the names of substances as explain the sense men use them in. And it would be well, where there is occasion, if they would afford us so much. This yet is not usually done; but men talk to one another and dispute in words whose meaning is not agreed between them, out of a mistake that the signification of common words are certainly established and the precise *ideas* they stand for perfectly known, and that it is a shame to be ignorant of them. Both which suppositions are false: no names of complex *ideas* having so settled determined significations that they are constantly used for the same precise *ideas*. Nor is it a shame for a man not to have a certain knowledge of anything but by the necessary ways of attaining it; and so it is no discredit not to know what precise *idea* any sound stands for in another man's mind, without he declare it to me by some other way than barely using that sound, there being no other way without such a declaration certainly to know it. Indeed, the necessity of communication by language brings men to an agreement in the signification of common words, within some tolerable latitude, that may serve for ordinary conversation; and so a man cannot be supposed wholly ignorant of the *ideas* which are annexed to words by common use, in a language familiar to him. But common use, being but a very uncertain rule, which reduces itself at last to the *ideas* of particular men, proves often but a very variable standard. But though such a dictionary as I have above mentioned will require too much time, cost, and pains to be hoped for in this age, yet methinks it is not unreasonable to propose that words standing for things which are known and distinguished by their outward shapes should be expressed by little draughts and prints made of them. A vocabulary made after this fashion would perhaps, with more ease and in less time, teach the true signification of many terms, especially in languages of remote countries or ages, and settle truer *ideas* in men's minds of several things, whereof we read the names in ancient authors, than all the large and laborious comments of learned critics. Naturalists that treat of plants and animals have found the benefit of this way; and he that has had occasion to consult them will have reason to confess that he has a clear *idea* of *apium* or *ibex*, from a little print of that herb or beast, than he could have from a long definition of the names of either of them. And so, no doubt, he would have of *strigil* and *sistrum* if, instead of a *currycomb* and *cymbal*, which are the English names dictionaries render them by, he could see stamped in the margin small pictures of these instruments as they were in use amongst the ancients. *Toga, tunica, pallium* are words easily translated by *gown, coat,* and *cloak*; but we have thereby no more true *ideas* of the fashion of those habits amongst the *Romans* than we have of the faces of the tailors who made them. Such things as these, which the eye distinguishes by their shapes, would be best let into the mind by draughts made of them, and more determine the signification of such words than any other words set for them or made use of to define them. But this only by the by.

26.   *Fifthly,* If men will not be at the pains to declare the meaning of their words, and definitions of their terms are not to be had, yet this is the least can be expected: that, in all discourses wherein one man pretends to instruct or convince another, he should *use the same word constantly in the same sense.* If this were done (which nobody can refuse without great disingenuity), many of the books extant might be spared; many of the controversies in dispute would be at an end; several of those great volumes, swollen with ambiguous words, now used in one sense, and by and by in another, would shrink into a very narrow compass; and many of the philosophers' (to mention no other) as well as poets' works might be contained in a nutshell.

27.   But after all, the provision of words is so scanty in respect of that infinite variety of thoughts that men, wanting terms to suit their precise notions, will, notwithstanding their utmost caution, be forced often to use the same word in somewhat different senses. And though in the continuation of a discourse or the pursuit of an argument, there be hardly room to digress into a particular definition as often as a man varies the signification of any term, yet the import of the discourse will, for the most part, if there be no designed fallacy, sufficiently lead candid and

intelligent readers into the true meaning of it; but where that is not sufficient to guide the reader, there it concerns the writer to explain his meaning and show in what sense he there uses that term.

THE ANALYTICAL CONTENTS

BOOK IV

CHAPTER I

OF KNOWLEDGE IN GENERAL

SECTION
1. Our knowledge conversant about our ideas .. 133
2. Knowledge is the perception of the agreement or disagreement of two ideas 133
3. This agreement four-fold 133
4. First, Of identity or diversity 133
5. Secondly, Of relation 134
6. Thirdly, Of co-existence 134
7. Fourthly, Of real existence 135
8. Knowledge actual or habitual 135
9. Habitual knowledge two-fold 136

CHAPTER II

OF THE DEGREES OF OUR KNOWLEDGE

SECTION
1. Intuitive 138
2. Demonstrative 139
3. Depends on proofs 139
4. But not so easy 139
5. Not without precedent doubt 140
6. Not so clear 140
7. Each step must have intuitive evidence 140
8. Hence the mistake *ex praecognitis et praeconcessis* .. 141
9. Demonstration not limited to quantity 141
10–13. Why it has been so thought 142
14. Sensitive knowledge of particular existence .. 143
15. Knowledge not always clear, where the ideas are so .. 144

CHAPTER III

OF THE EXTENT OF HUMAN KNOWLEDGE

SECTION
1. First, No further than we have ideas   145
2. Secondly, No further than we can perceive their agree-
   ment or disagreement   145
3. Thirdly, Intuitive knowledge extends itself not to all
   the relations of all our ideas   145
4. Fourthly, Nor demonstrative knowledge   146
5. Fifthly, Sensitive knowledge narrower than either   ..   146
6. Sixthly, Our knowledge therefore narrower than our
   ideas   146
7. How far our knowledge reaches   149
8. *First*, Our knowledge of identity and diversity, as far
   as our ideas   149
9. *Secondly*, Of co-existence a very little way   ..   149
10. Because the connexion between most simple ideas is
    unknown   150
11. Especially of secondary qualities   150
12-14. And further, because all connexion between any
    secondary and primary qualities is undiscoverable   ..   150
15. Of repugnancy to co-exist, larger..   152
16. Of the co-existence of powers, a very little way   ..   153
17. Of the spirits, yet narrower   153
18. *Thirdly*, Of other relations, it is not easy to say how
    far. Morality capable of demonstration   154
19. Two things have made moral ideas thought uncapable
    of demonstration: their complexedness, and want of
    sensible representations   155
20. Remedies of those difficulties   157
21. *Fourthly*, Of real existence we have an intuitive
    knowledge of our own, demonstrative of God's,
    sensible of some few other things..   157
22. Our ignorance great   158
23. First, One cause of it, want of ideas, either such as we
    have no conception of, or such as particularly we have not   158
24. Because of their remoteness, or, ...   159
25. Because of their minuteness   160
26. Hence no science of bodies   161
27. Much less of spirits   162
28. Secondly, Want of a discoverable connexion between
    ideas we have   162
29. Instances   163
30. Thirdly, Want of tracing our ideas   164
31. Extent in respect of universality   165

CHAPTER IV

OF THE REALITY OF KNOWLEDGE

SECTION
1. Objection, knowledge placed in ideas may be all bare
vision   166
2–3. Answer, not so, where ideas agree with things   ..   167
4. As, first, all simple ideas do   167
5. Secondly, all complex ideas except of substances   ..   168
6. Hence the reality of mathematical knowledge   ..   168
7. And of moral   169
8. Existence not required to make it real   169
9. Nor will it be less true or certain, because moral ideas
are of our own making and naming   170
10. Mis-naming disturbs not the certainty of the know-
ledge   171
11. Ideas of substances have their archetypes without us   171
12. So far as they agree with those, so far our knowledge
concerning them is real   171
13. In our inquiries about substances, we must consider
ideas and not confine our thoughts to names or species
supposed set out by names   172
14–16. Objection against a changeling being something
between man and beast, answered   173
17. Words and species   176
18. Recapitulation   176

CHAPTER V

OF TRUTH IN GENERAL

SECTION
1. What truth is   176
2. A right joining or separating of signs, i.e. ideas or words   176
3. Which make mental or verbal propositions..   ..   177
4. Mental propositions are very hard to be treated of   ..   177
5. Being nothing but the joining or separating ideas without words   178
6. When mental propositions contain real truth, and
when verbal   178
7. Objection against verbal truth, that thus it may all be
alchimerical   179

8. Answered, real truth is about ideas agreeing to things   180
9. Falsehood is the joining of names otherwise than their
     ideas agree   180
10. General propositions to be treated of more at large ..   180
11. Moral and metaphysical truth   181

CHAPTER VI

OF UNIVERSAL PROPOSITIONS, THEIR TRUTH AND CERTAINTY

SECTION

1. Treating of words necessary to knowledge   181
2. General truths hardly to be understood, but in verbal
     propositions   181
3. Certainty two-fold, of truth and of knowledge   ..   182
4. No proposition can be known to be true where the
     essence of each species mentioned is not known   ..   182
5. This more particularly concerns substances   ..   183
6. The truth of few universal propositions concerning
     substances is to be known   184
7. Because co-existence of ideas in few cases to be known   184
8–9. Instance in gold   184
10. As far as any such co-existence can be known, so far
     universal propositions may be certain. But this will go
     but a little way because,..   185
11–12. The qualities which make our complex ideas of sub-
     stances depend mostly on external, remote, and
     unperceived causes   187
13. Judgment may reach further, but that is not knowledge   189
14. What is requisite for our knowledge of substances ..   190
15. Whilst our ideas of substances contain not their real
     constitutions, we can make but few general certain
     propositions concerning them   191
16. Wherein lies the general certainty of propositions   ..   192

CHAPTER VII

OF MAXIMS

SECTION

1. They are self-evident   192
2. Wherein that self-evidence consists   192
3. Self-evidence not peculiar to received axioms   ..   193

4. First, As to identity and diversity, all propositions are equally self-evident 193

5. Secondly, In co-existence we have few self-evident propositions 195

6. Thirdly, In other relations we may have 195

7. Fourthly, Concerning real existence, we have none .. 195

8. These axioms do not much influence our other knowledge 196

9. Because they are not the truths we first knew .. 196

10. Because, on them the other parts of our knowledge do not depend 197

11. What use these general maxims have 198

12. Maxims, if care be not taken in the use of words, may prove contradictions 204

13. Influence in *vacuum* 204

14. They prove not the existence of things without us .. 205

15. Their application dangerous about complex ideas .. 206

16–18. Instance in man 206

19. Little use of these maxims in proofs where we have clear and distinct ideas 207

20. Their use dangerous where our ideas are confused .. 208

CHAPTER VIII

OF TRIFLING PROPOSITIONS

SECTION

1. Some propositions bring no increase to our knowledge 208

2–3. As, First, Identical propositions 208

4. Secondly, When a part of any complex idea is predicated of the whole 211

5. As part of the definition of the defined .. 212

6. Instance man and palfrey 212

7. For this teaches but the signification of words .. 213

8. But no real knowledge 213

9. General propositions concerning substances are often trifling 214

10. And why 215

11. Thirdly, Using words variously is trifling with them 215

12. Marks of verbal propositions. First, predication in abstract 215

13. Secondly, a part of the definition predicated of any term 216

CHAPTER IX

OF OUR KNOWLEDGE OF EXISTENCE

SECTION
1. General certain propositions concern not existence .. 216
2. A three-fold knowledge of existence   217
3. Our knowledge of our own existence is intuitive .. 217

CHAPTER X

OF OUR KNOWLEDGE OF THE EXISTENCE OF A GOD

SECTION
1. We are capable of knowing certainly that there is a
    GOD   217
2. Man knows that he himself is   218
3. He knows also that nothing cannot produce a being,
    therefore something eternal   218
4. That eternal being must be most powerful 219
5. And most knowing   219
6. And therefore GOD   219
7. Our idea of a most perfect being, not the sole proof of
    a GOD   220
8. Something from eternity   221
9. Two sorts of beings, cogitative and incogitative   .. 221
10. Incogitative being cannot produce a cogitative   .. 221
11–12. Therefore there has been an eternal wisdom   .. 223
13. Whether material or no 223
14. Not material, First, Because every particle of matter is
    not cogitative 224
15. Secondly, One particle alone of matter cannot be
    cogitative   224
16. Thirdly, A system of incogitative matter cannot be
    cogitative   224
17. Whether in motion or at rest   225
18–19. Matter not co-eternal with an eternal mind   .. 226

CHAPTER XI

OF OUR KNOWLEDGE OF THE EXISTENCE OF OTHER THINGS

SECTION
1. Is to be had only by sensation   228
2. Instance whiteness of this paper 228

3. This, though not so certain as demonstration, yet may be called knowledge, and proves the existence of things without us   ..   '..   ..   228
4. First, Because we cannot have them but by the inlet of the senses   229
5. Secondly, Because an idea from actual sensation and another from memory are very distinct perceptions ..   229
6. Thirdly, Pleasure or pain, which accompanies actual sensation, accompanies not the returning of those ideas without the external objects   230
7. Fourthly, Our senses assist one another's testimony of the existence of outward things   230
8. This certainty is as great as our condition needs   ..   231
9. But reaches no further than actual sensation   ..   232
10. Folly to expect demonstration in everything   ..   233
11. Past existence is known by memory   233
12. The existence of spirits not knowable   234
13. Particular propositions concerning existence are knowable   234
14. And general propositions concerning abstract ideas ..   235

CHAPTER XII

Of the Improvement of Our Knowledge

SECTION
1. Knowledge is not from maxims   236
2. The occasion of that opinion   236
3. But from the comparing clear and distinct ideas   ..   236
4. Dangerous to build upon precarious principles   ..   238
5. This no certain way to truth   238
6. But to compare clear complete ideas under steady names   239
7. The true method of advancing knowledge is by considering our abstract ideas   239
8. By which, morality also may be made clearer   ..   240
9. But knowledge of bodies is to be improved only by experience   240
10. This may procure us convenience, not science   ..   241
11. We are fitted for moral knowledge and natural improvements   242
12. But must beware of hypotheses and wrong principles   242
13. The true use of hypotheses   243

14. Clear and distinct ideas with settled names, and the
finding of those which show their agreement or disagreement are the ways to enlarge our knowledge   ..   244
15. Mathematics an instance of it   244

CHAPTER XIII

SOME FURTHER CONSIDERATIONS
CONCERNING OUR KNOWLEDGE

SECTION
1. Our knowledge partly necessary, partly voluntary   ..   245
2. The application voluntary; but we know as things are,
not as we please   246
3. Instance in numbers; in natural religion   246

CHAPTER XIV

OF JUDGMENT

SECTION
1. Our knowledge being short, we want something else   247
2. What use to be made of this twilight state   ..   247
3. Judgment supplies the want of knowledge   248
4. Judgment is the presuming things to be so, without
perceiving it   248

CHAPTER XV

OF PROBABILITY

SECTION
1. Probability is the appearance of agreement upon fallible proofs   249
2. It is to supply the want of knowledge   250
3. Being that which makes us presume things to be true,
before we know them to be so   250
4. The grounds of probability are two: conformity with
our own experience, or the testimony of others'
experience   250
5. In this all the agreements, *pro* and *con*, ought to be
examined, before we come to a judgment   251
6. They being capable of great variety   251

CHAPTER XVI

OF THE DEGREES OF ASSENT

SECTION
1. Our assent ought to be regulated by the grounds of probability 252
2. These cannot always be actually in view, and then we must content ourselves with the remembrance that we once saw ground for such a degree of assent .. 253
3. The ill consequence of this, if our former judgment were not rightly made 253
4. The right use of it, mutual charity and forbearance .. 254
5. Probability is either of matter of fact or speculation .. 255
6. The concurrent experience of all other men with ours produces assurance approaching to knowledge .. 255
7. Unquestionable testimony and experience for the most part produce confidence 256
8. Fair testimony, and the nature of the thing indifferent, produces also confident belief 257
9. Experiences and testimonies, clashing, infinitely vary degrees of probability 257
10. Traditional testimonies, the further removed, the less their proof 257
11. Yet history is of great use 258
12. In things which sense cannot discover, analogy is the great rule of probability 259
13. One case where contrary experience lessens not the testimony 261
14. The bare testimony of revelation is the highest certainty 261

CHAPTER XVII

OF REASON

SECTION
1. Various significations of the word reason 262
2. Wherein reasoning consists 262
3. Its four parts 263
4. Syllogism not the great instrument of reason .. 263
5. Helps little in demonstration, less in probability .. 271
6. Serves not to increase our knowledge, but to fence with it 272
7. Other helps should be sought 273
8. We reason about particulars 273

 9. First, Reason fails us for want of ideas   274
10. Secondly, Because of obscure and imperfect ideas   .. 275
11. Thirdly, For want of intermediate ideas   275
12. Fourthly, Because of wrong principles   275
13. Fifthly, Because of doubtful terms   275
14. Our highest degree of knowledge is intuitive without
    reasoning   276
15. The next is demonstration by reasoning   276
16. To supply the narrowness of this, we have nothing but
    judgment upon probable reasoning   277
17. Intuition, demonstration, judgment   277
18. Consequences of words and consequences of ideas .. 278
19. Four sorts of arguments: First, *ad verecundiam*   .. 278
20. Secondly, *ad ignorantiam*   278
21. Thirdly, *ad hominem*   278
22. Fourthly, *ad judicium* 279
23. Above, contrary, and according to reason 279
24. Reason and faith not opposite   279

CHAPTER XVIII

OF FAITH AND REASON,
AND THEIR DISTINCT PROVINCES

SECTION
 1. Necessary to know their boundaries   280
 2. Faith and reason what, as contra-distinguished   .. 281
 3. No new simple idea can be conveyed by traditional
    revelation   281
 4. Traditional revelation may make us know propositions
    knowable also by reason, but not with the same cer-
    tainty that reason doth 282
 5. Revelation cannot be admitted against the clear
    evidence of reason   283
 6. Traditional revelation much less 284
 7. Things above reason   285
 8. Or not contrary to reason, if revealed, are matter of
    faith 285
 9. Revelation, in matters where reason cannot judge or
    but probably, ought to be hearkened to   286
10. In matters where reason can afford certain knowledge,
    that is to be hearkened to   286
11. If the boundaries be not set between faith and reason,
    no enthusiasm or extravagancy in religion can be
    contradicted 287

CHAPTER XIX

OF ENTHUSIASM

SECTION

1. Love of truth necessary 288
2. A forwardness to dictate, from whence .. 289
3. Force of enthusiasm 289
4. Reason and revelation 289
5. Rise of enthusiasm 289
6–7. Enthusiasm 290
8–9. Enthusiasm mistaken for seeing and feeling .. 290
10. Enthusiasm how to be discovered .. 291
11. Enthusiasm fails of evidence that the proposition is from GOD 292
12. Firmness of persuasion, no proof that any proposition is from GOD 294
13. Light in the mind, what 294
14. Revelation must be judged of by reason 294
15–16. Belief no proof of revelation 295

CHAPTER XX

OF WRONG ASSENT, OR ERROR

SECTION

1. Causes of error 296
2. First, Want of proofs 297
3. Objection, what shall become of these who want them, answered 298
4. People hindered from inquiry 298
5. Secondly, Want of skill to use them 299
6. Thirdly, Want of will to use them 300
7. Fourthly, Wrong measures of probability, whereof .. 301
8–10. First, Doubtful propositions taken for principles .. 301
11. Secondly, Received hypothesis 303
12. Thirdly, Predominant passions 304
13. The means of evading probabilities: *first*, supposed fallacy 304
14. Secondly, supposed arguments for the contrary .. 305
15. What probabilities determine the assent 305
16. Where it is in our power to suspend it 306
17. Fourthly, Authority 307
18. Men not in so many errors as is imagined 308

CHAPTER XXI

OF THE DIVISION OF THE SCIENCES

SECTION
1. Three sorts 308
2. First, *Physica* 309
3. Secondly, *Practica* 309
4. Thirdly, Σημειωτικὴ 309
5. This is the first division of the objects of knowledge 310

BOOK IV

OF KNOWLEDGE AND OPINION

Chapter I

OF KNOWLEDGE IN GENERAL

1. SINCE *the mind*, in all its thoughts and reasonings, hath no other immediate object but its own *ideas*, which it alone does or can contemplate, it is evident that our knowledge is only conversant about them.

2. *Knowledge* then seems to me to be nothing but *the perception of the connexion and agreement, or disagreement and repugnancy, of any of our ideas.* In this alone it consists. Where this perception is, there is knowledge; and where it is not, there, though we may fancy, guess, or believe, yet we always come short of knowledge. For when we know that *white is not black*, what do we else but perceive that these two *ideas* do not agree? When we possess ourselves with the utmost security of the demonstration that *the three angles of a triangle are equal to two right ones*, what do we more but perceive that equality to two right ones does necessarily agree to and is inseparable from the three angles of a triangle?

3. But to understand a little more distinctly wherein this agreement or disagreement consists, I think we may reduce it all to these four sorts:

   1. *Identity*, or *diversity*.
   2. *Relation*.
   3. *Co-existence*, or *necessary connexion*.
   4. *Real existence*.

4. *First*, As to the first sort of agreement or disagreement, viz. *identity* or *diversity*. It is the first act of the mind, when it has any sentiments or *ideas* at all, to perceive its *ideas*, and so far as it perceives them, to know each what it is, and thereby also to perceive their difference and that one is not another. This is

133

so absolutely necessary that without it there could be no knowledge, no reasoning, no imagination, no distinct thoughts at all.
By this the mind clearly and infallibly perceives each *idea* to
agree with itself and to be what it is, and all distinct *ideas* to
disagree, i.e. the one not to be the other; and this it does without
pains, labour, or deduction, but at first view, by its natural
power of perception and distinction. And though men of art
have reduced this into those general rules, *What is, is,* and *It is
impossible for the same thing to be and not to be,* for ready application in all cases wherein there may be occasion to reflect on it:
yet it is certain that the first exercise of this faculty is about
particular *ideas.* A man infallibly knows, as soon as ever he has
them in his mind, that the *ideas* he calls *white* and *round* are the
very *ideas* they are, and that they are not other *ideas* which he
calls *red* or *square.* Nor can any maxim or proposition in the
world make him know it clearer or surer than he did before, and
without any such general rule. This then is the first agreement
or disagreement which the mind perceives in its *ideas,* which it
always perceives at first sight; and if there ever happen any doubt
about it, it will always be found to be about the names and not
the *ideas* themselves, whose identity and diversity will always be
perceived as soon and as clearly as the *ideas* themselves are; nor
can it possibly be otherwise.

5. *Secondly,* The next sort of agreement or disagreement the
mind perceives in any of its *ideas* may, I think, be called *relative,*
and is nothing but *the perception of the relation between any two
ideas,* of what kind soever, whether substances, modes, or any
other. For, since all distinct *ideas* must eternally be known not
to be the same, and so be universally and constantly denied one
of another, there could be no room for any positive knowledge at
all if we could not perceive any relation between our *ideas* and
find out the agreement or disagreement they have one with another, in several ways the mind takes of comparing them.

6. *Thirdly,* The third sort of agreement or disagreement to be
found in our *ideas,* which the perception of the mind is employed about, is *co-existence* or *non-co-existence* in the same
subject; and this belongs particularly to substances. Thus when
we pronounce, concerning *gold,* that it is fixed, our knowledge of
this truth amounts to no more but this: that fixedness, or a power
to remain in the fire unconsumed, is an *idea* that always accompanies and is joined with that particular sort of yellowness,

weight, fusibility, malleableness, and solubility in *aqua regia*, which make our complex *idea* signified by the word *gold*.

7. *Fourthly,* The fourth and last sort is that of *actual real existence* agreeing to any *idea*. Within these four sorts of agreement or disagreement is, I suppose, contained all the knowledge we have or are capable of; for all the inquiries that we can make concerning any of our *ideas*, all that we know or can affirm concerning any of them is that it is or is not the same with some other; that it does or does not always co-exist with some other *idea* in the same subject; that it has this or that relation to some other *idea*; or that it has a real existence without the mind. Thus, *Blue is not yellow* is of identity. *Two triangles upon equal bases between two parallels are equal* is of relation. *Iron is susceptible of magnetical impressions* is of co-existence. GOD *is* is of real existence. Though identity and co-existence are truly nothing but relations, yet they are so peculiar ways of agreement or disagreement of our *ideas* that they deserve well to be considered as distinct heads and not under relation in general, since they are so different grounds of affirmation and negation; as will easily appear to anyone who will but reflect on what is said in several places of this Essay. I should now proceed to examine the several degrees of our knowledge, but that it is necessary first to consider the different acceptations of the word *knowledge*.

8. There are several ways wherein the mind is possessed of truth, each of which is called *knowledge*.

(1) There is *actual knowledge*, which is the present view the mind has of the agreement or disagreement of any of its *ideas*, or of the relation they have one to another.

(2) A man is said to know any proposition, which having been once laid before his thoughts, he evidently perceived the agreement or disagreement of the *ideas* whereof it consists, and so lodged it in his memory that, whenever that proposition comes again to be reflected on, he, without doubt or hesitation, embraces the right side, assents to, and is certain of the truth of it. This, I think, one may call *habitual knowledge*; and thus a man may be said to know all those truths which are lodged in his memory, by a foregoing clear and full perception, whereof the mind is assured past doubt as often as it has occasion to reflect on them. For our finite understandings being able to think clearly and distinctly but on one thing at once, if men had no

knowledge of any more than what they actually thought on, they would all be very ignorant, and he that knew most would know but one truth, that being all he was able to think on at one time.

9. Of habitual knowledge there are, also, vulgarly speaking, two degrees:

First, The one is of *such truths laid up in the memory as, whenever they occur to the mind, it actually perceives the relation is between those* ideas. And this is in all those truths whereof we have an *intuitive knowledge,* where the *ideas* themselves, by an immediate view, discover their agreement or disagreement one with another.

Secondly, The other is of *such truths whereof the mind having been convinced, it retains the memory of the conviction, without the proofs.* Thus a man, that remembers certainly that he once perceived the demonstration that the three angles of a triangle are equal to two right ones, is certain that he knows it, because he cannot doubt of the truth of it. In his adherence to a truth where the demonstration by which it was at first known is forgot, though a man may be thought rather to believe his memory than really to know (and this way of entertaining a truth seemed formerly to me like something between opinion and knowledge, a sort of assurance which exceeds bare belief, for that relies on the testimony of another), yet upon a due examination I find it comes not short of perfect certainty and is in effect true knowledge. That which is apt to mislead our first thoughts into a mistake in this matter is that the agreement or disagreement of the *ideas* in this case is not perceived, as it was at first, by an actual view of all the intermediate *ideas* whereby the agreement or disagreement of those in the proposition was at first perceived, but by other intermediate *ideas* that show the agreement or disagreement of the *ideas* contained in the proposition whose certainty we remember. For example, in this proposition that the three angles of a triangle are equal to two right ones, one who has seen and clearly perceived the demonstration of this truth knows it to be true when that demonstration is gone out of his mind, so that at present it is not actually in view and possibly cannot be recollected; but he knows it in a different way from what he did before. The agreement of the two *ideas* joined in that proposition is perceived, but it is by the intervention of other *ideas* than those which at first produced that perception.

He remembers, i.e. he knows (for remembrance is but the reviving of some past knowledge) that he was once certain of the truth of this proposition, that the three angles of a triangle are equal to two right ones. The immutability of the same relations between the same immutable things is now the *idea* that shows him that, if the three angles of a triangle were once equal to two right ones, they will always be equal to two right ones. And hence he comes to be certain that what was once true in the case is always true, what *ideas* once agreed will always agree, and consequently what he once knew to be true he will always know to be true, as long as he can remember that he once knew it. Upon this ground it is that particular demonstrations in mathematics afford general knowledge. If then the perception that the same *ideas* will eternally have the same habitudes and relations be not a sufficient ground of knowledge, there could be no knowledge of general propositions in mathematics: for no mathematical demonstration would be any other than particular, and when a man had demonstrated any proposition concerning one triangle or circle, his knowledge would not reach beyond that particular diagram. If he would extend it further, he must renew his demonstration in another instance before he could know it to be true in another like triangle, and so on; by which means one could never come to the knowledge of any general propositions. Nobody, I think, can deny that Mr. *Newton* certainly knows any proposition that he now at any time reads in his book to be true, though he has not in actual view that admirable chain of intermediate *ideas* whereby he at first discovered it to be true. Such a memory as that, able to retain such a train of particulars, may be well thought beyond the reach of human faculties, when the very discovery, perception, and laying together that wonderful connexion of *ideas* is found to surpass most readers' comprehension. But yet it is evident the author himself knows the proposition to be true, remembering he once saw the connexion of those *ideas*: as certainly as he knows such a man wounded another, remembering that he saw him run him through. But because the memory is not always so clear as actual perception and does in all men more or less decay in length of time, this amongst other differences is one which shows that *demonstrative knowledge* is much more imperfect than *intuitive*, as we shall see in the following chapter.

CHAPTER II

OF THE DEGREES OF OUR KNOWLEDGE

1. ALL our knowledge consisting, as I have said, in the view
the mind has of its own *ideas*, which is the utmost light and
greatest certainty we, with our faculties and in our way of knowledge, are capable of, it may not be amiss to consider a little the
degrees of its evidence. The different clearness of our knowledge
seems to me to lie in the different way of perception the mind has
of the agreement or disagreement of any of its *ideas*. For if we
will reflect on our own ways of thinking, we shall find that sometimes the mind perceives the agreement or disagreement of two
ideas immediately by themselves, without the intervention of any
other; and this I think we may call *intuitive knowledge*. For in
this the mind is at no pains of proving or examining but perceives the truth, as the eye doth light, only by being directed
toward it.   Thus the mind perceives that *white* is not *black*,
that a *circle* is not a *triangle*, that *three* are more than *two* and
equal to *one* and *two*.   Such kind of truths the mind perceives at
the first sight of the *ideas* together, by bare *intuition*, without the
intervention of any other *idea*; and this kind of knowledge is the
clearest and most certain that human frailty is capable of. This
part of knowledge is irresistible and, like bright sunshine, forces
itself immediately to be perceived, as soon as ever the mind
turns its view that way; and leaves no room for hesitation, doubt,
or examination, but the mind is presently filled with the clear
light of it. It is on this *intuition* that depends all the certainty
and evidence of all our knowledge, which certainty everyone
finds to be so great that he cannot imagine, and therefore not
require, a greater; for a man cannot conceive himself capable of
a greater certainty than to know that any *idea* in his mind is such
as he perceives it to be, and that two *ideas* wherein he perceives
a difference are different and not precisely the same. He that
demands a greater certainty than this demands he knows not
what, and shows only that he has a mind to be a sceptic without
being able to be so. Certainty depends so wholly on this
intuition that in the next degree of *knowledge*, which I call

demonstrative, this intuition is necessary in all the connexions of
the intermediate *ideas,* without which we cannot attain knowledge
and certainty.

2. The next degree of knowledge is where the mind perceives
the agreement or disagreement of any *ideas,* but not immediately.
Though, wherever the mind perceives the agreement or disagreement of any of its *ideas,* there be certain knowledge: yet it
does not always happen that the mind sees that agreement or
disagreement which there is between them, even where it is
discoverable; and in that case, remains in ignorance, and at most
gets no further than a probable conjecture. The reason why the
mind cannot always perceive presently the agreement or disagreement of two *ideas* is because those *ideas,* concerning whose
agreement or disagreement the inquiry is made, cannot by the
mind be so put together as to show it. In this case then, when
the mind cannot so bring its *ideas* together as by their immediate
comparison and as it were juxtaposition or application one to
another, to perceive their agreement or disagreement, it is fain,
by the intervention of other *ideas* (one or more, as it happens) to
discover the agreement or disagreement which it searches; and
this is that which we call *reasoning.* Thus the mind, being willing
to know the agreement or disagreement in bigness between the
three angles of a triangle and two right ones, cannot by an
immediate view and comparing them do it, because the three
angles of a triangle cannot be brought at once and be compared
with any one or two angles; and so of this the mind has no
immediate, no intuitive knowledge. In this case the mind is
fain to find out some other angles to which the three angles of a
triangle have an equality, and finding those equal to two right
ones, comes to know their equality to two right ones.

3. Those intervening *ideas* which serve to show the agreement
of any two others are called *proofs*; and where the agreement or
disagreement is by this means plainly and clearly perceived, it
is called *demonstration*: it being *shown* to the understanding, and
the mind made see that it is so. A quickness in the mind to find
out these intermediate *ideas* (that shall discover the agreement
or disagreement of any other) and to apply them right is, I
suppose, that which is called *sagacity.*

4. *This knowledge by intervening proofs,* though it be certain,
yet the evidence of it is *not* altogether *so clear* and bright, nor
the assent so ready, *as in intuitive* knowledge. For, though in

demonstration the mind does at last perceive the agreement or disagreement of the *ideas* it considers, yet it is not without pains and attention: there must be more than one transient view to find it. A steady application and pursuit is required to this discovery, and there must be a progression by steps and degrees, before the mind can in this way arrive at certainty and come to perceive the agreement or repugnancy between two *ideas* that need proofs and the use of reason to show it.

5. *Another difference between intuitive and demonstrative knowledge* is that, though in the latter all doubt be removed when, by the intervention of the intermediate *ideas*, the agreement or disagreement is perceived, yet before the demonstration there was a doubt; which in intuitive knowledge cannot happen to the mind that has its faculty of perception left to a degree capable of distinct *ideas*, no more than it can be a doubt to the eye (that can distinctly see white and black) whether this ink and this paper be all of a colour. If there be sight in the eyes, it will at first glimpse, without hesitation, perceive the words printed on this paper, different from the colour of the paper; and so if the mind have the faculty of distinct perception, it will perceive the agreement or disagreement of those *ideas* that produce intuitive knowledge. If the eyes have lost the faculty of seeing, or the mind of perceiving, we in vain inquire after the quickness of sight in one or clearness of perception in the other.

6. It is true, the perception produced by *demonstration* is also very clear, yet it is often with a great abatement of that evident lustre and full assurance that always accompany that which I call *intuitive*: like a face reflected by several mirrors one to another, where, as long as it retains the similitude and agreement with the object, it produces a knowledge; but it is still in every successive reflection, with a lessening of that perfect clearness and distinctness which is in the first; till at last, after many removes, it has a great mixture of dimness and is not at first sight so knowable, especially to weak eyes. Thus it is with knowledge made out by a long train of proofs.

7. Now, *in every step reason makes in demonstrative knowledge, there is an intuitive knowledge* of that agreement or disagreement it seeks with the next intermediate *idea* which it uses as a proof; for if it were not so, that yet would need a proof, since without the perception of such agreement or disagreement, there is no knowledge produced. If it be perceived by itself, it is

intuitive knowledge; if it cannot be perceived by itself, there is need of some intervening *idea*, as a common measure to show their agreement or disagreement. By which it is plain that every step in reasoning that produces knowledge has intuitive certainty; which when the mind perceives, there is no more required but to remember it to make the agreement or disagreement of the *ideas*, concerning which we inquire, visible and certain. So that to make anything a *demonstration*, it is necessary to perceive the immediate agreement of the intervening *ideas* whereby the agreement or disagreement of the two *ideas* under examination (whereof the one is always the first, and the other the last in the account) is found. This intuitive perception of the agreement or disagreement of the intermediate *ideas*, in each step and progression of the *demonstration*, must also be carried exactly in the mind, and a man must be sure that no part is left out; which because, in long deductions and the use of many proofs, the memory does not always so readily and exactly retain, therefore it comes to pass that this is more imperfect than intuitive knowledge, and men embrace often falsehood for demonstrations.

8. The necessity of this intuitive knowledge in each step of scientifical or demonstrative reasoning gave occasion, I imagine, to that *mistaken axiom, that all reasoning was ex praecognitis et praeconcessis*; which, how far it is mistaken, I shall have occasion to show more at large, where I come to consider propositions, and particularly those propositions which are called maxims, and to show that it is by a mistake that they are supposed to be the foundations of all our knowledge and reasonings.

9. It has been generally taken for granted that mathematics alone are capable of demonstrative certainty; but to have such an agreement or disagreement as may intuitively be perceived being, as I imagine, not the privilege of the *ideas* of *number*, *extension*, and *figure* alone, it may possibly be the want of due method and application in us, and not of sufficient evidence in things, that demonstration has been thought to have so little to do in other parts of knowledge, and been scarce so much as aimed at by any but mathematicians. For whatever *ideas* we have wherein the mind can perceive the immediate agreement or disagreement that is between them, there the mind is capable of intuitive knowledge; and where it can perceive the agreement or disagreement of any two *ideas*, by an intuitive perception of the agreement or disagreement they have with any intermediate

ideas, there the mind is capable of demonstration, which is not limited to *ideas* of extension, figure, number, and their modes.
10.   The reason why it has been generally sought for and supposed to be only in those, I imagine, has been not only the general usefulness of those sciences, but because, in comparing their equality or excess, the modes of numbers have every the least difference very clear and perceivable; and though in extension every the least excess is not so perceptible, yet the mind has found out ways to examine and discover demonstratively the just equality of two angles, or extensions, or figures; and both these, i.e. numbers and figures, can be set down by visible and lasting marks wherein the *ideas* under consideration are perfectly determined, which for the most part they are not where they are marked only by names and words.
11.   But in other simple *ideas*, whose modes and differences are made and counted by degrees and not quantity, we have not so nice and accurate a distinction of their differences as to perceive or find ways to measure their just equality or the least differences.   For those other simple *ideas* being appearances or sensations produced in us by the size, figure, number, and motion of minute corpuscles singly insensible, their different degrees also depend upon the variation of some or all of those causes: which, since it cannot be observed by us in particles of matter whereof each is too subtle to be perceived, it is impossible for us to have any exact measures of the different degrees of these simple *ideas*.   For supposing the sensation or *idea* we name *whiteness* be produced in us by a certain number of globules which, having a verticity about their own centres, strike upon the *retina* of the eye with a certain degree of rotation as well as progressive swiftness: it will hence easily follow that the more the superficial parts of any body are so ordered as to reflect the greater number of globules of light and to give them that proper rotation which is fit to produce this sensation of white in us, the more white will that body appear that, from an equal space, sends to the *retina* the greater number of such corpuscles with that peculiar sort of motion.   I do not say that the nature of light consists in very small round globules, nor of whiteness in such a texture of parts as gives a certain rotation to these globules when it reflects them, for I am not now treating physically of light or colours; but this, I think I may say: that I cannot (and I would be glad anyone would make intelligible

that he did) conceive how bodies without us can anyways affect our senses but by the immediate contact of the sensible bodies themselves, as in tasting and feeling, or the impulse of some insensible particles coming from them, as in seeing, hearing, and smelling; by the different impulse of which parts, caused by their different size, figure, and motion, the variety of sensations is produced in us.

12.   Whether then they be globules or no, or whether they have a verticity about their own centres that produce the *idea* of *whiteness* in us, this is certain: that the more particles of light are reflected from a body, fitted to give them that peculiar motion which produces the sensation of whiteness in us, and possibly too, the quicker that peculiar motion is, the whiter does the body appear from which the greater number are reflected; as is evident in the same piece of paper put in the sunbeams, in the shade, and in a dark hole, in each of which it will produce in us the *idea* of whiteness in far different degrees.

13.   Not knowing, therefore, what number of particles nor what motion of them is fit to produce any precise degree of *whiteness*, we cannot demonstrate the certain equality of any two degrees of *whiteness*, because we have no certain standard to measure them by, nor means to distinguish every the least real difference, the only help we have being from our senses, which in this point fail us. But where the difference is so great as to produce in the mind clearly distinct *ideas* whose differences can be perfectly retained, there these *ideas* of colours, as we see in different kinds, as blue and red, are as capable of demonstration as *ideas* of number and extension. What I have here said of *whiteness* and colours I think holds true in all secondary qualities and their modes.

14.   These two, viz. intuition and demonstration, are the degrees of our knowledge; whatever comes short of one of these, with what assurance soever embraced, is but faith or opinion, but not knowledge, at least in all general truths. There is, indeed, another *perception* of the mind, employed about *the particular existence of finite beings* without us, which, going beyond bare probability and yet not reaching perfectly to either of the foregoing degrees of certainty, passes under the name of knowledge. There can be nothing more certain than that the *idea* we receive from an external object is in our minds: this is intuitive knowledge. But whether there be anything more than barely that *idea* in our minds, whether we can thence certainly infer the

existence of anything without us which corresponds to that *idea* is that whereof some men think there may be a question made: because men may have such *ideas* in their minds, when no such thing exists, no such object affects their senses. But yet here I think we are provided with an evidence that puts us past doubting: for I ask anyone whether he be not invincibly conscious to himself of a different perception, when he looks on the sun by day and thinks on it by night, when he actually tastes wormwood or smells a rose or only thinks on that savour or odour? We as plainly find the difference there is between any *idea* revived in our minds by our own memory and actually coming into our minds by our senses, as we do between any two distinct *ideas*. If anyone say a dream may do the same thing, and all these *ideas* may be produced in us without any external objects, he may please to dream that I make him this answer: (1) That it is no great matter whether I remove his scruple or no: where all is but dream, reasoning and arguments are of no use, truth and knowledge nothing. (2) That I believe he will allow a very manifest difference between dreaming of being in the fire and being actually in it. But yet if he be resolved to appear so sceptical as to maintain that what I call being actually in the fire is nothing but a dream, and that we cannot thereby certainly know that any such thing as fire actually exists without us, I answer: that we certainly finding that pleasure or pain follows upon the application of certain objects to us whose existence we perceive or dream that we perceive by our senses, this certainty is as great as our happiness or misery, beyond which we have no concernment to know or to be. So that, I think, we may add to the two former sorts of *knowledge* this also of the existence of particular external objects, by that perception and consciousness we have of the actual entrance of *ideas* from them, and allow these *three degrees of knowledge*, viz. *intuitive, demonstrative, and sensitive*, in each of which there are different degrees and ways of evidence and certainty.

15. But since our knowledge is founded on and employed about our *ideas* only, will it not follow from thence that it is conformable to our *ideas*; and that where our *ideas* are clear and distinct, or obscure and confused, our knowledge will be so too? To which I answer, No: for our knowledge consisting in the perception of the agreement or disagreement of any two *ideas*, its clearness or obscurity consists in the clearness or obscurity of

that perception, and not in the clearness or obscurity of the *ideas* themselves: v.g. a man that has as clear *ideas* of the angles of a triangle, and of equality to two right ones, as any mathematician in the world may yet have but a very obscure perception of their agreement, and so have but a very obscure knowledge of it. But *ideas* which, by reason of their obscurity or otherwise, are confused cannot produce any clear or distinct knowledge: because, as far as any *ideas* are confused, so far the mind cannot perceive clearly whether they agree or disagree. Or to express the same thing in a way less apt to be misunderstood: he that hath not determined *ideas* to the words he uses cannot make propositions of them of whose truth he can be certain.

Chapter III

OF THE EXTENT OF HUMAN KNOWLEDGE

1.   KNOWLEDGE, as has been said, lying in the perception of the agreement or disagreement of any of our *ideas*, it follows from hence that:

First, We can have *knowledge* no further than we have *ideas.*
2.   *Secondly,* That we can have no *knowledge* further than we can have perception of that agreement or disagreement; which perception being: (1) either by *intuition,* or the immediate comparing any two *ideas*; or (2) by *reason,* examining the agreement or disagreement of two *ideas* by the intervention of some others; or (3) by *sensation,* perceiving the existence of particular things. Hence it also follows:
3.   *Thirdly,* That we cannot have an *intuitive knowledge* that shall extend itself to all our *ideas* and all that we would know about them; because we cannot examine and perceive all the relations they have one to another, by juxtaposition or an immediate comparison one with another. Thus having the *ideas* of an obtuse and an acute angled triangle, both drawn from equal bases and between parallels, I can by intuitive knowledge perceive the one not to be the other, but cannot that way know whether they be equal or no, because their agreement or disagreement in equality can never be perceived by an immediate comparing them; the difference of figure makes their parts

incapable of an exact immediate application, and therefore there is need of some intervening quantities to measure them by, which is demonstration or rational knowledge.

4.   *Fourthly*, It follows, also, from what is above observed that our *rational knowledge* cannot reach to the whole extent of our *ideas*: because between two different *ideas* we would examine, we cannot always find such *mediums* as we can connect one to another with an intuitive knowledge in all the parts of the deduction; and wherever that fails, we come short of knowledge and demonstration.

5.   *Fifthly*, *Sensitive knowledge*, reaching no further than the existence of things actually present to our senses, is yet much narrower than either of the former.

6.   From all which it is evident that *the extent of our knowledge* comes not only short of the reality of things, but even of the extent of our own *ideas*. Though our knowledge be limited to our *ideas* and cannot exceed them either in extent or perfection; and though these be very narrow bounds in respect of the extent of all-being, and far short of what we may justly imagine to be in some even created understandings, not tied down to the dull and narrow information that is to be received from some few and not very acute ways of perception, such as are our senses: yet it would be well with us if our knowledge were but as large as our *ideas*, and there were not many doubts and inquiries concerning the *ideas* we have, whereof we are not nor, I believe, ever shall be in this world resolved. Nevertheless, I do not question but that human knowledge, under the present circumstances of our beings and constitutions, may be carried much further than it hitherto has been, if men would sincerely and with freedom of mind employ all that industry and labour of thought in improving the means of discovering truth, which they do for the colouring or support of falsehood, to maintain a system, interest, or party they are once engaged in. But yet after all I think I may, without injury to human perfection, be confident that our knowledge would never reach to all we might desire to know concerning those *ideas* we have, nor be able to surmount all the difficulties and resolve all the questions that might arise concerning any of them. We have the *ideas* of a *square*, a *circle*, and *equality*, and yet, perhaps, shall never be able to find a circle equal to a square, and certainly know that it is so. We have the *ideas* of *matter* and *thinking*, but possibly

shall never be able to know whether any mere material being thinks or no: it being impossible for us, by the contemplation of our own *ideas*, without revelation, to discover whether Omnipotency has not given to some systems of matter, fitly disposed, a power to perceive and think, or else joined and fixed to matter, so disposed, a thinking immaterial substance: it being, in respect of our notions, not much more remote from our comprehension to conceive that GOD can, if he pleases, superadd to matter a faculty of thinking, than that he should superadd to it another substance with a faculty of thinking, since we know not wherein thinking consists, nor to what sort of substances the Almighty has been pleased to give that power, which cannot be in any created being but merely by the good pleasure and bounty of the Creator. For I see no contradiction in it that the first eternal thinking Being should, if he pleased, give to certain systems of created senseless matter, put together as he thinks fit, some degrees of sense, perception, and thought: though, as I think I have proved, *lib. IV*, *ch. x*, it is no less than a contradiction to suppose matter (which is evidently in its own nature void of sense and thought) should be that eternal first thinking being. What certainty of knowledge can anyone have that some perceptions, such as, v.g. pleasure and pain, should not be in some bodies themselves, after a certain manner modified and moved, as well as that they should be in an immaterial substance upon the motion of the parts of body: body, as far as we can conceive, being able only to strike and affect body; and motion, according to the utmost reach of our *ideas*, being able to produce nothing but motion; so that when we allow it to produce pleasure or pain, or the *idea* of a colour or sound, we are fain to quit our reason, go beyond our *ideas*, and attribute it wholly to the good pleasure of our Maker. For since we must allow he has annexed effects to motion, which we can no way conceive motion able to produce, what reason have we to conclude that he could not order them as well to be produced in a subject we cannot conceive capable of them, as well as in a subject we cannot conceive the motion of matter can any way operate upon? I say not this that I would any way lessen the belief of the soul's immateriality; I am not here speaking of probability but knowledge, and I think not only that it becomes the modesty of philosophy not to pronounce magisterially where we want that evidence that can produce knowledge, but also that it is of use to us to discern how far our knowledge does reach; for the state we are at present in not being that of vision, we must, in many things, content ourselves with faith and probability; and in the present question about the immateriality of the soul, if our faculties cannot arrive at demonstrative certainty, we need not think it strange. All the great ends of morality and religion are well enough secured without philosophical proofs of the soul's immateriality, since it is evident that he who made us at first begin to subsist here, sensible intelligent beings, and for several years continued us in such a state, can and will restore us to the like state of sensibility in another world and make us capable there to receive the retribution he has designed to men, according to their doings in this life. And therefore it is not of such mighty necessity to determine one way or the other, as some, over zealous for or against the immateriality of the soul, have been forward to make the world believe: who, either on the one side, indulging too much their thoughts immersed altogether in matter, can allow no existence to what is not material; or who, on the other side, finding not *cogitation* within the natural powers of matter examined over and over again by the utmost intention of mind, have the confidence to conclude that omnipotency itself cannot give perception and thought to a substance which has the modification of solidity. He that considers how hardly sensation is, in our thoughts, reconcilable to extended matter, or existence to anything that has no extension at all, will confess that he is very far from certainly knowing what his soul is. It is a point which seems to me to be put out of the reach of our knowledge; and he who will give himself leave to consider freely and look into the dark and intricate part of each hypothesis, will scarce find his reason able to determine him fixedly for or against the soul's materiality: since, on which side soever he views it, either as an unextended substance or as a thinking extended matter, the difficulty to conceive either will, whilst either alone is in his thoughts, still drive him to the contrary side. An unfair way which some men take with themselves, who, because of the unconceivableness of something they find in one, throw themselves violently into the contrary hypothesis, though altogether as unintelligible to an unbiassed understanding. This serves not only to show the weakness and the scantiness of our knowledge, but the insignificant triumph of such sort of arguments, which, drawn from our own views, may satisfy us that we can find no certainty on one side of the question, but do not at all thereby help us to truth by running into the opposite opinion, which on examination will be found clogged with equal difficulties. For what safety, what advantage to anyone is it, for the avoiding the seeming absurdities and, to him, unsurmountable rubs he meets with in one opinion, to take refuge in the contrary, which is built on something altogether as inexplicable and as far remote from his comprehension? It is past controversy that we have in us something that thinks: our very doubts about what it is confirm the certainty of its being, though we must content ourselves in the ignorance of what kind of *being* it is; and it is in vain to go about to be sceptical in this, as it is unreasonable in most other cases to be positive against the being of anything because we cannot comprehend its nature. For I would fain know what substance exists that has not something in it which manifestly baffles our understandings. Other spirits, who see and know the nature and inward constitution of things, how much must they exceed us in knowledge? To which if we add larger comprehension, which enables them at one glance to see the connexion and agreement of very many *ideas* and readily supplies to them the intermediate proofs which we, by single and slow steps and long poring in the dark, hardly at last find out and are often ready to forget one before we have hunted out another, we may guess at some part of the happiness of superior ranks of spirits, who have a quicker and more penetrating sight, as well as a larger field of knowledge. But to return to the argument in hand: our *knowledge*, I say, is not only limited to the paucity and imperfections of the *ideas* we have and which we employ it about, but even comes short of that too; but how far it reaches let us now inquire.

7. The affirmations or negations we make concerning the *ideas* we have may, as I have before intimated in general, be reduced to these four sorts, viz. identity, co-existence, relation, and real existence. I shall examine how far our knowledge extends in each of these:

8. *First, As to identity and diversity*: in this way of the agreement or disagreement of our *ideas, our intuitive knowledge is as far extended as our ideas* themselves; and there can be no *idea* in the mind which it does not presently, by an intuitive knowledge, perceive to be what it is, and to be different from any other.

9. *Secondly, As to* the second sort, which is the *agreement or*

disagreement of our *ideas in co-existence*: in this our knowledge is very short, though in this consists the greatest and most material part of our knowledge concerning substances. For our *ideas* of the species of substances being, as I have shown, nothing but certain collections of simple *ideas* united in one subject, and so co-existing together: v.g. our *idea* of *flame* is a body hot, luminous, and moving upward; of *gold*, a body heavy to a certain degree, yellow, malleable, and fusible: these, or some such complex *ideas* as these, in men's minds, do these two names of the different substances, *flame* and *gold*, stand for. When we would know anything further concerning these or any other sort of substances, what do we inquire but what other qualities or powers these substances have or have not? Which is nothing else but to know what other simple *ideas* do or do not co-exist with those that make up that complex *idea*.

10.   This, how weighty and considerable a part soever of human science, is yet very narrow, and scarce any at all. The reason whereof is that the simple *ideas* whereof our complex *ideas* of substances are made up are, for the most part, such as carry with them, in their own nature, no visible necessary connexion or inconsistency with any other simple *ideas*, whose *co-existence* with them we would inform ourselves about.

11.   The *ideas* that our complex ones of substances are made up of, and about which our knowledge concerning substances is most employed, are those of their *secondary qualities*; which depending all (as has been shown) upon the primary qualities of their minute and insensible parts or, if not upon them, upon something yet more remote from our comprehension, it is impossible we should know which have a necessary union or inconsistency one with another; for, not knowing the root they spring from, not knowing what size, figure, and texture of parts they are on which depend and from which result those qualities which make our complex *idea* of gold, it is impossible we should know what other qualities result from or are incompatible with the same constitution of the insensible parts of *gold*, and so consequently must always *co-exist* with that complex *idea* we have of it, or else are *inconsistent* with it.

12.   Besides this ignorance of the primary qualities of the insensible parts of bodies, on which depend all their secondary qualities, there is yet another and more incurable part of ignorance, which sets us more remote from a certain knowledge of the

co-existence or *in-co-existence* (if I may so say) of different *ideas* in the same subject; and that is that there is no discoverable connexion between any *secondary quality and those primary qualities* that it depends on.

13. That the size, figure, and motion of one body should cause a change in the size, figure, and motion of another body is not beyond our conception; the separation of the parts of one body upon the intrusion of another, and the change from rest to motion upon impulse: these, and the like, seem to us to have some *connexion* one with another.   And if we knew these primary qualities of bodies, we might have reason to hope we might be able to know a great deal more of these operations of them one upon another; but our minds not being able to discover any *connexion* betwixt these primary qualities of bodies and the sensations that are produced in us by them, we can never be able to establish certain and undoubted rules of the consequence or *co-existence* of any secondary qualities, though we could discover the size, figure, or motion of those invisible parts which immediately produce them.   We are so far from knowing what figure, size, or motion of parts produce a yellow colour, a sweet taste, or a sharp sound that we can by no means conceive how any *size, figure, or motion* of any particles can possibly produce in us the *idea* of any *colour, taste,* or *sound* whatsoever: there is no conceivable *connexion* betwixt the one and the other.

14. In vain, therefore, shall we endeavour to discover by our *ideas* (the only true way of certain and universal knowledge) what other *ideas* are to be found constantly joined with that of our complex *idea* of any substance: since we neither know the real constitution of the minute parts on which their qualities do depend; nor, did we know them, could we discover any necessary *connexion* between them and any of the *secondary qualities;* which is necessary to be done before we can certainly know their *necessary co-existence*.   So that, let our complex *idea* of any species of substances be what it will, we can hardly, from the simple *ideas* contained in it, certainly determine the *necessary co-existence* of any other quality whatsoever. Our knowledge in all these inquiries reaches very little further than our experience. Indeed some few of the primary qualities have a necessary dependence and visible connexion one with another, as figure necessarily supposes extension, receiving or communicating

motion by impulse supposes solidity. But though these and perhaps some others of our *ideas* have, yet there are so *few* of them that have a *visible connexion* one with another, that we can by intuition or demonstration discover the co-existence of very few of the qualities that are to be found united in substances; and we are left only to the assistance of our senses to make known to us what qualities they contain. For of all the qualities that are *co-existent* in any subject, without this dependence and evident connexion of their *ideas* one with another, we cannot know certainly any two to *co-exist* any further than experience by our senses informs us. Thus though we see the yellow colour and upon trial find the weight, malleableness, fusibility, and fixed-ness that are united in a piece of gold: yet, because no one of these *ideas* has any evident *dependence* or necessary connexion with the other, we cannot certainly know that where any four of these are, the fifth will be there also, how highly probable soever it may be: because the highest probability amounts not to certainty, without which there can be no true knowledge. For this *co-existence* can be no further known than it is perceived; and it cannot be perceived but either in particular subjects, by the observation of our senses, or in general, by the necessary *connexion* of the *ideas* themselves.

15. *As to incompatibility or repugnancy to co-existence*, we may know that any subject can have of each sort of primary quali-ties but one particular at once: v.g. each particular extension, figure, number of parts, motion, excludes all other of each kind. The like also is certain of all sensible *ideas* peculiar to each sense; for whatever of each kind is present in any subject excludes all other of that sort: v.g. no one subject can have two smells or two colours at the same time. To this, perhaps, will be said, Has not an *opal*, or the infusion of *lignum nephriticum*, two colours at the same time? To which I answer that these bodies, to eyes differently placed, may at the same time afford different colours; but I take liberty also to say that, to eyes differently placed, it is different parts of the object that reflect the particles of light, and therefore it is not the same part of the object, and so not the very same subject which at the same time appears both yellow and azure. For it is as impossible that the very same particle of any body should at the same time differently modify or reflect the rays of light, as that it should have two different figures and textures at the same time.

16. But *as to the powers of substances* to change the sensible qualities of other bodies, which make a great part of our inquiries about them and is no inconsiderable branch of our knowledge: I doubt, as to these, whether *our knowledge reaches* much further than our experience, or whether we can come to the discovery of most of these powers and be certain that they are in any subject by the connexion with any of those *ideas* which to us make its essence. Because the active and passive powers of bodies and their ways of operating consisting in a texture and motion of parts which we cannot by any means come to discover, it is but in very few cases we can be able to perceive their dependence on or repugnance to any of those *ideas* which make our complex one of that sort of things. I have here instanced in the corpuscularian hypothesis, as that which is thought to go furthest in an intelligible explication of the qualities of bodies; and I fear the weakness of human understanding is scarce able to substitute another which will afford us a fuller and clearer discovery of the necessary connexion and *co-existence* of the powers which are to be observed united in several sorts of them. This at least is certain: that whichever hypothesis be clearest and truest (for of that it is not my business to determine), our knowledge concerning corporeal substances will be very little advanced by any of them, till we are made to see what qualities and powers of bodies have a *necessary connexion or repugnancy* one with another; which in the present state of philosophy I think we know but to a very small degree. And I doubt whether, with those faculties we have, we shall ever be able to carry our general knowledge (I say not particular experience) in this part much further. Experience is that which in this part we must depend on. And it were to be wished that it were more improved. We find the advantages some men's generous pains have this way brought to the stock of natural knowledge. And if others, especially the philosophers by fire, who pretend to it, had been so wary in their observations and sincere in their reports as those who call themselves philosophers ought to have been, our acquaintance with the bodies here about us and our insight into their powers and operations had been yet much greater.

17. If we are at a loss in respect of the powers and operations of bodies, I think it is easy to conclude *we are much more in the dark in reference to spirits*; whereof we naturally have no *ideas*

but what we draw from that of our own, by reflecting on the operations of our own souls within us as far as they can come within our observation. But how inconsiderable a rank the spirits that inhabit our bodies hold amongst those various and possibly innumerable kinds of nobler beings, and how far short they come of the endowments and perfections of cherubims and seraphims and infinite sorts of spirits above us is what, by a transient hint, in another place, I have offered to my reader's consideration.

18. As to the third sort of our knowledge, viz. *the agreement or disagreement of any of our* ideas *in any other relation*; this, as it is the largest field of our knowledge, so it is hard to determine how far it may extend: because the advances that are made in this part of knowledge depending on our sagacity in finding intermediate *ideas* that may show the *relations* and *habitudes* of *ideas* whose co-existence is not considered, it is a hard matter to tell when we are at an end of such discoveries, and when reason has all the helps it is capable of, for the finding of proofs or examining the agreement or disagreement of remote *ideas*. They that are ignorant of *algebra* cannot imagine the wonders in this kind that are to be done by it; and what further improvements and helps, advantageous to other parts of knowledge, the sagacious mind of man may yet find out, it is not easy to determine. This at least I believe: that the *ideas* of quantity are not those alone that are capable of demonstration and knowledge; and that other and perhaps more useful parts of contemplation would afford us certainty, if vices, passions, and domineering interest did not oppose or menace such endeavours.

The *idea* of a supreme Being, infinite in power, goodness, and wisdom, whose workmanship we are and on whom we depend, and the *idea* of ourselves as understanding rational beings, being such as are clear in us, would, I suppose, if duly considered and pursued, afford such foundations of our duty and rules of action as might place *morality amongst the sciences capable of demonstration*: wherein I doubt not but from self-evident propositions, by necessary consequences as incontestable as those in mathematics, the measures of right and wrong might be made out to anyone that will apply himself with the same indifference and attention to the one as he does to the other of these sciences. The *relation* of other *modes* may certainly be perceived, as well as those of number and extension; and I cannot see why they should not also be capable of demonstration, if due methods were thought on to examine or pursue their agreement or disagreement. *Where there is no property there is no injustice* is a proposition as certain as any demonstration in *Euclid*: for the *idea* of *property* being a right to anything, and the idea to which the name *injustice* is given being the invasion or violation of that right, it is evident that, these *ideas* being thus established, and these names annexed to them, I can as certainly know this proposition to be true as that a triangle has three angles equal to two right ones. Again, *No government allows absolute liberty*: the *idea* of government being the establishment of society upon certain rules or laws which require conformity to them, and the *idea* of absolute liberty being for anyone to do whatever he pleases, I am as capable of being certain of the truth of this proposition as of any in mathematics.

19. That which in this respect has given the advantage to the *ideas* of quantity and made them thought more capable of certainty and demonstration is,

First, That they can be set down and represented by sensible marks, which have a greater and nearer correspondence with them than any words or sounds whatsoever. Diagrams drawn on paper are copies of the *ideas* in the mind, and not liable to the uncertainty that words carry in their signification. An angle, circle, or square, drawn in lines, lies open to the view and cannot be mistaken: it remains unchangeable and may at leisure be considered and examined, and the demonstration be revised, and all the parts of it may be gone over more than once, without any danger of the least change in the *ideas*. This cannot be thus done in *moral ideas*: we have no sensible marks that resemble them whereby we can set them down, we have nothing but words to express them by; which, though when written they remain the same, yet the *ideas* they stand for may change in the same man; and it is very seldom that they are not different in different persons.

Secondly, Another thing that makes the greater difficulty in *ethics* is that *moral ideas* are commonly more complex than those of the figures ordinarily considered in mathematics. From whence these two inconveniences follow: *First*, that their names are of more uncertain signification, the precise collection of simple *ideas* they stand for not being so easily agreed on; and so the sign that is used for them in communication always, and in

thinking often, does not steadily carry with it the same *idea*.
Upon which the same disorder, confusion, and error follows as
would if a man, going to demonstrate something of an *heptagon*,
should, in the diagram he took to do it, leave out one of the angles
or by oversight make the figure with one angle more than the
name ordinarily imported or he intended it should, when at
first he thought of his demonstration. This often happens and
is hardly avoidable in very complex moral *ideas* where, the same
name being retained, one angle, i.e. one simple *idea*, is left out
or put in in the complex one (still called by the same name),
more at one time than another. *Secondly*, from the complexed-
ness of these moral *ideas* there follows another inconvenience,
(viz.) that the mind cannot easily retain those precise combinations so exact and perfectly as is necessary in the examination of
the habitudes and correspondences, agreements or disagreements, of several of them one with another, especially where it is
to be judged of, by long deductions and the intervention of
several other complex *ideas*, to show the agreement or disagreement of two remote ones.

The great help against this which mathematicians find in
diagrams and figures, which remain unalterable in their draughts,
is very apparent, and the memory would often have great difficulty otherwise to retain them so exactly, whilst the mind went
over the parts of them step by step to examine their several
correspondences. And though, in casting up a long sum, either
in *addition*, *multiplication*, or *division*, every part be only a progression of the mind, taking a view of its own *ideas* and considering their agreement or disagreement; and the resolution of
the question be nothing but the result of the whole, made up of
such particulars whereof the mind has a clear perception: yet
without setting down the several parts by marks whose precise
significations are known, and by marks that last and remain in
view when the memory had let them go, it would be almost
impossible to carry so many different *ideas* in mind without
confounding or letting slip some parts of the reckoning, and
thereby making all our reasonings about it useless. In which
case, the cyphers or marks help not the mind at all to perceive
the agreement of any two or more numbers, their equalities, or
proportions: that the mind has only by intuition of its own *ideas*
of the numbers themselves. But the numerical characters are
helps to the memory to record and retain the several *ideas* about

which the demonstration is made, whereby a man may know how far his intuitive knowledge in surveying several of the particulars has proceeded, that so he may without confusion go on to what is yet unknown, and at last have in one view before him the result of all his perceptions and reasonings.

20. One part of *these disadvantages* in moral *ideas*, which has made them be thought not capable of demonstration, may in a good measure be *remedied* by definitions, setting down that collection of simple *ideas* which every term shall stand for, and then using the terms steadily and constantly for that precise collection. And what methods *algebra*, or something of that kind, may hereafter suggest to remove the other difficulties is not easy to foretell. Confident I am that, if men would, in the same method and with the same indifferency, search after moral as they do mathematical truths, they would find them to have a stronger connexion one with another and a more necessary consequence from our clear and distinct *ideas*, and to come nearer perfect demonstration than is commonly imagined. But much of this is not to be expected, whilst the desire of esteem, riches, or power makes men espouse the well-endowed opinions in fashion, and then seek arguments either to make good their beauty, or varnish over and cover their deformity. Nothing being so beautiful to the eye as truth is to the mind; nothing so deformed and irreconcilable to the understanding as a lie. For though many a man can with satisfaction enough own a not very handsome wife in his bosom, yet who is bold enough openly to avow that he has espoused a falsehood and received into his breast so ugly a thing as a lie? Whilst the parties of men cram their tenets down all men's throats whom they can get into their power, without permitting them to examine their truth or falsehood, and will not let truth have fair play in the world nor men the liberty to search after it: what improvements can be expected of this kind? What greater light can be hoped for in the moral sciences? The subject part of mankind in most places might instead thereof, with *Egyptian* bondage, expect *Egyptian* darkness, were not the candle of the Lord set up by himself in men's minds, which it is impossible for the breath or power of man wholly to extinguish.

21. As to the fourth sort of our knowledge, viz. *of* the *real actual existence* of things: we have an intuitive knowledge of our own *existence*, a demonstrative knowledge of the *existence*

of a god; of the *existence* of anything else, we have no other but a sensitive knowledge, which extends not beyond the objects present to our senses.

22.   Our knowledge being so narrow, as I have shown, it will perhaps give us some light into the present state of our minds if we look a little into the dark side, and take a view of *our ignorance*; which, being infinitely larger than our knowledge, may serve much to the quieting of disputes and improvement of useful knowledge, if, discovering how far we have clear and distinct *ideas*, we confine our thoughts within the contemplation of those things that are within the reach of our understandings and launch not out into that abyss of darkness (where we have not eyes to see, nor faculties to perceive anything) out of a presumption that nothing is beyond our comprehension. But to be satisfied of the folly of such a conceit, we need not go far.   He that knows anything knows this in the first place: that he need not seek long for instances of his ignorance.   The meanest and most obvious things that come in our way have dark sides that the quickest sight cannot penetrate into.   The clearest and most enlarged understandings of thinking men find themselves puzzled and at a loss in every particle of matter.   We shall the less wonder to find it so, when we consider the *causes of our ignorance* which, from what has been said, I suppose will be found to be chiefly these three:

First, Want of *ideas*.

Secondly, Want of a discoverable connexion between the *ideas* we have.

Thirdly, Want of tracing and examining our *ideas*.

23.   *First*, There are some things, and those not a few, that we are ignorant of for *want of ideas*.

First, All the simple *ideas* we have are confined (as I have shown) to those we receive from corporeal objects by *sensation*, and from the operations of our own minds as the objects of *reflection*.   But how much these few and narrow inlets are disproportionate to the vast whole extent of all beings, will not be hard to persuade those who are not so foolish as to think their span the measure of all things.   What other simple *ideas* it is possible the creatures in other parts of the universe may have, by the assistance of senses and faculties more or perfecter than we have or different from ours, it is not for us to determine.   But to say or think there are no such, because we conceive nothing of them, is no better an argument than if a blind man should be positive in it, that there was no such thing as sight and colours, because he had no manner of *idea* of any such thing nor could by any means frame to himself any notions about seeing. The ignorance and darkness that is in us no more hinders nor confines the knowledge that is in others, than the blindness of a mole is an argument against the quick-sightedness of an eagle. He that will consider the infinite power, wisdom, and goodness of the Creator of all things will find reason to think it was not all laid out upon so inconsiderable, mean, and impotent a creature as he will find man to be, who in all probability is one of the lowest of all intellectual beings. What faculties therefore other species of creatures have to penetrate into the nature and inmost constitutions of things, what *ideas* they may receive of them, far different from ours, we know not. This we know and certainly find, that we want several other views of them, besides those we have, to make discoveries of them more perfect. And we may be convinced that the *ideas* we can attain to by our faculties are very disproportionate to things themselves, when a positive clear distinct one of substance itself, which is the foundation of all the rest, is concealed from us. But want of *ideas* of this kind, being a part as well as cause of our ignorance, cannot be described. Only this, I think, I may confidently say of it: that the intellectual and sensible world are in this perfectly alike; that that part, which we see of either of them, holds no proportion with what we see not; and whatsoever we can reach, with our eyes or our thoughts, of either of them is but a point, almost nothing, in comparison of the rest.

24. *Secondly*, Another great cause of ignorance is the *want of* ideas *we are capable of*. As the want of *ideas*, which our faculties are not able to give us, shuts us wholly from those views of things which it is reasonable to think other beings, perfecter than we, have, of which we know nothing, so the want of *ideas* I now speak of keeps us in ignorance of things we conceive capable of being known to us. *Bulk, figure*, and *motion* we have *ideas* of. But though we are not without *ideas* of these primary qualities of bodies in general, yet not knowing what is the particular *bulk, figure*, and *motion* of the greatest part of the bodies of the universe, we are ignorant of the several powers, efficacies, and ways of operation whereby the effects which we daily see are produced. These are hid from us, in some things by being *too*

remote, and in others by being too *minute.* When we consider
the vast distance of the known and visible parts of the world,
and the reasons we have to think that what lies within our ken is
but a small part of the immense universe, we shall then discover
an huge abyss of ignorance. What are the particular fabrics of
the great masses of matter which make up the whole stupendous
frame of corporeal beings; how far they are extended; what is
their motion, and how continued, or communicated; and what
influence they have one upon another are contemplations that,
at first glimpse, our thoughts lose themselves in. If we narrow
our contemplation and confine our thoughts to this little canton,
I mean this system of our sun and the grosser masses of matter
that visibly move about it, what several sorts of vegetables,
animals, and intellectual corporeal beings, infinitely different
from those of our little spot of earth, may there probably be in
the other planets, to the knowledge of which even of their outward figures and parts we can no way attain whilst we are confined to this earth, there being no natural means either by sensation or reflection to convey their certain *ideas* into our minds?
They are out of the reach of those inlets of all our knowledge;
and what sorts of furniture and inhabitants those mansions
contain in them we cannot so much as guess, much less have
clear and distinct *ideas* of them.

25. If a great, nay, far the greatest part of the several ranks of
bodies in the universe escape our notice by their remoteness,
there are others that are no less concealed from us by their
minuteness. These insensible corpuscles being the active parts
of matter and the great instruments of nature on which depend
not only all their secondary qualities but also most of their
natural operations, our want of precise distinct *ideas* of their
primary qualities keeps us in an incurable ignorance of what we
desire to know about them. I doubt not but, if we could discover the figure, size, texture, and motion of the minute con-
stituent parts of any two bodies, we should know without trial
several of their operations one upon another, as we do now the
properties of a square or a triangle. Did we know the mechanical
affections of the particles of *rhubarb, hemlock, opium,* and a *man,*
as a watchmaker does those of a watch, whereby it performs its
operations, and of a file, which by rubbing on them will alter the
figure of any of the wheels, we should be able to tell beforehand
that *rhubarb* will purge, *hemlock* kill, and *opium* make a man

sleep: as well as a watchmaker can that a little piece of paper laid on the balance will keep the watch from going till it be removed; or that some small part of it being rubbed by a file, the machine would quite lose its motion, and the watch go no more. The dissolving of silver in *aqua fortis* and gold in *aqua regia*, and not *vice versa*, would be then perhaps no more difficult to know than it is to a smith to understand why the turning of one key will open a lock and not the turning of another. But whilst we are destitute of senses acute enough to discover the minute particles of bodies and to give us *ideas* of their mechanical affections, we must be content to be ignorant of their properties and ways of operation; nor can we be assured about them any further than some few trials we make are able to reach. But whether they will succeed again another time, we cannot be certain. This hinders our certain knowledge of universal truths concerning natural bodies, and our reason carries us herein very little beyond particular matter of fact.

26. And therefore I am apt to doubt that, how far soever human industry may advance useful and *experimental* philosophy *in physical things, scientifical* will still be out of our reach: because we want perfect and adequate *ideas* of those very bodies which are nearest to us and most under our command. Those which we have ranked into classes under names and we think ourselves best acquainted with, we have but very imperfect and incomplete *ideas* of. Distinct *ideas* of the several sorts of bodies that fall under the examination of our senses perhaps we may have; but adequate *ideas*, I suspect, we have not of any one amongst them. And though the former of these will serve us for common use and discourse, yet, whilst we want the latter, we are not capable of *scientifical knowledge*, nor shall ever be able to discover general, instructive, unquestionable truths concerning them. *Certainty* and *demonstration* are things we must not, in these matters, pretend to. By the colour, figure, taste, and smell and other sensible qualities, we have as clear and distinct *ideas* of sage and hemlock as have of a circle and a triangle; but having no *ideas* of the particular primary qualities of the minute parts of either of these plants, nor of other bodies which we would apply them to, we cannot tell what effects they will produce nor, when we see those effects, can we so much as guess, much less know, their manner of production. Thus having no *ideas* of the particular mechanical affections of the

minute parts of bodies that are within our view and reach, we are ignorant of their constitutions, powers, and operations; and of bodies more remote, we are yet more ignorant, not knowing so much as their very outward shapes or the sensible and grosser parts of their constitutions.

27. This at first sight will show us how disproportionate our knowledge is to the whole extent even of material beings; to which if we add the consideration of that infinite number of *spirits* that may be, and probably are, which are yet more remote from our knowledge, whereof we have no cognizance nor can frame to ourselves any distinct *ideas* of their several ranks and sorts, we shall find this cause of ignorance conceal from us, in an impenetrable obscurity, almost the whole intellectual world: a greater, certainly, and more beautiful world than the material. For bating some very few and those, if I may so call them, superficial *ideas* of spirit, which by reflection we get of our own, and from thence the best we can collect of the Father of all spirits, the eternal independent Author of them and us and all things, we have no certain information so much as of the existence of other spirits but by revelation. Angels of all sorts are naturally beyond our discovery; and all those intelligences, whereof it is likely there are more orders than of corporeal substances, are things whereof our natural faculties give us no certain account at all. That there are minds and thinking beings in other men as well as himself, every man has a reason, from their words and actions, to be satisfied; and the knowledge of his own mind cannot suffer a man, that considers, to be ignorant that there is a GOD. But that there are degrees of spiritual beings between us and the great GOD, who is there that by his own search and ability can come to know? Much less have we distinct *ideas* of their different natures, conditions, states, powers, and several constitutions wherein they agree or differ from one another and from us. And therefore in what concerns their different species and properties, we are under an absolute ignorance.

28. *Secondly*, What a small part of the substantial beings that are in the universe the want of *ideas* leave open to our knowledge, we have seen. In the next place, another cause of ignorance, of no less moment, is a want of *a discoverable connexion* between those *ideas* which we have. For wherever we want that, we are utterly incapable of universal and certain knowledge and

are, as in the former case, left only to observation and experiment: which, how narrow and confined it is, how far from general knowledge, we need not be told. I shall give some few instances of this cause of our ignorance and so leave it. It is evident that the bulk, figure, and motion of several bodies about us produce in us several sensations, as of colours, sounds, tastes, smells, pleasure and pain, etc. These mechanical affections of bodies having no affinity at all with those *ideas* they produce in us (there being no conceivable connexion between any impulse of any sort of body and any perception of a colour or smell which we find in our minds), we can have no distinct knowledge of such operations beyond our experience and can reason no otherwise about them than as effects produced by the appointment of an infinitely wise agent, which perfectly surpass our comprehensions. As the *ideas* of sensible secondary qualities, which we have in our minds, can by us be no way deduced from bodily causes, nor any correspondence or connexion be found between them and those primary qualities which (experience shows us) produce them in us: so, on the other side, the operation of our minds upon our bodies is as inconceivable. How any thought should produce a motion in body is as remote from the nature of our *ideas*, as how any body should produce any thought in the mind. That it is so, if experience did not convince us, the consideration of the things themselves would never be able in the least to discover to us. These, and the like, though they have a constant and regular connexion in the ordinary course of things: yet, that connexion being not discoverable in the *ideas* themselves, which appearing to have no necessary dependence one on another, we can attribute their connexion to nothing else but the arbitrary determination of that all-wise Agent who has made them to be and to operate as they do, in a way wholly above our weak understandings to conceive.

29. In some of our *ideas* there are certain relations, habitudes, and connexions so visibly included in the nature of the *ideas* themselves, that we cannot conceive them separable from them by any power whatsoever. And in these only we are capable of certain and universal knowledge. Thus the *idea* of a right-lined triangle necessarily carries with it an equality most angles to two right ones. Nor can we conceive this relation, this connexion of these two *ideas*, to be possibly mutable or to depend on any arbitrary power, which of choice made it thus or could make it

otherwise. But the coherence and continuity of the parts of
matter, the production of sensation in us of colours and sounds,
etc., by impulse and motion, nay, the original rules and communication of motion being such wherein we can discover no
natural connexion with any *ideas* we have, we cannot but ascribe
them to the arbitrary will and good pleasure of the wise Architect.
I need not, I think, here mention the resurrection of the dead,
the future state of this globe of earth, and such other things,
which are by everyone acknowledged to depend wholly on the
determination of a free agent. The things that, as far as our
observation reaches, we constantly find to proceed regularly,
we may conclude do act by a law set them, but yet by a law
that we know not: whereby, though causes work steadily and
effects constantly flow from them, yet their *connexions* and
dependencies being not discoverable in our *ideas*, we can have
but an experimental knowledge of them. From all which it is
easy to perceive what a darkness we are involved in, how little
it is of being and the things that are that we are capable to know.
And therefore we shall do no injury to our knowledge, when
we modestly think with ourselves, that we are so far from being
able to comprehend the whole nature of the universe and all the
things contained in it that we are not capable of a philosophical
knowledge of the bodies that are about us and make a part of
us; concerning their secondary qualities, powers, and operations,
we can have no universal certainty. Several effects come every
day within the notice of our senses, of which we have so far
sensitive knowledge; but the causes, manner, and certainty of
their production, for the two foregoing reasons, we must be
content to be ignorant of. In these we can go no further than
particular experience informs us of matter of fact, and by analogy
to guess what effects the like bodies are, upon other trials, like
to produce. But as to a perfect *science* of natural bodies (not to
mention spiritual beings), we are, I think, so far from being
capable of any such thing that I conclude it lost labour to seek
after it.

30. *Thirdly,* Where we have adequate *ideas*, and where there
is a certain and discoverable connexion between them, yet we
are often ignorant for want of *tracing* those *ideas* which we have
or may have, and for want of finding out those intermediate
ideas which may show us what habitude of agreement or disagreement they have one with another. And thus many are

ignorant of mathematical truths, not out of any imperfection of their faculties or uncertainty in the things themselves, but for want of application in acquiring, examining, and by due ways comparing those *ideas*. That which has most contributed to hinder the due *tracing* of our *ideas* and finding out their relations and agreements or disagreements one with another, has been, I suppose, the ill use of *words*. It is impossible that men should ever truly seek or certainly discover the agreement or disagreement of *ideas* themselves, whilst their thoughts flutter about or stick only in sounds of doubtful and uncertain significations. Mathematicians, abstracting their thoughts from names and accustoming themselves to set before their minds the *ideas* themselves that they would consider, and not sounds instead of them, have avoided thereby a great part of that perplexity, puddering, and confusion which has so much hindered men's progress in other parts of knowledge. For, whilst they stick in words of undetermined and uncertain signification, they are unable to distinguish true from false, certain from probable, consistent from inconsistent, in their own opinions. This having been the fate or misfortune of a great part of the men of letters, the increase brought into the stock of real knowledge has been very little in proportion to the schools, disputes, and writings the world has been filled with: whilst students, being lost in the great wood of words, knew not whereabout they were, how far their discoveries were advanced, or what was wanting in their own or the general stock of knowledge. Had men in the discoveries of the material done as they have in those of the intellectual world, involved all in the obscurity of uncertain and doubtful ways of talking: volumes writ of navigation and voyages, theories and stories of zones and tides multiplied and disputed, nay, ships built and fleets set out would never have taught us the way beyond the line; and the antipodes would be still as much unknown as when it was declared heresy to hold there were any. But having spoken sufficiently of words and the ill or careless use that is commonly made of them, I shall not say anything more of it here.

31. Hitherto we have examined the *extent* of our knowledge in respect of the several sorts of beings that are. There is another *extent of it in respect of universality*, which will also deserve to be considered; and in this regard our knowledge follows the nature of our *ideas*. If the *ideas* are abstract whose agreement or

disagreement we perceive, our knowledge is universal. For what is known of such general *ideas* will be true of every particular thing in whom that essence, i.e. that abstract *idea*, is to be found; and what is once known of such *ideas* will be perpetually and forever true. So that as to all general knowledge, we must search and find it only in our own minds; and it is only the examining of our own *ideas* that furnisheth us with that. Truths belonging to essences of things (that is, to abstract *ideas*) are eternal, and are to be found out by the contemplation only of those essences: as the existence of things is to be known only from experience. But having more to say of this in the chapters where I shall speak of general and real knowledge, this may here suffice as to the universality of our knowledge in general.

Chapter IV

OF THE REALITY OF KNOWLEDGE

1. I DOUBT not but my reader, by this time, may be apt to think that I have been all this while only building a castle in the air and be ready to say to me: To what purpose all this stir? Knowledge, say you, is only the perception of the agreement or disagreement of our own *ideas*; but who knows what those *ideas* may be? Is there anything so extravagant as the imaginations of men's brains? Where is the head that has no *chimeras* in it? Or if there be a sober and a wise man, what difference will there be by your rules between his knowledge and that of the most extravagant fancy in the world? They both have their *ideas* and perceive their agreement and disagreement one with another. If there be any difference between them, the advantage will be on the warm-headed man's side, as having the more *ideas* and the more lively. And so, by your rules, he will be the more knowing. If it be true that all knowledge lies only in the perception of the agreement or disagreement of our own *ideas*, the visions of an enthusiast and the reasonings of a sober man will be equally certain. It is no matter how things are: so a man observe but the agreement of his own imaginations and talk conformably, it is all truth, all certainty. Such castles in the air will be as strongholds of truth as the demonstrations of

Euclid. That an harpy is not a centaur is by this way as certain knowledge, and as much a truth, as that a square is not a circle.

But *of what use is all this* fine *knowledge of men's own imaginations* to a man that inquires after the reality of things? It matters not what men's fancies are, it is the knowledge of things that is only to be prized: it is this alone gives a value to our reasonings and preference to one man's knowledge over another's, that it is of things as they really are and not of dreams and fancies.

2. To which I answer that, if our knowledge of our *ideas* terminate in them and reach no further where there is something further intended, our most serious thoughts will be of little more use than the reveries of a crazy brain, and the truths built thereon of no more weight than the discourses of a man who sees things clearly in a dream and with great assurance utters them. But I hope, before I have done, to make it evident that this way of certainty, by the knowledge of our own *ideas*, goes a little further than bare imagination; and I believe it will appear that all the certainty of general truths a man has lies in nothing else.

3. It is evident the mind knows not things immediately, but only by the intervention of the *ideas* it has of them. *Our knowledge*, therefore, is *real* only so far as there is a conformity between our *ideas* and the reality of things. But what shall be here the criterion? How shall the mind, when it perceives nothing but its own *ideas*, know that they agree with things themselves? This, though it seems not to want difficulty, yet, I think, there be two sorts of *ideas* that we may be assured agree with things.

4. *First*, The first are simple *ideas* which, since the mind, as has been shown, can by no means make to itself, must necessarily be the product of things operating on the mind in a natural way and producing therein those perceptions which by the wisdom and will of our Maker they are ordained and adapted to. From whence it follows that *simple* ideas *are not fictions* of our fancies, but the natural and regular productions of things without us, really operating upon us, and so carry with them all the conformity which is intended or which our state requires; for they represent to us things under those appearances which they are fitted to produce in us: whereby we are enabled to distinguish the sorts of particular substances, to discern the states they are in, and so to take them for our necessities and

apply them to our uses. Thus the *idea* of whiteness or bitterness, as it is in the mind, exactly answering that power which is in any body to produce it there, has all the real conformity it can or ought to have with things without us. And this conformity between our simple *ideas* and the existence of things is sufficient for real knowledge.

5. *Secondly, All our complex* ideas, *except those of substances,* being *archetypes* of the mind's own making, not intended to be the copies of anything nor referred to the existence of anything as to their originals, *cannot want any conformity necessary to real knowledge.* For that which is not designed to represent anything but itself can never be capable of a wrong representation nor mislead us from the true apprehension of anything by its dislikeness to it; and such, excepting those of substances, are all our complex *ideas.* Which, as I have shown in another place, are combinations of *ideas* which the mind, by its free choice, puts together, without considering any connexion they have in nature. And hence it is that in all these sorts the *ideas* themselves are considered as the *archetypes,* and things no otherwise regarded but as they are conformable to them. So that we cannot but be infallibly certain that all the knowledge we attain concerning these *ideas* is real and reaches things themselves. Because in all our thoughts, reasonings, and discourses of this kind, we intend things no further than as they are conformable to our *ideas.* So that in these we cannot miss of a certain undoubted reality.

6. I doubt not but it will be easily granted that the *knowledge* we have *of mathematical truths is* not only certain, but *real knowledge,* and not the bare empty vision of vain, insignificant *chimeras* of the brain; and yet, if we will consider, we shall find that it is only of our own *ideas.* The mathematician considers the truth and properties belonging to a rectangle or circle only as they are in *idea* in his own mind. For it is possible he never found either of them existing mathematically, i.e. precisely true, in his life. But yet the knowledge he has of any truths or properties belonging to a circle, or any other mathematical figure, are nevertheless true and certain, even of real things existing: because real things are no further concerned, nor intended to be meant by any such propositions, than as things really agree to those *archetypes* in his mind. Is it true of the *idea* of a *triangle,* that its three angles are equal to two right ones? It is true also

of a *triangle*, wherever it really exists. Whatever other figure exists, that is not exactly answerable to that *idea* of a *triangle* in his mind, is not at all concerned in that proposition. And therefore he is certain all his knowledge concerning such *ideas* is real knowledge: because, intending things no further than they agree with those his *ideas*, he is sure what he knows concerning those figures, when they have barely *an ideal existence* in his mind, will hold true of them also when they have a real existence in matter: his consideration being barely of those figures which are the same wherever or however they exist.

7. And hence it follows that *moral knowledge* is as *capable of real certainty* as mathematics. For certainty being but the perception of the agreement or disagreement of our *ideas*, and demonstration nothing but the perception of such agreement by the intervention of other *ideas* or mediums, our *moral ideas*, as well as mathematical, being *archetypes* themselves and so adequate and complete *ideas*, all the agreement or disagreement which we shall find in them will produce real knowledge, as well as in mathematical figures.

8. For the attaining of *knowledge* and certainty, it is requisite that we have determined *ideas*; and, to make our knowledge *real*, it is requisite that the *ideas* answer their *archetypes*. Nor let it be wondered that I place the certainty of our knowledge in the consideration of our *ideas*, with so little care and regard (as it may seem) to the real existence of things: since most of those discourses which take up the thoughts and engage the disputes of those who pretend to make it their business to inquire after truth and certainty will, I presume, upon examination, be found to be *general propositions* and notions in which existence is not at all concerned. All the discourses of the mathematicians about the squaring of a circle, conic sections, or any other part of mathematics *concern not* the *existence* of any of those figures; but their demonstrations, which depend on their *ideas*, are the same, whether there be any square or circle existing in the world nor no. In the same manner, the truth and certainty of *moral* discourses abstracts from the lives of men and the existence of those virtues in the world whereof they treat; nor are *Tully's* Offices less true, because there is nobody in the world that exactly practises his rules and lives up to that pattern of a virtuous man which he has given us, and which existed nowhere when he writ but in *idea*. If it be true in speculation, i.e. in

idea, that *murder deserves death*, it will also be true in reality of
any action that exists conformable to that *idea* of *murder*. As
for other actions, the truth of that proposition concerns them
not. And thus it is of all other species of things which have no
other essences but those *ideas* which are in the minds of men.

9.   But it will here be said that, if *moral knowledge* be placed in
the contemplation of our own *moral ideas*, and those, as other
modes, be of our own making, what strange notions will there
be of *justice* and *temperance*? What confusion of virtues and
vices, if everyone may make what *ideas* of them he pleases?
No confusion or disorder in the things themselves, nor the
reasonings about them; no more than (in mathematics) there
would be a disturbance in the demonstration, or a change in the
properties of figures and their relations one to another, if a man
should make a triangle with four corners, or a *trapezium* with
four right angles: that is in plain *English*, change the names of
the figures and call that by one name which mathematicians called
ordinarily by another. For let a man make to himself the *idea* of
a figure with three angles whereof one is a right one, and call it,
if he please, *equilaterum* or *trapezium* or anything else, the properties of and demonstrations about that *idea* will be the same
as if he called it a *rectangular-triangle*. I confess, the change of
the name, by the impropriety of speech, will at first disturb
him who knows not what *idea* it stands for; but as soon as the
figure is drawn, the consequences and demonstrations are plain
and clear. Just the same is it in *moral* knowledge: let a man have
the *idea* of taking from others, without their consent, what their
honest industry has possessed them of, and call this *justice* if he
please. He that takes the name here without the *idea* put to it
will be mistaken, by joining another *idea* of his own to that
name; but strip the *idea* of that name or take it such as it is in the
speaker's mind, and the same things will agree to it as if you
called it *injustice*. Indeed, wrong names in moral discourses
breed usually more disorder, because they are not so easily
rectified as in mathematics, where the figure once drawn and
seen makes the name useless and of no force. For what need of a
sign, when the thing signified is present and in view? But in
moral names, that cannot be so easily and shortly done, because
of the many decompositions that go to the making up the
complex *ideas* of those modes. But yet for all this, the *mis-
calling of* any of those *ideas*, contrary to the usual signification

of the words of that language, hinders not but that we may have certain and demonstrative knowledge of their several agreements and disagreements, if we will carefully, as in mathematics, keep to the same precise *ideas* and trace them in their several relations one to another, without being led away by their names. If we but separate the *idea* under consideration from the sign that stands for it, our knowledge goes equally on in the discovery of real truth and certainty, whatever sounds we make use of.

10.   One thing more we are to take notice of: that where GOD or any other law-maker hath defined any moral names, there they have made the essence of that species to which that name belongs, and there it is not safe to apply or use them otherwise; but in other cases it is bare impropriety of speech to apply them contrary to the common usage of the country. But yet even this too disturbs not the certainty of that knowledge, which is still to be had by a due contemplation and comparing of those even nicknamed *ideas*.

11.   *Thirdly*, There is another sort of *complex ideas* which, being referred to *archetypes* without us, may differ from them, and so our knowledge about them may come short of being real. Such are our *ideas* of substances, which, consisting of a collection of simple *ideas*, supposed taken from the works of nature, may yet vary from them by having more or different *ideas* united in them than are to be found united in the things themselves; from whence it comes to pass that they may, and often do, fail of being exactly conformable to things themselves.

12.   I say then that, to have *ideas* of *substances* which, by being conformable to things, may afford us *real* knowledge, it is not enough, as in modes, to put together such *ideas* as have no inconsistency, though they did never before so exist: v.g., the *ideas* of *sacrilege* or *perjury*, etc., were as real and true *ideas* before, as after, the existence of any such fact. But *our ideas of substances*, being supposed copies and referred to *archetypes* without us, must still be taken from something that does or has existed: they must not consist of *ideas* put together at the pleasure of our thoughts, without any real pattern they were taken from, though we can perceive no inconsistency in such a combination. The reason whereof is because, we knowing not what real constitution it is of substances whereon our simple *ideas* depend, and which really is the cause of the strict union of some

of them one with another and the exclusion of others, there are very few of them that we can be sure are or are not inconsistent in nature, any further than experience and sensible observation reaches. Herein, therefore, is founded the *reality* of our knowledge concerning *substances*: that all our complex *ideas* of them must be such, and such only, as are made up of such simple ones as have been discovered to co-exist in nature. And our *ideas*, being thus true though not perhaps very exact copies, are yet the subjects of *real* (as far as we have any) *knowledge* of them. Which (as has been already shown) will not be found to reach very far; but so far as it does, it will still be *real knowledge*. Whatever *ideas* we have, the agreement we find they have with others will still be knowledge. If those *ideas* be abstract, it will be general knowledge. But to make it *real* concerning substances, the *ideas* must be taken from the real existence of things. Whatever simple *ideas* have been found to co-exist in any substance, these we may with confidence join together again and so make abstract *ideas* of substances. For whatever have once had an union in nature may be united again.

13. This if we rightly consider, and *confine not our thoughts* and abstract *ideas* to names, as if there were *or* could be no other *sorts* of things than what known names had already determined and, as it were, set out, we should think of things with greater freedom and less confusion than perhaps we do. It would possibly be thought a bold paradox, if not a very dangerous falsehood, if I should say that some *changelings*, who have lived forty years together without any appearance of reason, are something between a man and a beast: which prejudice is founded upon nothing else but a false supposition that these two names, *man* and *beast*, stand for distinct species so set out by real essences that there can come no other species between them; whereas, if we will abstract from those names and the supposition of such specific essences made by nature wherein all things of the same denominations did exactly and equally partake, if we would not fancy that there were a certain number of these essences wherein all things, as in molds, were cast and formed, we should find that the *idea* of the shape, motion, and life of a man without reason is as much a distinct *idea* and makes as much a distinct *sort* of things from man and beast, as the *idea* of the shape of an *ass* with reason would be different from either that of man or beast, and be a species of an animal between or distinct from both.

14. Here everybody will be ready to ask: if *changelings* may be supposed something between man and beast, pray what are they? I answer, *changelings*, which is as good a word to signify something different from the signification of MAN or BEAST, as the names man and beast are to have significations different one from the other.   This, well considered, would resolve this matter and show my meaning without any more ado. But I am not so unacquainted with the zeal of some men, which enables them to spin consequences and to see religion threatened whenever anyone ventures to quit their forms of speaking, as not to foresee what names such a proposition as this is like to be charged with; and without doubt it will be asked: if *changelings* are something between man and beast, what will become of them in the other world? To which I answer: first, it concerns me not to know or inquire. To their own master they stand or fall. It will make their state neither better nor worse whether we determine anything of it or no. They are in the hands of a faithful Creator and a bountiful Father, who disposes not of his creatures according to our narrow thoughts or opinions, nor distinguishes them according to names and species of our contrivance. And we that know so little of this present world we are in may, I think, content ourselves without being peremptory in defining the different states which creatures shall come into when they go off this stage. It may suffice us that He hath made known, to all those who are capable of instruction, discourse, and reasoning, that they shall come to an account and receive according to what they have done in this body.

15. But secondly, I answer, the force of these men's question (viz., will you deprive *changelings* of a future state?) is founded on one of two suppositions, which are both false. The first is that all things that have the outward shape and appearance of a man must necessarily be designed to an immortal future being, after this life. Or, secondly, that whatever is of human birth must be so. Take away these imaginations, and such questions will be groundless and ridiculous. I desire then those who think there is no more but an accidental difference between themselves and *changelings*, the essence in both being exactly the same, to consider whether they can imagine immortality annexed to any outward shape of the body: the very proposing it is, I suppose, enough to make them disown it. No one yet, that ever I heard of, how much soever immersed in matter,

allowed that excellency to any figure of the gross sensible outward parts as to affirm eternal life due to it or necessary consequence of it, or that any mass of matter should, after its dis-
solution here, be again restored hereafter to an everlasting state
of sense, perception, and knowledge only because it was molded
into this or that figure and had such a particular frame of its
visible parts. Such an opinion as this, placing immortality in a
certain superficial figure, turns out-of-doors all consideration of
soul or spirit, upon whose account alone some corporeal beings
have hitherto been concluded immortal and others not. This
is to attribute more to the outside than inside of things, to place
the excellency of a man more in the external shape of his body
than internal perfections of his soul: which is but little better
than to annex the great and inestimable advantage of immortality and life everlasting, which he has above other material
beings, to annex it, I say, to the cut of his beard or the fashion of
his coat. For this or that outward make of our bodies no more
carries with it the hopes of an eternal duration, than the fashion
of a man's suit gives him reasonable grounds to imagine it will
never wear out, or that it will make him immortal. It will
perhaps be said that nobody thinks that the shape makes anything immortal, but it is the shape is the sign of a rational soul
within, which is immortal. I wonder who made it the sign of
any such thing: for barely saying it will not make it so. It would
require some proofs to persuade one of it. No figure that I know
speaks any such language. For it may as rationally be concluded
that the dead body of a man, wherein there is to be found no
more appearance or action of life than there is in a statue, has
yet nevertheless a living soul in it because of its shape, as that
there is a rational soul in a *changeling* because he has the outside
of a rational creature, when his actions carry far less marks of
reason with them in the whole course of his life than what are to
be found in many a beast.

16. But it is the issue of rational parents, and must therefore
be concluded to have a rational soul. I know not by what logic
you must so conclude. I am sure this is a conclusion that men
nowhere allow of. For if they did, they would not make bold,
as everywhere they do, to destroy ill-formed and misshaped
productions. Aye, but these are *monsters*. Let them be so;
what will your drivelling, unintelligent, intractable *changeling*
be? Shall a defect in the body make a *monster*: a defect in the

mind (the far more noble and, in the common phrase, the far more essential part) not? Shall the want of a nose or a neck make a *monster*, and put such issue out of the rank of men; the want of reason and understanding not? This is to bring all back again to what was exploded just now: this is to place all in the shape, and to take the measure of a man only by his outside. To show that, according to the ordinary way of reasoning in this matter, people do lay the whole stress on the figure and resolve the whole essence of the species of man (as they make it) into the outward shape, how unreasonable soever it be and how much soever they disown it, we need but trace their thoughts and practice a little further, and then it will plainly appear. The well-shaped *changeling* is a man, has a rational soul, though it appear not: this is past doubt, say you. Make the ears a little longer and more pointed, and the nose a little flatter than ordinary, and then you begin to boggle; make the face yet narrower, flatter, and longer, and then you are at a stand; add still more and more of the likeness of a brute to it, and let the head be perfectly that of some other animal, then presently it is a *monster*, and it is demonstration with you that it hath no rational soul and must be destroyed. Where now (I ask) shall be the just measure, which the utmost bounds of that shape that carries with it a rational soul? For since there have been human *foetuses* produced, half-beast and half-man, and others three parts one and one part the other, and so it is possible they may be in all the variety of approaches to the one or the other shape and may have several degrees of mixture of the likeness of a man or a brute, I would gladly know what are those precise lineaments which, according to this hypothesis, are or are not capable of a rational soul to be joined to them. What sort of outside is the certain sign that there is or is not such an inhabitant within? For till that be done, we talk at random of *man* and shall always, I fear, do so, as long as we give ourselves up to certain sounds and the imaginations of settled and fixed species in nature, we know not what. But after all, I desire it may be considered that those who think they have answered the difficulty, by telling us that a misshaped *foetus* is a *monster*, run into the same fault they are arguing against by constituting a species between man and beast. For what else, I pray, is their monster in the case (if the word *monster* signifies anything at all) but something neither man nor beast, but partaking somewhat of either; and just so is the *changeling* before-mentioned.   So necessary is it to quit the common notion of species and essences, if we will truly look into the nature of things and examine them by what our faculties can discover in them as they exist, and not by groundless fancies that have been taken up about them.

17.   I have mentioned this here, because I think we cannot be too cautious that *words* and *species*, in the ordinary notions which we have been used to of them, impose not on us. For I am apt to think therein lies one great obstacle to our clear and distinct knowledge, especially in reference to substances, and from thence has risen a great part of the difficulties about truth and certainty. Would we accustom ourselves to separate our contemplations and reasonings from words, we might in a great measure remedy this inconvenience within our own thoughts; but yet it would still disturb us in our discourse with others, as long as we retained the opinion that *species* and their essences were anything else but our abstract *ideas* (such as they are) with names annexed to them, to be the signs of them.

18.   Wherever we perceive the agreement or disagreement of any of our *ideas*, there is certain knowledge; and wherever we are sure those *ideas* agree with the reality of things, there is certain real knowledge. Of which agreement of our *ideas* with the reality of things having here given the marks, I think I have shown wherein it is that *certainty, real certainty*, consists. Which, whatever it was to others, was, I confess, to me heretofore one of those *desiderata* which I found great want of.

CHAPTER V

OF TRUTH IN GENERAL

1.   WHAT is *truth* was an inquiry many ages since; and it being that which all mankind either do or pretend to search after, it cannot but be worth our while carefully to examine wherein it consists, and so acquaint ourselves with the nature of it, as to observe how the mind distinguishes it from falsehood.

2.   *Truth* then seems to me, in the proper import of the word, to signify nothing but *the joining or separating of signs, as the things signified by them do agree or disagree one with another.*

The *joining* or *separating* of signs here meant is what by another name we call proposition. So that truth properly belongs only to propositions; whereof there are two sorts, viz. mental and verbal, as there are two sorts of signs commonly made use of, viz. *ideas* and words.

3. To form a clear notion of *truth*, it is very necessary to consider *truth* of thought and *truth* of words, distinctly one from another; but yet it is very difficult to treat of them asunder. Because it is unavoidable, in treating of mental propositions, to make use of words, and then the instances given of *mental propositions* cease immediately to be barely mental *and* become *verbal*. For a *mental proposition* being nothing but a bare consideration of the *ideas* as they are in our minds stripped of names, they lose the nature of purely *mental propositions* as soon as they are put into words.

4. And that which makes it yet *harder to treat of mental* and verbal *propositions separately* is that most men, if not all, in their thinking and reasonings within themselves, make use of words instead of *ideas*, at least when the subject of their meditation contains in it complex *ideas*. Which is a great evidence of the imperfection and uncertainty of our *ideas* of that kind and may, if attentively made use of, serve for a mark to show us what are those things we have clear and perfect established *ideas* of, and what not. For if we will curiously observe the way our mind takes in thinking and reasoning, we shall find, I suppose, that when we make any propositions within our own thoughts about *white* or *black*, *sweet* or *bitter*, a *triangle* or a *circle*, we can and often do frame in our minds the *ideas* themselves, without reflecting on the names. But when we would consider or make propositions about the more complex *ideas*, as of a *man*, *vitriol*, *fortitude*, *glory*, we usually put the name for the *idea*: because the *ideas* these names stand for being for the most part imperfect, confused, and undetermined, we reflect on the *names* themselves because they are more clear, certain, and distinct, and readier occur to our thoughts than the pure *ideas*; and so we make use of these words instead of the *ideas* themselves, even when we would meditate and reason within ourselves and make tacit mental propositions. In *substances*, as has been already noted, this is occasioned by the imperfection of our *ideas*: we making the name stand for the real essence of which we have no *idea* at all. In *modes*, it is occasioned by the great

number of simple *ideas* that go to the making them up. For many of them being compounded, the *name* occurs much easier than the complex *idea* itself, which requires time and attention to be recollected and exactly represented to the mind, even in those men who have formerly been at the pains to do it, and is utterly impossible to be done by those who, though they have ready in their memory the greatest part of the common words of their language, yet perhaps never troubled themselves in all their lives to consider what precise *ideas* the most of them stood for. Some confused or obscure notions have served their turns; and many who talk very much of *religion* and *conscience*, of *church* and *faith*, of *power* and *right*, of *obstructions* and *humours*, *melancholy* and *choler* would perhaps have little left in their thoughts and meditations if one should desire them to think only of the things themselves and lay by those words with which they so often confound others, and not seldom themselves also.

5.   But to return to the consideration of truth. We must, I say, observe two sorts of propositions that we are capable of making.

First, mental, wherein the *ideas* in our understandings *are*, without the use of words, *put together or separated* by the mind perceiving or judging of their agreement or disagreement.

Secondly, verbal propositions, which *are words* the signs of our *ideas put together or separated in affirmative or negative sentences.* By which way of affirming or denying, these signs made by sounds are, as it were, put together or separated one from another. So that: proposition consists in joining or separating signs, and truth consists in the putting together or separating these signs according as the things which they stand for agree or disagree.

6.   Everyone's experience will satisfy him that the mind, either by perceiving or supposing the agreement or disagreement of any of its *ideas*, does tacitly within itself put them into a kind of proposition affirmative or negative; which I have endeavoured to express by the terms *putting together* and *separating*. But this action of the mind, which is so familiar to every thinking and reasoning man, is easier to be conceived by reflecting on what passes in us when we affirm or deny, than to be explained by words. When a man has in his mind the *idea* of two lines, viz. the *side* and *diagonal* of a square, whereof the diagonal is an inch long, he may have the *idea* also of the division of that line

into a certain number of equal parts: v.g. into five, ten, an hundred, a thousand, or any other number, and may have the *idea* of that inch line being divisible or not divisible, into such equal parts as a certain number of them will be equal to the side line. Now whenever he perceives, believes, or supposes such a kind of divisibility to agree or disagree to his *idea* of that line, he as it were *joins* or *separates* those two *ideas*, viz. the *idea* of that line and the *idea* of that kind of divisibility, and so makes a mental proposition, which is true or false according as such a kind of divisibility, a divisibility into such *aliquot* parts, does really agree to that line or no. When *ideas* are so put together or separated in the mind as they or the things they stand for do agree or not, that is, as I may call it, *mental truth*. But *truth of words* is something more: and that is the affirming or denying of words one of another, as the *ideas* they stand for agree or disagree; and this again is twofold: either *purely verbal* and trifling, which I shall speak of, *chap. x*; or *real* and instructive, which is the object of that real knowledge which we have spoken of already.

7. But here again will be apt to occur the same doubt about truth that did about knowledge; and it will be objected that, if truth be nothing but the joining and separating of words in propositions as the *ideas* they stand for agree or disagree in men's minds, the knowledge of *truth is not so valuable a thing* as it is taken to be, nor worth the pains and time men employ in the search of it: since *by this account* it amounts to no more than the conformity of words to the *chimeras* of men's brains. Who knows not what odd notions many men's heads are filled with, and what strange *ideas* all men's brains are capable of? But if we rest here, we know the truth of nothing by this rule but of the visionary world in our own imaginations, nor have other truth but what as much concerns *harpies* and *centaurs* as men and horses. For those and the like may be *ideas* in our heads and have their agreement and disagreement there, as well as the *ideas* of real beings, and so have as true propositions made about them. And it will be altogether as true a proposition to say all *centaurs are animals*, as that *all men are animals*; and the certainty of one as great as the other. For in both the propositions, the words are put together according to the agreement of the *ideas* in our minds, and the agreement of the *idea* of *animal* with that of *centaur* is as clear and visible to the mind as the

agreement of the *idea* of *animal* with that of *man*; and so these two propositions are equally true, equally certain. But of what use is all such truth to us?

8. Though what has been said in the foregoing chapter, to distinguish real from imaginary knowledge, might suffice here in answer to this doubt, to distinguish *real truth* from *chimerical* or (if you please) *barely nominal*, they depending both on the same foundation: yet it may not be amiss here again to consider that, though our words signify nothing but our *ideas*, yet being designed by them to signify things, the *truth* they contain when put into propositions will be only *verbal* when they stand for *ideas* in the mind that have not an agreement with the reality of things.   And therefore truth as well as knowledge may well come under the distinction of *verbal* and *real*: that being only *verbal truth* wherein terms are joined according to the agreement or disagreement of the *ideas* they stand for, without regarding whether our *ideas* are such as really have or are capable of having an existence in nature. But then it is they contain *real truth*: when these signs are joined as our *ideas* agree, and when our *ideas* are such as we know are capable of having an existence in nature; which in substances we cannot know but by knowing that such have existed.

9. *Truth* is the marking down in words the agreement or disagreement of *ideas* as it is. *Falsehood* is the marking down in words the agreement or disagreement of *ideas* otherwise than it is. And so far as these *ideas*, thus marked by sounds, agree to their archetypes, so far only is the *truth real*. The knowledge of this truth consists in knowing what *ideas* the words stand for and the perception of the agreement or disagreement of those *ideas*, according as it is marked by those words.

10. But because words are looked on as the great conduits of truth and knowledge, and that in conveying and receiving of truth and commonly in reasoning about it we make use of words and propositions, I shall more at large inquire wherein the certainty of real truths contained in propositions consists, and where it is to be had, and endeavour to show in what sort of universal propositions we are capable of being *certain* of their real truth or falsehood.

I shall begin with general propositions, as those which most employ our thoughts and exercise our contemplation. *General truths* are most looked after by the mind as those that most

enlarge our knowledge and, by their comprehensiveness satisfy-
ing us at once of many particulars, enlarge our view and shorten
our way to knowledge.

11. Besides truth taken in the strict sense before-mentioned,
there are other sorts of truths: As (1) *Moral truth*, which is
speaking things according to the persuasion of our own minds,
though the proposition we speak agree not to the reality of
things. (2) *Metaphysical truth*, which is nothing but the real
existence of things, conformable to the *ideas* to which we have
annexed their names. This, though it seems to consist in the
very beings of things, yet when considered a little nearly, will
appear to include a tacit proposition whereby the mind joins
that particular thing to the *idea* it had before settled with a name
to it. But these considerations of truth either having been before
taken notice of or not being much to our present purpose, it
may suffice here only to have mentioned them.

Chapter VI

OF UNIVERSAL PROPOSITIONS, THEIR TRUTH AND CERTAINTY

1. THOUGH the examining and judging of *ideas* by themselves,
their names being quite laid aside, be the best and surest way to
clear and distinct knowledge: yet, through the prevailing custom
of using sounds for *ideas*, I think it is very seldom practised.
Everyone may observe how common it is for names to be made
use of, instead of the *ideas* themselves, even when men think and
reason within their own breasts, especially if the *ideas* be very
complex and made up of a great collection of simple ones. This
makes *the consideration of words and propositions* so *necessary
a part of the treatise of knowledge* that it is very hard to speak
intelligibly of the one without explaining the other.

2. All the knowledge we have being only of particular or
general truths, it is evident that whatever may be done in the
former of these, the latter, which is that which with reason is
most sought after, can never be well made known and is very
seldom apprehended but as conceived and expressed in words. It
is not therefore out of our way, in the examination of our knowledge, to inquire into the truth and certainty of universal
propositions.

3.   But that we may not be misled in this case by that which is the danger everywhere, I mean by the doubtfulness of terms, it is fit to observe that certainty is twofold: *certainty of truth* and *certainty of knowledge*.   *Certainty of truth* is when words are so put together in propositions as exactly to express the agreement or disagreement of the *ideas* they stand for as really it is.   *Certainty of knowledge* is to perceive the agreement or disagreement of *ideas* as expressed in any proposition.   This we usually call knowing, or being certain of the truth of any proposition.

4.   Now, because *we cannot be certain of the truth of any general proposition unless we know the precise bounds and extent of the species its terms stand for*, it is necessary we should know the essence of each *species*, which is that which constitutes and bounds it. This, in all simple *ideas* and modes, is not hard to do. For in these, the real and nominal essence being the same or, which is all one, the abstract *idea* which the general term stands for being the sole essence and boundary that is or can be supposed of the *species*, there can be no doubt how far the *species* extends or what things are comprehended under each term: which, it is evident, are all that have an exact conformity with the *idea* it stands for, and no other. But in substances, wherein a real essence, distinct from the nominal, is supposed to constitute, determine, and bound the species, the extent of the general word is very uncertain; because, not knowing this real essence, we cannot know what is or what is not of that *species*, and, consequently, what may or may not with certainty be affirmed of it. And thus speaking of a *man* or *gold* or any other *species* of natural substances, as supposed constituted by a precise real essence which nature regularly imparts to every individual of that kind whereby it is made to be of that species, we cannot be certain of the truth of any affirmation or negation made of it. For *man* or *gold*, taken in this sense and used for *species* of things constituted by real essences, different from the complex *idea* in the mind of the speaker, stand for we know not what; and the extent of these species with such boundaries are so unknown and undetermined that it is impossible with any certainty to affirm that all men are rational, or that all gold is yellow. But where the nominal essence is kept to, as the boundary of each species, and men extend the application of any general term no further than to the particular things in which the complex *idea* it stands for is to be found, there they are in no

danger to mistake the bounds of each *species* nor can be in doubt, on this account, whether any propositions be true or no. I have chosen to explain this uncertainty of propositions in this scholastic way, and have made use of the terms of *essences* and *species* on purpose, to show the absurdity and inconvenience there is to think of them as of any other sort of realities than barely abstract *ideas* with names to them. To suppose that the *species* of things are anything but the sorting of them under general names, according as they agree to several abstract *ideas* of which we make those names the signs, is to confound truth and introduce uncertainty into all general propositions that can be made about them. Though therefore these things might, to people not possessed with scholastic learning, be perhaps treated of in a better and clearer way: yet those wrong notions of *essences* or *species*, having got root in most people's minds who have received any tincture from the learning which has prevailed in this part of the world, are to be discovered and removed, to make way for that use of words which should convey certainty with it.

5. *The names of substances*, then, *whenever made to stand for species which are supposed to be constituted by real essences which* we know not, *are not capable to convey certainty to the understanding*: of the truth of general propositions made up of such terms we cannot be sure. The reason whereof is plain. For how can we be sure that this or that quality is in *gold*, when we know not what is or is not *gold*? Since in this way of speaking, nothing is *gold* but what partakes of an essence, which we, not knowing, cannot know where it is or is not and so cannot be sure that any parcel of matter in the world is or is not in this sense *gold*: being incurably ignorant whether it has or has not that which makes anything to be called *gold*, i.e. that real essence of *gold* whereof we have no *idea* at all. This being as impossible for us to know as it is for a blind man to tell in what flower the colour of a *pansy* is or is not to be found, whilst he has no *idea* of the colour of a *pansy* at all. Or if we could (which is impossible) certainly know where a real essence, which we know not, is, v.g. in what parcels of matter the real essence of *gold* is, yet could we not be sure that this or that quality could with truth be affirmed of *gold*: since it is impossible for us to know that this or that quality or *idea* has a necessary connexion with a real essence of which we have no *idea* at all, whatever

species that supposed real essence may be imagined to
constitute.

6. On the other side, the *names of substances*, when made use
of as they should be, for the *ideas* men have in their minds,
though they carry a clear and determinate signification with
them, *will not* yet *serve us to make many universal propositions of
whose truth we can be certain*. Not because in this use of them
we are uncertain what things are signified by them, but because
the complex *ideas* they stand for are such combinations of simple
ones as carry not with them any discoverable connexion or
repugnancy but with a very few other *ideas*.

7. The complex *ideas* that our names of the species of substances properly stand for are collections of such qualities as
have been observed to co-exist in an unknown *substratum*, which
we call *substance*; but what other qualities necessarily co-exist
with such combinations we cannot certainly know, unless we can
discover their natural dependence: which, in their primary
qualities, we can go but a very little way in; and in all their
secondary qualities we can discover no connexion at all, for the
reasons mentioned, *chap. iii*: viz. (1) Because we know not the
real constitutions of substances on which each *secondary
quality* particularly depends. (2) Did we know that, it would
serve us only for experimental (not universal) knowledge, and
reach with certainty no further than that bare instance. Because
our understandings can discover no conceivable connexion
between any *secondary quality* and any modification whatsoever
of any of the *primary* ones. And therefore there are very few
general propositions to be made concerning substances which
can carry with them *undoubted certainty*.

8. *All gold is fixed* is a proposition whose truth we cannot be
certain of, how universally soever it be believed. For if, according to the useless imagination of the Schools, anyone supposes
the term *gold* to stand for a species of things set out by nature by
a real essence belonging to it, it is evident he knows not what
particular substances are of that species, and so cannot with
certainty affirm anything universally of *gold*. But if he makes
gold stand for a species determined by its nominal essence, let
the nominal essence, for example, be the complex *idea* of a
body of a certain *yellow* colour, *malleable*, *fusible*, and *heavier*
than any other known: in this proper use of the word *gold*, there
is no difficulty to know what is or is not *gold*. But yet no other

quality can with certainty be universally affirmed or denied of *gold* but what hath a discoverable connexion or inconsistency with that nominal essence. *Fixedness*, for example, having no necessary connexion that we can discover with the colour, weight, or any other simple *idea* of our complex one, or with the whole combination together: it is impossible that we should certainly know the truth of this proposition, that *all gold is fixed*.

9.   As there is no discoverable connexion between *fixedness* and the colour, weight, and other simple *ideas* of that nominal essence of *gold*: so, if we make our complex *idea* of *gold* a *body yellow, fusible, ductile, weighty*, and *fixed*, we shall be at the same uncertainty concerning *solubility* in *aqua regia*, and for the same reason; since we can never, from consideration of the *ideas* themselves, with certainty affirm or deny, of a body whose complex *idea* is made up of yellow, very weighty, ductile, fusible, and fixed, that it is soluble in *aqua regia*; and so on of the rest of its qualities.   I would gladly meet with one general affirmation concerning any quality of *gold* that anyone can certainly know is true.   It will, no doubt, be presently objected, Is not this an universal certain proposition, *All gold is malleable*? To which I answer: It is a very certain proposition, if *malleableness* be a part of the complex *idea* the word *gold* stands for.   But then here is nothing affirmed of *gold* but that that sound stands for an *idea* in which *malleableness* is contained, and such a sort of truth and certainty as this it is to say *a centaur is four-footed*. But if *malleableness* makes not a part of the specific essence the name of *gold* stands for, it is plain, *All gold is malleable* is not a certain proposition.   Because let the complex *idea* of *gold* be made up of which soever of its other qualities you please, *malleableness* will not appear to depend on that complex *idea* nor follow from any simple one contained in it.   The connexion that *malleableness* has (if it has any) with those other qualities, being only by the intervention of the real constitution of its insensible parts, which since we know not, it is impossible we should perceive that connexion, unless we could discover that which ties them together.

10.   The more, indeed, of these co-existing qualities we unite into one complex *idea* under one name, the more precise and determinate we make the signification of that word; but yet never make it thereby more capable of *universal certainty* in

respect of other qualities not contained in our complex *idea*, since we perceive not their connexion or dependence one on another, being ignorant both of that real constitution in which they are all founded, and also how they flow from it. For the chief part of our knowledge concerning substances is not, as in other things, barely of the relation of two *ideas* that may exist separately, but is of the necessary connexion and co-existence of several distinct *ideas* in the same subject, or of their repugnancy so to co-exist. Could we begin at the other end and discover what it was wherein that colour consisted, what made a body lighter or heavier, what texture of parts made it malleable, fusible and fixed, and fit to be dissolved in this sort of liquor and not in another: if (I say) we had such an *idea* as this of bodies and could perceive wherein all sensible qualities originally consist and how they are produced, we might frame such abstract *ideas* of them as would furnish us with matter of more general knowledge and enable us to make universal propositions that should carry *general truth* and *certainty* with them. But whilst our complex *ideas* of the sorts of substances are so remote from that internal real constitution on which their sensible qualities depend, and are made up of nothing but an imperfect collection of those apparent qualities our senses can discover, there can be very few general propositions concerning substances of whose real truth we can be *certainly* assured, since there are but few simple *ideas* of whose connexion and necessary co-existence we can have certain and undoubted knowledge. I imagine, amongst all the *secondary qualities* of substances and the powers relating to them, there cannot any two be named whose necessary co-existence or repugnance to co-exist can certainly be known, unless in those of the same sense, which necessarily exclude one another, as I have elsewhere shown. No one, I think, by the colour that is in any body, can certainly know what smell, taste, sound, or tangible qualities it has, nor what alterations it is capable to make or receive, on or from other bodies. The same may be said of the sound or taste, etc. Our specific names of substances standing for any collections of such *ideas*, it is not to be wondered that we can, with them, make very few general propositions of *undoubted real certainty*. But yet so far as any complex *idea* of any sort of substances contains in it any simple *idea* whose necessary co-existence with any other may be discovered, so far *universal propositions* may *with certainty* be made concerning it: v.g. could anyone discover a necessary connexion between *malleableness* and the *colour* or *weight* of *gold* or any other part of the complex *idea* signified by that name, he might make a *certain* universal proposition concerning *gold* in this respect; and the real truth of this proposition, that *all gold is malleable*, would be as *certain* as of this, *the three angles of all right-lined triangles are equal to two right ones*.

11.   Had we such *ideas* of substances as to know what real constitutions produce those sensible qualities we find in them and how those qualities flowed from thence, we could, by the specific *ideas* of their real essences in our own minds, more certainly find out their properties and discover what qualities they had or had not, than we can now by our senses; and to know the properties of *gold*, it would be no more necessary that *gold* should exist and that we should make experiments upon it than it is necessary, for the knowing the properties of a triangle, that a triangle should exist in any matter: the *idea* in our minds would serve for the one as well as the other.   But we are so far from being admitted into the secrets of nature that we scarce so much as ever approach the first entrance towards them.   For we are wont to consider the substances we meet with, each of them, as an entire thing by itself, having all its qualities in itself and independent of other things, overlooking, for the most part, the operations of those invisible fluids they are encompassed with and upon whose motions and operations depend the greatest part of those qualities which are taken notice of in them and are made by us the inherent marks of distinction whereby we know and denominate them.   Put a piece of *gold* anywhere by itself, separate from the reach and influence of all other bodies, it will immediately lose all its colour and weight, and perhaps malleableness too, which, for aught I know, would be changed into a perfect friability.   *Water*, in which to us *fluidity* is an essential quality, left to itself, would cease to be fluid.   But if inanimate bodies owe so much of their present state to other bodies without them that they would not be what they appear to us were those bodies that environ them removed, it is yet more so in *vegetables*, which are nourished, grow, and produce leaves, flowers, and seeds in a constant succession.   And if we look a little nearer into the state of *animals*, we shall find that their dependence as to life, motion, and the most considerable

qualities to be observed in them is so wholly on extrinsical causes and qualities of other bodies that make no part of them, that they cannot subsist a moment without them: though yet those bodies on which they depend are little taken notice of, and make no part of the complex *ideas* we frame of those animals. Take the air but a minute from the greatest part of living creatures, and they presently lose sense, life, and motion. This the necessity of breathing has forced into our knowledge. But how many other extrinsical and possibly very remote bodies do the springs of those admirable machines depend on, which are not vulgarly observed or so much as thought on; and how many are there which the severest inquiry can never discover? The inhabitants of this spot of the universe, though removed so many millions of miles from the sun, yet depend so much on the duly tempered motion of particles coming from or agitated by it that, were this earth removed but a small part of that distance, out of its present situation, and placed a little further or nearer that source of heat, it is more than probable that the greatest part of the animals in it would immediately perish: since we find them so often destroyed by an excess or defect of the sun's warmth, which an accidental position, in some parts of this our little globe, exposes them to. The qualities observed in a *loadstone* must needs have their source far beyond the confines of that body; and the ravage made often on several sorts of animals by invisible causes, the certain death (as we are told) of some of them by barely passing the line or, as it is certain of others, by being removed into a neighbouring country, evidently show that the concurrence and operation of several bodies, with which they are seldom thought to have anything to do, is absolutely necessary to make them be what they appear to us and to preserve those qualities by which we know and distinguish them. We are then quite out of the way when we think that things contain within themselves the qualities that appear to us in them; and we in vain search for that constitution within the body of a fly or an elephant upon which depend those qualities and powers we observe in them. For which perhaps, to understand them aright, we ought to look not only beyond this our earth and atmosphere, but even beyond the sun or remotest star our eyes have yet discovered. For how much the being and operation of particular substances in this our globe depend on causes utterly beyond our view is impossible for us to determine.

We see and perceive some of the motions and grosser operations of things here about us, but whence the streams come that keep all these curious machines in motion and repair, how conveyed and modified, is beyond our notice and apprehension; and the great parts and wheels, as I may so say, of this stupendous structure of the universe, may, for aught we know, have such a connexion and dependence in their influences and operations one upon another, that perhaps things in this our mansion would put on quite another face and cease to be what they are, if some one of the stars or great bodies incomprehensibly remote from us should cease to be or move as it does. This is certain: things, however absolute and entire they seem in themselves, are but retainers to other parts of nature for that which they are most taken notice of by us. Their observable qualities, actions, and powers are owing to something without them; and there is not so complete and perfect a part that we know of nature which does not owe the being it has, and the excellencies of it, to its neighbours; and we must not confine our thoughts within the surface of any body, but look a great deal further, to comprehend perfectly those qualities that are in it.

12.   If this be so, it is not to be wondered that *we have very imperfect* ideas *of substances*, and that the real essences, on which depend their properties and operations, are unknown to us. We cannot discover so much as that *size, figure,* and *texture* of their minute and active parts, which is really in them: much less the different motions and impulses made in and upon them by bodies from without, upon which depends and by which is formed the greatest and most remarkable part of those qualities we observe in them, and of which our complex *ideas* of them are made up. This consideration alone is enough to put an end to all our hopes of ever having the *ideas* of their real essences; which whilst we want, the nominal essences we make use of instead of them will be able to furnish us but very sparingly with any *general knowledge* or universal propositions capable of real *certainty*.

13.   We are not therefore to wonder if *certainty* be to be found in very few general propositions made concerning substances: our knowledge of their qualities and properties go very seldom further than our senses reach and inform us. Possibly, inquisitive and observing men may by strength of *judgment* penetrate further and, on probabilities taken from wary observation and

hints well laid together, often guess right at what experience has
not yet discovered to them. But this is but guessing still: it
amounts only to opinion and has not that *certainty* which is
requisite to knowledge. For all *general knowledge* lies only in
our own thoughts and consists barely in the contemplation of
our own abstract *ideas*. Wherever we perceive any agreement or
disagreement amongst them, there we have *general knowledge*
and, by putting the names of those *ideas* together accordingly in
propositions, can with certainty pronounce *general truths*. But
because the abstract *ideas* of substances, for which their specific
names stand, whenever they have any distinct and determinate
signification, have a discoverable connexion or inconsistency
with but a very few other *ideas*: the *certainty of universal propositions concerning substances* is very narrow and scanty in that
part, which is our principal inquiry concerning them; and there
is scarce any of the names of substances, let the *idea* it is applied
to be what it will, of which we can generally and with certainty
pronounce that it has or has not this or that other quality
belonging to it and constantly co-existing or inconsistent with
that *idea*, wherever it is to be found.

14. Before we can have any tolerable knowledge of this kind,
we must first know what changes the *primary qualities* of one
body do regularly produce in the *primary qualities* of another,
and how. Secondly, we must know what *primary qualities* of any
body produce certain sensations or *ideas* in us. This is, in truth,
no less than to know all the effects of matter under its divers
modifications of bulk, figure, cohesion of parts, motion and
rest. Which, I think, everybody will allow is utterly impossible
to be known by us without revelation. Nor, if it were revealed
to us what sort of figure, bulk, and motion of corpuscles would
produce in us the sensation of a *yellow* colour; and what sort of
figure, bulk, and texture of parts in the superficies of any body
were fit to give such corpuscles their due motion to produce
that colour: would that be enough to make *universal* propositions with *certainty* concerning the several sorts of them, unless
we had faculties acute enough to perceive the precise bulk,
figure, texture, and motion of bodies in those minute parts, by
which they operate on our senses, that so we might by those
frame our abstract *ideas* of them? I have mentioned here only
corporeal substances, whose operations seem to lie more level to
our understandings; for, as to the *operations of spirits*, both their

thinking and moving of bodies, we at first sight find ourselves at a loss: though perhaps, when we have applied our thoughts a little nearer to the consideration of bodies and their operations and examined how far our notions, even in these, reach with any clearness beyond sensible matter of fact, we shall be bound to confess that, even in these too, our discoveries amount to very little beyond perfect ignorance and incapacity.

15. This is evident: *the abstract complex* ideas *of substances,* for which their general names stand, not comprehending their real constitutions, *can afford us but very little universal certainty.* Because our *ideas* of them are not made up of that on which those qualities we observe in them and would inform ourselves about do depend, or with which they have any certain connexion. V.g., let the *idea* to which we give the name *man* be, as it commonly is, a body of the ordinary shape, with sense, voluntary motion, and reason joined to it. This being the abstract *idea* and consequently the essence of our species *man,* we can make but very few general certain propositions concerning *man,* standing for such an *idea.* Because, not knowing the real constitution on which sensation, power of motion, and reasoning, with that peculiar shape, depend, and whereby they are united together in the same subject, there are very few other qualities with which we can perceive them to have a necessary connexion; and therefore we cannot with certainty affirm that *all men sleep by intervals,* that *no man can be nourished by wood or stones,* that *all men will be poisoned by hemlock*: because these *ideas* have no connexion nor repugnancy with this our nominal essence of *man,* with this abstract *idea* that name stands for. We must, in these and the like, appeal to trial in particular subjects, which can reach but a little way. We must content ourselves with probability in the rest; but can have no general certainty, whilst our specific *idea* of *man* contains not that real constitution which is the root wherein all his inseparable qualities are united, and from whence they flow. Whilst our *idea* the word *man* stands for is only an imperfect collection of some sensible qualities and powers in him, there is no discernible connexion or repugnance between our specific *idea* and the operation of either the parts of hemlock or stones upon his constitution. There are animals that safely eat hemlock, and others that are nourished by wood and stones; but as long as we want *ideas* of those real constitutions of different sorts of animals, whereon these and the like

qualities and powers depend, we must not hope to reach *certainty* in universal propositions concerning them. Those few *ideas* only, which have a discernible connexion with our nominal essence or any part of it, can afford us such propositions. But these are so few, and of so little moment, that we may justly look on our certain *general knowledge of substances* as almost none at all.

16.   To conclude: *General propositions*, of what kind soever, are then only capable of *certainty* when the terms used in them stand for such *ideas* whose agreement or disagreement, as there expressed, is capable to be discovered by us. And we are then certain of their truth or falsehood, when we perceive the *ideas* the terms stand for to agree or not agree, according as they are affirmed or denied one of another. Whence we may take notice that *general certainty* is never to be found but in our *ideas*. Whenever we go to seek it elsewhere, in experiment or observations without us, our knowledge goes not beyond particulars. It is the contemplation of our own abstract *ideas* that alone is able to afford us *general knowledge*.

Chapter VII

OF MAXIMS

1.   There are a sort of propositions which, under the name of *maxims* and *axioms*, have passed for principles of science and, because they are *self-evident*, have been supposed innate, without that anybody (that I know) ever went about to show the reason and foundation of their clearness or cogency. It may, however, be worthwhile to inquire into the reason of their evidence and see whether it be peculiar to them alone, and also examine how far they influence and govern our other knowledge.

2.   *Knowledge*, as has been shown, consists in the perception of the agreement or disagreement of *ideas*; now where that agreement or disagreement is perceived immediately by itself, without the intervention or help of any other, there our *knowledge is self-evident*. This will appear to be so to anyone who will but consider any of those propositions which, without any proof, he

assents to at first sight: for, in all of them, he will find that the reason of his assent is from that agreement or disagreement which the mind by an immediate comparing them, finds in those *ideas* answering the affirmation or negation in the proposition.

3. This being so, in the next place let us consider whether this *self-evidence* be peculiar only to those propositions which commonly pass under the name of maxims and have the dignity of axioms allowed them. And here it is plain that several other truths, not allowed to be axioms, partake equally with them in this *self-evidence*. This we shall see, if we go over these several sorts of agreement or disagreement of *ideas* which I have above mentioned, viz. identity, relation, co-existence, and real existence; which will discover to us that not only those few propositions which have had the credit of *maxims* are self-evident, but a great many, even almost an infinite number of *other propositions* are such.

4. For, *First*, the immediate perception of the agreement or disagreement of *identity* being founded in the mind's having distinct *ideas*, this affords us as many *self-evident* propositions as we have distinct *ideas*. Everyone that has any knowledge at all has, as the foundation of it, various and distinct *ideas*; and it is the first act of the mind (without which it can never be capable of any knowledge) to know every one of its *ideas* by itself, and distinguish it from others. Everyone finds in himself that he knows the *ideas* he has; that he knows also, when any one is in his understanding and what it is; and that, when more than one are there, he knows them distinctly and unconfusedly one from another. Which always being so (it being impossible but that he should perceive what he perceives) he can never be in doubt, when any *idea* is in his mind, that it is there and is that *idea* it is; and that two distinct *ideas*, when they are in his mind, are there and are not one and the same *idea*. So that all such affirmations and negations are made without any possibility of doubt, uncertainty, or hesitation, and must necessarily be assented to as soon as understood: that is, as soon as we have in our minds determined *ideas*, which the terms in the proposition stand for. And therefore wherever the mind with attention considers any proposition, so as to perceive the two *ideas* signified by the terms and affirmed or denied one of the other, to be the same or different, it is presently and infallibly certain of the truth of such

a proposition, and this equally whether these propositions
be in terms standing for more general *ideas*, or such as are less so,
v.g. whether the general *idea* of *being* be affirmed of itself, as in
this proposition, *Whatsoever is, is*; or a more particular *idea* be
affirmed of itself, as *A man is a man*, or *Whatsoever is white is
white*. Or whether the *idea* of *being* in general be denied of *not
being*, which is the only (if I may so call it) *idea* different from it,
as in this other proposition: *It is impossible for the same to be and
not to be*; or any *idea* of any particular being be denied of another different from it, as *A man is not a horse, Red is not blue*.
The difference of the *ideas*, as soon as the terms are understood,
makes the truth of the proposition presently visible, and that
with an equal certainty and easiness, in the less as well as the
more general propositions, and all for the same reason, viz.
because the mind perceives in any *ideas* that it has the same *idea*
to be the same with itself, and two different *ideas* to be different
and not the same. And this it is equally certain of: whether
these *ideas* be more or less general, abstract, and comprehensive. It is not therefore alone to these two general propositions,
Whatsoever is, is, and *It is impossible for the same thing to be and
not to be*, that this self-evidence belongs by any peculiar right.
The perception of being or not being belongs no more to these
vague *ideas*, signified by the terms *whatsoever* and *thing*, than
it does to any other *ideas*. These two general maxims, amount-
ing to no more in short but this, that *The same is the same* and
The same is not different, are truths known in more particular
instances as well as in these general maxims, and known also in
particular instances before these general maxims are ever
thought on; and draw all their force from the discernment of the
mind employed about particular *ideas*. There is nothing more
visible than that the mind, without the help of any proof or
reflection on either of these general propositions, perceives so
clearly and knows so certainly that the *idea* of *white* is the *idea*
of white and not the *idea* of blue, and that the *idea* of white,
when it is in the mind, is there and is not absent, that the consideration of these axioms can add nothing to the evidence or
certainty of its knowledge. Just so it is (as everyone may experiment in himself) in all the *ideas* a man has in his mind: he knows
each to be itself and not to be another, and to be in his mind and
not away when it is there, with a certainty that cannot be
greater; and therefore the truth of no general proposition can be

known with a greater certainty, nor add anything to this. So that, in respect of identity, our intuitive knowledge reaches as far as our *ideas*. And we are capable of making as many self-evident propositions as we have names for distinct *ideas*. And I appeal to everyone's own mind whether this proposition, *A circle is a circle*, be not as self-evident a proposition as that consisting of more general terms, *Whatsoever is, is*; and again, whether this proposition, *Blue is not red*, be not a proposition that the mind can no more doubt of, as soon as it understands the words, than it does of that axiom, *It is impossible for the same thing to be and not to be*? And so of all the like.

5. *Secondly*, As to *co-existence*, or such necessary connexion between two *ideas* that, in the subject where one of them is supposed, there the other must necessarily be also: of such agreement or disagreement as this, the mind has an immediate perception but in very few of them. And therefore in this sort we have but very little intuitive knowledge; nor are there to be found very many propositions that are self-evident, though some there are: v.g. the *idea* of filling a place equal to the contents of its superficies being annexed to our *idea* of body, I think it is a self-evident proposition *that two bodies cannot be in the same place.*

6. *Thirdly*, As to the *relations* of modes, mathematicians have framed many axioms concerning that one relation of equality. As, *Equals taken from equals, the remainder will be equals*; which, with the rest of that kind, however they are received for maxims by the mathematicians and are unquestionable truths, yet I think that anyone who considers them will not find that they have a clearer self-evidence than these: that *One and one are equal to two*; that *If you take from the five fingers of one hand two, and from the five fingers of the other hand two, the remaining numbers will be equal*. These and a thousand other such propositions may be found in numbers, which at very first hearing force the assent and carry with them an equal, if not greater clearness than those mathematical axioms.

7. *Fourthly*, As to *real existence*, since that has no connexion with any other of our *ideas* but that of ourselves and of a First Being, we have, in that concerning the real existence of all other beings, not so much as demonstrative, much less a self-evident knowledge; and, therefore, concerning those there are no maxims.

8. In the next place, let us consider what *influence* these received *maxims* have upon the other parts of our knowledge. The rules established in the Schools, that all reasonings are *ex praecognitis et praeconcessis*, seem to lay the foundation of all other knowledge in these maxims, and to suppose them to be *praecognita*; whereby, I think, is meant these two things: first, that these axioms are those truths that are first known to the mind; and, secondly, that upon them the other parts of our knowledge depend.

9. *First*, That they are not the *truths first known* to the mind is evident to experience, as we have shown in another place, Book I, Ch. ii. Who perceives not that a child certainly knows that a stranger is not its mother; that its sucking bottle is not the rod, long before he knows that *It is impossible for the same thing to be and not to be*? And how many truths are there about numbers, which it is obvious to observe that the mind is perfectly acquainted with and fully convinced of, before it ever thought on these general maxims, to which mathematicians in their arguings do sometimes refer them? Whereof the reason is very plain: for that which makes the mind assent to such propositions being nothing else but the perception it has of the agreement or disagreement of its *ideas*, according as it finds them affirmed or denied one of another, in words it understands; and every *idea* being known to be what it is; and every two distinct *ideas* being known not to be the same, it must necessarily follow that such self-evident truths must be *first* known which consist of *ideas* that are *first* in the mind; and the *ideas first* in the mind, it is evident, are those of particular things; from whence, by slow degrees, the understanding proceeds to some few general ones; which, being taken from the ordinary and familiar objects of sense, are settled in the minds with general names to them. Thus particular *ideas* are *first* received and distinguished, and so knowledge got about them; and next to them, the less general or specific, which are next to particular. For abstract *ideas* are not so obvious or easy, to children or the yet unexercised mind, as particular ones. If they seem so to grown men, it is only because by constant and familiar use they are made so. For when we nicely reflect upon them, we shall find that general *ideas* are fictions and contrivances of the mind that carry difficulty with them, and do not so easily offer themselves as we are apt to imagine. For example,

does it not require some pains and skill to form the *general idea*
of a *triangle* (which is yet none of the most abstract, comprehensive, and difficult), for it must be neither oblique nor
rectangle, neither equilateral, equicrural, nor scalenon; but all
and none of these at once. In effect, it is something imperfect
that cannot exist, an *idea* wherein some parts of several different
and inconsistent *ideas* are put together. It is true, the mind in
this imperfect state has need of such *ideas*, and makes all the
haste to them it can, for the conveniency of communication and
enlargement of knowledge, to both which it is naturally very
much inclined. But yet one has reason to suspect such *ideas* are
marks of our imperfection: at least, this is enough to show that
the most abstract and general *ideas* are not those that the mind
is *first* and most easily acquainted with, nor such as its earliest
knowledge is conversant about.

10.   *Secondly*, From what has been said, it plainly follows that
these magnified *maxims* are not the principles and *foundations*
of all our other *knowledge*. For if there be a great many other
truths which have as much self-evidence as they, and a great
many that we know before them, it is impossible they should be
the *principles* from which we deduce all other truths. Is it
impossible to know that *one* and *two* are equal to *three*, but by
virtue of this or some such axiom, viz. *The whole is equal to all
its parts taken together*? Many a one knows that *one* and *two* are
equal to *three*, without having heard or thought on that or any
other axiom by which it might be proved; and knows it as
certainly as any other man knows that *The whole is equal to all
its parts*, or any other maxim; and all from the same reason of
self-evidence: the equality of those *ideas* being as visible and
certain to him without that or any other axiom as with it, it
needing no proof to make it perceived. Nor, after the knowledge that *The whole is equal to all its parts*, does he know that
One and two are equal to three better or more certainly than he
did before. For if there be any odds in those *ideas*, the *whole*
and *parts* are more obscure or, at least, more difficult to be
settled in the mind than those of *one*, *two* and *three*. And
indeed, I think I may ask these men who will needs have all
knowledge, besides those general principles themselves, to
depend on general innate and self-evident principles, what
principle is requisite to prove that *one* and *one* are *two*, that *two*
and *two* are *four*, that *three* times *two* are *six*? Which, being

known without any proof, do evince that either all knowledge
does not *depend* on certain *praecognita* or general maxims, called
principles; or else that these are principles; and if these are to be
counted principles, a great part of numeration will be so. To
which if we add all the self-evident propositions which may be
made about all our distinct *ideas*, principles will be almost
infinite, at least innumerable, which men arrive to the knowledge of at different ages; and a great many of these innate
principles they never come to know all their lives. But whether
they come in view of the mind earlier or later, this is true of
them: that they are all known by their native evidence, are
wholly independent, receive no light, nor are capable of any
proof one from another, much less the more particular from the
more general, or the more simple from the more compounded:
the more simple and less abstract being the most familiar, and
the easier and earlier apprehended. But whichever be the
clearest *ideas*, the evidence and *certainty* of all such propositions
is in this, that a man sees the same *idea* to be the same *idea*, and
infallibly perceives two different *ideas* to be different *ideas*. For
when a man has in his understanding the *ideas* of *one* and of
two, the *idea* of *yellow* and the *idea* of *blue*, he cannot but
certainly know that the *idea* of one is the *idea* of one, and not the
idea of two; and that the *idea* of yellow is the *idea* of yellow, and
not the *idea* of blue. For a man cannot confound the *ideas* in
his mind which he has distinct: that would be to have them confused and distinct at the same time, which is a contradiction; and
to have none distinct is to have no use of our faculties, to have no
knowledge at all. And therefore what *idea* soever is affirmed of
itself, or whatsoever two entire distinct *ideas* are denied one of
another, the mind cannot but assent to such a proposition as
infallibly true as soon as it understands the terms, without hesitation, or need of proof, or regarding those made in more general
terms and called maxims.

11. What shall we then say? Are these *general maxims* of no
use? By no means, though perhaps their use is not that which
it is commonly taken to be. But, since doubting in the least of
what hath been by some men ascribed to these *maxims* may be
apt to be cried out against, as overturning the foundations of all
the sciences, it may be worthwhile to consider them with respect
to other parts of our knowledge, and examine more particularly
to what purposes they serve, and to what not.

(1) It is evident, from what has been already said, that they are of no use to prove or confirm less general self-evident propositions.

(2) It is as plain that they are not, nor have been, the foundations whereon any science hath been built. There is, I know, a great deal of talk, propagated from scholastic men, of sciences and the *maxims* on which they are built; but it has been my ill-luck never to meet with any such sciences, much less any one built upon these two *maxims*, *What is, is,* and *It is impossible for the same thing to be and not to be.* And I would be glad to be shown where any such science, erected upon these or any other general *axioms*, is to be found; and should be obliged to anyone who would lay before me the frame and system of any science, so built on these or any such like *maxims*, that could not be shown to stand as firm without any consideration of them. I ask whether these general *maxims* have not the same use in the study of divinity, and in theological questions, that they have in the other sciences. They serve here, too, to silence wranglers and put an end to dispute. But I think that nobody will therefore say that the *Christian* religion is built on these *maxims*, or that the knowledge we have of it is derived from these *principles*. It is from revelation we have received it, and without revelation these *maxims* had never been able to help us to it. When we find out an *idea* by whose intervention we discover the connexion of two others, this is a revelation from God to us, by the voice of reason. For we then come to know a truth that we did not know before. When God declares any truth to us, this is a revelation to us by the voice of his spirit, and we are advanced in our knowledge. But in neither of these do we receive our light or knowledge from *maxims*. But in the one the things themselves afford it, and we see the truth in them by perceiving their agreement or disagreement. In the other, God himself affords it immediately to us, and we see the truth of what he says in his unerring veracity.

(3) They are not of use to help men forwards in the advancement of sciences or new discoveries of yet unknown truths. Mr. *Newton*, in his never enough to be admired book, has demonstrated several propositions, which are so many new truths before unknown to the world, and are further advances in mathematical knowledge; but, for the discovery of these, it was not the general *maxims*, *What is, is* or *The whole is bigger*

than a part, or the like, that helped him. These were not the clues that led him into the discovery of the truth and certainty of those propositions. Nor was it by them that he got the knowledge of those demonstrations, but by finding out intermediate *ideas* that showed the agreement or disagreement of the *ideas* as expressed in the propositions he demonstrated. This is the great exercise and improvement of human understanding in the enlarging of knowledge and advancing the sciences; wherein they are far enough from receiving any help from the contemplation of these or the like magnified *maxims*. Would those who have this traditional admiration of these propositions, that they think no step can be made in knowledge without the support of an *axiom*, no stone laid in the building of the sciences without a general *maxim*, but distinguish between the method of acquiring knowledge and of communicating, between the method of raising any science and that of teaching it to others as far as it is advanced: they would see that those general *maxims* were not the foundations on which the first discoverers raised their admirable structures, nor the keys that unlocked and opened those secrets of knowledge. Though afterwards, when schools were erected, and sciences had their professors to teach what others had found out, they often made use of *maxims*, i.e. laid down certain propositions which were self-evident or to be received for true; which, being settled in the minds of their scholars as unquestionable verities, they on occasion made use of, to convince them of truths in particular instances that were not so familiar to their minds as those general *axioms* which had before been inculcated to them and carefully settled in their minds. Though these particular instances, when well reflected on, are no less self-evident to the understanding than the general *maxims* brought to confirm them; and it was in those particular instances that the first discoverer found the truth, without the help of the general *maxims*; and so may anyone else do who with attention considers them.

To come, therefore, to the use that is made of *maxims*.

(1) They are of use, as has been observed, in the ordinary methods of teaching sciences as far as they are advanced; but of little or none in advancing them further.

(2) They are of use in disputes, for the silencing of obstinate wranglers and bringing those contests to some conclusion. Whether a need of them to that end came not in in the manner

following, I crave leave to inquire. The Schools, having made disputation the touchstone of men's abilities and the *criterion* of knowledge, adjudged victory to him that kept the field, and he that had the last word was concluded to have the better of the argument, if not of the cause. But because by this means there was like to be no decision between skilful combatants, whilst one never failed of a *medius terminus* to prove any proposition, and the other could as constantly, without or with a distinction, deny the *major* or *minor*: to prevent, as much as could be, the running out of disputes into an endless train of syllogisms, certain general propositions, most of them indeed self-evident, were introduced into the Schools; which, being such as all men allowed and agreed in, were looked on as general measures of truth, and served instead of principles (where the disputants had not laid down any other between them) beyond which there was no going, and which must not be receded from by either side. And thus these *maxims*, getting the name of *principles*, beyond which men in dispute could not retreat, were by mistake taken to be the originals and sources from whence all knowledge began, and the foundations whereon the sciences were built. Because when in their disputes they came to any of these, they stopped there and went no further: the matter was determined. But how much this is a mistake hath been already shown.

This method of the Schools, which have been thought the fountains of knowledge, introduced, as I suppose, the like use of these maxims into a great part of conversation out of the Schools, to stop the mouths of cavillers, whom anyone is excused from arguing any longer with, when they deny these general self-evident principles received by all reasonable men who have once thought of them; but yet their use herein is but to put an end to wrangling. They in truth, when urged in such cases, teach nothing: that is already done by the intermediate *ideas* made use of in the debate, whose connexion may be seen without the help of those maxims, and so the truth known before the maxim is produced and the argument brought to a first principle. Men would give off a wrong argument before it came to that, if in their disputes they proposed to themselves the finding and embracing of truth, and not a contest for victory. And thus maxims have their use to put a stop to their perverseness, whose ingenuity should have yielded sooner. But the method of the Schools having allowed and encouraged men to oppose and resist evident truth till they are baffled, i.e. till they are reduced to contradict themselves or some established principle, it is no wonder that they should not in civil conversation be ashamed of that which in the Schools is counted a virtue and a glory: viz. obstinately to maintain that side of the question they have chosen, whether true or false, to the last extremity, even after conviction. A strange way to attain truth and knowledge, and that which I think the rational part of mankind not corrupted by education could scarce believe should ever be admitted amongst the lovers of truth and students of religion or nature, or introduced into the seminaries of those who are to propagate the truths of religion or philosophy amongst the ignorant and unconvinced. How much such a way of learning is likely to turn young men's minds from the sincere search and love of truth, nay, and to make them doubt whether there is any such thing, or at least worth the adhering to, I shall not now inquire. This I think: that, bating those places which brought the *peripatetic* philosophy into their Schools, where it continued many ages without teaching the world anything but the art of wrangling, these maxims were nowhere thought the foundations on which the sciences were built, nor the great helps to the advancement of knowledge.

As to these *general maxims* therefore, they are, as I have said, of great *use* in disputes, *to stop the mouths of wranglers*, but not of much *use* to the discovery of unknown truths or to help the mind forwards in its search after knowledge. For whoever began to build his knowledge on this general proposition, *What is, is,* or *It is impossible for the same thing to be and not to be*, and from either of these, as from a principle of science, deduced a *system* of useful knowledge? Wrong opinions often involving contradictions, one of these maxims, as a touch-stone, may *serve* well to show whither they lead. But yet, however fit to lay open the absurdity or mistake of a man's reasoning or opinion, they are of very little *use* for enlightening the understanding; and it will not be found that the mind receives much help from them in its progress in knowledge; which would be neither less, nor less certain, were these two *general propositions* never thought on. It is true, as I have said, they sometimes *serve* in argumentation to stop a wrangler's mouth, by showing the absurdity of what he saith, and by exposing him to the shame of contradicting what all the world knows and he himself cannot but own to be true. But it is one thing to show a man that he is in an error, and another to put him in possession of truth; and I would fain know what truths these two propositions are able to teach, and by their influence make us know, which we did not know before or could not know without them. Let us reason from them as well as we can, they are only about identical predications and *influence*, if any at all, none but such. Each particular proposition concerning identity or diversity is as clearly and certainly known in itself, if attended to, as either of these general ones: only, these general ones, as serving in all cases, are therefore more inculcated and insisted on. As to other less general maxims, many of them are no more than bare verbal propositions, and teach us nothing but the respect and import of names one to another. *The whole is equal to all its parts*: what real truth, I beseech you, does it teach us? What more is contained in that maxim than what the signification of the word *totum*, or the *whole*, does of itself import? And he that knows that the word *whole* stands for what is made up of all its parts knows very little less than that the *whole* is equal to all its *parts*. And upon the same ground, I think that this proposition, *A hill is higher than a valley*, and several the like, may also pass for maxims. But yet masters of *mathematics*, when they would, as teachers of what they know, initiate others in that science, do not without reason place this and some other such maxims, at the entrance of their *systems*: that their scholars, having in the beginning perfectly acquainted their thoughts with these propositions made in such general terms, may be used to make such reflections and have these more general propositions, as formed rules and sayings, ready to apply to all particular cases. Not that if they be equally weighed, they are more clear and evident than the particular instances they are brought to confirm; but that, being more familiar to the mind, the very naming them is enough to satisfy the understanding. But this, I say, is more from our custom of using them and the establishment they have got in our minds, by our often thinking of them, than from the different evidence of the things. But, before custom has settled methods of thinking and reasoning in our minds, I am apt to imagine it is quite otherwise; and that the child, when a part of his apple is taken away, knows it better in that particular instance than by this general proposition, *The whole is equal to all its parts*; and that if one of these have need to be confirmed to him

by the other, the general has more need to be let into his mind
by the particular, than the particular by the general. For in
particulars our knowledge begins, and so spreads itself, by
degrees, to generals: though afterwards the mind takes the
quite contrary course, and having drawn its knowledge into as
general propositions as it can, makes those familiar to its
thoughts, and accustoms itself to have recourse to them as to
the standards of truth and falsehood. By which familiar *use of
them*, as rules to measure the truth of other propositions, it
comes in time to be thought that more particular propositions
have their truth and evidence from their conformity to these
more general ones, which, in discourse and argumentation, are
so frequently urged and constantly admitted. And this I think
to be the reason why, amongst so many self-evident propositions,
the most general only have had the title of maxims.

12.   One thing further, I think, it may not be amiss to observe
concerning these general maxims: that they are so far from
improving or establishing our minds in true knowledge that, if
our notions be wrong, loose, or unsteady, and we resign up our
thoughts to the sound of words rather than fix them on settled,
determined *ideas* of things: I say, these *general maxims* will
serve to confirm us in mistakes, and in such a way of use of
words, which is most common, will *serve* to prove contradictions:
v.g. he that with *Descartes* shall frame in his mind an *idea* of
what he calls *body* to be nothing but extension, may easily
demonstrate that there is no *vacuum*, i.e. no space void of body,
by this maxim, *What is*, *is*. For the *idea* to which he annexes
the name *body* being bare extension, his knowledge that space
cannot be without body is certain. For he knows his own *idea*
of extension clearly and distinctly, and knows that it is *what it
is*, and not another *idea*, though it be called by these three
names, *extension*, *body*, *space*. Which three words, standing for
one and the same *idea*, may no doubt with the same evidence and
certainty be affirmed one of another, as each of itself; and it is as
certain that, whilst I use them all to stand for one and the same
idea, this predication is as true and identical in its signification,
that space is body, as this predication is true and identical, *that
body is body*, both in signification and sound.

13.   But if another shall come and make to himself another
idea, different from *Descartes's*, of the thing which yet with
Descartes he calls by the same name *body*, and make his *idea*,

which he expresses by the word *body*, to be of a thing that hath both *extension* and *solidity* together: he will as easily demonstrate that there may be a *vacuum* or space without a body, as *Descartes* demonstrated the contrary. Because the *idea* to which he gives the name *space* being barely the simple one of *extension*, and the *idea* to which he gives the name *body* being the complex *idea* of *extension* and *resistibility* or *solidity* together in the same subject, these two *ideas* are not exactly one and the same, but in the understanding as distinct as the *ideas* of one and two, white and black, or as of *corporeity* and *humanity*, if I may use those barbarous terms; and therefore the predication of them in our minds or in words standing for them is not identical, but the negation of them one of another: viz. this proposition, Extension or *space is not body*, is as true and evidently certain as this maxim, *It is impossible for the same thing to be and not to be*, can make any proposition.

14. But yet, though both these propositions (as you see) may be equally demonstrated, viz. that there may be a *vacuum* and that there cannot be a *vacuum*, by these two certain principles (viz.) *What is, is* and *The same thing cannot be and not be*: yet neither of these principles will serve to prove to us that any, or what, bodies do exist; for that we are left to our senses to discover to us, as far as they can. Those universal and self-evident principles, being only our constant, clear, and distinct knowledge of our own *ideas* more general or comprehensive, can assure us of nothing that passes without the mind: their certainty is founded only upon the knowledge we have of each *idea* by itself and of its distinction from others; about which we cannot be mistaken whilst they are in our minds, though we may, and often are mistaken, when we retain the names without the *ideas* or use them confusedly sometimes for one, and sometimes for another *idea*. In which cases, the force of these *axioms*, reaching only to the sound and not the signification of the words, *serves* only to lead us into confusion, mistake, and error. It is to show men that these maxims, however cried up for the great guards to truth, will not secure them from error in a careless loose use of their words, that I have made this remark. In all that is here suggested concerning their little use for the improvement of knowledge or dangerous use in undetermined *ideas*, I have been far enough from saying or intending they should be *laid aside*, as some have been too forward to charge

me. I affirm them to be truths, self-evident truths; and so
cannot be *laid aside*. As far as their influence will reach, it is in
vain to endeavour, nor would I attempt to, abridge it. But yet,
without any injury to truth or knowledge, I may have reason to
think their use is not answerable to the great stress which seems
to be laid on them; and I may warn men not to make an ill use of
them for the confirming themselves in errors.

15. But let them be of what *use* they will in verbal propositions,
they cannot discover or prove to us the least knowledge of the
nature of substances, as they are found and exist without us,
any further than grounded on experience. And though the
consequence of these two propositions, called principles, be
very clear, and their *use* not dangerous or hurtful in the probation of such things, wherein there is no need at all of them for
proof but such as are clear by themselves without them, viz.
where our *ideas* are determined and known by the names that
stand for them: yet, when these principles, viz. *What is, is*, and
It is impossible for the same thing to be and not to be, are made
use of in the probation of propositions wherein are words standing for complex *ideas*, v.g. *man, horse, gold, virtue*, there they
are of infinite danger, and most commonly make men receive
and retain falsehood for manifest truth and uncertainty for
demonstration; upon which follows error, obstinacy, and all the
mischiefs that can happen from wrong reasoning. The reason
whereof is not that these principles are less true, or of less force,
in proving propositions made of terms standing for complex
ideas than where the propositions are about simple *ideas*. But
because men mistake generally, thinking that, where the same
terms are preserved, the propositions are about the same things,
though the *ideas* they stand for are in truth different. Therefore
these maxims are made use of to support those which in sound
and appearance are contradictory propositions, as is clear in the
demonstrations above-mentioned about a *vacuum*. So that
whilst men take words for things, as usually they do, these
maxims may and do commonly serve to prove contradictory
propositions. As shall yet be further made manifest.

16. For instance: let *man* be that concerning which you would
by these first principles demonstrate anything, and we shall see
that, so far as demonstration is by these principles, it is only
verbal and gives us no certain, universal, true proposition or
knowledge of any being existing without us. First, a child

having framed the *idea* of a *man*, it is probable that his *idea* is just like that picture which the painter makes of the visible appearances joined together; and such a complication of *ideas* together in his understanding makes up the single complex *idea* which he calls *man*; whereof white or flesh-colour in *England* being one, the child can demonstrate to you that *a negro is not a man*, because white colour was one of the constant simple *ideas* of the complex *idea* he calls *man*; and therefore he can demonstrate, by the principle, *It is impossible for the same thing to be and not to be*, that *a negro is not a man*: the foundation of his certainty being not that universal proposition, which perhaps he never heard nor thought of, but the clear, distinct perception he hath of his own simple *ideas* of black and white, which he cannot be persuaded to take nor can ever mistake one for another, whether he knows that maxim or no; and to this child or anyone who hath such an *idea* which he calls *man*, can you never demonstrate that a *man* hath a soul, because his *idea* of man includes no such notion or *idea* in it. And therefore, to him, the principle of *What is, is* proves not this matter; but it depends upon collection and observation, by which he is to make his complex *idea* called *man*.

17. *Secondly*, another that hath gone further in framing and collecting the *idea* he calls *man*, and to the outward shape adds *laughter* and *rational discourse*, may demonstrate that infants and changelings are no men, by this maxim, *It is impossible for the same thing to be and not to be*; and I have discoursed with very rational men who have actually denied that they are *men*.

18. *Thirdly*, perhaps another makes up the complex *idea* which he calls *man*, only out of the *ideas* of body in general and the powers of language and reason, and leaves out the shape wholly: this man is able to demonstrate that a man may have no hands but be *quadrupes*, neither of those being included in his *idea* of *man*; and in whatever body or shape he found *speech* and *reason* joined, that was a *man*: because, having a clear knowledge of such a complex *idea*, it is certain that *What is, is*.

19. So that, if rightly considered, I think we may say that where our *ideas* are determined in our minds, and have annexed to them by us known and steady names under those settled determinations, there is *little need* or *no use* at all of these *maxims*, to prove the agreement or disagreement of any of them. He that cannot discern the truth or falsehood of such propositions,

without the help of these and the like maxims, will not be *helped* by these maxims to do it: since he cannot be supposed to know the truth of these maxims themselves without proof, if he cannot know the truth of others without proof, which are as self-evident as these. Upon this ground it is that intuitive knowledge neither requires nor admits any proof, one part of it more than another. He that will suppose it does takes away the foundation of all knowledge and certainty; and he that needs any proof to make him certain and give his assent to this proposition, that *Two are equal to two*, will also have need of a proof to make him admit that *What is, is.* He that needs a probation to convince him that *Two are not three*, that *White is not black*, that *A triangle is not a circle*, etc., or any other two determined distinct *ideas* are not one and the same, will need also a demonstration to convince him that It is impossible *for the same thing to be and not to be.*

20.   And as these maxims are of *little use* where we have determined *ideas*, so they are, as I have shown, of *dangerous use* where our *ideas* are not determined, and where we use words that are not annexed to determined *ideas* but such as are of a loose and wandering signification, sometimes standing for one, and sometimes for another *idea*; from which follows mistake and error, which these maxims (brought as proofs to establish propositions, wherein the terms stand for undetermined *ideas*) do by their authority confirm and rivet.

Chapter VIII

OF TRIFLING PROPOSITIONS

1.   Whether the maxims treated of in the foregoing chapter be of that use to real knowledge as is generally supposed, I leave to be considered. This, I think, may confidently be affirmed, that there are universal propositions; that, though they be certainly true, yet they add no light to our understandings, bring no increase to our knowledge. Such are,

2.   *First, All purely identical propositions.* These obviously and at first blush appear to contain no instruction in them; for when we affirm the said term of itself, whether it be barely verbal, or

whether it contains any clear and real *idea*, it shows us nothing but what we must certainly know before, whether such a proposition be either made by or proposed to us. Indeed, that most general one, *What is, is*, may serve sometimes to show a man the absurdity he is guilty of when, by circumlocution or equivocal terms, he would in particular instances deny the same thing of itself; because nobody will so openly bid defiance to common sense as to affirm visible and direct contradictions in plain words, or, if he does, a man is excused if he breaks off any further discourse with him. But yet, I think I may say that neither that received maxim nor any other identical proposition teaches us anything; and, though in such kind of propositions this great and magnified maxim, boasted to be the foundation of demonstration, may be and often is made use of to confirm them, yet all it proves amounts to no more than this: that the same word may with great certainty be affirmed of itself, without any doubt of the truth of any such proposition and, let me add also, without any real knowledge.

3. For at this rate, any very ignorant person, who can but make a proposition and knows what he means when he says *aye* or *no*, may make a million of propositions of whose truths he may be infallibly certain, and yet not know one thing in the world thereby: v.g. What is a soul, is a soul; or, *a soul is a soul*; *a spirit is a spirit*; *a fetiche is a fetiche*, etc. These all being equivalent to this proposition, viz. *What is, is*; i.e. *What hath existence, hath existence*; or *Who hath a soul, hath a soul*. What is this more than trifling with words? It is but like a monkey shifting his oyster from one hand to the other; and had he had but words, might no doubt have said: Oyster in right hand is *subject*, and oyster in left hand is *predicate*; and so might have made a self-evident proposition of oyster, i.e. *Oyster is oyster*, and yet, with all this, not have been one whit the wiser or more knowing; and that way of handling the matter would much at one have satisfied the monkey's hunger or a man's understanding, and they two would have improved in knowledge and bulk together.

I know there are some who, because *identical propositions* are self-evident, show a great concern for them and think they do great service to philosophy by crying them up, as if in them was contained all knowledge, and the understanding were led into all truth by them only. I grant as forwardly as anyone that they

are all true and self-evident. I grant further that the foundation
of all our knowledge lies in the faculty we have of perceiving the
same *idea* to be the same, and of discerning it from those that
are different, as I have shown in the foregoing chapter. But how
that vindicates the making use of *identical propositions* for the
improvement of knowledge from the imputation of trifling, I do
not see. Let anyone repeat as often as he pleases that *The will
is the will*, or lay what stress on it he thinks fit: of what use is
this, and an infinite the like propositions, for the enlarging our
knowledge? Let a man abound as much as the plenty of words
which he has will permit him in such propositions as these, *A
law is a law*, and *Obligation is obligation, Right is right*, and
Wrong is wrong: will these and the like ever help him to an
acquaintance with *ethics*, or instruct him or others in the knowledge of *morality*? Those who know not, nor perhaps ever will
know what is *right* and what is *wrong*, nor the measures of them,
can with as much assurance make and infallibly know the truth
of these and all such propositions as he that is best instructed in
morality can do. But what advance do such propositions give in
the knowledge of anything necessary or useful for their conduct?

He would be thought to do little less than trifle who, for the
enlightening the understanding in any part of knowledge, should
be busy with *identical propositions*, and insist on such maxims
as these: *Substance is substance* and *Body is body, A vacuum is a
vacuum* and *A vortex is a vortex, A centaur is a centaur* and *A
chimera is a chimera*, etc. For these and all such are equally
true, equally certain, and equally self-evident. But yet they
cannot but be counted trifling, when made use of as principles of
instruction, and stress laid on them as helps to knowledge,
since they teach nothing but what everyone who is capable of
discourse knows without being told: viz. that the same term is
the same term, and the same idea the same idea. And upon this
account it was that I formerly did and do still think the offering
and inculcating such propositions, in order to give the understanding any new light or inlet into the knowledge of things, no
better than trifling.

Instruction lies in something very different, and he that would
enlarge his own or another's mind to truths he does not yet
know must find out intermediate *ideas*, and then lay them in such
order one by another that the understanding may see the agreement or disagreement of those in question. Propositions that do

this are instructive; but they are far from such as affirm the same term of itself, which is no way to advance one's self or others in any sort of knowledge. It no more helps to that than it would help anyone, in his learning to read, to have such propositions as these inculcated to him, *an A is an A,* and *a B is a B;* which a man may know as well as any schoolmaster, and yet never be able to read a word as long as he lives. Nor do these or any such identical propositions help him one jot forwards in the skill of reading, let him make what use of them he can.

If those who blame my calling them *trifling propositions* had but read and been at the pains to understand what I had above writ in very plain *English,* they could not but have seen that by *identical propositions* I mean only such wherein the same term importing the same *idea* is affirmed of itself: which I take to be the proper signification of *identical proposition;* and concerning all such, I think I may continue safely to say that to propose them as instructive is no better than trifling. For no one who has the use of reason can miss them, where it is necessary they should be taken notice of, nor doubt of their truth when he does take notice of them.

But if men will call propositions *identical* wherein the same term is not affirmed of itself, whether they speak more properly than I, others must judge; this is certain: all that they say of propositions that are not *identical,* in my sense, concerns not me nor what I have said, all that I have said, relating to those propositions wherein the same term is affirmed of itself. And I would fain see an instance wherein any such can be made use of, to the advantage and improvement of anyone's knowledge. Instances of other kinds, whatever use may be made of them, concern not me, as not being such as I call *identical.*

4. *Secondly,* Another sort of trifling propositions is *when a part of the complex* idea *is predicated of the name of the whole:* a part of the definition of the word defined. Such are all propositions wherein the *genus* is predicated of the *species,* or more comprehensive of less comprehensive terms; for what information, what knowledge carries this proposition in it, viz. *Lead is a metal,* to a man who knows the complex *idea* the name *lead* stands for? All the simple *ideas* that go to the complex one signified by the term *metal* being nothing but what he before comprehended and signified by the name *lead.* Indeed, to a man that knows the signification of the word *metal,* and not of the word *lead,* it is a

shorter way to explain the signification of the word *lead*, be saying it is a *metal*, which at once expresses several of its simple *ideas*, than to enumerate them one by one, telling him it is a body very *heavy*, *fusible*, and *malleable*.

5.   A like trifling it is *to predicate any other part of the definition of the term defined*, or to affirm any one of the simple *ideas* of a complex one, of the name of the whole complex *idea*, as *All gold is fusible*. For *fusibility* being one of the simple *ideas* that goes to the making up the complex one the sound *gold* stands for, what can it be but playing with sounds, to affirm that of the name *gold* which is comprehended in its received signification? It would be thought little better than ridiculous to affirm gravely, as a truth of moment, that *gold is yellow*; and I see not how it is any jot more material to say *it is fusible*, unless that quality be left out of the complex *idea* of which the sound *gold* is the mark in ordinary speech. What instruction can it carry with it, to tell one that which he hath been told already or he is supposed to know before? For I am supposed to know the signification of the word another uses to me, or else he is to tell me. And if I know that the name *gold* stands for this complex *idea* of *body*, *yellow*, *heavy*, *fusible*, *malleable*, it will not much instruct me to put it solemnly afterwards in a proposition and gravely say *All gold is fusible*. Such propositions can only serve to show the disingenuity of one who will go from the definition of his own terms, by reminding him sometimes of it; but carry no knowledge with them but of the signification of words, however certain they be.

6.   *Every* man *is an animal* or living body, is as certain a proposition as can be; but no more conducing to the knowledge of things than to say *A palfrey is an ambling horse*, or a neighing, ambling *animal*: both being only about the signification of words, and make me know but this, that *body*, *sense*, and *motion* or power of sensation and moving, are three of those *ideas* that I always comprehend and signify by the word *man*; and where they are not to be found together, the name *man* belongs not to that thing; and so of the other, that *body*, *sense*, and *a certain way of going*, with *a certain kind of voice*, are some of those *ideas* which I always comprehend and signify by the word *palfrey*, and when they are not to be found together, the name *palfrey* belongs not to that thing. It is just the same, and to the same purpose, when any term, standing for any one or more of the simple

ideas that altogether make up that complex *idea* which is called a man, is affirmed of the term *man*: v.g. suppose a *Roman* signified by the word *homo* all these distinct *ideas* united in one subject, *corporietas, sensibilitas, potentia se movendi, rationalitas, risibilitas,* he might no doubt with great certainty universally affirm one, more, or all of these together of the word *homo*, but did no more than say that the word *homo* in his country comprehended in its signification all these *ideas*. Much like a *Romance* knight, who by the word *palfrey* signified these *ideas, body of a certain figure, four-legged, with sense, motion, ambling, neighing, white, used to have a woman on his back*, might with the same certainty universally affirm also any or all of these of the word *palfrey*; but did thereby teach no more but that the word *palfrey*, in his or Romance language, stood for all these, and was not to be applied to anything where any of these was wanting. But he that shall tell me that, in whatever thing *sense, motion, reason,* and *laughter* were united, that thing had actually a notion of GOD or would be cast into a sleep by *opium*, made indeed an instructive proposition: because, neither *having the notion of* GOD nor *being cast into sleep by opium* being contained in the *idea* signified by the word *man*, we are by such propositions taught something more than barely what the word *man* stands for; and therefore the knowledge contained in it is more than *verbal*.

7. Before a man makes any proposition, he is supposed to understand the terms he uses in it; or else he talks like a parrot, only making a noise by imitation and framing certain sounds which he has learnt of others, but not, as a rational creature, using them for signs of *ideas* which he has in his mind. The hearer also is supposed to understand the terms as the speaker uses them, or else he talks jargon and makes an unintelligible noise. And therefore he trifles with words who makes such a proposition which, when it is made, contains no more than one of the terms does, and which a man was supposed to know before: v.g. *A triangle hath three sides*, or *Saffron is yellow*. And this is no further tolerable than where a man goes to explain his terms to one who is supposed or declares himself not to understand him; and then *it teaches only the signification of that word* and the use of that sign.

8. We can know then the truth of two sorts of propositions with perfect *certainty*: the one is of those trifling propositions which have a certainty in them, but it is but a *verbal certainty*,

but not instructive. And, secondly, we can know the truth and so may be *certain* in propositions which affirm something of another, which is a necessary consequence of its precise complex *idea*, but not contained in it: as that *the external angle of all triangles is bigger than either of the opposite internal angles*; which relation of the outward angle to either of the opposite internal angles making no part of the complex *idea* signified by the name triangle, this is a real truth and conveys with it instructive *real knowledge*.

9. We having little or no knowledge of what combinations there be of simple *ideas* existing together in substances but by our senses, we cannot make any universal *certain* propositions concerning them, any further than our nominal essences lead us; which being to a very few and inconsiderable truths, in respect of those which depend on their real constitutions, the general *propositions* that are made *about substances, if they are certain, are for the most part but trifling*; and if they are instructive, are uncertain, and such as we can have no knowledge of their real truth, how much soever constant observation and analogy may assist our judgments in guessing. Hence it comes to pass that one may often meet with very clear and coherent discourses that amount yet to nothing. For it is plain that names of substantial beings, as well as others as far as they have relative significations affixed to them, may, with great truth, be joined negatively and affirmatively in propositions, as their relative definitions make them fit to be so joined; and propositions consisting of such terms may, with the same clearness, be deduced one from another as those that convey the most real truths, and all this without any knowledge of the nature or reality of things existing without us. By this method one may make demonstrations and undoubted propositions in words, and yet thereby advance not one jot in the knowledge of the truth of things: v.g. he that, having learnt these following words with their ordinary mutually relative acceptations annexed to them, v.g. *substance, man, animal, form, soul, vegetative, sensitive, rational*, may make several undoubted propositions about the soul without knowing at all what the soul really is; and of this sort a man may find an infinite number of propositions, reasonings, and conclusions, in books of metaphysics, school-divinity, and some sort of natural philosophy, and, after all, know as little of GOD, *spirits*, or *bodies* as he did before he set out.

10. He that hath liberty to define, i.e. determine, the signification of his names of substances (as certainly everyone does in effect, who makes them stand for his own *ideas*) and makes their significations at a venture, taking them from his own or other men's fancies and not from an examination or inquiry into the nature of things themselves, may with little trouble demonstrate them one of another, according to those several respects and mutual relations he has given them one to another wherein, however things agree or disagree in their own nature, he needs mind nothing but his own notions, with the names he hath bestowed upon them; but thereby no more increases his own knowledge than he does his riches who, taking a bag of counters, calls one in a certain place a *pound*, another in another place a *shilling*, and a third in a third place a *penny*, and so proceeding, may undoubtedly reckon right and cast up a great sum, according to his counters so placed and standing for more or less as he pleases, without being one jot the richer or without even knowing how much a pound, shilling, or penny is, but only that one is contained in the other twenty times, and contains the other twelve; which a man may also do in the signification of words, by making them, in respect of one another, more or less or equally comprehensive.

11. Though yet, concerning most words used in discourses, especially argumentative and controversial, there is this more to be complained of, which is the worst sort of *trifling* and which sets us yet further from the certainty of knowledge we hope to attain by them or find in them, viz. that most writers are so far from instructing us in the nature and knowledge of things that they *use their words loosely* and uncertainly, and do not, by using them constantly and steadily in the same significations, make plain and clear deductions of words one from another and make their discourses coherent and clear (how little soever it were instructive), which were not difficult to do, did they not find it convenient to shelter their ignorance or obstinacy under the obscurity and perplexedness of their terms; to which perhaps inadvertency and ill custom does in many men much contribute.

12. To conclude, *Barely verbal propositions* may be known by these following *marks*:

First, All propositions wherein two abstract terms are affirmed one of another are barely about the signification of sounds. For since no abstract *idea* can be the same with any other but itself, when its abstract name is affirmed of any other term, it can signify no more but this: that it may or ought to be called by that name, or that these two names signify the same *idea*. Thus, should anyone say that *Parsimony is frugality*, that *Gratitude is justice*, that this or that action is or is not *temperance*: however specious these and the like propositions may at first sight seem, yet when we come to press them and examine nicely what they contain, we shall find that it all amounts to nothing but the signification of those terms.

13.   *Secondly,* All *propositions wherein a part of the complex* idea which any term stands for *is predicated of that term, are only* verbal, v.g. to say *that gold is a metal,* or *heavy.* And thus all propositions wherein more comprehensive words, called *genera,* are *affirmed* of subordinate or less comprehensive, called *species or individuals,* are barely verbal.

When by these two rules we have examined the propositions that make up the discourses we ordinarily meet with, both in and out of books, we shall perhaps find that a greater part of them than is usually suspected are purely about the signification of words, and contain nothing in them but the use and application of these signs.

This I think I may lay down for an infallible rule: that wherever the distinct *idea* any word stands for is not known and considered, and something not contained in the *idea* is not affirmed or denied of it, there our thoughts stick wholly in sounds and are able to attain no real truth or falsehood. This, perhaps, if well heeded, might save us a great deal of useless amusement and dispute, and very much shorten our trouble and wandering in the search of real and true knowledge.

Chapter IX

OF OUR KNOWLEDGE OF EXISTENCE

1.   HITHERTO we have only considered the essences of things; which, being only abstract *ideas* and thereby removed in our thoughts from particular existence (that being the proper opera-

tion of the mind in abstraction, to consider an *idea* under no other existence but what it has in the understanding) give us no knowledge of real existence at all. Where, by the way, we may take notice that *universal propositions* of whose truth or falsehood we can have certain knowledge concern not *existence*; and further, that all *particular affirmations or negations* that would not be certain if they were made general are only concerning *existence*: they declaring only the accidental union or separation of *ideas* in things existing, which, in their abstract natures, have no known necessary union or repugnancy.

2. But, leaving the nature of propositions and different ways of predication to be considered more at large in another place, let us proceed now to inquire concerning our knowledge of the *existence* of things, and how we come by it. I say, then, that we have the knowledge of *our own existence* by intuition, of the *existence* of GOD by demonstration, and of other things by sensation.

3. As for *our own existence*, we perceive it so plainly and so certainly that it neither needs nor is capable of any proof. For nothing can be more evident to us than our own existence. *I think, I reason, I feel pleasure and pain*: can any of these be more evident to me than my own existence? If I doubt of all other things, that very doubt makes me perceive my own *existence*, and will not suffer me to doubt of that. For if I know *I feel pain*, it is evident I have as certain perception of my own existence as of the existence of the pain I feel; or, if I know *I doubt*, I have as certain perception of the existence of the thing doubting, as of that thought which I call *doubt*. Experience then convinces us that *we have an intuitive knowledge of our own existence* and an internal infallible perception that we are. In every act of sensation, reasoning, or thinking, we are conscious to ourselves of our own being and, in this matter, come not short of the highest degree of *certainty*.

CHAPTER X

OF OUR KNOWLEDGE OF THE EXISTENCE OF A GOD

1. THOUGH GOD has given us no innate *ideas* of himself, though he has stamped no original characters on our minds

wherein we may read his being: yet, having furnished us with those faculties our minds are endowed with, he hath not left himself without witness, since we have sense, perception, and reason and cannot want a clear proof of him, as long as we carry ourselves about us. Nor can we justly complain of our ignorance in this great point, since he has so plentifully provided us with the means to discover and know him, so far as is necessary to the end of our being and the great concernment of our happiness. But, though this be the most obvious truth that reason discovers, and though its evidence be (if I mistake not) equal to mathematical certainty: yet it requires thought and attention, and the mind must apply itself to a regular deduction of it from some part of our intuitive knowledge, or else we shall be as uncertain and ignorant of this as of other propositions which are in themselves capable of clear demonstration. To show, therefore, that we are capable of *knowing*, i.e. *being certain, that there is a* GOD and how we may come by this certainty, I think we need go no further than ourselves and that undoubted knowledge we have of our own existence.

2. I think it is beyond question that *man has a clear perception of his own being*: he knows certainly that he exists and that he is something. He that can doubt whether he be anything or no, I speak not to, no more than I would argue with pure nothing, or endeavour to convince nonentity that it were something. If anyone pretends to be so sceptical as to deny his own existence (for really to doubt of it is manifestly impossible), let him for me enjoy his beloved happiness of being nothing, until hunger or some other pain convince him of the contrary. This, then, I think I may take for a truth, which everyone's certain knowledge assures him of, beyond the liberty of doubting, viz. that he is something that actually exists.

3. In the next place, man knows, by an intuitive certainty, that bare *nothing can no more produce any real being than it can be equal to two right angles*. If a man knows not that nonentity, or the absence of all being, cannot be equal to two right angles, it is impossible he should know any demonstration in *Euclid*. If, therefore, we know there is some real being, and that nonentity cannot produce any real being, it is an evident demonstration that from eternity there has been something, since what was not from eternity had a beginning, and what had a beginning must be produced by something else.

4. Next, it is evident that what had its being and beginning from another must also have all that which is in and belongs to its being from another too. All the powers it has must be owing to and received from the same source. This eternal source, then, of all being must also be the source and original of all power: and so *this eternal being must be also the most powerful*.

5. Again, a man finds in himself *perception* and *knowledge*. We have then got one step further, and we are certain now that there is not only some being, but some knowing, intelligent being in the world.

There was a time, then, when there was no knowing being, and when knowledge began to be; or else there has been also *a knowing being from eternity*. If it be said there was a time when no being had any knowledge, when that eternal being was void of all understanding, I reply that then it was impossible there should ever have been any knowledge: it being as impossible that things wholly void of knowledge, and operating blindly and without any perception, should produce a knowing being, as it is impossible that a triangle should make itself three angles bigger than two right ones . For it is as repugnant to the *idea* of senseless matter that it should put into itself sense, perception, and knowledge, as it is repugnant to the *idea* of a triangle that it should put into itself greater angles than two right ones.

6. Thus, from the consideration of ourselves and what we infallibly find in our own constitutions, our reason leads us to the knowledge of this certain and evident truth: that *there is an eternal, most powerful, and most knowing being*, which whether anyone will please to call *God*, it matters not. The thing is evident, and, from this *idea* duly considered, will easily be deduced all those other attributes which we ought to ascribe to this eternal being. If nevertheless anyone should be found so senselessly arrogant as to suppose man alone knowing and wise, but yet the product of mere ignorance and chance; and that all the rest of the universe acted only by that blind haphazard: I shall leave with him that very rational and emphatical rebuke of *Tully, lib. ii, De Leg.*, to be considered at his leisure. 'What can be more sillily arrogant and misbecoming than for a man to think that he has a mind and understanding in him, but yet in all the universe beside there is no such thing? Or that those

things, which with the utmost stretch of his reason he can scarce
comprehend, should be moved and managed without any reason
at all?' *Quid est enim verius quam neminem esse oportere tam
stulte arrogantem, ut in se mentem & rationem putet inesse, in
caelo mundoque non putet? Aut ea quae vix summa ingenii
ratione comprehendat nulla ratione moveri putet?*

From what has been said, it is plain to me we have a more
certain knowledge of the existence of a GOD than of anything
our senses have not immediately discovered to us. Nay, I presume I may say that we more certainly know that there is a GOD
than that there is anything else without us. When I say we *know*,
I mean there is such a knowledge within our reach, which we
cannot miss if we will but apply our minds to that, as we do to
several other inquiries.

7. *How far the* idea *of a most perfect being*, which a man may
frame in his mind, does or does not prove the *existence of a* GOD,
I will not here examine. For in the different make of men's
tempers and application of their thoughts, some arguments prevail more on one, and some on another, for the confirmation of
the same truth. But yet I think this I may say, that it is an ill
way of establishing this truth and silencing atheists: to lay the
whole stress of so important a point as this upon that sole
foundation; and take some men's having that *idea* of GOD in
their minds (for it is evident some men have none, and some
worse than none, and the most very different) for the only
proof of a deity; and, out of an overfondness of that darling
invention, cashier or at least endeavour to invalidate all other
arguments and forbid us to hearken to those proofs as being
weak or fallacious, which our own existence and the sensible
parts of the universe offer so clearly and cogently to our thoughts,
that I deem it impossible for a considering man to withstand
them. For I judge it as certain and clear a truth as can anywhere
be delivered, that *the invisible things of* GOD *are clearly seen from
the creation of the world, being understood, by the things that are
made, even his eternal power and godhead.* Though our own
being furnishes us, as I have shown, with an evident and incontestable proof of a deity, and I believe nobody can avoid the
cogency of it who will but as carefully attend to it as to any other
demonstration of so many parts: yet, this being so fundamental
a truth and of that consequence that all religion and genuine ·
morality depend thereon, I doubt not but I shall be forgiven by

my reader if I go over some parts of this argument again and enlarge a little more upon them.

8.   There is no truth more evident than that *something* must be *from eternity*. I never yet heard of anyone so unreasonable, or that could suppose so manifest a contradiction, as a time wherein there was perfectly nothing: this being of all absurdities the greatest, to imagine that pure nothing, the perfect negation and absence of all beings, should ever produce any real existence.

It being then unavoidable for all rational creatures to conclude that something has existed from eternity, let us next see what kind of thing that must be.

9.   There are but two sorts of beings in the world that man knows or conceives.

First, Such as are purely material, without sense, perception, or thought, as the clippings of our beards, and parings of our nails.

Secondly, Sensible, thinking, perceiving beings, such as we find ourselves to be. Which, if you please, we will hereafter call *cogitative and incogitative* beings; which to our present purpose, if for nothing else, are perhaps better terms than material and immaterial.

10.   If, then, there must be something eternal, let us see what sort of being it must be. And to that, it is very obvious to reason that it must necessarily be a *cogitative* being. For it is as impossible to conceive that ever bare incogitative matter should produce a thinking intelligent being, as that nothing should of itself produce matter. Let us suppose any parcel of matter eternal, great or small; we shall find it, in itself, able to produce nothing. For example: let us suppose the matter of the next pebble we meet with eternal, closely united, and the parts firmly at rest together; if there were no other being in the world, must it not eternally remain so, a dead inactive lump? Is it possible to conceive it can add motion to itself, being purely matter, or produce anything? Matter, then, by its own strength, cannot produce in itself so much as motion; the motion it has must also be from eternity, or else be produced and added to matter by some other being more powerful than matter: matter, as is evident, having not power to produce motion in itself. But let us suppose motion eternal too, yet matter, *incogitative matter* and motion, whatever changes it might produce of figure and bulk, *could never produce thought*: knowledge will still be as far

beyond the power of motion and matter to produce, as matter is beyond the power of *nothing* or *nonentity* to produce. And I appeal to everyone's own thoughts whether he cannot as easily conceive matter produced by *nothing* as thought to be produced by pure matter, when before there was no such thing as thought or an intelligent being existing. Divide matter into as minute parts as you will (which we are apt to imagine a sort of spiritual-izing, or making a thinking thing of it), vary the figure and motion of it as much as you please: a globe, cube, cone, prism, cylinder, etc., whose diameters are but 1,000,000th part of a *gry*[1], will operate no otherwise upon other bodies of proportion-able bulk than those of an inch or foot diameter; and you may as rationally expect to produce sense, thought, and knowledge by putting together in a certain figure and motion gross particles of matter, as by those that are the very minutest that do anywhere exist. They knock, impel, and resist one another just as the greater do, and that is all they can do. So that if we will suppose nothing first or eternal, *matter* can never begin to be; if we suppose bare matter without motion eternal, *motion* can never begin to be; if we suppose only matter and motion first or eternal, *thought* can never begin to be. For it is impossible to conceive that matter either with or without motion could have originally, in and from itself, sense, perception, and knowledge: as is evident from hence, that then sense, perception, and know-ledge must be a property eternally inseparable from matter and every particle of it. Not to add that, though our general or specific conception of matter makes us speak of it as one thing, yet really all matter is not one individual thing, neither is there any such thing existing as one material being or one single body that we know or can conceive. And therefore if matter were the eternal first cogitative being, there would not be one eternal infinite cogitative being, but an infinite number of eternal finite cogitative beings, independent one of another, of limited force and distinct thoughts, which could never produce that order, harmony, and beauty which is to be found in nature. Since therefore whatsoever is the first eternal *being* must necessarily

---

[1] A gry is one-tenth of a line, a line one-tenth of an inch, an inch one-tenth of a philosophical foot, a philosophical foot one-third of a pendulum whose diadroms, in the latitude of 45 degrees, are each equal to one second of time or one-sixtieth of a minute. I have affectedly made use of this measure here, and the parts of it under a decimal division with names to them, because I think it would be of general con-venience that this should be the common measure in the commonwealth of letters.

be cogitative; and whatsoever is first of all things must necessarily contain in it and actually have, at least, all the perfections that can ever after exist; nor can it ever give to another any perfection that it hath not, either actually in itself or at least in a higher degree: it necessarily follows that the first eternal being cannot be matter.

11. If, therefore, it be evident that *something* necessarily must *exist from eternity*, it is also as evident that *that something must* necessarily *be a cogitative being*: for it is as impossible that incogitative matter should produce a cogitative being as that nothing, or the negation of all being, should produce a positive being or matter.

12. Though this discovery of the *necessary existence of an eternal mind* does sufficiently lead us into the knowledge of GOD, since it will hence follow that all other knowing beings that have a beginning must depend on him, and have no other ways of knowledge or extent of power than what he gives them; and therefore, if he made those, he made also the less excellent pieces of this universe, all inanimate beings: whereby his *omniscience*, *power*, and *providence* will be established, and all his other attributes necessarily follow; yet, to clear up this a little further, we will see what doubts can be raised against it.

13. *First*, Perhaps it will be said that, though it be as clear as demonstration can make it that there must be an eternal being, and that being must also be knowing, yet it does not follow but that thinking being may also be material. Let it be so; it equally still follows that there is a GOD. For if there be an eternal, omniscient, omnipotent being, it is certain that there is a GOD, whether you imagine that being to be material or no. But herein I suppose lies the danger and deceit of that supposition: there being no way to avoid the demonstration that there is an eternal knowing being, men, devoted to matter, would willingly have it granted that this knowing being is material; and then, letting slide out of their minds or the discourse the demonstration whereby an eternal knowing being was proved necessarily to exist, would argue all to be matter and so deny a GOD, that is, an eternal cogitative being: whereby they are so far from establishing, that they destroy their own hypothesis. For if there can be, in their opinion, eternal matter without any eternal cogitative being, they manifestly separate matter and thinking and suppose no necessary connexion of the one with

the other, and so establish the necessity of an eternal spirit, but not of matter: since it has been proved already that an eternal cogitative being is unavoidably to be granted. Now if thinking and matter may be separated, *the eternal existence of matter will not follow from the eternal existence of a cogitative being*, and they suppose it to no purpose.

14. But now let us see how they can satisfy themselves, or others, that this *eternal thinking being is material*.

First, I would ask them whether they imagine that all matter, *every particle of matter, thinks*? This, I suppose, they will scarce say, since then there would be as many eternal thinking beings as there are particles of matter, and so an infinity of gods. And yet, if they will not allow matter as matter, that is, every particle of matter, to be as well cogitative as extended, they will have as hard a task to make out to their own reasons a cogitative being out of incogitative particles, as an extended being out of unextended parts, if I may so speak.

15. *Secondly*, if all matter does not think, I next ask whether it be *only one atom that does so*? This has as many absurdities as the other, for then this atom of matter must be alone eternal or not. If this alone be eternal, then this alone, by its powerful thought or will, made all the rest of matter. And so we have the creation of matter by a powerful thought, which is that the materialists stick at. For if they suppose one single thinking atom to have produced all the rest of matter, they cannot ascribe that pre-eminence to it upon any other account than that of its thinking, the only supposed difference. But allow it to be by some other way which is above our conception, it must be still creation, and these men must give up their great maxim, *Ex nihilo nil fit*. If it be said that all the rest of matter is equally eternal as that thinking atom, it will be to say anything at pleasure, though never so absurd; for to suppose all matter eternal, and yet one small particle in knowledge and power infinitely above all the rest, is without any the least appearance of reason to frame any hypothesis. Every particle of matter, as matter, is capable of all the same figures and motions of any other; and I challenge anyone, in his thoughts, to add anything else to one above another.

16. *Thirdly*, if then neither one peculiar atom alone can be this eternal thinking being; nor all matter, as matter, i.e. every particle of matter, can be it: it only remains that it is *some certain*

system of matter, duly put together, that is this *thinking eternal being*. This is that which, I imagine, is that notion which men are aptest to have of GOD, who would have him a material being, as most readily suggested to them by the ordinary conceit they have of themselves and other men, which they take to be material thinking beings. But this imagination, however more natural, is no less absurd than the other: for to suppose the eternal thinking being to be nothing else but a composition of particles of matter, each whereof is incogitative, is to ascribe all the wisdom and knowledge of that eternal being only to the *juxta-position* of parts, than which nothing can be more absurd. For unthinking particles of matter, however put together, can have nothing thereby added to them but a new relation of position, which it is impossible should give thought and knowledge to them.

17. But further, this *corporeal system* either has all its parts at rest, or it is a certain motion of the parts wherein its thinking consists. If it be perfectly at rest, it is but one lump, and so can have no privileges above one atom.

If it be the motion of its parts on which its thinking depends, all the thoughts there must be unavoidably accidental and limited: since all the particles that by motion cause thought, being each of them in itself without any thought, cannot regulate its own motions, much less be regulated by the thought of the whole: since that thought is not the cause of motion (for then it must be antecedent to it and so without it), but the consequence of it whereby freedom, power, choice, and all rational and wise thinking or acting will be quite taken away; so that such a thinking being will be no better nor wiser than pure blind matter, since to resolve all into the accidental unguided motions of blind matter, or into thought depending on unguided motions of blind matter, is the same thing, not to mention the narrowness of such thoughts and knowledge that must depend on the motion of such parts. But there needs no enumeration of any more absurdities and impossibilities in this hypothesis (however full of them it be) than that before-mentioned: since, let this thinking system be all or a part of the matter of the universe, it is impossible that any one particle should either know its own or the motion of any other particle, or the whole know the motion of every particular, and so regulate its own thoughts or motions, or indeed have any thought resulting from such motion.

18.   Others would have *matter* to be *eternal*, notwithstanding that they allow an eternal, cogitative, immaterial being. This, though it take not away the being of a GOD, yet since it denies one and the first great piece of his workmanship, the creation, let us consider it a little. *Matter* must be allowed eternal; why? Because you cannot conceive how it can be made out of nothing; why do you not also think yourself eternal? You will answer, perhaps, because about twenty or forty years since, you began to be. But if I ask you what that *you* is which began then to be, you can scarce tell me. The matter whereof you are made began not then to be, for if it did, then it is not eternal: but it began to be put together in such a fashion and frame as makes up your body; but yet that frame of particles is not you, it makes not that thinking thing you are (for I have now to do with one who allows an eternal, immaterial, thinking being, but would have unthinking matter eternal too): therefore, when did that thinking thing begin to be? If it did never begin to be, then have you always been a thinking thing from eternity: the absurdity whereof I need not confute till I meet with one who is so void of understanding as to own it.   If, therefore, you can allow a thinking thing to be made out of nothing (as all things that are not eternal must be), why also can you not allow it possible for a material being to be made out of nothing by an equal power, but that you have the experience of the one in view, and not of the other? Though, when well considered, creation of a spirit will be found to require no less power than the creation of matter. Nay possibly, if we would emancipate ourselves from vulgar notions and raise our thoughts as far as they would reach to a closer contemplation of things, we might be able to aim at some dim and seeming conception how matter might at first be made and begin to exist by the power of that eternal first being; but to give beginning and being to a spirit would be found a more inconceivable effect of omnipotent power. But this being what would perhaps lead us too far from the notions on which the philosophy now in the world is built, it would not be pardonable to deviate so far from them or to inquire, so far as grammar itself would authorize, if the common settled opinion opposes it, especially in this place where the received doctrine serves well enough to our present purpose and leaves this past doubt: that the creation or beginning of any one SUB-STANCE out of nothing being once admitted, the creation of

all other but the CREATOR himself may, with the same ease, be supposed.

19.   But you will say, Is it not impossible to admit of the *making anything out of nothing*, since we cannot possibly conceive it?   I answer, No, because it is not reasonable to deny the power of an infinite being because we cannot comprehend its operations.   We do not deny other effects upon this ground, because we cannot possibly conceive the manner of their production.   We cannot conceive how anything but impulse of body can move body; and yet that is not a reason sufficient to make us deny it possible, against the constant experience we have of it in ourselves, in all our voluntary motions, which are produced in us only by the free action or thought of our own minds, and are not, nor can be the effects of the impulse or determination of the motion of blind matter in or upon our bodies: for then it could not be in our power or choice to alter it.   For example, my right hand writes whilst my left hand is still.   What causes rest in one and motion in the other?   Nothing but my will, a thought of my mind; my thought only changing, the right hand rests, and the left hand moves.   This is matter of fact which cannot be denied.   Explain this and make it intelligible, and then the next step will be to understand creation.   For the giving a new determination to the motion of the animal spirits (which some make use of to explain voluntary motion) clears not the difficulty one jot, to alter the determination of motion being in this case no easier nor less than to give motion itself, since the new determination given to the animal spirits must be either immediately by thought, or by some other body put in their way by thought which was not in their way before, and so must owe its motion to thought: either of which leaves voluntary motion as unintelligible as it was before.   In the meantime, it is an overvaluing ourselves to reduce all to the narrow measure of our capacities, and to conclude all things impossible to be done whose manner of doing exceeds our comprehension.   This is to make our comprehension infinite or GOD finite, when what he can do is limited to what we can conceive of it.   If you do not understand the operations of your own finite mind, that thinking thing within you, do not deem it strange that you cannot comprehend the operations of that eternal infinite mind who made and governs all things and whom the heaven of heavens cannot contain.

* H 984

CHAPTER XI

OF OUR KNOWLEDGE OF THE EXISTENCE OF OTHER THINGS

1.   THE knowledge of our own being we have by intuition. The existence of a GOD, reason clearly makes known to us, as has been shown.

The *knowledge of the existence* of any other thing we can have only by *sensation*: for, there being no necessary connexion of *real existence* with any *idea* a man hath in his memory, nor of any other existence but that of GOD with the existence of any particular man, no particular man can know the *existence* of any other being but only when, by actual operating upon him, it makes itself perceived by him.   For the having the *idea* of anything in our mind no more proves the existence of that thing, than the picture of a man evidences his being in the world, or the visions of a dream make thereby a true history.

2.   It is therefore the actual receiving of *ideas* from without that gives us notice of the *existence* of other things and makes us know that something doth exist at that time without us which causes that *idea* in us, though perhaps we neither know nor consider how it does it; for it takes not, from the certainty of our senses and the *ideas* we receive by them, that we know not the manner wherein they are produced: v.g. whilst I write this, I have, by the paper affecting my eyes, that *idea* produced in my mind which, whatever object causes, I call *white*, by which I know that that quality or accident (i.e. whose appearance before my eyes always causes that *idea*) doth really exist and hath a being without me.   And of this, the greatest assurance I can possibly have and to which my faculties can attain is the testimony of my eyes, which are the proper and sole judges of this thing whose testimony I have reason to rely on, as so certain that I can no more doubt whilst I write this that I see white and black, and that something really exists that causes that sensation in me, than that I write or move my hand: which is a certainty as great as human nature is capable of concerning the existence of anything but a man's self alone and of GOD.

3.   *The notice we have by our senses of the existing of things*

without us, though it be not altogether so certain as our intuitive knowledge or the deductions of our reason employed about the clear abstract *ideas* of our own minds, yet it is an assurance that *deserves the name of knowledge*. If we persuade ourselves that our faculties act and inform us right concerning the existence of those objects that affect them, it cannot pass for an ill-grounded confidence: for I think nobody can, in earnest, be so sceptical as to be uncertain of the existence of those things which he sees and feels. At least, he that can doubt so far (whatever he may have with his own thoughts) will never have any controversy with me, since he can never be sure I say anything contrary to his own opinion. As to myself, I think GOD has given me assurance enough of the existence of things without me, since, by their different application, I can produce in myself both pleasure and pain, which is one great concernment of my present state. This is certain: the confidence that our faculties do not herein deceive us is the greatest assurance we are capable of concerning the existence of material beings. For we cannot act anything but by our faculties, nor talk of knowledge itself but by the help of those faculties which are fitted to apprehend even what knowledge is. But besides the assurance we have from our senses themselves, that they do not err in the information they give us of the existence of things without us when they are affected by them, we are further confirmed in this assurance by other concurrent reasons.

4. *First*, It is plain those perceptions are produced in us by exterior causes affecting our senses, because *those that want the organs of any sense never can have the* ideas *belonging to that sense* produced in their minds. This is too evident to be doubted, and therefore we cannot but be assured that they come in by the organs of that sense, and no other way. The organs themselves, it is plain, do not produce them: for then the eyes of a man in the dark would produce colours, and his nose smell roses in the winter; but we see nobody gets the relish of a pineapple till he goes to the *Indies*, where it is, and tastes it.

5. *Secondly*, Because *sometimes I find that I cannot avoid the having those* ideas *produced in my mind*. For though, when my eyes are shut, or windows fast, I can at pleasure recall to my mind the *ideas* of *light*, or the *sun*, which former sensations had lodged in my memory: so I can at pleasure lay by that *idea*, and take into my view that of the *smell* of a rose, or *taste* of sugar. But, if

I turn my eyes at noon towards the sun, I cannot avoid the *ideas* which the light or sun then produces in me. So that there is a manifest difference between the *ideas* laid up in my memory (over which, if they were there only, I should have constantly the same power to dispose of them and lay them by at pleasure) and those which force themselves upon me and I cannot avoid having. And therefore it must needs be some exterior cause and the brisk acting of some objects without me, whose efficacy I cannot resist, that produces those *ideas* in my mind, whether I will or no. Besides, there is nobody who doth not perceive the difference in himself between contemplating the sun as he hath the *idea* of it in his memory, and actually looking upon it: of which two, his perception is so distinct that few of his *ideas* are more distinguishable one from another, and therefore he hath certain knowledge that they are not both memory or the actions of his mind and fancies only within him, but that actual seeing hath a cause without.

6. *Thirdly,* Add to this, that *many of those* ideas *are produced in us with pain, which afterwards we remember without the least offence.* Thus, the pain of heat or cold, when the *idea* of it is revived in our minds, gives us no disturbance, which when felt was very troublesome, and is again when actually repeated: which is occasioned by the disorder the external object causes in our bodies when applied to them; and we remember the pain of *hunger, thirst,* or the *headache* without any pain at all: which would either never disturb us, or else constantly do it as often as we thought of it, were there nothing more but *ideas* floating in our minds and appearances entertaining our fancies, without the real existence of things affecting us from abroad. The same may be said of pleasure accompanying several actual sensations; and though mathematical demonstration depends not upon sense, yet the examining them by diagrams gives great credit to the evidence of our sight and seems to give it a certainty approaching to that of the demonstration itself. For it would be very strange that a man should allow it for an undeniable truth that two angles of a figure, which he measures by lines and angles of a diagram, should be bigger one than the other, and yet doubt of the existence of those lines and angles which, by looking on, he makes use of to measure that by.

7. *Fourthly,* Our *senses* in many cases bear *witness* to the truth of each other's report concerning the existence of sensible

things without us. He that sees a *fire* may, if he doubt whether
it be anything more than a bare fancy, feel it too and be convinced by putting his hand in it. Which certainly could never
be put into such exquisite pain by a bare *idea* or phantom,
unless that the pain be a fancy too: which yet he cannot, when
the burn is well, by raising the *idea* of it, bring upon himself
again.

Thus I see, whilst I write this, I can change the appearance of
the paper and, by designing the letters, tell beforehand what
new *idea* it shall exhibit the very next moment, barely by drawing my pen over it: which will neither appear (let me fancy as
much as I will) if my hand stand still or, though I move my
pen, if my eyes be shut; nor, when those characters are once
made on the paper, can I choose afterwards but see them as
they are, that is, have the *ideas* of such letters as I have made.
Whence it is manifest that they are not barely the sport and
play of my own imagination, when I find that the characters
that were made at the pleasure of my own thoughts do not obey
them, nor yet cease to be whenever I shall fancy it, but continue to affect my senses constantly and regularly, according to
the figures I made them. To which if we will add that the sight
of those shall, from another man, draw such sounds as I beforehand design they shall stand for, there will be little reason left to
doubt that those words I write do really exist without me, when
they cause a long series of regular sounds to affect my ears,
which could not be the effect of my imagination, nor could my
memory retain them in that order.

8. But yet, if after all this anyone will be so sceptical as to
distrust his senses and to affirm that all we see and hear, feel and
taste, think and do during our whole being is but the series and
deluding appearances of a long dream, whereof there is no
reality, and therefore will question the existence of all things or
our knowledge of anything: I must desire him to consider that,
if all be a dream, then he doth but dream that he makes the
question, and so it is not much matter that a waking man should
answer him. But yet if he pleases he may dream that I make
him this answer, that *the certainty of* things existing *in rerum
natura*, when we have *the testimony of our senses* for it, is not
only *as great* as our frame can attain to, but *as our condition
needs*. For our faculties being suited not to the full extent of
being, nor to a perfect, clear, comprehensive knowledge of

things free from all doubt and scruple, but to the preservation of us in whom they are, and accommodated to the use of life: they serve to our purpose well enough if they will but give us certain notice of those things which are convenient or inconvenient to us. For he that sees a candle burning and hath experimented the force of its flame by putting his finger in it will little doubt that this is something existing without him which does him harm and puts him to great pain: which is assurance enough, when no man requires greater certainty to govern his actions by than what is as certain as his actions themselves. And if our dreamer pleases to try whether the glowing heat of a glass furnace be barely a wandering imagination in a drowsy man's fancy, by putting his hand into it, he may perhaps be wakened into a certainty greater than he could wish that it is something more than bare imagination. So that this evidence is as great as we can desire, being as certain to us as our pleasure or pain, i.e. happiness or misery, beyond which we have no concernment, either of knowing or being. Such an assurance of the existence of things without us is sufficient to direct us in the attaining the good and avoiding the evil which is caused by them, which is the important concernment we have of being made acquainted with them.

9.   In fine then, when our senses do actually convey into our understandings any *idea*, we cannot but be satisfied that there doth something at that time really exist without us which doth affect our senses, and by them give notice of itself to our apprehensive faculties, and actually produce that *idea* which we then perceive; and we cannot so far distrust their testimony as to doubt that such collections of simple *ideas*, as we have observed by our senses to be united together, do really exist together. But *this knowledge extends as far as the present testimony of our senses*, employed about particular objects that do then affect them, *and no further*. For if I saw such a collection of simple *ideas* as is wont to be called *man*, existing together one minute since, and am now alone, I cannot be certain that the same man exists now, since there is no necessary connexion of his existence a minute since with his existence now: by a thousand ways he may cease to be since I had the testimony of my senses for his existence. And if I cannot be certain that the man I saw last today is now in being, I can less be certain that he is so who hath been longer removed from my senses and I have not seen

since yesterday or since the last year; and much less can I be certain of the existence of men that I never saw. And, therefore, though it be highly probable that millions of men do now exist, yet, whilst I am alone, writing this, I have not that certainty of it which we strictly call knowledge: though the great likelihood of it puts me past doubt, and it be reasonable for me to do several things upon the confidence that there are men (and men also of my acquaintance, with whom I have to do) now in the world; but this is but probability, not knowledge.

10.   Whereby yet we may observe how foolish and vain a thing it is for a man of a narrow knowledge who, having reason given him to judge of the different evidence and probability of things and to be swayed accordingly, how *vain*, I say, it is *to expect demonstration* and certainty *in things not capable of it*, and refuse assent to very rational propositions and act contrary to very plain and clear truths because they cannot be made out so evident as to surmount every the least (I will not say reason, but) pretence of doubting. He that, in the ordinary affairs of life, would admit of nothing but direct plain demonstration would be sure of nothing in this world but of perishing quickly. The wholesomeness of his meat or drink would not give him reason to venture on it, and I would fain know what it is he could do upon such grounds as were capable of no doubt, no objection.

11.   As, when our senses are actually employed about any object, we do know that it does exist, so *by our memory* we may be assured that heretofore things that affected our senses have existed. And thus *we have knowledge of the past existence* of several things whereof, our senses having informed us, our memories still retain the *ideas*; and of this we are past all doubt, so long as we remember well. But this knowledge also reaches no further than our senses have formerly assured us. Thus, seeing water at this instant, it is an unquestionable truth to me that water doth exist; and remembering that I saw it yesterday, it will also be always true and, as long as my memory retains it, always an undoubted proposition to me that water did exist 10th *July*, 1688; as it will also be equally true that a certain number of very fine colours did exist, which at the same time I saw upon a bubble of that water; but, being now quite out of the sight both of the water and bubbles too, it is no more certainly known to me that the water doth now exist than that the bubbles

or colours therein do so: it being no more necessary that water should exist today because it existed yesterday, than that the colours or bubbles exist today because they existed yesterday, though it be exceedingly much more probable: because water hath been observed to continue long in existence, but bubbles, and the colours on them, quickly cease to be.

12. What *ideas* we have of spirits, and how we come by them, I have already shown. But though we have those *ideas* in our minds and know we have them there, the having the *ideas* of spirits does not make us *know* that any such things do exist without us, or *that there are any finite spirits* or any other spiritual beings but the eternal GOD. We have ground from revelation, and several other reasons, to believe with assurance that there are such creatures; but our senses not being able to discover them, we want the means of knowing their particular existences. For we can no more know that there are finite spirits really existing, by the *idea* we have of such beings in our minds, than by the *ideas* anyone has of fairies or centaurs he can come to know that things answering those *ideas* do really exist.

And therefore, concerning the existence of finite spirits as well as several other things, we must content ourselves with the evidence of faith : but universal certain propositions concerning this matter are beyond our reach. For however true it may be, v.g. that all the intelligent spirits that GOD ever created do still exist, yet it can never make a part of our certain knowledge. These and the like propositions we may assent to, as highly probable, but are not, I fear, in this state capable of knowing. We are not, then, to put others upon demonstrating, nor ourselves upon search of universal certainty in all those matters wherein we are not capable of any other knowledge but what our senses give us in this or that particular.

13. By which it appears that there are two sorts of *propositions*: (1) There is one sort of propositions *concerning* the *existence* of anything answerable to such an *idea*: as having the *idea* of an *elephant, phoenix, motion,* or an *angel* in my mind, the first and natural inquiry is whether such a thing does anywhere exist? And this knowledge is only of *particulars*. No existence of anything without us, but only of GOD, can certainly be known further than our senses inform us. (2) There is another sort of

propositions, wherein is expressed the agreement or disagreement of our abstract *ideas* and their dependence one on another. Such propositions may be *universal* and certain. So, having the *idea* of GOD and myself, of fear and obedience, I cannot but be sure that GOD is to be feared and obeyed by me; and this proposition will be certain concerning *man* in general, if I have made an abstract *idea* of such a species whereof I am one particular. But yet this proposition, how certain soever, that men ought to fear and obey GOD, proves not to me the existence of men in the world, but will be true of all such creatures whenever they do exist: which *certainty* of such general propositions depends on the agreement or disagreement to be discovered in those abstract *ideas.*

14. In the former case, our knowledge is the consequence of the existence of things producing *ideas* in our minds by our senses; in the latter, knowledge is the consequence of the *ideas* (be they what they will) that are in our minds producing there general certain propositions. Many of these are called *aeternae veritates,* and all of them indeed are so: not from being written, all or any of them, in the minds of all men, or that they were any of them propositions in anyone's mind till he, having got the abstract *ideas,* joined or separated them by affirmation or negation. But wheresoever we can suppose such a creature as *man* is, endowed with such faculties and thereby furnished with such *ideas* as we have, we must conclude he must needs, when he applies his thoughts to the consideration of his *ideas,* know the truth of certain propositions that will arise from the agreement or disagreement which he will perceive in his own *ideas.* Such propositions are therefore called *eternal truths*: not because they are eternal propositions actually formed, and antecedent to the understanding that at any time makes them; nor because they are imprinted on the mind from any patterns that are anywhere out of the mind, and existed before: but because, being once made about abstract *ideas* so as to be true, they will, whenever they can be supposed to be made again at any time, past or to come, by a mind having those *ideas,* always actually be true. For names being supposed to stand perpetually for the same *ideas,* and the same *ideas* having immutably the same habitudes one to another, propositions concerning any abstract *ideas* that are once true must needs be *eternal verities.*

CHAPTER XII

OF THE IMPROVEMENT OF OUR KNOWLEDGE

1.   IT having been the common received opinion amongst men
of letters that *maxims* were the foundation of all knowledge, and
that the sciences were each of them built upon certain *praecognita*, from whence the understanding was to take its rise and
by which it was to conduct itself in its inquiries into the matters
belonging to that science, the beaten road of the Schools has been
to lay down in the beginning one or more general propositions as
foundations whereon to build the knowledge that was to be had
of that subject. These doctrines, thus laid down for foundations
of any science, were called *principles*, as the beginnings from
which we must set out and look no further backwards in our
inquiries, as we have already observed.
2.   One thing which might probably give an occasion to this
way of proceeding in other sciences was (as I suppose) the good
success it seemed to have in *mathematics*, wherein men being
observed to attain a great certainty of knowledge, these sciences
came by pre-eminence to be called μαθήματα and μάθησις,
learning, or things learned, thoroughly learned, as having
of all others the greatest certainty, clearness, and evidence in
them.
3.   But if anyone will consider, he will (I guess) find that *the
great advancement* and certainty of *real knowledge*, which men
arrived to in these sciences, was not owing to the influence of
these principles nor derived from any peculiar advantage they
received from two or three general maxims laid down in the
beginning, but *from* the *clear, distinct, complete ideas* their
thoughts were employed about and the relation of equality and
excess, so clear between some of them that they had an intuitive
knowledge, and by that a way to discover it in others, and this
without the help of those *maxims*. For I ask, Is it not possible
for a young lad to know that his whole body is bigger than his
little finger, but by virtue of this axiom, that *The whole is bigger
than a part*, nor be assured of it until he has learned that *maxim*?
Or cannot a country-wench know that, having received a shilling

from one that owes her three, and a shilling also from another that owes her three, that the remaining debts in each of their hands are equal? Cannot she know this, I say, without she fetch the certainty of it from this maxim, that *If you take equals from equals, the remainder will be equals*, a maxim which possibly she never heard or thought of? I desire anyone to consider, from what has been elsewhere said, which is known first and clearest by most people: the particular instance or the general rule; and which it is that gives life and birth to the other. These general rules are but the comparing our more general and abstract *ideas*, which are the workmanship of the mind, made and names given to them for the easier dispatch in its reasonings, and drawing into comprehensive terms and short rules its various and multiplied observations. But knowledge began in the mind and was founded on particulars, though afterwards, perhaps, no notice be taken thereof: it being natural for the mind (forward still to enlarge its knowledge) most attentively to lay up those general notions and make the proper use of them, which is to disburden the memory of the cumbersome load of particulars. For I desire it may be considered what more certainty there is to a child or anyone that his body, little finger and all, is bigger than his little finger alone, after you have given to his body the name *whole* and to his little finger the name *part*, than he could have had before; or what new knowledge concerning his body can these two relative terms give him which he could not have without them? Could he not know that his body was bigger than his little finger if his language were yet so imperfect that he had no such relative terms as *whole* and *part*? I ask further, when he has got these names, how is he more certain that his body is a *whole* and his little finger a *part* than he was or might be certain, before he learnt those terms, that his body was bigger than his little finger? Anyone may as reasonably doubt or deny that his little finger is a part of his body as that it is less than his body. And he that can doubt whether it be less will as certainly doubt whether it be a part. So that the maxim, *The whole is bigger than a part*, can never be made use of, to prove the little finger less than the body, but when it is useless, by being brought to convince one of a truth which he knows already. For he that does not certainly know that any parcel of matter, with another parcel of matter joined to it, is bigger than either of them alone will never be able to know it by the help of these two relative terms *whole* and *part*, make of them what maxim you please.

4. But be it in the mathematics as it will, whether it be clearer that, taking an inch from a black line of two inches and an inch from a red line of two inches, the remaining parts of the two lines will be equal, or that *if you take equals from equals, the remainder will be equals*: which, I say, of these two is the clearer and first known I leave to anyone to determine, it not being material to my present occasion. That which I have here to do is to inquire whether, if it be the readiest way to knowledge to begin with general maxims and build upon them, it be yet a safe way to take the *principles* which are laid down in any other science as unquestionable truths, and so receive them without examination and adhere to them without suffering them to be doubted of, because mathematicians have been so happy, or so fair, to use none but self-evident and undeniable. If this be so, I know not what may not pass for truth in morality, what may not be introduced and proved in natural philosophy.

Let that principle of some of the philosophers, that all is matter and that there is nothing else, be received for certain and indubitable, and it will be easy to be seen, by the writings of some that have revived it again in our days, what consequences it will lead us into. Let anyone, with *Polemo*, take the world; or, with the *Stoics*, the *aether* or the sun; or with *Anaximenes*, the air, to be *God*: and what a divinity, religion, and worship must we needs have! *Nothing* can be *so dangerous as principles* thus *taken up without questioning or examination*, especially if they be such as concern morality, which influence men's lives and give a bias to all their actions. Who might not justly expect another kind of life in *Aristippus*, who placed happiness in bodily pleasure; and in *Antisthenes*, who made virtue sufficient to felicity? And he, who with *Plato* shall place beatitude in the knowledge of GOD, will have his thoughts raised to other contemplations than those who look not beyond this spot of earth and those perishing things which are to be had in it. He that, with *Archelaus*, shall lay it down as a principle that right and wrong, honest and dishonest, are defined only by laws, and not by nature, will have other measures of moral rectitude and pravity than those who take it for granted that we are under obligations antecedent to all human constitutions.

5. If, therefore, those that pass for *principles* are *not certain*

(which we must have some way to know, that we may be able to distinguish them from those that are doubtful) but are only made so to us by our blind assent, we are liable to be misled by them and, instead of being guided into truth, we shall, by principles, be only confirmed in mistake and error.

6. But since the knowledge of the certainty of principles, as well as of all other truths, depends only upon the perception we have of the agreement or disagreement of our *ideas, the way to improve our knowledge* is not, I am sure, blindly and with an implicit faith, to receive and swallow principles; but is, I think, to get and *fix in our minds clear, distinct, and complete* ideas, as far as they are to be had, *and annex to them proper and constant names.* And thus, perhaps, without any other principles, but barely considering those *ideas* and, by *comparing them one with another,* finding their agreement and disagreement and their several relations and habitudes, we shall get more true and clear knowledge by the conduct of this one rule, than by taking up principles and thereby putting our minds into the disposal of others.

7. *We must,* therefore, if we will proceed as reason advises, *adapt our methods of inquiry to the nature of the* ideas *we examine* and the truth we search after. General and certain truths are only founded in the habitudes and relations of abstract *ideas.* A sagacious and methodical application of our thoughts, for the finding out these relations, is the only way to discover all that can be put with truth and certainty concerning them into general propositions. By what steps we are to proceed in these is to be learned in the schools of the mathematicians who, from very plain and easy beginnings, by gentle degrees and a continued chain of reasonings, proceed to the discovery and demonstration of truths that appear at first sight beyond human capacity. The art of finding proofs, and the admirable methods they have invented for the singling out and laying in order those inter-mediate *ideas* that demonstratively show the equality or in-equality of inapplicable quantities, is that which has carried them so far and produced such wonderful and unexpected dis-coveries; but whether something like this, in respect of other *ideas,* as well as those of magnitude, may not in time be found out, I will not determine. This, I think, I may say: that, if other *ideas* that are the real as well as nominal essences of their species were pursued in the way familiar to mathematicians, they would

carry our thoughts further and with greater evidence and clearness than possibly we are apt to imagine.

8. This gave me the confidence to advance that conjecture
which I suggest, Chap. iii, viz. that *morality is capable of demonstration*, as well as mathematics. For the *ideas* that ethics are
conversant about being all real essences, and such as I imagine
have a discoverable connexion and agreement one with another:
so far as we can find their habitudes and relations, so far we shall
be possessed of certain, real, and general truths; and I doubt not
but, if a right method were taken, a great part of morality might
be made out with that clearness that could leave, to a considering
man, no more reason to doubt, than he could have to doubt of
the truth of propositions in mathematics which have been
demonstrated to him.

9. In our search after the knowledge of *substances*, our want of
ideas that are suitable to such a way of proceeding obliges us to
a quite different method. We advance not here as in the other
(where our abstract *ideas* are real as well as nominal essences),
by contemplating our *ideas* and considering their relations and
correspondences: that helps us very little, for the reasons that in
another place we have at large set down. By which I think it is
evident that substances afford matter of very little general
knowledge; and the bare contemplation of their abstract *ideas*
will carry us but a very little way in the search of truth and
certainty. What, then, are we to do for the improvement of our
knowledge in substantial beings? Here we are to take a quite
contrary course, the want of *ideas* of their real *essences* sends us
from our own thoughts to the things themselves as they exist.
Experience here must teach me what reason cannot; and it is by
trying alone that I can certainly know what other qualities co-
exist with those of my complex *idea*, v.g. whether that *yellow,
heavy, fusible* body I call *gold* be *malleable* or no; which experience (which way ever it prove, in that particular body I examine)
makes me not certain that it is so in all or any other *yellow,
heavy, fusible* bodies but that which I have tried. Because it is no
consequence one way or the other from my complex *idea*: the
necessity or inconsistency of *malleability* hath no visible connexion with the combination of that *colour, weight,* and *fusibility*
in any body. What I have said here of the nominal essence of
gold, supposed to consist of a body of such a determinate *colour,
weight,* and *fusibility*, will hold true if *malleableness, fixedness,*

and *solubility* in *aqua regia* be added to it. Our reasonings from these *ideas* will carry us but a little way in the certain discovery of the other properties in those masses of matter wherein all these are to be found. Because the other properties of such bodies depending not on these, but on that unknown real essence on which these also depend, we cannot by them discover the rest: we can go no further than the simple *ideas* of our nominal essence will carry us, which is very little beyond themselves and so afford us but very sparingly any certain, universal, and useful truths. For upon trial, having found that particular piece (and all others of that colour, weight, and fusibility that I ever tried) *malleable*, that also makes now perhaps a part of my complex *idea*, part of my nominal essence of *gold*; whereby though I make my complex *idea* to which I affix the name *gold* to consist of more simple *ideas* than before: yet still, it not containing the real essence of any species of bodies, it helps me not certainly to know (I say to know, perhaps it may to conjecture) the other remaining properties of that body, further than they have a visible connexion with some or all of the simple *ideas* that make up my nominal essence. For example, I cannot be certain from this complex *idea* whether *gold* be fixed or no: because, as before, there is no necessary connexion or inconsistency to be discovered betwixt a complex *idea* of a body *yellow, heavy, fusible, malleable,* betwixt these, I say, and *fixedness*, so that I may certainly know that in whatsoever body these are found, there *fixedness* is sure to be. Here again for assurance I must apply myself to *experience*: as far as that reaches I may have certain knowledge, but no further.

10. I deny not but a man, accustomed to rational and regular experiments, shall be able to see further into the nature of bodies and guess righter at their yet unknown properties than one that is a stranger to them; but yet, as I have said, this is but judgment and opinion, not knowledge and certainty. This *way of* getting and *improving our knowledge in substances only by experience* and history, which is all that the weakness of our faculties in this state of *mediocrity* which we are in in this world can attain to, makes me suspect that natural philosophy is not capable of being made a science. We are able, I imagine, to reach very little general knowledge concerning the species of bodies and their several properties. Experiments and historical observations we may have, from which we may draw advantages of

ease and health, and thereby increase our stock of conveniences
for this life; but beyond this I fear our talents reach not, nor are
our faculties, as I guess, able to advance.

11. From whence it is obvious to conclude that, since our
faculties are not fitted to penetrate into the internal fabric and
real essences of bodies, but yet plainly discover to us the being
of a GOD and the knowledge of ourselves, enough to lead us into
a full and clear discovery of our duty and great concernment, it
will become us, as rational creatures, to employ those faculties
we have about what they are most adapted to, and follow the
direction of nature where it seems to point us out the way. For
it is rational to conclude that our proper employment lies in those
inquiries, and in that sort of knowledge which is most suited to
our natural capacities and carries in it our greatest interest, i.e.
the condition of our eternal estate. Hence I think I may conclude that *morality* is *the proper science and business of mankind
in general* (who are both concerned and fitted to search out their
summum bonum) as several arts, conversant about several parts
of nature, are the lot and private talent of particular men, for the
common use of human life and their own particular subsistence
in this world. Of what consequence the discovery of one natural
body and its properties may be to human life, the whole great
continent of *America* is a convincing instance: whose ignorance
in useful arts and want of the greatest part of the conveniences of
life, in a country that abounded with all sorts of natural plenty,
I think may be attributed to their ignorance of what was to be
found in a very ordinary, despicable stone, I mean the mineral
of *iron*. And whatever we think of our parts or improvements in
this part of the world, where knowledge and plenty seem to vie
with each other, yet to anyone that will seriously reflect on it,
I suppose it will appear past doubt that, were the use of *iron* lost
among us, we should in a few ages be unavoidably reduced to
the wants and ignorance of the ancient savage *Americans*, whose
natural endowments and provisions come no way short of those
of the most flourishing and polite nations. So that he who first
made known the use of that one contemptible mineral may be
truly styled the father of arts and author of plenty.

12. I would *not therefore* be thought to disesteem or *dissuade
the study of nature*. I readily agree the contemplation of his
works gives us occasion to admire, revere, and glorify their
Author and, if rightly directed, may be of greater benefit to

mankind than the monuments of exemplary charity that have at so great charge been raised by the founders of hospitals and almshouses. He that first invented printing, discovered the use of the compass, or made public the virtue and right use of *quinquina*, did more for the propogation of knowledge, for the supply and increase of useful commodities, and saved more from the grave than those who built colleges, workhouses, and hospitals. All that I would say is that we should not be too forwardly possessed with the opinion or expectation of knowledge where it is not to be had, or by ways that will not attain it; that we should not take doubtful systems for complete sciences, nor unintelligible notions for scientifical demonstrations. In the knowledge of bodies, we must be content to glean what we can from particular experiments, since we cannot from a discovery of their real essences grasp at a time whole sheaves, and in bundles comprehend the nature and properties of whole species together. Where our inquiry is concerning co-existence or repugnancy to co-exist, which by contemplation of our *ideas* we cannot discover, there experience, observation, and natural history must give us by our senses and by detail an insight into corporeal substances. The knowledge of bodies we must get by our senses warily employed in taking notice of their qualities and operations on one another; and what we hope to know of separate spirits in this world we must, I think, expect only from revelation. He that shall consider *how little general maxims, precarious principles, and hypotheses laid down at pleasure have promoted true knowledge* or helped to satisfy the inquiries of rational men after real improvements, how little, I say, the setting out at that end has for many ages together advanced men's progress towards the knowledge of natural philosophy, will think we have reason to thank those who in this latter age have taken another course and have trod out to us, though not an easier way to learned ignorance, yet a surer way to profitable knowledge.

13.   Not that we may not, to explain any *phenomena* of nature, make use of any probable *hypothesis* whatsoever: *hypotheses*, if they are well made, are at least great helps to the memory and often direct us to new discoveries. But my meaning is that we should *not take up any one too hastily* (which the mind, that would always penetrate into the causes of things and have principles to rest on, is very apt to do) till we have very well examined particulars and made several experiments in that thing which

we would explain by our hypothesis and see whether it will agree to them all, whether our principles will carry us quite through and not be as inconsistent with one *phenomenon* of nature, as they seem to accommodate and explain another. And at least that we take care that the name of *principles* deceive us not, nor impose on us, by making us receive that for an unquestionable truth which is really at best but a very doubtful conjecture, such as are most (I had almost said all) of the *hypotheses* in natural philosophy.

14. But whether natural philosophy be capable of certainty or no, the *ways to enlarge our knowledge*, as far as we are capable, seem to me, in short, to be these two:

First, The *first* is *to get and settle in our minds* determined *ideas* of those things whereof we have general or specific names, at least, of so many of them as we would consider and improve our knowledge in or reason about. And if they be *specific* ideas of *substances*, we should endeavour also to make them as complete as we can, whereby I mean that we should put together as many simple *ideas* as, being constantly observed to co-exist, may perfectly determine the *species*; and each of those simple *ideas* which are the ingredients of our complex ones should be clear and distinct in our minds. For it being evident that our knowledge cannot exceed our *ideas*: as far as they are either imperfect, confused, or obscure, we cannot expect to have certain, perfect, or clear knowledge.

Secondly, The other is the art of *finding out* those *intermediate ideas*, which may show us the agreement or repugnancy of other *ideas* which cannot be immediately compared.

15. That these two (and not the relying on maxims, and drawing consequences from some general propositions) are the right method of improving our knowledge in the *ideas* of other modes besides those of quantity, the consideration of mathematical knowledge will easily inform us. Where first we shall find that he that has not a perfect and clear *idea* of those angles or figures of which he desires to know anything is utterly thereby incapable of any knowledge about them. Suppose a man not to have a perfect exact *idea* of a *right angle*, a *scalene*, or *trapezium*; and there is nothing more certain than that he will in vain seek any demonstration about them. Further, it is evident that it was not the influence of those maxims, which are taken for principles in mathematics, that hath led the masters of that science into those

wonderful discoveries they have made. Let a man of good parts know all the maxims generally made use of in mathematics ever so perfectly, and contemplate their extent and consequences as much as he pleases, he will by their assistance, I suppose, scarce ever come to know that *The square of the hypotenuse in a right-angled triangle is equal to the squares of the two other sides.* The knowledge that *The whole is equal to all its parts,* and *If you take equals from equals, the remainder will be equal,* etc., helped him not, I presume, to this demonstration; and a man may, I think, pore long enough on those axioms without ever seeing one jot the more of mathematical truths. They have been discovered by the thoughts otherways applied: the mind had other objects, other views before it, far different from those maxims, when it first got the knowledge of such kind of truths in mathematics which men, well enough acquainted with those received axioms but ignorant of their method, who first made these demonstrations, can never sufficiently admire. And who knows what methods, to enlarge our knowledge in other parts of science, may hereafter be invented, answering that of *algebra* in mathematics, which so readily finds out *ideas* of quantities to measure others by, whose equality or proportion we could otherwise very hardly or perhaps never come to know?

CHAPTER XIII

SOME FURTHER CONSIDERATIONS CONCERNING OUR KNOWLEDGE

1. OUR *knowledge,* as in other things, so in this, has a great conformity with our sight that it is *neither wholly necessary, nor wholly voluntary.* If our knowledge were altogether necessary, all men's knowledge would not only be alike, but every man would know all that is knowable; and if it were wholly voluntary, some men so little regard or value it that they would have extreme little, or none at all. Men that have senses cannot choose but receive some *ideas* by them; and if they have memory, they cannot but retain some of them; and if they have any distinguishing faculty, cannot but perceive the agreement or disagreement of some of them one with another: as he that has eyes, if

he will open them by day, cannot but see some objects and perceive a difference in them. But though a man with his eyes open in the light cannot but see, yet there be certain objects which he may choose whether he will turn his eyes to: there may be in his reach a book containing pictures and discourses, capable to delight or instruct him, which yet he may never have the will to open, never take the pains to look into.

2. There is also another thing in a man's power, and that is, though he turns his eyes sometimes towards an object, yet he may choose whether he will curiously survey it and with an intent application endeavour to observe accurately all that is visible in it. But yet, what he does see, he cannot see otherwise than he does. It depends not on his will to see that *black* which appears *yellow*, nor to persuade himself that what actually *scalds* him feels *cold*; the earth will not appear painted with flowers, nor the fields covered with verdure, whenever he has a mind to it: in the cold winter, he cannot help seeing it white and hoary, if he will look abroad. Just thus is it with our understanding: all that is *voluntary* in our knowledge is the *employing* or withholding any of *our faculties* from this or that sort of objects, and a more or less accurate survey of them; but they being employed, *our will hath no power to determine the knowledge of the mind* one way or other: that is done only by the objects themselves, as far as they are clearly discovered. And therefore, as far as men's senses are conversant about external objects, the mind cannot but receive those *ideas* which are presented by them, and be informed of the existence of things without; and so far as men's thoughts converse with their own determined *ideas*, they cannot but in some measure observe the agreement and disagreement that is to be found amongst some of them, which is so far knowledge; and if they have names for those *ideas* which they have thus considered, they must needs be assured of the truth of those propositions which express that agreement or disagreement they perceive in them, and be undoubtedly convinced of those truths. For what a man sees, he cannot but see; and what he perceives, he cannot but know that he perceives.

3. Thus he that has got the *ideas* of numbers and hath taken the pains to compare *one*, *two*, and *three* to *six*, cannot choose but know that they are equal; he that hath got the *idea* of a triangle and found the ways to measure its angles and their magnitudes is certain that its three angles are equal to two right ones. And

can as little doubt of that, as of this truth, that *It is impossible for the same to be, and not to be.*

He also that hath the *idea* of an intelligent, but frail and weak being, made by and depending on another who is eternal, omnipotent, perfectly wise and good, will as certainly know that man is to honour, fear, and obey GOD, as that the sun shines when he sees it. For if he hath but the *ideas* of two such beings in his mind, and will turn his thoughts that way and consider them, he will as certainly find that the inferior, finite, and dependent is under an obligation to obey the supreme and infinite, as he is certain to find that *three, four,* and *seven* are less than *fifteen,* if he will consider and compute those numbers; nor can he be surer in a clear morning that the sun is risen, if he will but open his eyes and turn them that way. But yet these truths being never so certain, never so clear, he may be ignorant of either or all of them, who will never take the pains to employ his faculties as he should to inform himself about them.

Chapter XIV

of judgment

1. The understanding faculties being given to man, not barely for speculation, but also for the conduct of his life, man would be at a great loss if he had nothing to direct him but what has the certainty of true *knowledge.* For that being very short and scanty, as we have seen, he would be often utterly in the dark, and in most of the actions of his life perfectly at a stand, had he nothing to guide him in the absence of clear and certain knowledge. He that will not eat till he has demonstration that it will nourish him, he that will not stir till he infallibly knows the business he goes about will succeed, will have little else to do but sit still and perish.

2. Therefore, as God has set some things in broad daylight, as he has given us some certain knowledge, though limited to a few things in comparison, probably as a taste of what intellectual creatures are capable of, to excite in us a desire and endeavour after a better state: so, in the greatest part of our concernment, he has afforded us only the twilight, as I may so say, of *pro-*

bability, suitable, I presume, to that state of mediocrity and probationership he has been pleased to place us in here; wherein to check our over-confidence and presumption, we might by every day's experience be made sensible of our short-sightedness and liableness to error; the sense whereof might be a constant admonition to us to spend the days of this our pilgrimage with industry and care in the search and following of that way which might lead us to a state of greater perfection. It being highly rational to think, even were revelation silent in the case, that as men employ those talents God has given them here, they shall accordingly receive their rewards at the close of the day, when their sun shall set and night shall put an end to their labours.

3. The faculty which God has given man to supply the want of clear and certain knowledge, in cases where that cannot be had, is *judgment*: whereby the mind takes its *ideas* to agree or disagree or, which is the same, any proposition to be true or false, without perceiving a demonstrative evidence in the proofs. The mind sometimes exercises this *judgment* out of necessity, where demonstrative proofs and certain knowledge are not to be had; and sometimes out of laziness, unskilfulness, or haste, even where demonstrative and certain proofs are to be had. Men often stay not warily to examine the agreement or disagreement of two *ideas* which they are desirous or concerned to know; but, either incapable of such attention as is requisite in a long train of gradations or impatient of delay, lightly cast their eyes on or wholly pass by the proofs; and so, without making out the demonstration, determine of the agreement or disagreement of two *ideas*, as it were, by a view of them as they are at a distance, and take it to be the one or the other, as seems most likely to them upon such a loose survey. This faculty of the mind, when it is exercised immediately about things, is called *judgment*; when about truths delivered in words, is most commonly called *assent* or *dissent*; which being the most usual way wherein the mind has occasion to employ this faculty, I shall under these terms treat of it as least liable in our language to equivocation.

4. Thus the mind has two faculties conversant about truth and falsehood:

First, Knowledge, whereby it certainly perceives and is undoubtedly satisfied of the agreement or disagreement of any *ideas*.

Secondly, Judgment, which is the putting *ideas* together or separating them from one another in the mind, when their certain agreement or disagreement is not perceived but *presumed* to be so; which is, as the word imports, taken to be so before it certainly appears. And if it so unites or separates them as in reality things are, it is *right judgment*.

CHAPTER XV

OF PROBABILITY

1. As demonstration is the showing the agreement or disagreement of two *ideas* by the intervention of one or more proofs which have a constant, immutable, and visible connexion one with another, so *probability* is nothing but the appearance of such an agreement or disagreement by the intervention of proofs whose connexion is not constant and immutable, or at least is not perceived to be so, but is or appears for the most part to be so, and is enough to induce the mind to *judge* the proposition to be true or false, rather than the contrary. For example: In the demonstration of it a man perceives the certain, immutable connexion there is of equality between the three angles of a *triangle* and those intermediate ones which are made use of to show their equality to two right ones; and so, by an intuitive knowledge of the agreement or disagreement of the intermediate *ideas* in each step of the progress, the whole series is continued with an evidence which clearly shows the agreement or disagreement of those three angles in equality to two right ones; and thus he has certain knowledge that it is so. But another man, who never took the pains to observe the demonstration, hearing a mathematician, a man of credit, affirm the three angles of a triangle to be equal to two right ones, *assents* to it, i.e. receives it for true. In which case the foundation of his assent is the probability of the thing: the proof being such as for the most part carries truth with it, the man on whose testimony he receives it not being wont to affirm anything contrary to or besides his knowledge, especially in matters of this kind. So that that which causes his assent to this proposition, that the three angles of a triangle are equal to two right ones, that which makes him take these *ideas* to agree, without knowing them to do so, is the wonted veracity

of the speaker in other cases, or his supposed veracity in this.
2. Our knowledge, as has been shown, being very narrow, and
we not happy enough to find certain truth in everything which
we have occasion to consider: most of the propositions we think,
reason, discourse, nay, act upon, are such as we cannot have
undoubted knowledge of their truth; yet some of them border
so near upon certainty that we make no doubt at all about them,
but *assent* to them as firmly and act according to that assent as
resolutely as if they were infallibly demonstrated, and that our
knowledge of them was perfect and certain. But there being
degrees herein, from the very neighbourhood of certainty and
demonstration quite down to improbability and unlikeliness,
even to the confines of impossibility, and also degrees of *assent*
from full *assurance* and confidence quite down to *conjecture,*
doubt, and *distrust,* I shall come now (having, as I think, found
out the bounds of human knowledge and certainty) in the next
place to consider *the several degrees and grounds of probability,*
and assent or faith.
3. *Probability* is likeliness to be true, the very notation of the
word signifying such a proposition for which there be arguments
or proofs to make it pass or be received for true. The entertainment the mind gives this sort of propositions is called *belief,*
assent, or *opinion,* which is the admitting or receiving any proposition for true, upon arguments or proofs that are found to
persuade us to receive it as true, without certain knowledge that
it is so. And herein lies the *difference between probability* and
certainty, faith and *knowledge,* that in all the parts of knowledge
there is intuition; each immediate *idea,* each step has its visible
and certain connexion: in belief, not so. That which makes me
believe is something extraneous to the thing I believe, something
not evidently joined on both sides to, and so not manifestly
showing the agreement or disagreement of, those *ideas* that are
under consideration.
4. *Probability,* then, being to supply the defect of our knowledge and to guide us where that fails, is always conversant
about propositions whereof we have no certainty, but only some
inducements to receive them for true. The *grounds of it* are, in
short, these *two* following:
   First, The conformity of anything with our own knowledge,
observation, and experience.
   Secondly, The testimony of others, vouching their observation

and experience. In the testimony of others is to be considered: (1) The number. (2) The integrity. (3) The skill of the witnesses. (4) The design of the author, where it is a testimony out of a book cited. (5) The consistency of the parts, and circumstances of the relation. (6) Contrary testimonies.

5. Probability wanting that intuitive evidence which infallibly determines the understanding and produces certain knowledge, *the mind, if it will proceed rationally, ought to examine all the grounds of probability* and see how they make more or less *for or against* any probable proposition, before it assents to or dissents from it; and, upon a due balancing the whole, reject or receive it, with a more or less firm assent, proportionably to the preponderancy of the greater grounds of probability on one side or the other. For example:

If I myself see a man walk on the ice, it is past *probability*, it is knowledge; but if another tells me he saw a man in *England* in the midst of a sharp winter walk upon water hardened with cold, this has so great conformity with what is usually observed to happen that I am disposed by the nature of the thing itself to assent to it, unless some manifest suspicion attend the relation of that matter of fact. But if the same thing be told to one born between the tropics, who never saw nor heard of any such thing before, there the whole probability relies on testimony; and as the relators are more in number and of more credit and have no interest to speak contrary to the truth, so that matter of fact is like to find more or less belief. Though to a man whose experience has been always quite contrary, and has never heard of anything like it, the most untainted credit of a witness will scarce be able to find belief. And as it happened to a *Dutch* ambassador who, entertaining the King of *Siam* with the particularities of *Holland*, which he was inquisitive after, amongst other things told him that the water in his country would sometimes, in cold weather, be so hard that men walked upon it and that it would bear an elephant, if he were there. To which the King replied, *Hitherto I have believed the strange things you have told me because I look upon you as a sober fair man, but now I am sure you lie.*

6. Upon these grounds depends the *probability* of any proposition; and as the conformity of our knowledge, as the certainty of observations, as the frequency and constancy of experience and the number and credibility of testimonies do more or less agree

or disagree with it, so is any proposition in itself more or less probable. There is another, I confess, which, though by itself it be no true ground of *probability*, yet is often made use of for one, by which men most commonly regulate their assent and upon which they pin their faith more than anything else, and that is *the opinion of others*, though there cannot be a more dangerous thing to rely on, nor more likely to mislead one, since there is much more falsehood and error among men than truth and knowledge. And if the opinions and persuasions of others whom we know and think well of be a ground of assent, men have reason to be Heathens in *Japan*, Mahometans in *Turkey*, Papists in *Spain*, Protestants in *England*, and Lutherans in *Sweden*. But of this wrong ground of assent, I shall have occasion to speak more at large in another place.

CHAPTER XVI

OF THE DEGREES OF ASSENT

1. THE grounds of probability we have laid down in the foregoing chapter, as they are the foundations on which our *assent* is built: so are they also the measure whereby its several degrees are or ought to be *regulated*; only we are to take notice that, whatever grounds of probability there may be, they yet operate no further on the mind, which searches after truth and endeavours to judge right, than they appear, at least in the first judgment or search that the mind makes. I confess, in the opinions men have and firmly stick to in the world, their *assent* is not always from an actual view of the reasons that at first prevailed with them: it being in many cases almost impossible, and in most very hard, even for those who have very admirable memories, to retain all the proofs which upon a due examination made them embrace that side of the question. It suffices that they have once with care and fairness sifted the matter as far as they could; and that they have searched into all the particulars that they could imagine to give any light to the question; and with the best of their skill cast up the account upon the whole evidence; and thus, having once found on which side the probability appeared to them, after as full and exact an inquiry as they can make, they lay up the conclusion in their memories as a

truth they have discovered; and for the future they remain satisfied with the testimony of their memories that this is the opinion that, by the proofs they have once seen of it, deserves such a *degree* of their *assent* as they afford it.

2. This is all that the greatest part of men are capable of doing, in regulating their *opinions* and judgments, unless a man will exact of them either to retain distinctly in their memories all the proofs concerning any probable truth, and that too in the same order and regular deduction of consequences in which they have formerly placed or seen them (which sometimes is enough to fill a large volume upon one single question), or else they must require a man, for every opinion that he embraces, every day to examine the proofs: both which are impossible. It is unavoidable therefore that the memory be relied on in the case, and that *men be persuaded of several opinions whereof the proofs are not actually in their thoughts*, nay, which perhaps they are not able actually to recall. Without this, the greatest part of men must be either very sceptics, or change every moment and yield themselves up to whoever, having lately studied the question, offers them arguments which, for want of memory, they are not able presently to answer.

3. I cannot but own that men's *sticking* to their *past judgment* and adhering firmly to conclusions formerly made is often the cause of great obstinacy in error and mistake. But the fault is not that they rely on their memories for what they have before well judged, but because they judged before they had well examined. May we not find a great number (not to say the greatest part) of men that think they have formed right judgments of several matters, and that for no other reason but because they never thought otherwise? That imagine themselves to have judged right only because they never questioned, never examined their own opinions? Which is indeed to think they judged right because they never judged at all; and yet these of all men hold their opinions with the greatest stiffness, those being generally the most fierce and firm in their tenets who have least examined them. What we once know, we are certain is so; and we may be secure that there are no latent proofs undiscovered which may overturn our knowledge or bring it in doubt. But, in matters of probability, it is not in every case we can be sure that we have all the particulars before us that any way concern the question, and that there is no evidence behind and yet unseen, which may

cast the probability on the other side and outweigh all that at
present seems to preponderate with us. Who almost is there
that hath the leisure, patience, and means to collect together all
the proofs concerning most of the opinions he has, so as safely
to conclude that he hath a clear and full view, and that there is
no more to be alleged for his better information? And yet we
are forced to determine ourselves on the one side or other. The
conduct of our lives and the management of our great concerns
will not bear delay: for those depend, for the most part, on the
determination of our judgment in points wherein we are not
capable of certain and demonstrative knowledge, and wherein it
is necessary for us to embrace the one side or the other.

4. Since, therefore, it is unavoidable to the greatest part of
men, if not all, to have several *opinions* without certain and
indubitable proofs of their truth; and it carries too great an
imputation of ignorance, lightness, or folly for men to quit and
renounce their former tenets presently upon the offer of an
argument which they cannot immediately answer and show the
insufficiency of: it would, methinks, become all men to maintain
peace, and the common offices of humanity, *and friendship*, *in
the diversity of opinions*, since we cannot reasonably expect that
anyone should readily and obsequiously quit his own opinion
and embrace ours, with a blind resignation to an authority which
the understanding of man acknowledges not. For however it
may often mistake, it can own no other guide but reason, nor
blindly submit to the will and dictates of another. If he you
would bring over to your sentiments be one that examines
before he assents, you must give him leave at his leisure to go
over the account again and, recalling what is out of his mind,
examine all the particulars to see on which side the advantage
lies; and if he will not think our arguments of weight enough to
engage him anew in so much pains, it is but what we do often
ourselves in the like case, and we should take it amiss if others
should prescribe to us what points we should study. And if he
be one who takes his opinions upon trust, how can we imagine
that he should renounce those tenets, which time and custom
have so settled in his mind, that he thinks them self-evident and
of an unquestionable certainty, or which he takes to be impressions he has received from GOD himself or from men sent by
Him? How can we expect, I say, that opinions thus settled
should be given up to the arguments of authority of a stranger

Of the Degrees of Assent

or adversary, especially if there be any suspicion of interest or design, as there never fails to be where men find themselves ill-treated? We should do well to commiserate our mutual ignorance and endeavour to remove it in all the gentle and fair ways of information, and not instantly treat others ill, as obstinate and perverse, because they will not renounce their own and receive our opinions, or at least those we would force upon them, when it is more than probable that we are no less obstinate in not embracing some of theirs. For where is the man that has incontestable evidence of the truth of all that he holds, or of the falsehood of all he condemns, or can say that he has examined to the bottom all his own or other men's opinions? The necessity of believing without knowledge, nay, often upon very slight grounds, in this fleeting state of action and blindness we are in, should make us more busy and careful to inform ourselves than constrain others. At least, those who have not thoroughly examined to the bottom all their own tenets must confess they are unfit to prescribe to others, and are unreasonable in imposing that as truth on other men's belief which they themselves have not searched into nor weighed the arguments of probability on which they should receive or reject it. Those who have fairly and truly examined, and are thereby got past doubt in all the doctrines they profess and govern themselves by, would have a juster pretence to require others to follow them; but these are so few in number and find so little reason to be magisterial in their opinions that nothing insolent and imperious is to be expected from them; and there is reason to think that, if men were better instructed themselves, they would be less imposing on others.

5. But, to return to the grounds of assent and the several degrees of it, we are to take notice that the propositions we receive upon inducements of *probability* are *of two sorts*: either concerning some particular existence or, as it is usually termed, matter of fact which, falling under observation, is capable of human testimony; or else concerning things which, being beyond the discovery of our senses, are not capable of any such testimony.

6. Concerning the *first* of these, viz. *particular matter of fact*.

First, Where any particular thing, consonant to the constant observation of ourselves and others in the like case, comes attested by the concurrent reports of all that mention it, we receive it as easily and build as firmly upon it as if it were certain knowledge; and we reason and act thereupon with as little doubt as if it were perfect demonstration. Thus, if all *Englishmen*, who have occasion to mention it, should affirm that it froze in *England* the last winter, or that there were swallows seen there in the summer, I think a man could almost as little doubt of it as that seven and four are eleven. The first, therefore, and *highest degree of probability* is when the general consent of all men in all ages, as far as it can be known, concurs with a man's constant and never-failing experience, in like cases, to confirm the truth of any particular matter of fact attested by fair witnesses: such are all the stated constitutions and properties of bodies, and the regular proceedings of causes and effects in the ordinary course of nature. This we call an argument from the nature of things themselves. For what our own and other men's constant observation has found always to be after the same manner, that we with reason conclude to be the effects of steady and regular causes, though they come not within the reach of our knowledge. Thus, that fire warmed a man, made lead fluid, and changed the colour or consistency in wood or charcoal, that iron sunk in water and swam in quicksilver: these and the like propositions about particular facts, being agreeable to our constant experience as often as we have to do with these matters, and being generally spoke of (when mentioned by others) as things found constantly to be so and therefore not so much as controverted by anybody, we are put past doubt that a relation affirming any such thing to have been or any predication that it will happen again in the same manner is very true. These *probabilities* rise so near to *certainty* that they govern our thoughts as absolutely and influence all our actions as fully as the most evident demonstration; and in what concerns us we make little or no difference between them and certain knowledge; our belief, thus grounded, rises to *assurance*.

7.   *Secondly, The next degree of probability* is when I find, by my own experience and the agreement of all others that mention it, a thing to be for the most part so, and that the particular instance of it is attested by many and undoubted witnesses: v.g. history giving us such an account of men in all ages, and my own experience, as far as I had an opportunity to observe, confirming it, that most men prefer their private advantage to the public. If all historians that write of *Tiberius* say that *Tiberius* did so, it is extremely probable. And in this case, our assent has

a sufficient foundation to raise itself to a degree which we may call *confidence*.

8.   *Thirdly*, In things that happen indifferently, as that a bird should fly this or that way, that it should thunder on a man's right or left hand, etc., when any particular matter of fact is vouched by the concurrent testimony of unsuspected witnesses, there our assent is also unavoidable. Thus: that there is such a city in *Italy* as *Rome*; that about 1700 years ago, there lived in it a man called *Julius Caesar*; that he was a general, and that he won a battle against another called *Pompey*. This, though in the nature of the thing there be nothing for nor against it, yet being related by historians of credit and contradicted by no one writer, a man cannot avoid believing it and can as little doubt of it as he does of the being and actions of his own acquaintance, whereof he himself is a witness.

9.   Thus far the matter goes easy enough. Probability upon such grounds carries so much evidence with it that it naturally determines the judgment and leaves us as little liberty to believe or disbelieve, as a demonstration does, whether we will know or be ignorant.   The difficulty is when testimonies contradict common experience, and the reports of history and witnesses clash with the ordinary course of nature or with one another: there it is where diligence, attention, and exactness are required, to form a right judgment and to proportion the *assent* to the different evidence and probability of the thing, which rises and falls according as those two foundations of credibility, viz. common observation in like cases and particular testimonies in that particular instance, favour or contradict it.   These are liable to so great variety of contrary observations, circumstances, reports, different qualifications, tempers, designs, oversights, etc., of the reporters, that it is impossible to reduce to precise rules the various degrees wherein men give their assent. This only may be said in general, that as the arguments and proofs *pro* and *con*, upon due examination, nicely weighing every particular circumstance, shall to anyone appear upon the whole matter in a greater or less degree to preponderate on either side, so they are fitted to produce in the mind such different entertainment as we call *belief, conjecture, guess, doubt, wavering, distrust, disbelief*, etc.

10.   This is what concerns *assent* in matters wherein testimony is made use of: concerning which, I think, it may not be amiss

to take notice of a rule observed in the law of *England*, which is that, though the attested copy of a record be good proof, yet the copy of a copy, never so well attested and by never so credible witnesses, will not be admitted as a proof in judicature. This is so generally approved as reasonable and suited to the wisdom and caution to be used in our inquiry after material truths that I never yet heard of anyone that blamed it. This practice, if it be allowable in the decisions of right and wrong, carries this observation along with it, viz. that any testimony, the further off it is from the original truth, the less force and proof it has. The being and existence of the thing itself is what I call the original truth. A credible man vouching his knowledge of it is a good proof; but if another, equally credible, do witness it from his report, the testimony is weaker; and a third, that attests the hearsay of an hearsay, is yet less considerable. So that *in traditional truths, each remove weakens the force of the proof*; and the more hands the tradition has successively passed through, the less strength and evidence does it receive from them. This I thought necessary to be taken notice of, because I find amongst some men the quite contrary commonly practised, who look on opinions to gain force by growing older; and what a thousand years since would not, to a rational man contemporary with the first voucher, have appeared at all probable, is now urged as certain beyond all question, only because several have since, from him, said it one after another. Upon this ground propositions, evidently false or doubtful enough in their first beginning, come by an inverted rule of probability, to pass for authentic truths; and those which found or deserved little credit from the mouths of their first authors are thought to grow venerable by age and are urged as undeniable.

11.   I would not be thought here to lessen the credit and use of *history*: it is all the light we have in many cases, and we receive from it a great part of the useful truths we have, with a convincing evidence. I think nothing more valuable than the records of antiquity: I wish we had more of them and more uncorrupted. But this truth itself forces me to say that no *probability* can rise higher than its first original. What has no other evidence than the single testimony of one only witness must stand or fall by his only testimony, whether good, bad, or indifferent; and though cited afterwards by hundreds of others, one after another, is so far from receiving any strength thereby, that it is only the

weaker. Passion, interest, inadvertency, mistake of his meaning, and a thousand odd reasons or capriccios men's minds are acted by (impossible to be discovered) may make one man quote another man's words or meaning wrong. He that has but ever so little examined the citations of writers cannot doubt how little credit the quotations deserve where the originals are wanting, and consequently how much less quotations of quotations can be relied on. This is certain, that what in one age was affirmed upon slight grounds can never after come to be more valid in future ages by being often repeated. But the further still it is from the original, the less valid it is, and has always less force in the mouth or writing of him that last made use of it than in his from whom he received it.

12. The probabilities we have hitherto mentioned are only such as concern matter of fact, and such things as are capable of observation and testimony. There remains that other sort *concerning* which men entertain opinions with variety of assent, though the *things* be such *that, falling not under the reach of our senses, they are not capable of testimony.* Such are: (1) The existence, nature, and operations of finite immaterial beings without us; as spirits, angels, devils, etc. Or the existence of material beings which, either for their smallness in themselves or remoteness from us, our senses cannot take notice of, as whether there be any plants, animals, and intelligent inhabitants in the planets and other mansions of the vast universe. (2) Concerning the manner of operation in most parts of the works of nature wherein, though we see the sensible effects, yet their causes are unknown, and we perceive not the ways and manner how they are produced. We see animals are generated, nourished, and move; the loadstone draws iron; and the parts of a candle, successively melting, turn into flame and give us both light and heat. These and the like effects we see and know; but the causes that operate, and the manner they are produced in, we can only guess and probably conjecture. For these and the like, coming not within the scrutiny of human senses, cannot be examined by them or be attested by anybody, and therefore can appear more or less probable only as they more or less agree to truths that are established in our minds and as they hold proportion to other parts of our knowledge and observation. *Analogy* in these matters is the only help we have, and it is from that alone we draw all our grounds of probability. Thus,

observing that the bare rubbing of two bodies violently one upon another produces heat, and very often fire itself, we have reason to think that what we call heat and fire consists in a violent agitation of the imperceptible minute parts of the burning matter; observing likewise that the different refractions of pellucid bodies produce in our eyes the different appearances of several colours, and also that the different ranging and laying the superficial parts of several bodies, as of velvet, watered silk, etc., does the like, we think it probable that the colour and shining of bodies is in them nothing but the different arrangement and refraction of their minute and insensible parts. Thus, finding in all parts of the creation that fall under human observation that there is a gradual connexion of one with another, without any great or discernible gaps between, in all that great variety of things we see in the world, which are so closely linked together that, in the several ranks of beings, it is not easy to discover the bounds betwixt them: we have reason to be persuaded that, by such gentle steps, things ascend upwards in degrees of perfection. It is an hard matter to say where sensible and rational begin, and where insensible and irrational end; and who is there quick-sighted enough to determine precisely which is the lowest species of living things, and which the first of those which have no life? Things, as far as we can observe, lessen and augment as the quantity does in a regular cone where, though there be a manifest odds betwixt the bigness of the diameter at remote distance, yet the difference between the upper and under, where they touch one another, is hardly discernible. The difference is exceeding great between some men and some animals; but, if we will compare the understanding and abilities of some men and some brutes, we shall find so little difference that it will be hard to say that that of the man is either clearer or larger. Observing, I say, such gradual and gentle descents downwards in those parts of the creation that are beneath man, the rule of analogy may make it probable that it is so also in things above us and beyond our observation, and that there are several ranks of intelligent beings, excelling us in several degrees of perfection, ascending upwards towards the infinite perfection of the creator by gentle steps and differences that are every one at no great distance from the next to it. This sort of probability, which is the best conduct of rational experiments, and the rise of hypothesis has also its use and influence; and a wary reasoning from analogy leads us often into the discovery of truths and useful productions, which would otherwise lie concealed.

13.   Though the common experience and the ordinary course of things have justly a mighty influence on the minds of men to make them give or refuse credit to anything proposed to their belief, yet there is one case wherein the strangeness of the fact lessens not the assent to a fair testimony given of it. For where such supernatural events are suitable to ends aimed at by him who has the power to change the course of nature, there, under such circumstances, they may be the fitter to procure belief by how much the more they are beyond or contrary to ordinary observation. This is the proper case of *miracles* which, well attested, do not only find credit themselves, but give it also to other truths which need such confirmation.

14.   Besides those we have hitherto mentioned, there is one sort of propositions that challenge the highest degree of our assent, upon bare testimony, whether the thing proposed agree or disagree with common experience and the ordinary course of things or no. The reason whereof is because the testimony is of such an one as cannot deceive nor be deceived, and that is of God himself. This carries with it assurance beyond doubt, evidence beyond exception. This is called by a peculiar name, *revelation*; and our assent to it, *faith*; which as absolutely determines our minds, and as perfectly excludes all wavering as our knowledge itself; and we may as well doubt of our own being as we can whether any revelation from GOD be true. So that faith is a settled and sure principle of assent and assurance, and leaves no manner of room for doubt or hesitation. Only we must be sure that it be a divine revelation, and that we understand it right; else we shall expose ourselves to all the extravagancy of enthusiasm and all the error of wrong principles, if we have faith and assurance in what is not divine revelation. And therefore in those cases, our assent can be rationally no higher than the evidence of its being a revelation, and that this is the meaning of the expressions it is delivered in. If the evidence of its being a revelation, or that this its true sense be only on probable proofs, our assent can reach no higher than an assurance or diffidence, arising from the more or less apparent probability of the proofs. But of faith and the precedency it ought to have before other arguments of persuasion, I shall speak more hereafter, where I treat of it as it is ordinarily placed in

contradistinction to reason, though in truth it be nothing else but
an assent founded on the highest reason.

CHAPTER XVII

OF REASON

1.   THE *word reason* in the *English* language *has different significations*: sometimes it is taken for true and clear principles;
sometimes for clear and fair deductions from those principles;
and sometimes for the cause, and particularly the final cause.
But the consideration I shall have of it here is in a signification
different from all these, and that is as it stands for a faculty in
man, that faculty whereby man is supposed to be distinguished
from beasts, and wherein it is evident he much surpasses them.
2.   If general knowledge, as has been shown, consists in a perception of the agreement or disagreement of our own *ideas*, and
the knowledge of the existence of all things without us (except
only of a GOD, whose existence every man may certainly know
and demonstrate to himself from his own existence) be had only
by our senses, what room then is there for the exercise of any
other faculty but outward sense and inward perception? What
need is there of reason? Very much: both for the enlargement of
our knowledge and regulating our assent; for it hath to do both
in knowledge and opinion, and is necessary and assisting to all
our other intellectual faculties, and indeed contains two of them,
viz. *sagacity and illation*. By the one, it finds out; and by the
other, it so orders the intermediate *ideas* as to discover what
connexion there is in each link of the chain whereby the
extremes are held together, and thereby, as it were, to draw
into view the truth sought for: which is that we call *illation* or
inference, and consists in nothing but the perception of the connexion there is between the *ideas* in each step of the deduction,
whereby the mind comes to see either the certain agreement or
disagreement of any two *ideas*, as in demonstration, in which it
arrives at knowledge, or their probable connexion on which it
gives or withholds its assent, as in opinion. Sense and intuition
reach but a very little way. The greatest part of our knowledge
depends upon deductions and intermediate *ideas*; and in those

cases where we are fain to substitute assent instead of knowledge, and take propositions for true without being certain they are so, we have need to find out, examine, and compare the grounds of their probability. In both these cases, the faculty which finds out the means and rightly applies them, to discover certainty in the one and probability in the other, is that which we call reason. For as reason perceives the necessary and indubitable connexion of all the *ideas* or proofs one to another, in each step of any demonstration that produces knowledge: so it likewise perceives the probable connexion of all the *ideas* or proofs one to another, in every step of a discourse to which it will think assent due. This is the lowest degree of that which can be truly called reason. For where the mind does not perceive this probable connexion, where it does not discern whether there be any such connexion or no, there men's opinions are not the product of judgment or the consequence of reason, but the effects of chance and hazard, of a mind floating at all adventures, without choice and without direction.

3. So that we may in *reason* consider these *four degrees*: the first and highest is the discovering and finding out of proofs; the second, the regular and methodical disposition of them and the laying them in a clear and fit order, to make their connexion and force be plainly and easily perceived; the third is the perceiving their connexion; and the fourth, a making a right conclusion. These several degrees may be observed in any mathematical demonstration: it being one thing to perceive the connexion of each part as the demonstration is made by another; another to perceive the dependence of the conclusion on all the parts; a third to make out a demonstration clearly and neatly one's self and, something different from all these, to have first found out those intermediate *ideas* or proofs by which it is made.

4. There is one thing more which I shall desire to be considered concerning reason, and that is whether *syllogism*, as is generally thought, be the proper instrument of it and the usefullest way of exercising this faculty. The causes I have to doubt are these:

First, Because syllogism serves our reason but in one only of the forementioned parts of it, and that is to show the connexion of the proofs in any one instance, and no more; but in this it is of no great use, since the mind can perceive such connexion where it really is as easily, nay, perhaps better, without it.

If we will observe the actings of our own minds, we shall find that we reason best and clearest when we only observe the connexion of the proof, without reducing our thoughts to any rule of syllogism. And therefore we may take notice that there are many men, that reason exceeding clear and rightly, who know not how to make a syllogism. He that will look into many parts of *Asia* and *America* will find men reason there perhaps as acutely as himself, who yet never heard of a syllogism nor can reduce any one argument to those forms; and I believe scarce anyone ever makes syllogisms in reasoning within himself. Indeed syllogism is made use of on occasion to discover a fallacy hid in a rhetorical flourish or cunningly wrapped up in a smooth period and, stripping an absurdity of the cover of wit and good language, show it in its naked deformity. But the weakness or fallacy of such a loose discourse it shows, by the artificial form it is put into, only to those who have thoroughly studied *mode and figure* and have so examined the many ways that three propositions may be put together as to know which of them does certainly conclude right and which not, and upon what grounds it is that they do so. All who have so far considered *syllogism* as to see the reason why, in three propositions laid together in one form, the conclusion will be certainly right but in another not certainly so, I grant, are certain of the conclusion they draw from the premisses in the allowed *modes* and *figures*; but they who have not so far looked into those forms are not sure by virtue of syllogism that the conclusion certainly follows from the premisses: they only take it to be so by an implicit faith in their teachers and a confidence in those forms of argumentation; but this is still but believing, not being certain. Now if of all mankind those who can make syllogisms are extremely few in comparison of those who cannot; and if of those few who have been taught logic there is but a very small number who do any more than believe that syllogisms in the allowed *modes* and *figures* do conclude right, without knowing certainly that they do so; if syllogisms must be taken for the only proper instrument of reason and means of knowledge, it will follow that before *Aristotle* there was not one man that did or could know anything by reason, and that since the invention of syllogisms there is not one of ten thousand that doth.

But God has not been so sparing to men, to make them barely two-legged creatures, and left it to *Aristotle* to make them rational, i.e. those few of them that he could get so to examine the grounds of syllogisms as to see that, in above threescore ways that three propositions may be laid together, there are but about fourteen wherein one may be sure that the conclusion is right, and upon what ground it is that in these few the conclusion is certain and in the other not. God has been more bountiful to mankind than so. He has given them a mind that can reason without being instructed in methods of syllogizing; the understanding is not taught to reason by these rules, it has a native faculty to perceive the coherence or incoherence of its *ideas*, and can range them right without any such perplexing repetitions. I say not this any way to lessen *Aristotle*, whom I look on as one of the greatest men amongst the ancients; whose large views, acuteness, and penetration of thought and strength of judgment, few have equalled; and who, in this very invention of forms of argumentation wherein the conclusion may be shown to be rightly inferred, did great service against those who were not ashamed to deny anything. And I readily own that all right reasoning may be reduced to his forms of syllogism. But yet I think, without any diminution to him, I may truly say that they are not the only nor the best way of reasoning, for the leading of those into truth who are willing to find it and desire to make the best use they may of their reason for the attainment of knowledge. And he himself, it is plain, found out some forms to be conclusive and others not, not by the forms themselves but by the original way of knowledge, i.e. by the visible agreement of *ideas*. Tell a country gentlewoman that the wind is south-west, and the weather louring, and like to rain, and she will easily understand it is not safe for her to go abroad thin clad in such a day after a fever: she clearly sees the probable connexion of all these, viz. south-west wind and clouds, rain, wetting, taking cold, relapse, and danger of death, without tying them together in those artificial and cumbersome fetters of several syllogisms that clog and hinder the mind, which proceeds from one part to another quicker and clearer without them; and the probability which she easily perceives in things thus in their native state would be quite lost, if this argument were managed learnedly and proposed in mode and figure. For it very often confounds the connexion; and, I think, everyone will perceive in mathematical demonstrations that the knowledge gained thereby comes shortest and clearest without syllogism.

Inference is looked on as the great act of the rational faculty, and so it is when it is rightly made; but the mind, either very desirous to enlarge its knowledge, or very apt to favour the sentiments it has once imbibed, is very forward to make inferences, and therefore often makes too much haste before it perceives the connexion of the *ideas* that must hold the extremes together.

To infer is nothing but, by virtue of one proposition laid down as true, to draw in another as true, i.e. to see or suppose such a connexion of the two *ideas* of the inferred proposition. V.g., Let this be the proposition laid down, *Men shall be punished in another world*, and from thence be inferred this other, *Then men can determine themselves*. The question now is to know whether the mind has made this inference right or no; if it has made it by finding out the intermediate *ideas* and taking a view of the connexion of them placed in a due order, it has proceeded rationally and made a right inference. If it has done it without such a view, it has not so much made an inference that will hold or an inference of right reason as shown a willingness to have it be, or be taken for such. But in neither case is it *syllogism* that discovered those *ideas* or showed the connexion of them, for they must be both found out and the connexion everywhere perceived before they can rationally be made use of in *syllogism*: unless it can be said that any *idea*, without considering what connexion it hath with the two other whose agreement should be shown by it, will do well enough in a *syllogism* and may be taken at a venture for the *medius terminus*, to prove any conclusion. But this nobody will say, because it is by virtue of the perceived agreement of the intermediate *idea* with the extremes that the extremes are concluded to agree; and therefore each intermediate *idea* must be such as in the whole chain hath a visible connexion with those two it is placed between, or else thereby the conclusion cannot be inferred or drawn in; for wherever any link of the chain is loose and without connexion, there the whole strength of it is lost, and it hath no force to infer or draw in anything. In the instance above-mentioned, what is it shows the force of the inference and, consequently, the reasonableness of it, but a view of the connexion of all the intermediate *ideas* that draw in the conclusion or proposition inferred? V.g., *Men shall be punished, — God the punisher, — just punishment, — the punished guilty — could have done otherwise —*

freedom — self-determination: by which chain of *ideas* thus visibly
linked together in train, i.e. each intermediate *idea* agreeing on
each side with those two it is immediately placed between, the
ideas of men and self-determination appear to be connected:
i.e. this proposition, *Men can determine themselves*, is drawn in
or inferred from this, *that they shall be punished in the other
world*. For here the mind, seeing the connexion there is between the *idea of men's punishment in the other world* and the
idea of God punishing, between *God punishing* and *the justice
of the punishment*, between *justice of punishment* and *guilt*,
between *guilt* and a *power to do otherwise*, between a *power to do
otherwise* and *freedom*, and between *freedom* and *self-determination*, sees the connexion between *men* and *self-determination*.

Now I ask whether the connexion of the extremes be not
more clearly seen in this simple and natural disposition than in
the perplexed repetitions and jumble of five or six *syllogisms*.
I must beg pardon for calling it jumble, till somebody shall put
these *ideas* into so many *syllogisms* and then say that they are less
jumbled and their connexion more visible when they are trans-
posed and repeated and spun out to a greater length in artificial
forms, than in that short natural plain order they are laid down
in here, wherein everyone may see it, and wherein they must be
seen before they can be put into a train of *syllogisms*. For the
natural order of the connecting *ideas* must direct the order of the
syllogisms, and a man must see the connexion of each intermediate *idea* with those that it connects, before he can with
reason make use of it in a *syllogism*. And when all those syllogisms are made, neither those that are nor those that are not
logicians will see the force of the argumentation, i.e. the connexion of the extremes, one jot the better. [For those that are
not men of art, not knowing the true forms of *syllogism*, nor
the reasons of them, cannot know whether they are made in
right and conclusive *modes* and *figures* or no, and so are not at all
helped by the forms they are put into, though by them the
natural order, wherein the mind could judge of their respective
connexion, being disturbed renders the illation much more
uncertain than without them.] And as for logicians themselves,
they see the connexion of each intermediate *idea* with those it
stands between (on which the force of the inference depends) as
well before as after the *syllogism* is made, or else they do not see it
all. For a *syllogism* neither shows nor strengthens the connexion

of any two *ideas* immediately put together, but, only by the connexion seen in them, shows what connexion the extremes have one with another. But what connexion the intermediate has with either of the extremes in that syllogism, that no syllogism does or can show. That the mind only doth or can perceive, as they stand there in that *juxtaposition*, only by its own view, to which the syllogistical form it happens to be in gives no help or light at all: it only shows that, if the intermediate *idea* agrees with those it is on both sides immediately applied to, then those two remote ones or, as they are called, *extremes* do certainly agree; and therefore the immediate connexion of each *idea* to that which it is applied to on each side, on which the force of the reasoning depends, is as well seen before as after the *syllogism* is made, or else he that makes the syllogism could never see it at all. This, as has been already observed, is seen only by the eye, or the perceptive faculty of the mind, taking a view of them laid together, in a *juxtaposition*: which view of any two it has equally, whenever they are laid together in any proposition, whether that proposition be placed as a *major* or a *minor*, in a *syllogism* or no.

Of what use, then, are *syllogisms*? I answer, Their chief and main use is in the Schools, where men are allowed without shame to deny the agreement of *ideas* that do manifestly agree; or out of the Schools, to those who from thence have learned without shame to deny the connexion of *ideas*, which even to themselves is visible. But to an ingenuous searcher after truth, who has no other aim but to find it, there is no need of any such form to force the allowing of the inference: the truth and reasonableness of it is better seen in ranging of the *ideas* in a simple and plain order; and hence it is that men, in their own inquiries after truth, never use *syllogisms* to convince themselves [or in teaching others to instruct willing learners]. Because, before they can put them into a *syllogism*, they must see the connexion that is between the intermediate *idea* and the two other *ideas* it is set between and applied to, to show their agreement; and when they see that, they see whether the inference be good or no; and so *syllogism* comes too late to settle it. For to make use again of the former instance, I ask whether the mind considering the *idea* of justice placed as an intermediate *idea* between the *punishment* of men and the guilt of the punished (and till it does so consider it, the mind cannot make use of it as a *medius terminus*) does not as plainly see the force and strength of the inference, as when it is formed into syllogism. To show it in a very plain and easy example, let *animal* be the intermediate *idea* or *medius terminus* that the mind makes use of to show the connexion of *homo* and *vivens*; I ask whether the mind does not more readily and plainly see that connexion in the simple and proper position of the connecting *idea* in the middle, thus:

Homo — *Animal* — *vivens*,

than in this perplexed one,

Animal — *vivens* — *Homo* — *Animal*;

which is the position these *ideas* have in a syllogism, to show the connexion between *homo* and *vivens* by the intervention of *animal*.

Indeed syllogism is thought to be of necessary use, even to the lovers of truth, to show them the fallacies that are often concealed in florid, witty, or involved discourses. But that this is a mistake will appear, if we consider that the reason why sometimes men, who sincerely aim at truth, are imposed upon by such loose and, as they are called, rhetorical discourses is that, their fancies being struck with some lively metaphorical representations, they neglect to observe or do not easily perceive what are the true *ideas* upon which the inference depends. Now to show such men the weakness of such an argumentation, there needs no more but to strip it of the superfluous *ideas* which, blended and confounded with those on which the inference depends, seem to show a connexion where there is none or, at least, do hinder the discovery of the want of it, and then to lay the naked *ideas* on which the force of the argumentation depends in their due order; in which position the mind, taking a view of them, sees what connexion they have, and so is able to judge of the inference without any need of a syllogism at all.

I grant that *mode* and *figure* is commonly made use of in such cases, as if the detection of the incoherence of such loose discourses were wholly owing to the syllogistical form; and so I myself formerly thought, till upon a stricter examination I now find that laying the intermediate *ideas* naked in their due order shows the incoherence of the argumentation better than syllogism: not only as subjecting each link of the chain to the immediate view of the mind in its proper place, whereby its connexion is best observed, but also because syllogism shows the incoherence only to those (who are not one of ten thousand) who perfectly understand *mode* and *figure* and the reason upon which

those forms are established; whereas a due and orderly placing
of the *ideas* upon which the inference is made makes everyone,
both logician or not logician, who understands the terms and
hath the faculty to perceive the agreement or disagreement of
such *ideas* (without which, in or out of syllogism, he cannot
perceive the strength or weakness, coherence or incoherence of
the discourse) see the want of connexion in the argumentation
and the absurdity of the inference.

And thus I have known a man, unskilful in syllogism, who at
first hearing could perceive the weakness and inconclusiveness of
a long artificial and plausible discourse, wherewith others better
skilled in syllogism have been misled. And I believe there are
few of my readers who do not know such. And indeed, if it were
not so, the debates of most princes' councils and the business of
assemblies would be in danger to be mismanaged, since those
who are relied upon and have usually a great stroke in them are
not always such who have the good luck to be perfectly knowing
in the forms of *syllogism* or expert in *mode* and *figure*. And if
syllogism were the only or so much as the surest way to detect
the fallacies of artificial discourses, I do not think that all
mankind, even princes in matters that concern their crowns and
dignities, are so much in love with falsehood and mistake that
they would everywhere have neglected to bring syllogism into
the debates of moment, or thought it ridiculous so much as to
offer them in affairs of consequence: a plain evidence to me that
men of parts and penetration, who were not idly to dispute at
their ease, but were to act according to the result of their
debates and often pay for their mistakes with their heads or
fortunes, found those scholastic forms were of little use to discover truth or fallacy, whilst both the one and the other might be
shown, and better shown without them, to those who would not
refuse to see what was visibly shown them.

Secondly, Another reason that makes me doubt whether
syllogism be the only proper instrument of reason, in the discovery of truth, is that, of whatever use *mode* and *figure* is pretended to be in the laying open of fallacy (which has been above
considered), those scholastic forms of discourse are not less
liable to fallacies than the plainer ways of argumentation; and
for this I appeal to common observation, which has always
found these artificial methods of reasoning more adapted to
catch and entangle the mind than to instruct and inform the

understanding. And hence it is that men, even when they are baffled and silenced in this scholastic way, are seldom or never convinced, and so brought over to the conquering side: they perhaps acknowledge their adversary to be the more skilful disputant, but rest nevertheless persuaded of the truth on their side, and go away, worsted as they are, with the same opinion they brought with them: which they could not do if this way of argumentation carried light and conviction with it, and made men see where the truth lay. And therefore syllogism has been thought more proper for the attaining victory in dispute, than for the discovery or confirmation of truth in fair inquiries. And if it be certain that fallacies can be couched in syllogisms, as it cannot be denied, it must be something else and not syllogism that must discover them.

I have had experience how ready some men are, when all the use which they have been wont to ascribe to anything is not allowed, to cry out that I am for laying it wholly aside. But to prevent such unjust and groundless imputations, I tell them that I am not for taking away any helps to the understanding in the attainment of knowledge. And if men skilled in and used to syllogisms find them assisting to their reason in the discovery of truth, I think they ought to make use of them. All that I aim at is that they should not ascribe more to these forms than belongs to them, and think that men have no use, or not so full a use, of their reasoning faculty without them. Some eyes want spectacles to see things clearly and distinctly: but let not those that use them therefore say nobody can see clearly without them; those who do so will be thought in favour with art (which perhaps they are beholding to) a little too much to depress and discredit nature. Reason, by its own penetration where it is strong and exercised, usually sees quicker and clearer without syllogism. If use of those spectacles has so dimmed its sight that it cannot without them see consequences or inconsequences in argumentation, I am not so unreasonable as to be against the using them. Everyone knows what best fits his own sight. But let him not thence conclude all in the dark, who use not just the same helps that he finds a need of.

5. But however it be in knowledge, I think I may truly say it is of *far* less or *no use* at all *in probabilities*. For the assent there being to be determined by the preponderancy, after a due weighing of all the proofs, with all circumstances on both sides,

nothing is so unfit to assist the mind in that as syllogism: which, running away with one assumed probability or one topical argument, pursues that till it has led the mind quite out of sight of the thing under consideration; and forcing it upon some remote difficulty, holds it fast there, entangled perhaps and as it were manacled in the chain of syllogisms, without allowing it that liberty, much less affording it the helps requisite to show on which side, all things considered, is the greater probability.

6. But let it help us (as perhaps may be said) in convincing men of their errors and mistakes (and yet I would fain see the man that was forced out of his opinion by dint of *syllogism*): yet still it fails *our reason* in that part which, if not its highest perfection, is yet certainly its hardest task, and that which we most need its help in, and that is *the finding out of proofs and making new discoveries*. The rules of *syllogism* serve not to furnish the mind with those intermediate *ideas* that may show the connexion of remote ones. This way of reasoning discovers no new proofs, but is the art of marshalling and ranging the old ones we have already. The 47th proposition of the First Book of *Euclid* is very true, but the discovery of it, I think, not owing to any rules of common logic. A man knows first, and then he is able to prove syllogistically. So that *syllogism* comes after knowledge, and then a man has little or no need of it. But it is chiefly by the finding out those *ideas* that show the connexion of distant ones that our stock of knowledge is increased, and that useful arts and sciences are advanced. *Syllogism*, at best, is but the art of fencing with the little knowledge we have, without making any addition to it. And if a man should employ his reason all this way, he will not do much otherwise than he who, having got some iron out of the bowels of the earth, should have it beaten up all into swords and put it into his servants' hands to fence with and bang one another. Had the king of *Spain* employed the hands of his people and his *Spanish* iron so, he had brought to light but little of that treasure that lay so long hid in the dark entrails of *America*. And I am apt to think that he who shall employ all the force of his reason only in brandishing of *syllogisms* will discover very little of that mass of knowledge which lies yet concealed in the secret recesses of nature, and which, I am apt to think, native rustic reason (as it formerly has done) is likelier to open a way to and add to the common stock

of mankind, rather than any scholastic proceeding by the strict rules of mode and figure.

7.   I doubt not nevertheless but there are ways to be found to assist our reason in this most useful part; and this the judicious *Hooker* encourages me to say who, in his *Eccl. Pol. lib.* I, §6, speaks thus: *If there might be added the right helps of true art and learning (which helps, I must plainly confess, this age of the world, carrying the name of a learned age, doth neither much know nor generally regard), there would undoubtedly be almost as much difference in maturity of judgment between men therewith inured, and that which now men are, as between men that are now, and innocents.*   I do not pretend to have found or discovered here any of those *right helps of art* this great man of deep thought mentions; but this is plain, that *syllogism* and the logic now in use, which were as well known in his days, can be none of those he means.   It is sufficient for me if by a discourse, perhaps something out of the way (I am sure as to me wholly new and unborrowed), I shall have given occasion to others to cast about for new discoveries and to seek in their own thoughts for those *right helps of art* which will scarce be found, I fear, by those who servilely confine themselves to the rules and dictates of others. For beaten tracks lead this sort of cattle (as an observing *Roman* calls them) whose thoughts reach only to imitation, *non quo eundem est, sed quo itur.*   But I can be bold to say that this age is adorned with some men of that strength of judgment and largeness of comprehension that, if they would employ their thoughts on this subject, could open new and undiscovered ways to the advancement of knowledge.

8.   Having here had an occasion to speak of *syllogism* in general and the use of it in reasoning, and the improvement of our knowledge, it is fit, before I leave this subject, to take notice of one manifest mistake in the rules of *syllogism*: viz. that no syllogistical reasoning can be right and conclusive, but what has at least one general proposition in it.   As if we could not *reason* and have knowledge *about particulars*.   Whereas, in truth, the matter rightly considered, the immediate object of all our reasoning and knowledge is nothing but particulars.   Every man's reasoning and knowledge is only about the *ideas* existing in his own mind, which are truly, every one of them, particular existences; and our knowledge and reasoning about other things is only as they correspond with those our particular *ideas*.   So

that the perception of the agreement or disagreement of our
particular *ideas* is the whole and utmost of all our knowledge.
Universality is but accidental to it and consists only in this, that
the particular *ideas* about which it is are such as more than one
particular thing can correspond with and be represented by. But
the perception of the agreement or disagreement of any two *ideas*,
and consequently our knowledge, is equally clear and certain
whether either or both or neither of those *ideas* be capable of
representing more real beings than one or no. One thing more I
crave leave to offer about syllogism, before I leave it, viz. may
one not upon just ground inquire whether the form syllogism
now has is that which in reason it ought to have? For the *medius
terminus* being to join the extremes, i.e. the intermediate *ideas*
by its intervention, to show the agreement or disagreement of
the two in question, would not the position of the *medius
terminus* be more natural and show the agreement or disagreement of the extremes clearer and better if it were placed in the
middle between them? Which might be easily done by trans-
posing the propositions and making the *medius terminus* the
predicate of the first, and the subject of the second. As thus:

> *Omnis homo est animal,*
> *Omne animal est vivens,*
> *Ergo omnis homo est vivens.*

> *Omne corpus est extensum & solidum,*
> *Nullum extensum & solidum est pura extensio,*
> *Ergo corpus non est pura extensio.*

I need not trouble my reader with instances in *syllogisms*, whose
conclusions are particular. The same reason holds for the same
form in them as well as in the general.

9. *Reason*, though it penetrates into the depths of the sea and
earth, elevates our thoughts as high as the stars, and leads us
through the vast spaces and large rooms of this mighty fabric,
yet it comes far short of the real extent of even corporeal being;
and there are many instances wherein it *fails us*: as,

First, It perfectly fails us *where our* ideas *fail*. It neither does
nor can extend itself further than they do. And therefore,
wherever we have no *ideas*, our reasoning stops, and we are at
an end of our reckoning; and if at any time we reason about

words which do not stand for any *ideas*, it is only about those sounds and nothing else.

10.   *Secondly*, Our reason is often puzzled and at a loss *because of the obscurity, confusion, or imperfection of the* ideas *it is employed about*; and there we are involved in difficulties and contradictions.   Thus, not having any perfect *idea* of the least extension of matter nor of infinity, we are at a loss about the divisibility of matter; but having perfect, clear, and distinct *ideas* of number, our reason meets with none of those inextricable difficulties in numbers, nor finds itself involved in any contradictions about them.   Thus we, having but imperfect *ideas* of the operations of our minds and of the beginning of motion or thought how the mind produces either of them in us, and much imperfecter yet of the operation of GOD, run into great difficulties about free created agents, which reason cannot well extricate itself out of.

11.   *Thirdly*, Our reason is often at a stand, *because it perceives not those* ideas *which could serve to show the certain or probable agreement or disagreement of any two other* ideas; and in this some men's faculties far outgo others.   Till *algebra*, that great instrument and instance of human sagacity, was discovered, men with amazement looked on several of the demonstrations of ancient mathematicians and could scarce forbear to think the finding several of those proofs to be something more than human.

12.   *Fourthly*, The mind, *by proceeding upon false principles*, is often engaged in absurdities and difficulties, brought into straits and contradictions, without knowing how to free itself; and in that case it is in vain to implore the help of reason, unless it be to discover the falsehood and reject the influence of those wrong principles.   Reason is so far from clearing the difficulties which the building upon false foundations brings a man into that, if he will pursue it, it entangles him the more and engages him deeper in perplexities.

13.   *Fifthly*, As obscure and imperfect *ideas* often involve our reason, so upon the same ground do *dubious words* and uncertain signs *often*, in discourses and arguings, when not warily attended to, *puzzle men's reason* and bring them to a *nonplus*.   But these two latter are our fault and not the fault of reason.   But yet the consequences of them are nevertheless obvious, and the perplexities or errors they fill men's minds with are everywhere observable.

14.   Some of the *ideas* that are in the mind are so there that
they can be by themselves immediately compared one with
another; and in these the mind is able to perceive that they agree
or disagree as clearly as that it has them.   Thus the mind perceives that an arc of a circle is less than the whole circle, as
clearly as it does the *idea* of a circle; and this, therefore, as has
been said, I call *intuitive knowledge*: which is certain beyond all
doubt, and needs no probation, nor can have any, this being the
highest of all human certainty.   In this consists the evidence of
all those *maxims* which nobody has any doubt about, but every
man (does not, as is said, only assent to, but) knows to be true,
as soon as ever they are proposed to his understanding.   In the
discovery of and assent to these truths there is no use of the
discursive faculty, *no need of reasoning*, but they are known by a
superior and higher degree of evidence.   And such, if I may
guess at things unknown, I am apt to think that angels have now,
and the spirits of just men made perfect shall have, in a future
state, of thousands of things which now either wholly escape our
apprehensions or which, our short-sighted reason having got
some faint glimpse of, we, in the dark, grope after.
15.   But though we have, here and there, a little of this clear
light, some sparks of bright knowledge, yet the greatest part of
our *ideas* are such that we cannot discern their agreement or
disagreement by an immediate comparing them.   And in all
these, we have *need of reasoning* and must by discourse and
inference make our discoveries.   Now of these there are two
sorts, which I shall take the liberty to mention here again.
First, Those whose agreement or disagreement, though it
cannot be seen by an immediate putting them together, yet may
be examined by the intervention of other *ideas* which can be
compared with them.   In this case, when the agreement or disagreement of the intermediate *idea* on both sides with those
which we would compare is plainly discerned, there it amounts
to demonstration, whereby knowledge is produced; which,
though it be certain, yet it is not so easy nor altogether so clear
as *intuitive knowledge*.   Because in that there is barely one
simple intuition wherein there is no room for any the least
mistake or doubt: the truth is seen all perfectly at once.   In
demonstration, it is true, there is intuition too, but not altogether at once: for there must be a remembrance of the intuition
of the agreement of the *medium*, or intermediate *idea*, with that

we compared it with before, when we compare it with the other; and where there be many *mediums*, there the danger of the mistake is the greater. For each agreement or disagreement of the *ideas* must be observed and seen in each step of the whole train, and retained in the memory just as it is, and the mind must be sure that no part of what is necessary to make up the demonstration is omitted or overlooked. This makes some demonstrations long and perplexed, and too hard for those who have not strength of parts distinctly to perceive and exactly carry so many particulars orderly in their heads. And even those who are able to master such intricate speculations are fain sometimes to go over them again, and there is need of more than one review before they can arrive at certainty. But yet where the mind clearly retains the intuition it had of the agreement of any *idea* with another, and that with a third, and that with a fourth, etc., there the agreement of the first and the fourth is a demonstration, and produces certain knowledge, which may be called *rational knowledge*, as the other is *intuitive*.

16. *Secondly*, There are other *ideas* whose agreement or disagreement can no otherwise be judged of but by the intervention of others, which have not a certain agreement with the extremes but an usual or likely one; and in these it is that the *judgment* is properly exercised, which is the acquiescing of the mind that any *ideas* do agree, by comparing them with such probable *mediums*. This, though it never amounts to knowledge, no, not to that which is the lowest degree of it: yet sometimes the intermediate *ideas* tie the extremes so firmly together, and the probability is so clear and strong, that assent as necessarily follows it as knowledge does demonstration. The great excellency and use of the judgment is to observe right and take a true estimate of the force and weight of each probability and, then casting them up all right together, choose that side which has the overbalance.

17. *Intuitive knowledge* is the perception of the certain agreement or disagreement of two *ideas* immediately compared together.

Rational knowledge is the perception of the certain agreement or disagreement of any two *ideas* by the intervention of one or more other *ideas*.

Judgment is the thinking or taking two *ideas* to agree or disagree by the intervention of one or more *ideas*, whose certain agreement or disagreement with them it does not perceive, but hath observed to be frequent and usual.

18. Though the deducing one proposition from another, or making *inferences in words*, be a great part of reason and that which it is usually employed about, yet the principal act of ratiocination is the finding the agreement or disagreement of two *ideas* one with another by the intervention of a third. As a man, by a yard, finds two houses to be of the same length, which could not be brought together to measure their equality by *juxtaposition*. Words have their consequences as the signs of such *ideas*, and things agree or disagree as really they are; but we observe it only by our *ideas*.

19. Before we quit this subject, it may be worth our while a little to reflect on *four sorts of arguments* that men, in their reasonings with others, do ordinarily make use of to prevail on their assent, or at least so to awe them as to silence their opposition.

First, The first is to allege the opinions of men whose parts, learning, eminency, power, or some other cause has gained a name and settled their reputation in the common esteem with some kind of authority. When men are established in any kind of dignity, it is thought a breach of modesty for others to derogate any way from it, and question the authority of men who are in possession of it. This is apt to be censured as carrying with it too much of pride, when a man does not readily yield to the determination of approved authors which is wont to be received with respect and submission by others; and it is looked upon as insolence for a man to set up and adhere to his own opinion against the current stream of antiquity, or to put it in the balance against that of some learned doctor or otherwise approved writer. Whoever backs his tenets with such authorities thinks he ought thereby to carry the cause, and is ready to style it impudence in anyone who shall stand up against them. This I think may be called *argumentum ad verecundiam*.

20. *Secondly*, Another way that men ordinarily use to drive others and force them to submit their judgments and receive the opinion in debate is to require the adversary to admit what they allege as a proof, or to assign a better. And this I call *argumentum ad ignorantiam*.

21. *Thirdly*, A third way is to press a man with consequences drawn from his own principles or concessions. This is already known under the name of *argumentum ad hominem*.

22. *Fourthly*, The fourth is the using of proofs drawn from any of the foundations of knowledge or probability. This I call *argumentum ad judicium*. This alone of all the four brings true instruction with it and advances us in our way to knowledge. For: (1) It argues not another man's opinion to be right because I, out of respect or any other consideration but that of conviction, will not contradict him. (2) It proves not another man to be in the right way, nor that I ought to take the same with him, because I know not a better. (3) Nor does it follow that another man is in the right way because he has shown me that I am in the wrong. I may be modest and therefore not oppose another man's persuasion; I may be ignorant and not be able to produce a better; I may be in an error and another may show me that I am so. This may dispose me, perhaps, for the reception of truth but helps me not to it; that must come from proofs and arguments and light arising from the nature of things themselves, and not from my shamefacedness, ignorance, or error.

23. By what has been before said of *reason*, we may be able to make some guess at the distinction of things into those that are according to, above, and contrary to reason. (1) *According to reason* are such propositions whose truth we can discover by examining and tracing those *ideas* we have from *sensation* and *reflection*, and by natural deduction find to be true or probable. (2) *Above reason* are such propositions whose truth or probability we cannot by reason derive from those principles. (3) *Contrary to reason* are such propositions as are inconsistent with or irreconcilable to our clear and distinct *ideas*. Thus the existence of one GOD is according to reason; the existence of more than one GOD, contrary to reason; the resurrection of the dead, above reason. Further, as *above reason* may be taken in a double sense, viz. either as signifying above probability, or above certainty: so in that large sense also, *contrary to reason* is, I suppose, sometimes taken.

24. There is another use of the word *reason*, wherein it is *opposed to faith*, which, though it be in itself a very improper way of speaking, yet common use has so authorized it that it would be folly either to oppose or hope to remedy it; only I think it may not be amiss to take notice that, however *faith* be opposed to reason, *faith* is nothing but a firm assent of the mind; which, if it be regulated, as is our duty, cannot be afforded to

anything but upon good reason, and so cannot be opposite to
it. He that believes without having any reason for believing may
be in love with his own fancies; but neither seeks truth as he
ought, nor pays the obedience due to his Maker, who would
have him use those discerning faculties he has given him, to
keep him out of mistake and error. He that does not this to the
best of his power, however he sometimes lights on truth, is in the
right but by chance; and I know not whether the luckiness of
the accident will excuse the irregularity of his proceeding. This
at least is certain, that he must be accountable for whatever
mistakes he runs into; whereas he that makes use of the light and
faculties GOD has given him, and seeks sincerely to discover
truth by those helps and abilities he has, may have this satisfaction in doing his duty as a rational creature: that, though he
should miss truth, he will not miss the reward of it. For he
governs his assent right and places it as he should who, in any
case or matter whatsoever, believes or disbelieves according as
reason directs him. He that does otherwise transgresses against
his own light, and misuses those faculties which were given him
to no other end but to search and follow the clearer evidence and
greater probability. But since reason and faith are by some
men opposed, we will so consider them in the following
chapter.

CHAPTER XVIII

OF FAITH AND REASON, AND THEIR DISTINCT PROVINCES

1. IT has been above shown: (1) That we are of necessity
ignorant and want knowledge of all sorts where we want *ideas*.
(2) That we are ignorant and want rational knowledge where we
want proofs. (3) That we want general knowledge and certainty,
as far as we want clear and determined specific *ideas*. (4) That
we want probability to direct our assent in matters where we
have neither knowledge of our own nor testimony of other men
to bottom our reason upon.

From these things thus premised, I think we may come to lay down the measures and *boundaries between faith and reason*: the want whereof may possibly have been the cause, if not of great disorders, yet at least of great disputes, and perhaps mistakes, in the world. For till it be resolved how far we are to be guided by reason, and how far by faith, we shall in vain dispute and endeavour to convince one another in matters of religion.

2. I find every sect, as far as reason will help them, makes use of it gladly; and where it fails them, they cry out, *It is matter of faith, and above reason*. And I do not see how they can argue with anyone, or ever convince a gainsayer who makes use of the same plea, without setting down strict boundaries between *faith* and *reason*, which ought to be the first point established in all questions where *faith* has anything to do.

Reason, therefore, here, as contradistinguished to *faith*, I take to be the discovery of the certainty or probability of such propositions or truths, which the mind arrives at by deduction made from such *ideas* which it has got by the use of its natural faculties, viz. by sensation or reflection.

Faith, on the other side, is the assent to any proposition, not thus made out by the deductions of reason, but upon the credit of the proposer as coming from GOD, in some extraordinary way of communication. This way of discovering truths to men we call *revelation*.

3. First, then, I say that *no man inspired by* GOD *can by any revelation communicate to others any new simple ideas* which they had not before from sensation or reflection. For, whatsoever impressions he himself may have from the immediate hand of GOD, this revelation, if it be of new simple *ideas*, cannot be conveyed to another, either by words or any other signs. Because words, by their immediate operation on us, cause no other *ideas* but of their natural sounds; and it is by the custom of using them for signs that they excite and revive in our minds latent *ideas*, but yet only such *ideas* as were there before. For words seen or heard recall to our thoughts those *ideas* only which to us they have been wont to be signs of, but cannot introduce any perfectly new and formerly unknown simple *ideas*. The same holds in all other signs, which cannot signify to us things of which we have before never had any *idea* at all.

Thus whatever things were discovered to St. *Paul*, when he was rapt up into the third heaven, whatever new *ideas* his mind there received, all the description he can make to others of that place is only this, that there are such things *as eye hath not seen, nor ear heard, nor hath it entered into the heart of man to conceive.* And supposing GOD should discover to anyone supernaturally, a species of creatures inhabiting, for example, *Jupiter* or *Saturn* (for that it is possible there may be such, nobody can deny) which had six senses, and imprint on his mind the *ideas* conveyed to theirs by that sixth sense: he could no more, by words, produce in the minds of other men those *ideas* imprinted by that sixth sense, than one of us could convey the *idea* of any colour, by the sounds of words, into a man who, having the other four senses perfect, had always totally wanted the fifth, of seeing. For our simple *ideas*, then, which are the foundation and sole matter of all our notions and knowledge, we must depend wholly on our reason, I mean, our natural faculties; and can by no means receive them, or any of them, from *traditional revelation*, I say *traditional revelation* in distinction to *original revelation.* By the one, I mean that first impression which is made immediately by GOD on the mind of any man, to which we cannot set any bounds; and by the other, those impressions delivered over to others in words and the ordinary ways of conveying our conceptions one to another.

4.   *Secondly,* I say that *the same truths may be discovered and conveyed down from revelation, which are discoverable to us by reason,* and by those *ideas* we naturally may have. So GOD might, by revelation, discover the truth of any proposition in *Euclid*; as well as men, by the natural use of their faculties, come to make the discovery themselves. In all things of this kind there is little need or use of *revelation,* GOD having furnished us with natural and surer means to arrive at the knowledge of them. For whatsoever truth we come to the clear discovery of, from the knowledge and contemplation of our own *ideas,* will always be certainer to us than those which are conveyed to us by *traditional revelation.* For the knowledge we have that this *revelation* came at first from GOD can never be so sure as the knowledge we have from the clear and distinct perception of the agreement or disagreement of our own *ideas*: v.g. if it were revealed, some ages since, that the three angles of a triangle were equal to two right ones, I might assent to the truth of that proposition upon the credit of the tradition that it was revealed; but that would never amount to so great a

certainty as the knowledge of it upon the comparing and measuring
my own *ideas* of two right angles and the three angles of a
triangle. The like holds in matter of fact knowable by our senses:
v.g. the history of the deluge is conveyed to us by writings
which had their original from revelation; and yet nobody, I
think, will say he has as certain and clear a knowledge of the
flood as *Noah*, that saw it, or that he himself would have had,
had he then been alive and seen it. For he has no greater an
assurance than that of his senses, that it is writ in the book
supposed writ by *Moses* inspired; but he has not so great an
assurance that *Moses* wrote that book as if he had seen *Moses*
write it. So that the assurance of its being a revelation is less
still than the assurance of his senses.

5. In propositions, then, whose certainty is built upon the
clear perception of the agreement or disagreement of our *ideas*,
attained either by immediate intuition, as in self-evident propositions, or by evident deductions of reason in demonstrations, we
need not the assistance of *revelation*, as necessary to gain our
assent and introduce them into our minds. Because the natural
ways of knowledge could settle them there, or had done it
already; which is the greatest assurance we can possibly have of
anything, unless where GOD immediately reveals it to us; and
there too our assurance can be no greater than our knowledge is,
that it is a *revelation* from GOD. But yet nothing, I think, can
under that title shake or overrule plain knowledge, or rationally
prevail with any man to admit it for true in a direct contradiction
to the clear evidence of his own understanding. For since no
evidence of our faculties, by which we receive such *revelations*,
can exceed, if equal, the certainty of our intuitive knowledge, we
can never receive for a truth anything that is directly contrary to
our clear and distinct knowledge: v.g. the *ideas* of one body and
one place do so clearly agree, and the mind has so evident a
perception of their agreement, that we can never assent to a
proposition that affirms the same body to be in two distant
places at once, however it should pretend to the authority of a
divine *revelation*: since the evidence, *first*, that we deceive not
ourselves in ascribing it to GOD; *secondly*, that we understand it
right, can never be so great as the evidence of our own intuitive
knowledge whereby we discern it impossible for the same body
to be in two places at once. And therefore *no proposition can be
received for divine revelation* or obtain the assent due to all such,

if it be contradictory to our clear intuitive knowledge. Because this would be to subvert the principles and foundations of all knowledge, evidence, and assent whatsoever; and there would be left no difference between truth and falsehood, no measures of credible and incredible in the world, if doubtful propositions shall take place before self-evident, and what we certainly know give way to what we may possibly be mistaken in. In propositions therefore contrary to the clear perception of the agreement or disagreement of any of our *ideas*, it will be in vain to urge them as matters of *faith*. They cannot move our assent under that or any other title whatsoever. For *faith* can never convince us of anything that contradicts our knowledge. Because, though *faith* be founded on the testimony of GOD (who cannot lie) revealing any proposition to us: yet we cannot have an assurance of the truth of its being a divine revelation greater than our own knowledge: since the whole strength of the certainty depends upon our knowledge that GOD revealed it; which, in this case, where the proposition supposed revealed contradicts our knowledge or reason, will always have this objection hanging to it, (viz.) that we cannot tell how to conceive that to come from GOD, the bountiful Author of our being, which, if received for true, must overturn all the principles and foundations of knowledge he has given us; render all our faculties useless; wholly destroy the most excellent part of his workmanship, our understandings; and put a man in a condition wherein he will have less light, less conduct than the beast that perisheth. For if the mind of man can never have a clearer (and, perhaps, not so clear) evidence of anything to be a divine *revelation*, as it has of the principles of its own reason, it can never have a ground to quit the clear evidence of its reason, to give place to a proposition whose *revelation* has not a greater evidence than those principles have.

6.   Thus far a man has use of reason and ought to hearken to it, even in immediate and original *revelation*, where it is supposed to be made to himself. But to all those who pretend not to immediate *revelation*, but are required to pay obedience and to receive the truths revealed to others which, by the tradition of writings or word of mouth, are conveyed down to them, reason has a great deal more to do, and is that only which can induce us to receive them. For matter of faith being only divine revelation and nothing else, *faith*, as we use the word (called commonly,

divine faith) has to do with no propositions but those which are supposed to be divinely revealed. So that I do not see how those who make revelation alone the sole object of *faith* can say that it is a matter of *faith*, and not of *reason*, to believe that such or such a proposition, to be found in such or such a book, is of divine inspiration, unless it be revealed that that proposition, or all in that book, was communicated by divine inspiration. Without such a *revelation*, the believing or not believing that proposition or book to be of divine authority can never be matter of *faith*, but matter of reason, and such as I must come to an assent to only by the use of my reason, which can never require or enable me to believe that which is contrary to itself: it being impossible for reason ever to procure any assent to that which to itself appears unreasonable.

In all things, therefore, where we have clear evidence from our *ideas* and those principles of knowledge I have above mentioned, *reason* is the proper judge; and *revelation*, though it may, in consenting with it, confirm its dictates, yet cannot in such cases invalidate its decrees; *nor can we be obliged, where we have the clear and evident sentence of reason, to quit it for the contrary opinion, under a pretence that it is matter of faith*, which can have no authority against the plain and clear dictates of *reason*.

7. But, *thirdly*, there being many things wherein we have very imperfect notions, or none at all; and other things, of whose past, present, or future existence, by the natural use of our faculties, we can have no knowledge at all: these, as being beyond the discovery of our natural faculties and above *reason*, are, when revealed, *the proper matter of faith*. Thus, that part of the angels rebelled against GOD and thereby lost their first happy state, and that the dead shall rise and live again: these and the like, being beyond the discovery of *reason*, are purely matters of *faith*, with which *reason* has, directly, nothing to do.

8. But since GOD, in giving us the light of *reason*, has not thereby tied up his own hands from affording us, when he thinks fit, the light of *revelation* in any of those matters wherein our natural faculties are able to give a probable determination: *revelation*, where God has been pleased to give it, *must carry it against the probable conjectures of reason*. Because the mind, not being certain of the truth of that it does not evidently know, but

only yielding to the probability that appears in it, is bound to
give up its assent to such a testimony which, it is satisfied, comes
from one who cannot err and will not deceive. But yet, it still
belongs to *reason* to judge of the truth of its being a revelation
and of the signification of the words wherein it is delivered. Indeed, if anything shall be thought *revelation* which is contrary to
the plain principles of reason and the evident knowledge the
mind has of its own clear and distinct *ideas*, there *reason* must be
hearkened to, as to a matter within its province: since a man can
never have so certain a knowledge that a proposition which contradicts the clear principles and evidence of his own knowledge
was divinely revealed, or that he understands the words rightly
wherein it is delivered, as he has that the contrary is true;
and so is bound to consider and judge of it as a matter of
reason and not swallow it, without examination, as a matter of
faith.

9.   *First*, Whatever proposition is revealed of whose truth our
mind, by its natural faculties and notions, cannot judge, that is
purely *matter of faith*, and above reason.

Secondly, All propositions whereof the mind, by the use of
its natural faculties, can come to determine and judge, from
naturally acquired *ideas*, are *matter of reason*, with this difference
still: that, in those concerning which it has but an uncertain
evidence and so is persuaded of their truth only upon probable
grounds, which still admit a possibility of the contrary to be true
without doing violence to the certain evidence of its own knowledge and overturning the principles of all reason, in such
probable propositions, I say, an evident *revelation* ought to determine our assent, even against probability. For where the principles of reason have not evidenced a proposition to be certainly
true or false, there clear *revelation*, as another principle of truth
and ground of assent, may determine; and so it may be matter of
faith and be also above *reason*. Because *reason*, in that particular
matter, being able to reach no higher than probability, *faith*
gave the determination where *reason* came short, and *revelation*
discovered on which side the truth lay.

10.   Thus far the dominion of *faith* reaches, and that without
any violence or hindrance to *reason*, which is not injured or
disturbed, but assisted and improved by new discoveries of truth
coming from the eternal fountain of all knowledge. Whatever
GOD hath revealed is certainly true: no doubt can be made of it.

This is the proper object of *faith*; but whether it be a divine revelation or no, *reason* must judge, which can never permit the mind to reject a greater evidence to embrace what is less evident, nor allow it to entertain probability in opposition to knowledge and certainty. There can be no evidence that any traditional revelation is of divine original, in the words we receive it and in the sense we understand it, so clear and so certain as that of the principles of reason; and therefore *nothing that is contrary to, and inconsistent with, the clear and self-evident dictates of reason has a right to be urged or assented to as a matter of faith, wherein reason hath nothing to do.* Whatsoever is divine *revelation*, ought to overrule all our opinions, prejudices, and interests, and hath a right to be received with full assent; such a submission as this, of our *reason* to *faith*, takes not away the landmarks of knowledge: this shakes not the foundations of reason, but leaves us that use of our faculties for which they were given us.

11. *If the provinces of faith and reason are not kept distinct by these boundaries,* there will, in matter of religion, be no room for *reason* at all, and those extravagant opinions and ceremonies that are to be found in the several religions of the world will not deserve to be blamed. For, to this crying up of *faith* in opposition to *reason*, we may, I think, in good measure ascribe those absurdities that fill almost all the religions which possess and divide mankind. For men, having been principled with an opinion that they must not consult *reason* in the things of religion, however apparently contradictory to common sense and the very principles of all their knowledge, have let loose their fancies and natural superstition, and have been by them led into so strange opinions and extravagant practices in religion that a considerate man cannot but stand amazed at their follies and judge them so far from being acceptable to the great and wise GOD, that he cannot avoid thinking them ridiculous and offensive to a sober, good man. So that in effect religion, which should most distinguish us from beasts and ought most peculiarly to elevate us as rational creatures above brutes, is that wherein men often appear most irrational and more senseless than beasts themselves. *Credo, quia impossibile est: I believe, because it is impossible,* might, in a good man, pass for a sally of zeal, but would prove a very ill rule for men to choose their opinions or religion by.

Chapter XIX

OF ENTHUSIASM

1.   He that would seriously set upon the search of truth ought
in the first place to prepare his mind with a love of it. For he
that loves it not will not take much pains to get it, nor be much
concerned when he misses it. There is nobody in the commonwealth of learning who does not profess himself a lover of truth;
and there is not a rational creature that would not take it amiss
to be thought otherwise of. And yet, for all this, one may truly
say there are very few lovers of truth for truth's sake, even
amongst those who persuade themselves that they are so. How
a man may know whether he be so in earnest, is worth inquiry;
and I think there is this one unerring mark of it, viz. the not
entertaining any proposition with greater assurance than the
proofs it is built upon will warrant. Whoever goes beyond this
measure of assent, it is plain, receives not truth in the love of it,
loves not truth for truth's sake but for some other by-end. For
the evidence that any proposition is true (except such as are self-
evident) lying only in the proofs a man has of it, whatsoever
degrees of assent he affords it beyond the degrees of that
evidence, it is plain all that surplusage of assurance is owing to
some other affection and not to the love of truth: it being as
impossible that the love of truth should carry my assent above
the evidence that there is to me that it is true, as that the love of
truth should make me assent to any proposition for the sake of
that evidence which it has not, that it is true; which is in effect
to love it as a truth because it is possible or probable that it may
not be true. In any truth that gets not possession of our minds
by the irresistible light of self-evidence or by the force of
demonstration, the arguments that gain it assent are the vouchers
and gauge of its probability to us; and we can receive it for no
other than such as they deliver it to our understandings. Whatsoever credit or authority we give to any proposition more than
it receives from the principles and proofs it supports itself upon
is owing to our inclinations that way, and is so far a derogation
from the love of truth as such; which, as it can receive no

evidence from our passions or interests, so it should receive no tincture from them.

2. The assuming an authority of dictating to others and a forwardness to prescribe to their opinions is a constant concomitant of this bias and corruption of our judgments. For how almost can it be otherwise but that he should be ready to impose on another's belief, who has already imposed on his own? Who can reasonably expect arguments and conviction from him in dealing with others whose understanding is not accustomed to them in his dealing with himself? Who does violence to his own faculties, tyrannizes over his own mind, and usurps the prerogative that belongs to truth alone, which is to command assent by only its own authority, i.e. by and in proportion to that evidence which it carries with it.

3. Upon this occasion I shall take the liberty to consider a third ground of assent, which with some men has the same authority and is as confidently relied on as either *faith* or *reason*, I mean *enthusiasm*. Which, laying by reason, would set up revelation without it. Whereby in effect it takes away both reason and revelation, and substitutes in the room of them the ungrounded fancies of a man's own brain, and assumes them for a foundation both of opinion and conduct.

4. *Reason* is natural *revelation*, whereby the eternal Father of light and fountain of all knowledge communicates to mankind that portion of truth which he has laid within the reach of their natural faculties; *revelation* is natural *reason* enlarged by a new set of discoveries communicated by GOD immediately, which *reason* vouches the truth of, by the testimony and proofs it gives that they come from GOD. So that he that takes away *reason*, to make way for *revelation*, puts out the light of both, and does much what the same as if he would persuade a man to put out his eyes, the better to receive the remote light of an invisible star by a telescope.

5. Immediate *revelation* being a much easier way for men to establish their opinions and regulate their conduct than the tedious and not always successful labour of strict reasoning, it is no wonder that some have been very apt to pretend to revelation, and to persuade themselves that they are under the peculiar guidance of heaven in their actions and opinions, especially in those of them which they cannot account for by the ordinary methods of knowledge and principles of reason. Hence we see

that, in all ages, men in whom melancholy has mixed with devotion, or whose conceit of themselves has raised them into an opinion of a greater familiarity with GOD and a nearer admittance to his favour than is afforded to others, have often flattered themselves with a persuasion of an immediate intercourse with the Deity and frequent communications from the Divine Spirit. GOD I own cannot be denied to be able to enlighten the understanding by a ray darted into the mind immediately from the fountain of light; this they understand he has promised to do; and who then has so good a title to expect it as those who are his peculiar people, chosen by him and depending on him?

6.   Their minds being thus prepared, whatever groundless opinion comes to settle itself strongly upon their fancies is an illumination from the Spirit of GOD, and presently of divine authority; and whatsoever odd action they find in themselves a strong inclination to do, that impulse is concluded to be a call or direction from heaven and must be obeyed: it is a commission from above, and they cannot err in executing it.

7.   This I take to be properly enthusiasm, which, though founded neither on reason nor divine revelation, but rising from the conceits of a warmed or overweening brain, works yet, where it once gets footing, more powerfully on the persuasions and actions of men than either of those two, or both together: men being most forwardly obedient to the impulses they receive from themselves, and the whole man is sure to act more vigorously where the whole man is carried by a natural motion. For strong conceit, like a new principle, carries all easily with it when, got above common sense and freed from all restraint of reason and check of reflection, it is heightened into a divine authority, in concurrence with our own temper and inclination.

8.   Though the odd opinions and extravagant actions *enthusiasm* has run men into were enough to warn them against this wrong principle, so apt to misguide them both in their belief and conduct: yet the love of something extraordinary, the ease and glory it is to be inspired and be above the common and natural ways of knowledge, so flatters many men's laziness, ignorance, and vanity that, when once they are got into this way of immediate revelation, of illumination without search, and of certainty without proof and without examination, it is a hard matter to get them out of it. Reason is lost upon them, they are above it; they see the light infused into their understandings, and cannot be

mistaken: it is clear and visible there, like the light of bright sunshine, shows itself, and needs no other proof but its own evidence; they feel the hand of GOD moving them within and the impulses of the Spirit, and cannot be mistaken in what they feel. Thus they support themselves and are sure reason hath nothing to do with what they see and feel in themselves: what they have a sensible experience of admits no doubt, needs no probation. Would he not be ridiculous who should require to have it proved to him that the light shines and that he sees it? It is its own proof and can have no other. When the spirit brings light into our minds, it dispels darkness. We see it as we do that of the sun at noon, and need not the twilight of reason to show it us. This light from heaven is strong, clear, and pure, carries its own demonstration with it, and we may as rationally take a glow-worm to assist us to discover the sun as to examine the celestial ray by our dim candle, reason.

9. This is the way of talking of these men: they are sure because they are sure, and their persuasions are right only because they are strong in them. For, when what they say is stripped of the metaphor of seeing and feeling, this is all it amounts to; and yet these similes so impose on them that they serve them for certainty in themselves and demonstration to others.

10. But to examine a little soberly this internal light, and this feeling on which they build so much. These men have, they say, clear light, and they see; they have an awakened sense, and they feel: this cannot, they are sure, be disputed them. For when a man says he sees or he feels, nobody can deny it him that he does so. But here let me ask: This seeing, is it the perception of the truth of the proposition, or of this, that it is a revelation from GOD? This feeling, is it a perception of an inclination or fancy to do something, or of the Spirit of GOD moving that inclination? These are two very different perceptions, and must be carefully distinguished, if we would not impose upon ourselves. I may perceive the truth of a proposition, and yet not perceive that it is an immediate revelation from GOD. I may perceive the truth of a proposition in *Euclid*, without its being, or my perceiving it to be, a revelation: nay, I may perceive I came not by this knowledge in a natural way, and so may conclude it revealed, without perceiving that it is a revelation from GOD. Because there be spirits which, without being divinely commissioned, may excite those *ideas* in me and lay them in such

order before my mind, that I may perceive their connexion. So that the knowledge of any proposition coming into my mind, I know not how, is not a perception that it is from GOD. Much less is a strong persuasion that it is true, a perception that it is from GOD, or so much as true. But however it be called light and seeing, I suppose it is at most but belief and assurance: and the proposition taken for a revelation is not such as they know to be true, but take to be true. For where a proposition is known to be true, revelation is needless; and it is hard to conceive how there can be a revelation to anyone of what he knows already. If therefore it be a proposition which they are persuaded, but do not know, to be true, whatever they may call it, it is not seeing, but believing. For these are two ways whereby truth comes into the mind, wholly distinct, so that one is not the other. What I see, I know to be so, by the evidence of the thing itself; what I believe, I take to be so upon the testimony of another; but this testimony I must know to be given, or else what ground have I of believing? I must see that it is GOD that reveals this to me, or else I see nothing. The question then here is: How do I know that GOD is the revealer of this to me, that this impression is made upon my mind by his Holy Spirit, and that therefore I ought to obey it? If I know not this, how great soever the assurance is that I am possessed with, it is groundless: whatever light I pretend to, it is but *enthusiasm*. For, whether the proposition supposed to be revealed be in itself evidently true or visibly probable or, by the natural ways of knowledge, uncertain, the proposition that must be well grounded and manifested to be true is this, that GOD is the revealer of it, and that what I take to be a revelation is certainly put into my mind by him, and is not an illusion dropped in by some other spirit or raised by my own fancy. For, if I mistake not, these men receive it for true because they presume GOD revealed it. Does it not, then, stand them upon to examine upon what grounds they presume it to be a revelation from GOD? or else all their confidence is mere presumption, and this light they are so dazzled with is nothing but an *ignis fatuus* that leads them continually round in this circle: *it is a revelation, because they firmly believe it*; and *they believe it, because it is a revelation*.

11.   In all that is of divine *revelation*, there is need of no other proof but that it is an inspiration from GOD: for he can neither deceive nor be deceived. But how shall it be known that any

proposition in our minds is a truth infused by GOD; a truth that is revealed to us by him, which he declares to us, and therefore we ought to believe? Here it is that *enthusiasm* fails of the evidence it pretends to. For men thus possessed boast of a light whereby they say they are enlightened and brought into the knowledge of this or that truth. But if they know it to be a truth, they must know it to be so either by its own self-evidence to natural reason, or by the rational proofs that make it out to be so. If they see and know it to be a truth either of these two ways, they in vain suppose it to be a revelation. For they know it to be true by the same way that any other man naturally may know that it is so, without the help of revelation. For thus all the truths, of what kind soever, that men uninspired are enlightened with came into their minds and are established there. If they say they know it to be true because it is a *revelation* from GOD, the reason is good; but then it will be demanded how they know it to be a revelation from GOD. If they say by the light it brings with it, which shines bright in their minds and they cannot resist, I beseech them to consider whether this be any more than what we have taken notice of already, viz. that it is a revelation because they strongly believe it to be true. For all the light they speak of is but a strong, though ungrounded, persuasion of their own minds that it is a truth. For rational grounds from proofs that it is a truth, they must acknowledge to have none: for then it is not received as a *revelation*, but upon the ordinary grounds that other truths are received; and if they believe it to be true because it is a *revelation*, and have no other reason for its being a *revelation* but because they are fully persuaded, without any other reason, that it is true, they believe it to be a revelation only because they strongly believe it to be a revelation; which is a very unsafe ground to proceed on, either in our tenets or actions; and what readier way can there be to run ourselves into the most extravagant errors and miscarriages than thus to set up fancy for our supreme and sole guide, and to believe any proposition to be true, any action to be right, only because we believe it to be so? The strength of our persuasions are no evidence at all of their own rectitude: crooked things may be as stiff and inflexible as straight, and men may be as positive and peremptory in error as in truth. How come else the intractable zealots in different and opposite parties? For if the light which everyone thinks he has in his mind, which in this case is nothing but the strength of his own persuasion, be an evidence that it is from GOD, contrary opinions may have the same title to be inspirations; and GOD will be not only the father of lights but of opposite and contradictory lights, leading men contrary ways; and contradictory propositions will be divine truths, if an ungrounded strength of assurance be an evidence that any proposition is a divine revelation.

12.   This cannot be otherwise, whilst firmness of persuasion is made the cause of believing, and confidence of being in the right is made an argument of truth: St. *Paul* himself believed he did well and that he had a call to it, when he persecuted the Christians, whom he confidently thought in the wrong; but yet it was he and not they who were mistaken.   Good men are men still, liable to mistakes, and are sometimes warmly engaged in errors, which they take for divine truths, shining in their minds with the clearest light.

13.   Light, true light, in the mind is, or can be, nothing else but the evidence of the truth of any proposition; and if it be not a self-evident proposition, all the light it has or can have is from the clearness and validity of those proofs upon which it is received.   To talk of any other light in the understanding is to put ourselves in the dark, or in the power of the Prince of Darkness, and, by our own consent, to give ourselves up to delusion to believe a lie.   For if strength of persuasion be the light which must guide us, I ask how shall anyone distinguish between the delusions of Satan and the inspirations of the Holy Ghost?   He can transform himself into an angel of light.   And they who are led by this son of the morning are as fully satisfied of the illumination, i.e. are as strongly persuaded, that they are enlightened by the spirit of God as anyone who is so: they acquiesce and rejoice in it, are acted by it, and nobody can be more sure nor more in the right (if their own strong belief may be judge) than they.

14.   He, therefore, that will not give himself up to all the extravagancies of delusion and error must bring this guide of his *light within* to the trial.   God when he makes the prophet does not unmake the man.   He leaves all his faculties in their natural state, to enable him to judge of his inspirations, whether they be of divine original or no.   When he illuminates the mind with supernatural light, he does not extinguish that which is natural. If he would have us assent to the truth of any proposition, he

either evidences that truth by the usual methods of natural reason, or else makes it known to be a truth which he would have us assent to by his authority, and convinces us that it is from him by some marks which reason cannot be mistaken in. *Reason* must be our last judge and guide in everything. I do not mean that we must consult reason and examine whether a proposition revealed from God can be made out by natural principles, and if it cannot, that then we may reject it; but consult it we must, and by it examine whether it be a *revelation* from God or no; and if *reason* finds it to be revealed from GOD, *reason* then declares for it as much as for any other truth, and makes it one of her dictates. Every conceit that thoroughly warms our fancies must pass for an inspiration, if there be nothing but the strength of our persuasions whereby to judge of our persuasions; if *reason* must not examine their truth by something extrinsical to the persuasions themselves, inspirations and delusions, truth and falsehood will have the same measure and will not be possible to be distinguished.

15. If this internal light, or any proposition which under that title we take for inspired, be conformable to the principles of reason or to the word of GOD, which is attested revelation, *reason* warrants it and we may safely receive it for true and be guided by it in our belief and actions; if it receive no testimony nor evidence from either of these rules, we cannot take it for a revelation or so much as for true, till we have some other mark that it is a *revelation*, besides our believing that it is so. Thus we see the holy men of old, who had *revelations* from GOD, had something else besides that internal light of assurance in their own minds to testify to them that it was from GOD. They were not left to their own persuasions alone that those persuasions were from GOD, but had outward signs to convince them of the author of those revelations. And when they were to convince others, they had a power given them to justify the truth of their commission from heaven, and by visible signs to assert the divine authority of a message they were sent with. *Moses* saw the bush burn without being consumed, and heard a voice out of it. This was something besides finding an impulse upon his mind to go to *Pharaoh*, that he might bring his brethren out of *Egypt*; and yet he thought not this enough to authorize him to go with that message, till GOD by another miracle, of his rod turned into a serpent, had assured him of a power to testify his

mission by the same miracle repeated before them whom he was sent to. *Gideon* was sent by an angel to deliver *Israel* from the *Midianites*, and yet he desired a sign to convince him that this commission was from GOD. These and several the like instances to be found among the prophets of old are enough to show that they thought not an inward seeing or persuasion of their own minds, without any other proof, a sufficient evidence that it was from GOD, though the Scripture does not everywhere mention their demanding or having such proofs.

16.   In what I have said I am far from denying that GOD can or doth sometimes enlighten men's minds in the apprehending of certain truths, or excite them to good actions by the immediate influence and assistance of the Holy Spirit, without any extra-ordinary signs accompanying it. But in such cases too we have reason and the Scripture, unerring rules to know whether it be from GOD or no. Where the truth embraced is consonant to the *revelation* in the written word of GOD, or the action conformable to the dictates of right *reason* or Holy Writ, we may be assured that we run no risk in entertaining it as such, because, though perhaps it be not an immediate revelation from GOD extra-ordinarily operating on our minds, yet we are sure it is war-ranted by that revelation which he has given us of truth. But it is not the strength of our private persuasion within ourselves that can warrant it to be a light or motion from heaven: nothing can do that but the written word of GOD without us, or that standard of reason which is common to us with all men. Where reason or Scripture is express for any opinion or action, we may receive it as of divine authority; but it is not the strength of our own persuasions which can by itself give it that stamp. The bent of our own minds may favour it as much as we please: that may show it to be a fondling of our own, but will by no means prove it to be an offspring of heaven and of divine original.

CHAPTER XX

OF WRONG ASSENT, OR ERROR

1.   KNOWLEDGE being to be had only of visible certain truth, *error* is not a fault of our knowledge, but a mistake of our judg-ment giving assent to that which is not true.

But if assent be grounded on likelihood, if the proper object and motive of our assent be probability, and that probability consists in what is laid down in the foregoing chapters, it will be demanded how men come to give their assents contrary to probability. For there is nothing more common than contrariety of opinions, nothing more obvious than that one man wholly disbelieves what another only doubts of and a third steadfastly believes and firmly adheres to. The reasons whereof, though they may be very various, yet, I suppose, may all be reduced to these four:

1. *Want of proofs.*
2. *Want of ability to use them.*
3. *Want of will to use them.*
4. *Wrong measures of probability.*

2. *First,* By *want of proofs,* I do not mean only the want of those proofs which are nowhere extant and so are nowhere to be had, but the want even of those proofs which are in being, or might be procured. And thus men want proofs, who have not the convenience or opportunity to make experiments and observations themselves tending to the proof of any proposition, nor likewise the convenience to inquire into and collect the testimonies of others; and in this state are the greatest part of mankind, who are given up to labour and enslaved to the necessity of their mean condition, whose lives are worn out only in the provisions for living. These men's opportunities of knowledge and inquiry are commonly as narrow as their fortunes; and their understandings are but little instructed, when all their whole time and pains is laid out to still the croaking of their own bellies or the cries of their children. It is not to be expected that a man, who drudges on all his life in a laborious trade, should be more knowing in the variety of things done in the world than a packhorse, who is driven constantly forwards and backwards in a narrow lane and dirty road only to market, should be skilled in the geography of the country. Nor is it at all more possible that he who wants leisure, books, and languages, and the opportunity of conversing with variety of men should be in a condition to collect those testimonies and observations which are in being and are necessary to make out many, nay most, of the propositions that, in the societies of men, are judged of the greatest moment, or to find out grounds of assurance so great as the belief of the points he would build on them is thought necessary. So that a

great part of mankind are, by the natural and unalterable state
of things in this world and the constitution of human affairs,
unavoidably given over to invincible ignorance of those proofs
on which others build, and which are necessary to establish those
opinions: the greatest part of men, having much to do to get the
means of living, are not in a condition to look after those of
learned and laborious inquiries.

3. What shall we say then? Are the greatest part of mankind,
by the necessity of their condition, subjected to unavoidable
ignorance in those things which are of greatest importance to
them (for of those it is obvious to inquire)? Have the bulk of
mankind no other guide but accident and blind chance to conduct them to their happiness or misery? Are the current opinions
and licensed guides of every country sufficient evidence and
security to every man to venture his greatest concernments on,
nay, his everlasting happiness or misery? Or can those be the
certain and infallible oracles and standards of truth which teach
one thing in *Christendom* and another in *Turkey*? Or shall a
poor countryman be eternally happy for having the chance to be
born in *Italy*; or a day-labourer be unavoidably lost because he
had the ill luck to be born in *England*? How ready some men
may be to say some of these things, I will not here examine; but
this I am sure, that men must allow one or other of these to be
true (let them choose which they please) or else grant that GOD
has furnished men with faculties sufficient to direct them in the
way they should take, if they will but seriously employ them that
way, when their ordinary vocations allow them the leisure. No
man is so wholly taken up with the attendance on the means of
living, as to have no spare time at all to think of his soul and
inform himself in matters of religion. Were men as intent upon
this as they are on things of lower concernment, there are none
so enslaved to the necessities of life who might not find many
vacancies that might be husbanded to this advantage of their
knowledge.

4. Besides those whose improvements and informations are
straitened by the narrowness of their fortunes, there are others
whose largeness of fortune would plentifully enough supply
books and other requisites for clearing of doubts and discovering
of truth; but they are *cooped in* close, *by the laws* of their
countries and the strict guards of those whose interest it is to
keep them ignorant, lest, knowing more, they should believe the

less in them. These are as far, nay further, *from the liberty and opportunities of a fair inquiry* than those poor and wretched labourers we before spoke of, and, however they may seem high and great, are confined to narrowness of thought and enslaved in that which should be the freest part of man, their understandings. This is generally the case of all those who live in places where care is taken to propagate truth without knowledge; where men are forced, at a venture, to be of the religion of the country; and must therefore swallow down opinions, as silly people do empirics' pills, without knowing what they are made of or how they will work, and having nothing to do but believe that they will do the cure; but in this are much more miserable than they, in that they are not at liberty to refuse swallowing what perhaps they had rather let alone, or to choose the physician to whose conduct they would trust themselves.

5. *Secondly,* Those who *want skill to use those evidences they have* of probabilities, who cannot carry a train of consequences in their heads, nor weigh exactly the preponderancy of contrary proofs and testimonies, making every circumstance its due allowance, may be easily misled to assent to positions that are not probable. There are some men of one, some but of two syllogisms, and no more; and others that can but advance one step further. These cannot always discern that side on which the strongest proofs lie, cannot constantly follow that which in itself is the more probable opinion. Now that there is such a difference between men in respect of their understandings, I think nobody who has had any conversation with his neighbours will question, though he never was at *Westminster-Hall* or the *Exchange* on the one hand, nor at *alms-houses* or *Bedlam* on the other. Which great difference in men's intellectuals, whether it rises from any defect in the organs of the body particularly adapted to thinking, or in the dullness or intractableness of those faculties for want of use, or, as some think, in the natural differences of men's souls themselves, or some or all these together, it matters not here to examine; only this is evident, that there is a difference of degrees in men's understandings, apprehensions, and reasonings, to so great a latitude that one may, without doing injury to mankind, affirm that there is a greater distance between some men and others in this respect, than between some men and some beasts. But how this comes about is a speculation, though of great consequence, yet not necessary to our present purpose.

6. *Thirdly,* There are another sort of people that *want proofs,* not because they are out of their reach, but *because they will not use them*: who, though they have riches and leisure enough and want neither parts nor other helps, are yet never the better for them. Their hot pursuit of pleasure or constant drudgery in business engages some men's thoughts elsewhere; laziness and oscitancy in general, or a particular aversion for books, study, and meditation keep others from any serious thoughts at all; and some, out of fear that an impartial inquiry would not favour those opinions which best suit their prejudices, lives, and designs, content themselves without examination to take upon trust what they find convenient and in fashion. Thus most men, even of those that might do otherwise, pass their lives without an acquaintance with, much less a rational assent to probabilities they are concerned to know, though they lie so much within their view that to be convinced of them they need but turn their eyes that way. But we know some men will not read a letter which is supposed to bring ill news; and many men forbear to cast up their accounts or so much as think upon their estates, who have reason to fear their affairs are in no very good posture. How men, whose plentiful fortunes allow them leisure to improve their understandings, can satisfy themselves with a lazy ignorance, I cannot tell; but methinks they have a low opinion of their souls, who lay out all their incomes in provisions for the body and employ none of it to procure the means and helps of knowledge; who take great care to appear always in a neat and splendid outside, and would think themselves miserable in coarse clothes or a patched coat, and yet contentedly suffer their minds to appear abroad in a piebald livery of coarse patches and borrowed shreds, such as it has pleased chance or their country tailor (I mean the common opinion of those they have conversed with) to clothe them in. I will not here mention how unreasonable this is for men that ever think of a future state and their concernment in it, which no rational man can avoid to do sometimes; nor shall I take notice what a shame and confusion it is, to the greatest contemners of knowledge, to be found ignorant in things they are concerned to know. But this at least is worth the consideration of those who call themselves gentlemen, that, however they may think credit, respect, power, and authority the concomitants of their birth and fortune, yet they will find all these still carried

away from them by men of lower condition, who surpass them
in knowledge. They who are blind will always be led by those
that see, or else fall into the ditch; and he is certainly the most
subjected, the most enslaved, who is so in his understanding.
In the foregoing instances, some of the causes have been shown
of wrong assent, and how it comes to pass that probable doctrines
are not always received with an assent proportionable to the
reasons which are to be had for their probability; but hitherto
we have considered only such probabilities whose proofs do
exist, but do not appear to him that embraces the error.

7. *Fourthly*, There remains yet the last sort, who, even where
the real probabilities appear and are plainly laid before them,
do not admit of the conviction nor yield unto manifest reasons,
but do either ἐπέχειν, suspend their assent, or give it to the less
probable opinion. And to this danger are those exposed who
have taken up *wrong measures of probability*, which are:

1. *Propositions that are not in themselves certain and evident,
   but doubtful and false, taken up for principles.*
2. *Received hypotheses.*
3. *Predominant passions or inclinations.*
4. *Authority.*

8. *First*, The first and firmest ground of probability is the conformity anything has to our own knowledge, especially that part
of our knowledge which we have embraced and continue to look
on as *principles*. These have so great an influence upon our
opinions that it is usually by them we judge of truth and measure
probability, to that degree: that what is inconsistent with our
principles is so far from passing for probable with us that it will
not be allowed possible. The reverence borne to these *principles*
is so great, and their authority so paramount to all other, that the
testimony not only of other men but the evidence of our own
senses are often rejected, when they offer to vouch anything
contrary to these established rules. How much the doctrine of
innate *principles*, and that *principles* are not to be proved or
questioned, has contributed to this, I will not here examine.
This I readily grant, that one truth cannot contradict another;
but withal I take leave also to say that everyone ought very carefully to beware what he admits for a *principle*, to examine it
strictly and see whether he certainly knows it to be true of itself
by its own evidence, or whether he does only with assurance
believe it to be so, upon the authority of others. For he hath a

strong bias put into his understanding, which will unavoidably
misguide his assent, who hath imbibed *wrong principles* and has
blindly given himself up to the authority of any opinion in itself
not evidently true.

9.   There is nothing more ordinary than that *children* should
receive into their minds propositions (especially about matters of
religion) from their parents, nurses, or those about them: which,
being insinuated into their unwary as well as unbiased understandings, and fastened by degrees, are at last (equally whether
true or false) riveted there by long custom and education,
beyond all possibility of being pulled out again. For men, when
they are grown up, reflecting upon their opinions, and finding
those of this sort to be as ancient in their minds as their very
memories, not having observed their early insinuation, nor by
what means they got them, they are apt to reverence them as
sacred things, and not to suffer them to be profaned, touched,
or questioned: they look on them as the *Urim* and *Thummim*
set up in their minds immediately by GOD himself, to be the
great and unerring deciders of truth and falsehood, and the
judges to which they are to appeal in all manner of controversies.

10.   This opinion of his *principles* (let them be what they will)
being *once established in anyone's mind,* it is easy to be imagined
what reception any proposition shall find, how clearly soever
proved, that shall invalidate their authority or at all thwart with
these internal oracles; whereas the grossest absurdities and
improbabilities, being but agreeable to such principles, go down
glibly and are easily digested. The great obstinacy that is to be
found in men firmly believing quite contrary opinions, though
many times equally absurd, in the various religions of mankind,
are as evident a proof as they are an unavoidable consequence of
this way of reasoning from received traditional principles. So
that men will disbelieve their own eyes, renounce the evidence
of their senses, and give their own experience the lie, rather
than admit of anything disagreeing with these sacred tenets.
Take an intelligent *Romanist* that, from the first dawning of any
notions in his understanding, hath had this principle constantly
inculcated, viz. that he must believe as the church (i.e. those of
his communion) believes, or that the pope is infallible, and this
he never so much as heard questioned, till at forty or fifty years
old he met with one of other principles: how is he prepared
easily to swallow, not only against all probability, but even the

clear evidence of his senses, the doctrine of *transubstantiation*? This principle has such an influence on his mind, that he will believe that to be flesh which he sees to be bread. And what way will you take to convince a man of any improbable opinion he holds, who, with some philosophers, hath laid down this as a foundation of reasoning, that he must believe his reason (for so men improperly call arguments drawn from their principles) against his senses? Let an *enthusiast* be principled that he or his teacher is inspired and acted by an immediate communication of the divine spirit, and you in vain bring the evidence of clear reasons against his doctrine. Whoever therefore have imbibed wrong *principles* are not, in things inconsistent with these principles, to be moved by the most apparent and convincing probabilities, till they are so candid and ingenuous to themselves as to be persuaded to examine even those very *principles*, which many never suffer themselves to do.

11. *Secondly*, Next to these are men whose understandings are cast into a mould, and fashioned just to the size of a *received hypothesis*. The difference between these and the former is that they will admit of matter of fact, and agree with dissenters in that; but differ only in assigning of reasons and explaining the manner of operation. These are not at that open defiance with their senses, as the former; they can endure to hearken to their information a little more patiently, but will by no means admit of their reports in the explanation of things, nor be prevailed on by probabilities, which would convince them that things are not brought about just after the same manner that they have decreed within themselves that they are. Would it not be an insufferable thing for a learned professor, and that which his scarlet would blush at, to have his authority of forty years' standing, wrought out of hard rock, Greek and Latin, with no small expense of time and candle and confirmed by general tradition and a reverend beard, in an instant overturned by an upstart novelist? Can anyone expect that he should be made to confess that what he taught his scholars thirty years ago was all error and mistake, and that he sold them hard words and ignorance at a very dear rate? What probabilities, I say, are sufficient to prevail in such a case? And whoever, by the most cogent arguments, will be prevailed with to disrobe himself at once of all his old opinions and pretences to knowledge and learning, which with hard study he hath all his time been labouring for; and turn himself out

stark naked, in quest afresh of new notions? All the arguments
that can be used will be as little able to prevail, as the wind did
with the traveller to part with his cloak, which he held only the
faster. To this, of wrong hypothesis, may be reduced the errors
that may be occasioned by a true *hypothesis*, or right principles,
but not rightly understood. There is nothing more familiar than
this. The instances of men contending for different opinions,
which they all derive from the infallible truth of the Scripture,
are an undeniable proof of it. All that call themselves Christians
allow the text, that says μετανοεῖτε, to carry in it the obligation
to a very weighty duty. But yet however erroneous will one of
their practices be who, understanding nothing but the *French*,
take this rule with one translation to be *repentez-vous*, repent; or
with the other, *faites pénitence*, do penance.

12.   *Thirdly*, Probabilities which cross men's appetites and
prevailing passions run the same fate. Let never so much probability hang on one side of a covetous man's reasoning, and
money on the other: and it is easy to foresee which will outweigh.
Earthly minds, like mud walls, resist the strongest batteries: and
though, perhaps, sometimes the force of a clear argument may
make some impression, yet they nevertheless stand firm,
keep out the enemy, truth, that would captivate or disturb them.
Tell a man passionately in love that he is jilted, bring a score of
witnesses of the falsehood of his mistress: it is ten to one but
three kind words of hers shall invalidate all their testimonies.
Quod volumus, facile credimus; *what suits our wishes is forwardly
believed* is, I suppose, what everyone hath more than once
experimented; and though men cannot always openly gainsay or
resist the force of manifest probabilities that make against them,
yet yield they not to the argument. Not but that it is the nature
of the understanding constantly to close with the more probable
side, but yet a man hath a power to suspend and restrain its
inquiries, and not permit a full and satisfactory examination, as
far as the matter in question is capable and will bear it to be
made. Until that be done, there will be always these *two ways
left of evading the most apparent probabilities*:

13.   *First*, That the arguments being (as for the most part they
are) brought in words, *there may be a fallacy latent* in them; and
the consequences being, perhaps, many in train, they may be
some of them incoherent. There be very few discourses are so
short, clear, and consistent to which most men may not, with

satisfaction enough to themselves, raise this doubt; and from whose *conviction* they may not, without reproach of disingenuity or unreasonableness, set themselves free with the old reply, *Non persuadebis, etiamsi persuaseris; though I cannot answer, I will not yield.*

14. *Secondly,* Manifest probabilities may be evaded and the assent withheld upon this suggestion, that *I know not yet all that may be said on the contrary side.* And therefore, though I be beaten, it is not necessary I should yield, not knowing what forces there are in reserve behind. This is a refuge against *conviction* so open and so wide, that it is hard to determine when a man is quite out of the verge of it.

15. But yet there is some end of it; and a man, having carefully inquired into all the grounds of probability and unlikeliness, done his utmost to inform himself in all particulars fairly, and cast up the sum total on both sides, may, in most cases, come to acknowledge, upon the whole matter, on which side the probability rests: wherein some proofs in matter of reason, being suppositions upon universal experience, are so cogent and clear, and some testimonies in matter of fact so universal, that he cannot refuse his assent. So that I think we may conclude that in propositions where, though the proofs in view are of most moment, yet there are sufficient grounds to suspect that there is either fallacy in words, or certain proofs as considerable to be produced on the contrary side: there assent, suspense, or dissent are often voluntary actions; but *where* the proofs are such as make it highly probable and there is not sufficient ground to suspect that there is either fallacy of words (which sober and serious consideration may discover) nor equally valid proofs yet undiscovered latent on the other side (which also the nature of the thing may, in some cases, make plain to a considerate man): there, I think, *a man* who has weighed them *can scarce refuse his assent* to the side on which the greater probability appears. Whether it be probable that a promiscuous jumble of printing letters should often fall into a method and order, which should stamp on paper a coherent discourse; or that a blind fortuitous concourse of atoms, not guided by an understanding agent, should frequently constitute the bodies of any species of animals: in these and the like cases, I think, nobody that considers them can be one jot at a stand which side to take, nor at all waver in his assent. Lastly, when there can be no supposition (the thing

in its own nature indifferent, and wholly depending upon the testimony of witnesses) that there is as fair testimony against, as for the matter of fact attested, which by inquiry is to be learned, v.g. whether there was 1700 years agone such a man at *Rome* as *Julius Caesar*: in all such cases, I say, I think it is not in any rational man's power to refuse his assent, but that it necessarily follows and closes with such probabilities. In other less clear cases, I think, it is in a man's power to suspend his assent and, perhaps, content himself with the proofs he has, if they favour the opinion that suits with his inclination or interest, and so stop from further search. But that a man should afford his assent to that side on which the less probability appears to him seems to me utterly impracticable, and as impossible as it is to believe the same thing probable and improbable at the same time.

16. As knowledge is no more arbitrary than perception: so, I think, assent is no more in our power than knowledge. When the agreement of any two *ideas* appears to our minds, whether immediately or by the assistance of reason, I can no more refuse to perceive, no more avoid knowing it, than I can avoid seeing those objects which I turn my eyes to and look on in day-light; and what upon full examination I find the most probable, I cannot deny my assent to. But, though we cannot hinder our knowledge where the agreement is once perceived, nor our assent where the probability manifestly appears upon due con-sideration of all the measures of it: yet *we can hinder both know-ledge and assent by stopping our inquiry* and not employing our faculties in the search of any truth. If it were not so, ignorance, error, or infidelity could not in any case be a fault. Thus, in some cases we can prevent or suspend our assent; but can a man versed in modern or ancient history doubt whether there be such a place as *Rome* or whether there was such a man as *Julius Caesar*? Indeed, there are millions of truths that a man is not or may not think himself concerned to know, as whether our King *Richard* the Third was crook-backed or no, or whether *Roger Bacon* was a mathematician or a magician. In these and such like cases, where the assent one way or other is of no importance to the interest of anyone, no action, no concernment of his following or depending thereon: there it is not strange that the mind should give itself up to the common opinion or render itself to the first comer. These and the like opinions are of so little weight and moment that, like motes in the sun, their

tendencies are very rarely taken notice of. They are there, as it were, by chance, and the mind lets them float at liberty. But where the mind judges that the proposition has concernment in it; where the assent, or not assenting, is thought to draw consequences of moment after it, and good or evil to depend on choosing or refusing the right side, and the mind sets itself seriously to inquire and examine the probability: there, I think, it is not in our choice to take which side we please, if manifest odds appear on either. The greater probability, I think, in that case will determine the assent; and a man can no more avoid assenting, or taking it to be true, where he perceives the greater probability, than he can avoid knowing it to be true where he perceives the agreement or disagreement of any two *ideas*.

If this be so, the foundation of error will lie in wrong measures of probability; as the foundation of vice in wrong measures of good.

17. *Fourthly*, The fourth and last *wrong measure of probability* I shall take notice of, and which keeps in ignorance or error more people than all the other together, is that which I have mentioned in the foregoing chapter, I mean the *giving up our assent to the common received opinions*, either of our friends or party, neighbourhood or country. How many men have no other ground for their tenets than the supposed honesty or learning or number of those of the same profession? As if honest or bookish men could nor err, or truth were to be established by the vote of the multitude; yet this with most men serves the turn. The tenet has had the attestation of reverend antiquity, it comes to me with the passport of former ages, and therefore I am secure in the reception I give it; other men have been and are of the same opinion (for that is all is said), and therefore it is reasonable for me to embrace it. A man may more justifiably throw up cross and pile for his opinion, than take them up by such measures. All men are liable to error, and most men are in many points, by passion or interest, under temptation to it. If we could but see the secret motives that influenced the men of name and learning in the world and the leaders of parties, we should not always find that it was the embracing of truth for its own sake that made them espouse the doctrines they owned and maintained. This at least is certain, there is not an opinion so absurd which a man may not receive upon this ground. There is no error to be named which has not had its professors; and a man shall

never want crooked paths to walk in, if he thinks that he is in the right way wherever he has the footsteps of others to follow.

18.   But, notwithstanding the great noise is made in the world about errors and opinions, I must do mankind that right as to say, *There are not so many men in errors and wrong opinions as is commonly supposed.* Not that I think they embrace the truth; but indeed, because concerning those doctrines they keep such a stir about, they have no thought, no opinion at all. For if anyone should a little catechize the greatest part of the partisans of most of the sects in the world, he would not find, concerning those matters they are so zealous for, that they have any opinions of their own: much less would he have reason to think that they took them upon the examination of arguments and appearance of probability. They are resolved to stick to a party that education or interest has engaged them in; and there, like the common soldiers of an army, show their courage and warmth as their leaders direct, without ever examining or so much as knowing the cause they contend for. If a man's life shows that he has no serious regard for religion, for what reason should we think that he beats his head about the opinions of his church and troubles himself to examine the grounds of this or that doctrine? It is enough for him to obey his leaders, to have his hand and his tongue ready for the support of the common cause, and thereby approve himself to those who can give him credit, preferment, or protection in that society. Thus men become professors of and combatants for those opinions they were never convinced of nor proselytes to, no, nor ever had so much as floating in their heads; and though one cannot say there are fewer improbable or erroneous opinions in the world than there are, yet this is certain: there are fewer that actually assent to them and mistake them for truths, than is imagined.

Chapter XXI

OF THE DIVISION OF THE SCIENCES

1.   ALL that can fall within the compass of human understanding being either, *first*, the nature of things, as they are in themselves, their relations, and their manner of operation; or,

secondly, that which man himself ought to do, as a rational and voluntary agent, for the attainment of any end, especially happiness; or, *thirdly*, the ways and means whereby the knowledge of both the one and the other of these is attained and communicated: I think *science* may be divided properly into these *three sorts*:

2. *First*, The knowledge of things as they are in their own proper beings, their constitution, properties, and operations; whereby I mean not only matter and body, but spirits also, which have their proper natures, constitutions, and operations, as well as bodies. This, in a little more enlarged sense of the word, I call φυσική, or *natural philosophy*. The end of this is bare speculative truth; and whatsoever can afford the mind of man any such, falls under this branch, whether it be God himself, angels, spirits, bodies, or any of their affections, as number, and figure, etc.

3. *Secondly*, Πρακτική, the skill of right applying our own powers and actions, for the attainment of things good and useful. The most considerable under this head is *ethics*, which is the seeking out those rules and measures of human actions which lead to happiness, and the means to practise them. The end of this is not bare speculation and the knowledge of truth, but right, and a conduct suitable to it.

4. *Thirdly*, The third branch may be called σημειωτική, or *the doctrine of signs*; the most usual whereof being words, it is aptly enough termed also λογική, *logic*: the business whereof is to consider the nature of signs the mind makes use of for the understanding of things, or conveying its knowledge to others. For, since the things the mind contemplates are none of them, besides itself, present to the understanding, it is necessary that something else, as a sign or representation of the thing it considers, should be present to it: and these are *ideas*. And because the scene of *ideas* that makes one man's thoughts cannot be laid open to the immediate view of another, nor laid up anywhere but in the memory, a no very sure repository: therefore to communicate our thoughts to one another, as well as record them for our own use, signs of our *ideas* are also necessary. Those which men have found most convenient, and therefore generally make use of, are articulate sounds. The consideration, then, of *ideas* and *words* as the great instruments of knowledge makes no despicable part of their contemplation who would take a view of

human knowledge in the whole extent of it. And perhaps if they were distinctly weighed and duly considered, they would afford us another sort of logic and critique than what we have been hitherto acquainted with.

5. *This* seems to me *the first and most general, as well as natural, division* of the objects of our understanding. For a man can employ his thoughts about nothing but either the contemplation of *things* themselves, for the discovery of truth; or about the things in his own power, which are his own *actions*, for the attainment of his own ends; or the *signs* the mind makes use of, both in the one and the other, and the right ordering of them, for its clearer information. All which three, viz. *things* as they are in themselves knowable; *actions* as they depend on us, in order to happiness; and the right use of *signs* in order to knowledge, being *toto coelo* different: they seemed to me to be the three great provinces of the intellectual world, wholly separate and distinct one from another.

FINIS

INDEX

Abraham, I. 155
abstraction, I. **126-127**, 130; II. 34, 37
  61-62, 74, 217
Alexander, I. 158; II. 17
algebra, II. 154, 157, 245, 275
America and Americans, I. 140, 152
  169; II. 242, 264, 272
Anaximenes, II. 238
angels, I. 47, 121, 158, 163, 166, 253,
  II. 10, 43, 49, 162, 234, 259, 276, 294,
  309
Anglerius, *see* Martyrus, Petrus
Antisthenes, II. 238
Apochancana, *king*, I. 50
Archelaus, II. 238
Aristides, II. 114
Aristippus, II. 238
Aristotle, I. 59; II. 98, **264-265**
atheism, I. 42, 46, 47; II. 220
atom, I. 85, 91, 258, 276; II. 96, 224
atomists, II. 28
attention, I. 80, 99, **112**, 115, 118, 123,
  187, 188; II. 103, 140
Augustine, St., I. 278
Augustus, II. 14

Bacon, Roger, II. 306
Baumgarten, M., I. 31
Bedlam, I. 127; II. 299
being, I. 8, 91, 101, 166; II. 18, 22, 33,
  46, 50, 149, **194**, 218, 219, 221, 223,
  232
Beryte, bishop of, *see* La Motte-Lam-
  bert, P. de
blindmen, I. 55, 91, **114**, 119, 153; II. 28,
  30-31, 48, 78, 159, 183, 301
Bodleian Library, I. 136
Boranday, I. 46
Borgia, Caesar, I. 278
Bourges, J. de, I. 51 n.7
Boyle, R., I. xxxv
brain, I. 58, 84, 92, 105, 119, 122, 145;
  II. 104, 166, 167, 168
Brazil, I. 46, 279
brutes, I. **124-127**, 277, 283, 294; II. 50
  175, 287

Caesar, J., I. 153, 309; II. 257, 306
Caius, I. 266, 268, 305
Caribbees, I. 30, 46
Cartesians, I. 283; II. 28-29
cassowaries, I. 269; II. 48, 62,115,

Castor, I. 82-83
certainty, I. 6, 7, 8, 9, 11, 26, 34, 58, 123,
  233; II. 136, 138, 139, 140, 143, 144,
  149, 161, 164, 166, 167, 169, 171, 176,
  186, 189, 190, 192, 208, 213, 217, 235,
  276, 283
changelings, II. 23, 53, 65, 113, **172-175**
Chinese, I. 46, 47, 158
Choisy, F. T. de, abbé, I. 51
chorea Sancti Viti, I. 198
Churchill, A. & J., I. 47
Cicero, I. 299
conception, I. 90, 91, 247, 259, 264; II.
  12, 14, 26, 36, 97, 105, 116, 150, 222,
  224, 226
conscience, I. 29, 30, 289; II, 178
consciousness, I. 54, 55, 83, 87, **281-293**
contemplation, I. 112, **117**, 147, 175, 183,
  198, 210, 211, 216, 224; II. 154, 160,
  166, 180, 192, 226, 240, 243, 309, 310

definition, II. **19**, 20, **26-27**, 28-31, 43,
  71, 114, 115, 116, 118
demonstration, I. 13, 25, 26, 58, 60, 87,
  115, 168; II. **136-142**, 144, 146, 152,
  154, 155, 157, 161, 166, 169-171, 200,
  206, 214, 217, 218, 220, 223, 230, 233,
  239, **240**, 243, 245, 249, 250, 256, 257,
  263, 265, 276, 277, 288, 291
Descartes, II. 29, 204-205
dreaming, I. 82, 83, 84, 147, 187, 188,
  283; II. 144, 167, 231
duty, I. 33, 34, 46, 50; II. 154

ecstasy, I. 187
education, I. 24, 40; II. 94
Egypt and the Egyptians, I. 158; II. **157**,
  295
Elizabeth, *queen*, I. 272
Enoch, I. 158
Epicureans, II. 96
essence, I. 5, 81, 144, 189, 246, 263,
  320-325, 327, 333, 334; II. **20-25**, 26,
  32-41, **42-71**, 74, 75, 85, 87, 98-100,
  105, 113, 153, 166, 170, 171, 172,
  175-177, 181, 183, 185, 187, 189, 191,
  192, 214, 216, 239, 240, 241
Euclid, II. 155, 167, 218, 272, 282, 291
Euphorbus, I. 45
Eurialus, I. 136

existence, I. **98**, 101, 120, 130, 136, 178-179, 237, 246, 254, 262; II. 48, 133, **216-217**

experience, I. 18, 44, 49, 60, **77-81**, 84, 87, 88, 97, 115, 128, 150, 185, 188, 189, 208, 210, 221, 238, 241, 245, 259, 260, 284; II. 19, 28, 31, 46, 55, 83, **151-153**, 163, 164, 166, 172, 178, 190, 206, 217, 226, 227, 240, 241, 243, 250, 251, 256, 257, 261, 271

faculties of the mind, I. 5, 10, 16, 42, 52, 57, 91, **98**, 117, **128**, 132, 196, 200, 201, 202, 213, 251; II. 43, 82, 137, 138, 140, 148, 158, 162, 176, 218, 228, 232, 235, 242, 246, 247, 262, 280, 281, 282, 284, 294

Fernandez-Navarrete, D., I. 47

Florence, I. 96

Garcilasso de la Vega, I. 30

Gideon, II. 296

Greeks, I. 33, 240, 243

Grüber, G., I. 30 n.1

gry, II. 222

happiness, I. 27, 28, 29, 82, 83, 99, 190, **210-215**, 217, 220, 221, 222, 224, 225-232, 234, 262, 263, 283, 291, 304; II. 218, 232, 238

hawking and hunting, I. xxxi, 222

Heliogabalus, I. 278

Herbert of Cherbury, I. 36-37

Hercules, I. 83

Historia Cultus Sinensium, I. 47

Hobbist, I. 28

Hooker, II. 273

Horace, I. 161

Hottentots, I. 50

Huygenius, I. xxxv

identity, I. xxxvi, 44-45, 82, 83, **274-293**; II. 133, 134, 135, 149, 193

idiots, I. 10, 11, 23, 24, 127, 128

illation, II. 262, 267

images, I. 84, 104, 119

imagination, I. xxxiii; II. 225, 231, 232

immortality, II. 173-174

impression, I. 10, 11, 19, 20, 22, 23, 25, 27, 44, 50, 56, 84, 85, 88, 89, 90, 112, 116, 117, 118, 120, 123, 128, 143, 149, 187, 188, 193, 213, 236, 303, 306; II. 29, 33, 96, 281

Indians, I. 24, 140, 245

individuationis principium, I. 276

intention, I. **187-188**, 189; II. 79, 111, 148

Ishmael, I. 278

Japan, I. 38, 155; II. 252

Jesuits, I. 47

Jews, I. 52; II. 37

judgment, I. 115, 123; II. **247-249**, 253, 257, 273, **277**, 289

Julian calendar, I. 155, 163

La Loubère, S. de, *marquis*, I. 46 n. 5; 47

La Martinière, P. M. de, I. 46 n. 3

Lambert, I. 30 n.2

La Motte-Lambert, P. de, *bishop of Beryte*, I. 51

language, I. xxxv, xxxviii, 126, 127; II. **9-120**, 237

law, I. **32-34**, 35, 36, **46**, **296-297**, 300; II. 35, 37, 80, 81, 88, 95, 110, 112, 113, 155, 164, 238, 258, 298

law of nature, I. 28, 35

Léry, J. de, I. 30 n.6, 46 n.2, 169 n.1

liberty, I. xxxvi, **196-205**, **217-220**, 223, 230, **233-235**, 254; II. 155

Liceto, F., II. 57

logic, II. 19, 92, 95, 174, 270, 272, **309**

Lowde, J., I. 298 n.1

Lucian, II. 93

Mahometans, I. 52; II. 252

Martyrus, Petrus, i.e. Anglerius, I. 30 n.4

maxims, I. 10, 11, 12, 14-17, 19, 20, 23-27, 57; II. 75, 134, **192-208**, 209, 224, **236-239**, 243, 244, 276

mechanism, I. 36, 116; II. 160-161, 163

Meliboeus, I. 292

memory, I. 16, 41, **54-56**, 79, 83, 84, 85, 116, **117-122**, 125, 157, 168, 243, 287, 290, 291, 292, 306, 339; II. 12, 15, 29, 36, 44, 76, 105, **135-137**, 144, 156, 229, 230, 233, 237, 243, 245, 252-253, 277, 302

Ménage, G., II. 56

metaphysics, II. 90, 181, 214

Methusalem, I. 158

Midas, I. 200

Midianites, II. 296

Mingrelians, I. 30, 33

miracles, II. 261, 295-296

Molyneux, W., I. 114

monsters, I. 42; II. 23, **51**, **54**, **56-57**, 100, 115, **174-175**

morality, I. 28, 29, 31, 36, 39, 40, 50; II. 88, 95, 112-114, 148, 154, **157**, **169-171**, 210, 220, 238, **240**, 242

Moses, I. 158; II. 283, 295

names, I. 15, 21, 38, 93, 99, 103, 126, 130, 139, 145, 161, 165, 168-169, 170, **186**, 213, 239, 240, 242, 245, 247, 253, 267, 269, 308, 310, 311, 326; II. **9-72**, 75, 78-87, 95-105, 108, 110-114, 117, 118, 134, 142, 155, 161, 170, 171, 172, 176, 177, 178, 183, 190, 206, 235, 236

natural philosophy, I. 18, 109; II. 238, 241, 243, 244, 309

naturals, I. 24, 127; II. 53

Navarrete, D., *see* Fernandez-Navarrete, D.

Nestor, I. 284, 285

Newton, I. xxxv; II. 137, 199

Nisus, I. 136

Noah, I. 286; II. 283

notions, I. xxxiv, xxxvii, 6, 7, **9**, 11, 23, 24, 25, 37, 46-52, 57, 89, 91, 94, 123, 129, 131, 145, 147, 157, 180, 198, 199, 202, 206, 232, 235, 240, 244, 246, 253, 261, 263, 265, 267, 300, 301, 334; II. 10, 17, 18, 19, **40**, 44, 48, 71, 77, 80, 88, 91, 94, 97, 101, 104, 106, 116, 159, 169, 170, 176, 177, 178, 183, 215, 225, 237, 286, 304

objects, corporeal, I. 91; II. 158

objects, external, I. 16, 77, 78, 89; II. 34, 143, 144, 230, 246

objects, particular, II. 16, 20, 21, 44, 46, 47, 145

objects, sensible, I. 21, 77, 78, 100; II. 10, 29, 49, 114, 230

objects, visible, I. 91; II. 30, 88

obligation, I. xxxvii, 29, 31, 33, 46, 220, 238, 294; II. 210, 238

opinion, I. 5, 6, 10, 40, 42, 58, 81, 91, 102; II. 90, 97, 136, 165, 202, 241, 253, 254, 278

Ovington, Sir J., I. 46 n.3

Papists, *see* Romanists

parrot, talking, I. **278-280**; II. 9, 14, 213

particles of matter, I. 100, **104-107**, 110, 238, 277; II. 23, 24, 43, 44, 142, **150-152**, **160-162**, 185, 224, 260

Pascal, I. 121

Paul, St., I. 49, 144, 209; II. 281, 294

perception, I. 27, 55, 78, 80, 98, 99, 103, **111-117**, 120, 122, 123, 147, 184, 188, **196**, 237, 252, 253, 302, 306, 327, 331; II. 10, 29, 31, 116, **133-157**, 163, 166, 169, 174, 192-196, 207, 217-222, 229, 230, 239, 248, 262, 268, 274, 277, 284, 292

Peru, I. 30, 33

Pilate, I. 278

Plato, I. 83, 289; II. 98, 115, 238

Platonists, I. 284; II. 96

pleasure, I. xxxi, 82, 98, 99, 100, 118, **189-192**, 213, 214, 226-227, 228; II. 48, 144, 147, 163, 217, **229-230**, 232

plenum, I. 141, 142

Polemo, II. 238

Pollux, I. 83

Pompey, I. 309; II. 257

power, I. 8, 9, 48, 57, 85, 98, 99, 101, 104, 105, 109-111, 118, 130, 173, 174, 185, **193-238**, 242, 243, 247, **248-250**, 262, 317, 323; II. 14, 75, 85, 86, 116, 148, 150, 153, 159, 219, 223

principles, first, I. 20, 25, 39, 40; II. 236

principles, innate, I. xxxvi, **9-60**, 113, 116, 129; II. 301

principles, moral, I. 25, 26, 30, 36, 46, 50

principles, practical, I. 10, **25-43**, 46, 54

principles, speculative, I. **9-53**

punishment, I. 32, 34, 38, 47, 223, 291, 292, 296-297, 300; II. 36, 267

Pythagoras and Pythagoreans, I. 45, 284

qualities, primary, I. **104-111**, 249, 260; II. **150-152**, 159, 163, 184, 190

qualities, real, I. 107, 109, 110

qualities, secondary, I. **105-111**, 249, 317; II. 143, **150-152**, 163, 164, 184, 186

qualities, sensible, I. 78, 106, 113, 118, 130, 194, 237, 246, 248, 250, 252, 254, 322, 328; II. 14, 23, 48, 50, 54, 55, 64, 69, 84, 115, 118, 153, 161, 186, 187, 191

qualities, tangible, I. 79, 143; II. 186

reason, faculty of, I. 13, 18, 32, 110, 123, 127, 219; II. 43, 145, **262-280**, 281-287, 289, 295, 306

reason, light of, I. 28, 48; II. 89

reason, use of, I. **12-18**, 22, 48

reflection, I. 53, 56, 78, 79, 80, 86, **89-91**, 92, **98-102**, 111, 125, 128, 129, 132, 144, 146, 158, 184, 188, 193, 242, 244, 254, 262, 264, 270, 274, 301; II. 48, 158, 160, 279

relation, I. 45, 124, 131, 201, **266-270**, 293-305, 319; II. 20, **33-42**, 66, 75, 105, 133-137, 145, 149, 154, 240

religion, I. 40, 47, 340; II. 88, 89, 90, 95, 148, 173, 178, 199, 202, 220, 238, 281, 287, 298, 299, 308

resurrection, I. 45, 285; II. 35, 164, 279

revelation, I. 35, 87; II. 89, 147, 162, 199, 234, 243, 248, 261, **281-287**, 289, 291-296

rhetoric, II. 105, 106, 269

Richard III, *king*, II. 306
Roe, Sir T., I. 46 n.1
Romanists, I. 49; II. 252, 302
Rome and Romans, I. 33, 153, 240; II. 37, 76, 119, 213, 257, 273, 306
Rosicrucians, I. 87

St. James' Park, I. 269; II. 62
St. Martin, abbot of, II. 56
Saldanha, I. 46, 50
savages, I. 14, 24, 54; II. 242
scepticism, I. 8; II. 138, 218, 231
Schools, The, II. 18, 19, 22, 27-28, 54, 75, 76, 93, 103, 106, 184, **196, 201-202**, 236, 268
self, I. 282, 285-293
Sempronia, I. 266, 304-305
sensation, I. 53, 56, 78, 85, 86, 90, 91, 93, 99, 102, 109, 112, 114, 116, 125, 128, 132, 144, 158, 159, 184, 193, 238, 242, 252, 254, 260, 262, 264, 274, 301, 302, 324; II. 10, 29, 31, 142, 143, 145, 151, 158, 160, 163, 164, 190, 229, 279
Seth, I. 278
Siam and Siamites, I. 46, 51
signs, I. xxxviii, xxxix, 125, **126-127**, 168, 170, 196, 242, 278, 309, 332; II. **9, 12-15**, 17, 20, 27, 29, 31, 39, 42, 61, 62, 64, 68, 72, 74, 76, 81, 85, 89, 91, 99-103, 110, 111, 174, **176-178**, 180, 183, 275, 281, 295, 309, 310
Socrates, I. 82-83, 278, 284, 287-289
Solomon, I. 144, 160
soul, I. 9, 11, 44, 45, **80-87**, 88, 139, 189, 196, 255, 259, 278, 286; II. 96, 115, **147-148**, 154, 174, 175, 207, 209, 214, 298, 299, 300
species, I. 9, 127, 186, 247, 327; II. 11, 18, **20-25**, 32-41, **42-71**, 96, 98, 99, 100, 115, 117, 150, 162, 171, 175, 176, 181, 183, 184, 211, 216, 241, 243, 244
spirits, I. xxxvi, 5, 86, 121, 122, 166, 253-256, 259-263, 275, 293; II. 10, 11, **48-49**, 116, 149, **153-154**, 162, 190, 191, 214, 224, 226, 234, 243, 259, 276, 290-292, 296, 309
spirits, animal, I. 85, 103, 119, 122, 283, 292, 336, 337; II. 227
Stoics, II. 238
substance, I. 53, 81, 87, 94, **131-132**, 139, 140, 141, 194, 200, 236, 243, **244-265**, 267, 269-271, 316, 318,

320-325, 328, 332, 334; II. 13, 18, 21, 22, 24, 26, 32, 33, 40, **42-71**, 75, **81-86**, 95, 98, 99, 104, 105, 110-115, **116-117**, 118, 134, 147, 150, 151, 159, **168**, 171, 172, 177, 182, **183-184**, 186-191, 214, 226, **240-241**, 244
syllogism, II. **263-275**
Sydenham, I. xxxv

Techo, N. del, I. 46
Temple, Sir W., I. 279
terms, general, I. 16, 21; II. **9, 15-25**, 32, 44, 60, 182, 195
Terry, E., I. 46 n.3
Thersites, I. 284, 285
Thévenot, M., I. 30 n.1-2, 46 n.1
things, *see* objects
thinking, I. 99, **112**, 131, 137, 146, 185, **187-189**, 194, 201, 236, 237, 242, 243, 246, 254, 257, 261, 282; II. 10, 49, 138, 146, 147, 221, 223, 225, 226
Tiberius, II. 253
time, I. 79, 88, **146-167**, 272, 274-275; II. 17
Titus, I. 305
Tououpinambos, I. 30, 169
transmigration of souls, I. 278
truth, I. xxviii, xxxi, xxxv-xxxvi, 6, 10, 24-27, 34, 41-43, 57, 58, 60, 124, 193, 235, **326-334**; II. 42, 87, 89, 92, 93, 95, 97, 102, 103, 106, 108, 109, 136-138, 143, 145, 157, 166, 171, **176-181**, 182, 268, 271, 288, 296, 310
Tully, II. 27, 169
Turkey and Turks, I. 31, 52; II. 298

uneasiness, I. 78, **98-99, 190-192, 206-217**, 221, 224, 225, 228, 233

vacuum, I. **94-96, 141-145**; II. 204, 205, 206, 210
Valle, P. della, I. 31
Virgil, I. 136, 299
virtue, I. 27, 29, 30, 37, 39, 297-298; II. 105, 108, 169
volition, I. 98, 188, **196-207**
Voss, I., I. 30

will, the, I. xxxvi, 27, 98, 99, 120, 195, 197, 199, 200, 201, 206, 208, 210-213, 216, 217, 220, 224, 233-235, 254
William the Conqueror, I. 272

EVERYMAN'S LIBRARY: A Selected List

BIOGRAPHY

Baxter, Richard (1615–91).
THE AUTOBIOGRAPHY OF RICHARD BAXTER.   868
Boswell, James (1740–95). *See* Johnson.
Brontë, Charlotte (1816–55).
LIFE, 1857. By *Mrs Gaskell*. Introduction by *May Sinclair*. (*See also* Fiction.) 318
Burns, Robert (1759–96).
LIFE, 1828. By *J. G. Lockhart* (1794–1854). With Introduction by *Prof. James Kinsley*, M.A., PH.D.   (*See also* Poetry and Drama.) 156
Byron, Lord (1788–1824).
LETTERS. Edited by *R. G. Howarth*, B.LITT., and with an Introduction by *André Maurois.*   (*See also* Poetry and Drama.) 931
Canton, William (1845–1926).
A CHILD'S BOOK OF SAINTS, 1898.   (*See also* Essays.) 61
Cellini, Benvenuto (1500–71).
THE LIFE OF BENVENUTO CELLINI, written by himself. Translated by *Anne Macdonell*. Introduction by *William Gaunt.*   51
Cowper, William (1731–1800).
SELECTED LETTERS. Edited, with Introduction, by *W. Hadley*, M.A.   774
        (*See also* Poetry and Drama.)
Dickens, Charles (1812–70).
LIFE, 1874. By *John Forster* (1812–76). Introduction by *G. K. Chesterton*. 2 vols.
        (*See also* Fiction.) 781–2
Evelyn, John (1620–1706).
DIARY. Edited by *William Bray*, 1819. Intro. by *G. W. E. Russell*. 2 vols.   220–1
Fox, George (1624–91).
JOURNAL, 1694. Revised by *Norman Penney*, with Account of Fox's last years. Introduction by *Rufus M. Jones*.   754
Franklin, Benjamin (1706–90).
AUTOBIOGRAPHY, 1817. With Introduction and Account of Franklin's later life by *W. Macdonald*. Reset new edition (1949), with a newly compiled Index.   316
Goethe, Johann Wolfgang von (1749–1832).
LIFE, 1855. By *G. H. Lewes* (1817–78). Introduction by *Havelock Ellis*. Index.
        (*See also* Poetry and Drama.) 269
Hudson, William Henry (1841–1922).
FAR AWAY AND LONG AGO, 1918. Intro. by *John Galsworthy.*   956
Johnson, Samuel (1709–84).
LIVES OF THE ENGLISH POETS, 1781. Introduction by *Mrs L. Archer-Hind*. 2 vols.
        (*See also* Essays, Fiction.) 770–1
BOSWELL'S LIFE OF JOHNSON, 1791. A new edition (1949), with Introduction by *S. C. Roberts*, M.A., LL.D., and a 30-page Index by Alan Dent. 2 vols.   1–2
Keats, John (1795–1821).
LIFE AND LETTERS, 1848. By *Lord Houghton* (1809–85). Introduction by *Robert Lynd*. Note on the letters by Lewis Gibbs.   (*See also* Poetry and Drama.) 801
Lamb, Charles (1775–1834).
LETTERS. New edition (1945) arranged from the Complete Annotated Edition of the Letters. 2 vols.   (*See also* Essays and Belles-Lettres, Fiction.) 342–3
Napoleon Buonaparte (1769–1821).
HISTORY OF NAPOLEON BUONAPARTE, 1829. By *J. G. Lockhart* (1794–1854).   3
        (*See also* Essays and Belles-Lettres.)
Nelson, Horatio, Viscount (1758–1805).
LIFE, 1813. By *Robert Southey* (1774–1843).   (*See also* Essays.) 52
Outram, General Sir James (1803–63), 'the Bayard of India.'
LIFE, 1903. Deals with important passages in the history of India in the nineteenth century. By *L. J. Trotter* (1827–1912).   396
Pepys, Samuel (1633–1703).
DIARY. Newly edited (1953), with modernized spelling, by *John Warrington*, from the edition of Mynors Bright (1875–9). 3 vols.   53–5
Plutarch (46?–120).
LIVES OF THE NOBLE GREEKS AND ROMANS. Dryden's edition, 1683–6. Revised, with Introduction, by *A. H. Clough* (1819–61). 3 vols.   407–9
Rousseau, Jean Jacques (1712–78).
CONFESSIONS, 1782. 2 vols. Complete and unabridged English translation. New Introduction by *Prof. R. Niklaus*, B.A., PH.D., of Exeter University.   859–60
        (*See also* Essays, Theology and Philosophy.)
Scott, Sir Walter (1771–1832).
LOCKHART'S LIFE OF SCOTT. An abridgement by *J. G. Lockhart* himself from the original 7 volumes. New Introduction by *W. M. Parker*, M.A.   39

Swift, Jonathan (1667–1745).
    JOURNAL TO STELLA, 1710–13. Deciphered by *J. K. Moorhead*. Introduction by *Sir Walter Scott*. Sir Walter Scott's essay 'Swift, Stella and Vanessa' is included.   757
                                                   (*See also* Essays, Fiction.)

Walpole, Horace (1717–97).
    SELECTED LETTERS. Edited, with Introduction, by *W. Hadley*, M.A.   775
Wellington, Arthur Wellesley, Duke of (1769–1852).
    LIFE, 1862. By *G. R. Gleig* (1796–1888).   341

CLASSICAL

Aeschylus (525–455 B.C.).
    PLAYS. Translated into English Verse by *G. M. Cookson*. New Introduction by *John Warrington*, and notes on each play.   62
Aristophanes (450 ?–385 ? B.C.).
    THE COMEDIES. Translated by *J. Hookham Frere*, etc. Edited, with Introduction, by *J. P. Maine* and *J. H. Frere*. 2 vols.   (*Vol. 1 temporarily out of print.*) 516
Aristotle (384–322 B.C.).
    POLITICS and THE ATHENIAN CONSTITUTION. Edited and translated by *John Warrington*.   605
    METAPHYSICS. Edited and translated by *John Warrington*. Introduction by *Sir David Ross*, K.B.E., M.A., D.LITT.   1000
Caesar, Julius (102 ?–44 B.C.).
    WAR COMMENTARIES. 'The Gallic Wars' and 'The Civil War.' Newly translated and edited by *John Warrington*.   702
Cicero, Marcus Tullius (106–43 B.C.).
    THE OFFICES (translated by *Thomas Cockman*, 1699); LAELIUS, ON FRIENDSHIP; CATO, ON OLD AGE; AND SELECT LETTERS (translated by *W. Melmoth*, 1753). With Note on Cicero's Character by De Quincey. Introduction by *John Warrington*. 345
Demetrius (fl. late first century A.D.). (*See under* Aristotle.)
Demosthenes (384–322 B.C.). (*See under* Oratory, p. 11.)
Epictetus (*b. c.* A.D. 60).
    MORAL DISCOURSES. THE ENCHIRIDION AND FRAGMENTS. Translated by *Elizabeth Carter* (1717–1806). Edited by *W. H. D. Rouse*, M.A.   404
Euripides (484 ?–407 B.C.).
    PLAYS. New Introduction by *John Warrington*. Translated by *A. S. Way*, D.LITT. 2 vols.   63, 271
Herodotus (484 ?–425 ? B.C.).
    HISTORY. The 'History' deals with the period covering the Persian invasion of Greece, 492–480 B.C. Rawlinson's Translation, additional notes and Introduction, by *E. H. Blakeney*. 2 vols. (*Vol. II temporarily out of print.*)   405–6
Homer (? ninth century B.C.).
    ILIAD. New verse translation by *S. O. Andrew* and *Michael Oakley*.   453
    ODYSSEY. The new verse translation (first published 1953) by *S. O. Andrew*. Introduction by *John Warrington*.   454
Juvenal (*c.* A.D. 50–*c.* 130).
    SATIRES: with THE SATIRES OF PERSIUS. Introduction by *Prof. H. J. Rose*, M.A., F.B.A. William Gifford Translation, 1802. Revised by *John Warrington*.   997
Lucretius (*c.* 99 ?–50 ? B.C.).
    ON THE NATURE OF THINGS. Metrical Translation by *W. E. Leonard*.   750
Ovid (43 B.C.–A.D. 18).
    SELECTED WORKS. Chosen by *J. C.* and *M. J. Thornton*. Selections from the *Metamorphoses*, *Heroical Epistles*, the *Festivals*, the *Ibis*, and his epistles written in exile: also his *Art of Love*.   955
Persius (34–62). *See* Juvenal.
Plato (427–347 B.C.).
    THE REPUBLIC. Translated, with an Introduction, by *A. D. Lindsay*, C.B.E., LL.D. The greatest achievement of the Greek intellect in philosophy.   64
    SOCRATIC DISCOURSES OF PLATO AND XENOPHON. Introduction by *A. D. Lindsay*, C.B.E., LL.D.   457
    THE LAWS. The last of Plato's dialogues is here printed in the A. E. Taylor (1869–1945) Translation.   275
Sophocles (496 ?–406 B.C.).
    DRAMAS. This volume contains the seven surviving dramas.   114
Thucydides (*c.* 460–401 B.C.).
    HISTORY OF THE PELOPONNESIAN WAR. Translation by *Richard Crawley*. Introduction by *John Warrington*. Index and five plans.   455
Virgil (70–19 B.C.).
    AENEID. Verse translation by *Michael Oakley*. Introduction by *E. M. Forster*.   161
    ECLOGUES AND GEORGICS. Verse Translation by *T. F. Royds*. The 'Eclogues' were inspired by Theocritus; the 'Georgics' describe a countryman's life.   222
Xenophon (430 ?–360 ? B.C.). (*See under* Plato.)

ESSAYS AND BELLES-LETTRES

Anthology OF ENGLISH PROSE, FROM BEDE TO STEVENSON.   675

Bacon, Francis, Lord Verulam (1561–1626).
  ESSAYS, 1597–1626. Introduction by *Oliphant Smeaton*. Index of Quotations and
  Foreign Phrases and Glossary.   (*See also* Theology and Philosophy.) 10

Bagehot, Walter (1826–77).
  LITERARY STUDIES, 1879. Introduction by *George Sampson*. 2 vols.   520–1

Belloc, Hilaire (1870–1953).
  STORIES, ESSAYS AND POEMS. Edited with Introduction by *J. B. Morton*, C.B.E.,
  the volume now contains a new selection from the *Sonnets, Verses* and celebrated
  Epigrams.   948

Burke, Edmund (1729–97).
  REFLECTIONS ON THE REVOLUTION IN FRANCE (1790) AND OTHER ESSAYS. Introduction and Notes by *A. J. Grieve*, M.A.   (*See also* Oratory.) 460

Canton, William (1845–1926).
  THE INVISIBLE PLAYMATE, 1894; W. V., HER BOOK, 1896; and IN MEMORY OF
  W. V., 1901.   (*See also* Biography.) 566

Carlyle, Thomas (1795–1881).
  ESSAYS. Introduction by *J. R. Lowell*. 2 vols. Essays on men and affairs.   703–4
  PAST AND PRESENT, 1843. New Introduction by *Douglas Jerrold*.   608
  SARTOR RESARTUS, 1838; and HEROES AND HERO-WORSHIP, 1841.
                                                       (*See also* History.) 278

Castiglione, Baldassare (1478–1529).
  THE BOOK OF THE COURTIER, 1528. *Sir Thomas Hoby's* Translation, 1561. Introduction by *W. H. D. Rouse* and Notes by *Prof. W. B. Drayton Henderson*.   807

Century. A CENTURY OF ENGLISH ESSAYS, FROM CAXTON TO BELLOC.   653

Chesterfield, Philip Dormer Stanhope, Earl of (1694–1773).
  LETTERS TO HIS SON; AND OTHERS. Introduction by *Prof. R. K. Root*.   823

Chesterton, Gilbert Keith (1874–1936).
  STORIES, ESSAYS AND POEMS. Introduction by *Maisie Ward*. An 'omnibus' volume
  including four 'Father Brown' stories.   913

Coleridge, Samuel Taylor (1772–1834).
  BIOGRAPHIA LITERARIA, 1817. Edited with a new Introduction by *George Watson*,
  M.A. Coleridge described the work as 'sketches of my literary life and opinions.' 11
  SHAKESPEAREAN CRITICISM, 1849. Edited with a long Introduction by *Prof.
  T. M. Raysor* (1960), a distinguished Coleridge scholar of the University of
  Nebraska. 2 vols.   (*See also* Poetry and Drama.) 162, 183

De la Mare, Walter (1873–1956).
  STORIES, ESSAYS AND POEMS. An anthology arranged by *Mildred Bozman*.   940

De Quincey, Thomas (1785–1859).
  CONFESSIONS OF AN ENGLISH OPIUM-EATER, 1822. Edited with Introduction by
  Prof. J. E. Jordan (1960).   223

Eckermann, Johann Peter (1792–1854).
  CONVERSATIONS WITH GOETHE, 1836–8. Translated by *John Oxenford*, 1850.
  Edited by *J. K. Moorhead*, with Introduction by *Havelock Ellis*.   851
                                        (*See also* Poetry and Drama, Biography.)

Emerson, Ralph Waldo (1803–82).
  ESSAYS, 1841–4. New Introduction by *Prof. Sherman Paul*.   12

Florio, John (1553?–1625). (*See* Montaigne.)

Gilfillan, George (1813–78).
  A GALLERY OF LITERARY PORTRAITS, 1845–54.   348

Gray, Thomas (1716–71).
  ESSAYS. (*See* Poetry.)

Hamilton, Alexander (1757–1804), and Others.
  THE FEDERALIST, OR THE NEW CONSTITUTION, 1787–8. Introduction by *Prof. W. J.
  Ashley*.   519

Hazlitt, William (1778–1830).
  LECTURES ON THE ENGLISH COMIC WRITERS, 1819; and MISCELLANEOUS ESSAYS.
  Introduction by *W. E. Henley*.   411
  LECTURES ON THE ENGLISH POETS, 1818; and THE SPIRIT OF THE AGE, 1825.
  Introduction by *Catherine Macdonald Maclean*, M.A., D.LITT., F.R.S.L.   459
  THE ROUND TABLE and CHARACTERS OF SHAKESPEAR'S PLAYS, 1817–18. New
  Introduction by *Catherine Macdonald Maclean*.   65
  TABLE TALK, 1821–2, 1824. New Introduction by *Catherine Macdonald Maclean*.
                                                                             321

Holmes, Oliver Wendell (1809–94).
  THE AUTOCRAT OF THE BREAKFAST-TABLE, 1858. Introduction by *Van Wyck
  Brooks*.   66

Hunt, Leigh (1784–1859).
  SELECTED ESSAYS. 78 essays with Introduction by *J. B. Priestley*.   829

Huxley, Aldous Leonard (*b.* 1894).
  STORIES, ESSAYS AND POEMS.   935

Johnson, Samuel (1709–84).
  THE RAMBLER. Introduction by *S. C. Roberts*. (*See also* Biography, Fiction.) 994

Lamb, Charles (1775–1834).
ESSAYS OF ELIA AND LAST ESSAYS OF ELIA, 1823–33. Introduction by *Augustine Birrell*. Includes the first and the last Essays of Elia.   14
    (See also Biography, Fiction.)

Landor, Walter Savage (1775–1864).
IMAGINARY CONVERSATIONS, AND POEMS, 1824–9, 1853. Edited, with Introduction, by *Havelock Ellis*.   890

Lawrence, David Herbert (1885–1930).
STORIES, ESSAYS AND POEMS. Selected by *Desmond Hawkins*. Poetry, Essays, Travel Sketches and Letters.   958
    (See also Fiction.)

Locke, John (1632–1704).
AN ESSAY CONCERNING HUMAN UNDERSTANDING, 1690. Abridged and edited by *Raymond Wilburn*, presenting the whole sweep of the work.   984
    (See also Theology and Philosophy.)

Lynd, Robert (1879–1949).
ESSAYS ON LIFE AND LITERATURE. Introduction by *Desmond MacCarthy*.   990

Macaulay, Thomas Babington, Lord (1800–59).
CRITICAL AND HISTORICAL ESSAYS, 1843. New Introduction by *Douglas Jerrold*. 2 vols.   225–6
MISCELLANEOUS ESSAYS, 1823–59; LAYS OF ANCIENT ROME, 1842; and MISCELLANEOUS POEMS, 1812–47. Introduction by *Prof. G. M. Trevelyan*, O.M.   439
    (See also History.)

Machiavelli, Niccolò (1469–1527).
THE PRINCE, 1513. New Introduction by *Prof. H. Butterfield*, M.A., HON. D.LITT. Translated by *W. K. Marriott*.   280

Mazzini, Joseph (1805–72).
THE DUTIES OF MAN (translated by *Miss E. Noyes*); and OTHER ESSAYS. New Introduction by *Dr Thomas Jones*, C.H., LL.D.   224

Milton, John (1608–74).
PROSE WRITINGS. Introduction by *K. M. Burton*, M.A. The contents of this volume include 'Areopagitica,' 1644, and other important prose works.   795
    (See also Poetry, etc.)

Mitford, Mary Russell (1787–1855).
OUR VILLAGE, 1824–32. Edited, with an Introduction, by *Sir John Squire*.   927

Modern Humour. An Anthology in Prose and Verse from over sixty authors.   957

Montaigne, Michel de (1533–92).
ESSAYS, 1580–8. John Florio's version, 1603. Edited (from the third edition, 1632), with Intro. by *A. R. Waller*, 3 vols.   *(Vol. I temporarily out of print.)* 440–2

Napoleon Buonaparte (1769–1821).
LETTERS. Some 300 of the most interesting of the Emperor's letters, chosen and translated by *J. M. Thompson*, F.B.A., F.R.HIST.S.   *(See also* Biography.) 995

Nelson, Horatio, Viscount (1758–1805).
NELSON'S LETTERS. Compiled by *Geoffrey Rawson*.   *(See also* Biography.) 244

Newman, John Henry (1801–90).
ON THE SCOPE AND NATURE OF UNIVERSITY EDUCATION; and CHRISTIANITY AND SCIENTIFIC INVESTIGATION, 1852. Introduction by *Wilfrid Ward*.   723
    (See also Theology and Philosophy.)

Poe, Edgar Allan (1809–49).
ESSAYS. *(See* Poetry.)

Quiller-Couch, Sir Arthur (1863–1944).
CAMBRIDGE LECTURES, from 'Q.'s' well-known books *The Art of Reading*, 1920; *The Art of Writing*, 1916; *Studies in Literature*, 1918; and *Shakespeare's Workmanship*, 1918.   *(See also* Fiction.) 974

Rousseau, Jean Jacques (1712–78).
ÉMILE; OR, EDUCATION. Translated by *Barbara Foxley*, M.A. Intro. (1955) by *Prof. André Boutet de Monvel*.   *(See also* Biography, Theology and Philosophy.) 518

Ruskin, John (1819–1900).
SESAME, AND LILIES, 1864; THE TWO PATHS, 1859; and THE KING OF THE GOLDEN RIVER; OR THE BLACK BROTHERS, 1851. Introduction by *Sir Oliver Lodge*.   219
THE SEVEN LAMPS OF ARCHITECTURE, 1849. With an Introduction (1956) by *Sir Arnold Lunn*. Illustrated with 14 plates of engravings.   207

Sévigné, Marie de Rabutin-Chantal, Marquise de (1626–96).
SELECTED LETTERS. Selected and translated by *H. T. Barnwell*, M.A.   98

Spectator, The, 1711–14. By Joseph Addison (1672–1719), Sir Richard Steele (1672–1729) and Others. Edited by *Prof. Gregory Smith*. New Introduction by *P. Smithers*, D.PHIL., M.P., and a Biographical and General Index by *Prof. Gregory Smith*. Reset with minor revisions, 1945. 4 vols.   *(See also* Essays *under* Steele.) 164–7

Spencer, Herbert (1820–1903).
ESSAYS ON EDUCATION, 1861. Introduction by *C. W. Eliot*.   504

Steele, Sir Richard (1672–1729).
THE TATLER, 1709–11.   993

Sterne, Laurence (1713–68).
A SENTIMENTAL JOURNEY THROUGH FRANCE AND ITALY, 1768; JOURNAL TO ELIZA, written in 1767; and LETTERS TO ELIZA, 1766–7. Introduction by *Daniel George*.   *(See also* Fiction.) 796

Stevenson, Robert Louis (1850–94).
    VIRGINIBUS PUERISQUE, 1881; and FAMILIAR STUDIES OF MEN AND BOOKS, 1882.
Swift, Jonathan (1667–1745).   (See also Fiction, Poetry and Drama, Travel.) 765
    A TALE OF A TUB, 1704; THE BATTLE OF THE BOOKS, 1704; and OTHER SATIRES.
    Introduction by *Louis Melville*.   (See also Biography, Fiction.) 347
Swinnerton, Frank (b. 1884).
    THE GEORGIAN LITERARY SCENE, 1935. A panorama, revised 1951, of English
    writers (novelists, essayists, dramatists, poets) from 1919.   943
Thackeray, William Makepeace (1811–63).
    THE ENGLISH HUMORISTS, 1851; CHARITY AND HUMOUR, 1853; and THE FOUR
    GEORGES, 1855. Introduction by *Walter Jerrold*.   (See also Fiction.) 610
Thoreau, Henry David (1817–62).
    WALDEN, OR LIFE IN THE WOODS, 1854. Introduction by *Prof. Basil Willey*. 281
Trench, Richard Chevenix (1807–86).
    ON THE STUDY OF WORDS, 1851; and ENGLISH PAST AND PRESENT, 1855. Intro-
    duction by *George Sampson*.   788
Tytler, Alexander Fraser (1747–1814).
    ESSAY ON THE PRINCIPLES OF TRANSLATION, 1791.   168
Walton, Izaak (1593–1683).
    THE COMPLETE ANGLER, 1653. Introduction by *Andrew Lang*.   70

                                    FICTION
Ainsworth, William Harrison (1805–82).
    OLD SAINT PAUL'S, 1841. Introduction by *W. E. Axon*, LL.D. Great Fire of London.
                                                                        522
    ROOKWOOD, 1834. Introduction by *Frank Swinnerton*. Dick Turpin.   870
    THE TOWER OF LONDON, 1840. Lady Jane Grey.   400
    WINDSOR CASTLE, 1843. Intro. by *Ernest Rhys*. Henry VIII and Ann Boleyn. 709
American Short Stories of the Nineteenth Century. Edited, with an Introduction, by
    John Cournos. Twenty stories from representative writers.   840
Andersen, Hans Christian (1805–75).
    FAIRY TALES AND STORIES. This represents a completely new selection and in the
    Reginald Spink Translation.   4
Austen, Jane (1775–1817). Each volume has an Introduction by *R. Brimley Johnson*.
    EMMA, 1816.   24   PRIDE AND PREJUDICE, 1823.   22
    MANSFIELD PARK, 1814.   23   SENSE AND SENSIBILITY, 1811.   21
    NORTHANGER ABBEY, 1818; and PERSUASION, 1818.   25
Balzac, Honoré de (1799–1850).
    AT THE SIGN OF THE CAT AND RACKET, 1830; and OTHER STORIES. Translated by
    Clara Bell. Introduction by *George Saintsbury*.   349
    EUGÉNIE GRANDET, 1834. Translated by *Ellen Marriage*. New Introduction by
    Prof. Marcel Girard.   169
    OLD GORIOT, 1835. Translated by *Ellen Marriage*. New Introduction by *Prof.
    Marcel Girard*.   170
    THE WILD ASS'S SKIN, 1831. A youth makes a bargain with destiny. New Introduction
    by *Prof. Marcel Girard*.   26
Barbusse, Henri (1874–1935).
    UNDER FIRE, THE STORY OF A SQUAD, 1916. Introduction by *Brian Rhys*.   798
Beaconsfield, Benjamin Disraeli, Earl of (1804–81).
    CONINGSBY, 1844. Introduction and Notes (with a Key to the Characters) by *B. N.
    Langdon-Davies*.   535
Bennett, Arnold (1867–1931).
    THE OLD WIVES' TALE, 1908. The most durable novel of Bennett's.   919
Blackmore, Richard Doddridge (1825–1900).
    LORNA DOONE: A ROMANCE OF EXMOOR, 1869. Introduction by *Ernest Rhys*. 304
Borrow, George (1803–81).
    THE ROMANY RYE, 1857. Practically a sequel to *Lavengro*. (See also Travel.) 120
Brontë, Anne (1820–49).
    THE TENANT OF WILDFELL HALL and AGNES GREY. With a new Introduction by
    Margaret Lane.   685
Brontë, Charlotte (1816–55). For Mrs Gaskell's 'Life' see Biography.
    JANE EYRE, 1847. Introduction by *Margaret Lane*.   287
    THE PROFESSOR, 1857. Introduction by *Margaret Lane*.   417
    SHIRLEY, 1849. Introduction by *Margaret Lane*.   288
    VILLETTE, 1853. Introduction by *Margaret Lane*.   351
Brontë, Emily (1818–48).
    WUTHERING HEIGHTS, 1848; and POEMS. Introduction by *Margaret Lane*.   243
Burney, Fanny (Madame Frances d'Arblay, 1753–1849).
    EVELINA, 1778. Introduction by *Lewis Gibbs*.   352
Butler, Samuel (1835–1902).
    EREWHON, 1872 (revised 1901); and EREWHON REVISITED, 1901. Introduction by
    Desmond MacCarthy.   881
    THE WAY OF ALL FLESH, 1903. Introduction by *A. J. Hoppé*.   895

Collins, Wilkie (1824–89).
THE MOONSTONE, 1868. Introduction by *Dorothy L. Sayers*. 979
THE WOMAN IN WHITE, 1860. New Introduction by *Maurice Richardson*. 464
Conrad, Joseph (1857–1924).
LORD JIM, 1900. Characteristically set in the East Indies. Introduction by *R. B. Cunninghame Graham*. 925
THE NIGGER OF THE 'NARCISSUS,' 1897; TYPHOON, 1903; and THE SHADOW LINE, 1917. Introduction by *A. J. Hoppé*. Three of Conrad's best-known stories. 980
NOSTROMO, 1904. New edition of Conrad's greatest novel with an Introduction by *Richard Curle*. 38
Cooper, James Fenimore (1789–1851).
THE LAST OF THE MOHICANS, 1826, A NARRATIVE OF 1757. With an Introduction by *Ernest Rhys*. 79
THE PRAIRIE, 1827. The last of the 'Leatherstocking Tales.' 172
Craik, Mrs. *See* Mulock.
Daudet, Alphonse (1840–97).
TARTARIN OF TARASCON, 1872; and TARTARIN ON THE ALPS, 1885. Two light episodic novels, some of the funniest episodes ever written in French. 423
Defoe, Daniel (1661 ?–1731).
THE FORTUNES AND MISFORTUNES OF MOLL FLANDERS, 1722. Introduction by *G. A. Aitken*. One of Defoe's greatest books, famous for its picture of low life. 837
JOURNAL OF THE PLAGUE YEAR, 1722. Introduction by *G. A. Aitken*. 289
LIFE, ADVENTURES AND PIRACIES OF THE FAMOUS CAPTAIN SINGLETON, 1720. Introduction by *Edward Garnett*. A supposed record of a journey across Africa. 74
ROBINSON CRUSOE, 1719. Parts 1 and 2 complete. Introduction by *Guy N. Pocock*. (*See also* Travel.) 59
De Rojas, Fernando (15th century).
CELESTINA: OR THE TRAGI-COMEDY OF CALISTO AND MELIBEA, attributed to Fernando de Rojas. Translated, with an Introduction, by *Phyllis Hartnoll*, M.A., L. ÉS L. This is a new translation (1958). 100
Dickens, Charles (1812–70). Each of the following volumes of Dickens's works has an Introduction by *G. K. Chesterton*:

BARNABY RUDGE, 1841.	76	LITTLE DORRIT, 1857.	293
BLEAK HOUSE, 1852–3.	236	MARTIN CHUZZLEWIT, 1843–4.	241
CHRISTMAS BOOKS, 1843–8.	239	NICHOLAS NICKLEBY, 1838–9.	238
CHRISTMAS STORIES, 1850–67.	414	OLD CURIOSITY SHOP, 1841.	173
DAVID COPPERFIELD, 1849–50.	242	OLIVER TWIST, 1838.	233
DOMBEY AND SON, 1846–8.	240	OUR MUTUAL FRIEND, 1864–5.	294
GREAT EXPECTATIONS, 1861.	234	PICKWICK PAPERS, 1836–7.	235
HARD TIMES, 1854.	292	A TALE OF TWO CITIES, 1859.	102

(*See also* Biography.)
Disraeli, Benjamin. *See* Beaconsfield.
Dostoyevsky, Fyodor (1821–81).
THE BROTHERS KARAMAZOV, 1879–80. Translated by *Constance Garnett*. Introduction by *Edward Garnett*. 2 vols. 802–3
CRIME AND PUNISHMENT, 1866. *Constance Garnett* translation. 501
THE IDIOT, 1873. Translated by *Eva M. Martin*. New Introduction by *Richard Curle*. 682
LETTERS FROM THE UNDERWORLD, 1864; and OTHER TALES (THE GENTLE MAIDEN; THE LANDLADY). Translated, with Introduction, by *C. J. Hogarth*. 654
POOR FOLK, 1845; and THE GAMBLER, 1867. Translated, with Introduction, by *C. J. Hogarth*. 711
THE POSSESSED, 1871. Translated by *Constance Garnett*. Introduction by *Nikolay Andreyev*, PH.D., M.A. 2 vols. 861–2
Dumas, Alexandre (1802–70).
THE BLACK TULIP, 1850. The brothers De Witt in Holland, 1672–5. New Introduction by *Prof. Marcel Girard*. 174
COUNT OF MONTE CRISTO, 1844. 2 vols. Napoleon's later phase. New Introduction by *Prof. Marcel Girard*. 393–4
MARGUERITE DE VALOIS, 1845. The Eve of St Bartholomew. 326
THE THREE MUSKETEERS, 1844. The France of Cardinal Richelieu. 81
Du Maurier, George Louis Palmella Busson (1834–96).
TRILBY, 1894. Illustrated by the author. Preface by *Sir Gerald Du Maurier*. *Trilby* breathes the air of Paris in the eighties and is drawn largely from the author's own experience. 863
Edgeworth, Maria (1767–1849).
CASTLE RACKRENT, 1800; and THE ABSENTEE, 1812. Introduction by *Prof. Brander Matthews*. 410
Eliot, George (pseudonym of Mary Ann Evans, 1819–80).
ADAM BEDE, 1859. New Introduction by *Robert Speaight*. 27
MIDDLEMARCH, 1872. New Introduction by *Gerald Bullett*. 2 vols. 854–5
THE MILL ON THE FLOSS, 1860. Introduction by *Sir W. Robertson Nicoll*. 325
ROMOLA, 1863. Intro. by *Rudolph Dircks*. The Florence of Savonarola. 231
SILAS MARNER, THE WEAVER OF RAVELOE, 1861. Introduction by *A. Matheson*. 12

English Short Stories. Thirty-six selected stories from Middle Ages to present time.
Introduction by *Richard Wilson*, B.A., D.LITT.   743

Fielding, Henry (1707–54). *George Saintsbury* has written an Introduction to the Everyman Fielding.
    AMELIA, 1751. 2 vols. Amelia is drawn from Fielding's first wife.   852–3
    JONATHAN WILD, 1743; and JOURNAL OF A VOYAGE TO LISBON, 1755. *Jonathan Wild* is a satire on false hero-worship; the *Journal* (published posthumously) narrates the incidents of Fielding's last voyage.   877
    JOSEPH ANDREWS, 1742. A skit on Richardson's *Pamela*.   467
    TOM JONES, 1749. 2 vols. The first great English novel of humour.   355–6

Flaubert, Gustave (1821–80).
    MADAME BOVARY, 1857. Translated by *Eleanor Marx-Aveling*. Introduction by *George Saintsbury*.   808
    SALAMMBO, 1862. Translated by *J. C. Chartres*. Introduction by *Prof. F. C. Green*, M.A., PH.D. The war of the Mercenaries against Carthage.   869
    SENTIMENTAL EDUCATION, 1869. Modern translation, with Introduction and Notes by *Anthony Goldsmith*.   969

Forster, Edward Morgan (*b.* 1879).
    A PASSAGE TO INDIA, 1924. With an Introduction by *Peter Burra*.   972

Galsworthy, John (1867–1933).
    THE COUNTRY HOUSE.   917

Gaskell, Mrs Elizabeth (1810–65).
    CRANFORD, 1853. Introduction by *Frank Swinnerton*.   (*See also* Biography.) 83

Ghost Stories. Introduction by *John Hampden*. Eighteen stories.   952

Gogol, Nikolay (1809–52).
    DEAD SOULS, 1842. Introduction by *Nikolay Andreyev*, PH.D., M.A.   726

Goldsmith, Oliver (1728–74).
    THE VICAR OF WAKEFIELD, 1766. Introduction by *J. M. Dent*.   295
    (*See also* Poetry.)

Goncharov, Ivan (1812–91).
    OBLOMOV, 1857. First complete English translation by *Natalie Duddington*. New Introduction by *Nikolay Andreyev*, PH.D., M.A.   878

Gorky, Maxim (pseudonym of Alexei Maximovitch Pieshkov, 1868–1936).
    THROUGH RUSSIA. Translated, with an Introduction, by *C. J. Hogarth*.   741

Grossmith, George (1847–1912), and Weedon (1853–1919).
    THE DIARY OF A NOBODY, 1894. With Weedon Grossmith's illustrations.   963

Hawthorne, Nathaniel (1804–64).
    THE HOUSE OF THE SEVEN GABLES, 1851. New Introduction by *Prof. Roy Harvey Pearce*.   176
    THE SCARLET LETTER: A ROMANCE, 1850. With new Introduction by *Prof. Roy Harvey Pearce*.   122
    TWICE-TOLD TALES, 1837–42. With a new Introduction by *Prof. Roy Harvey Pearce*.   531

Hugo, Victor Marie (1802–85).
    LES MISÉRABLES, 1862. Introduction by *Denis Saurat*.   2 vols. 363–4
    NOTRE DAME DE PARIS, 1831. Introduction by *Denis Saurat*.   422
    TOILERS OF THE SEA, 1866. Introduction by *Ernest Rhys*.   509

Huxley, Aldous.
    STORIES, ESSAYS AND POEMS. (*See under* Essays.)

James, Henry (1843–1916).
    THE AMBASSADORS, 1903. Introduction by *Frank Swinnerton*.   987
    THE TURN OF THE SCREW, 1898; and THE ASPERN PAPERS, 1888. Two famous short novels. Introduction by *Prof. Kenneth B. Murdock*, A.M., PH.D.   912

Jefferies, Richard (1848–87).
    AFTER LONDON, 1884; and AMARYLLIS AT THE FAIR, 1886. Introduction by *Richard Garnett*.   951

Jerome, Jerome K. (1859–1927).
    THREE MEN IN A BOAT and THREE MEN ON THE BUMMEL. Introduction by *D. C. Browning*, M.A., B.LITT.   118

Kingsley, Charles (1819–75).
    HEREWARD THE WAKE, 1866. Introduction by *Ernest Rhys*.   296
    WESTWARD HO!, 1855. Introduction by *Dr J. A. Williamson*, M.A.   20

Lamb, Charles (1775–1834), and Mary (1764–1847).
    TALES FROM SHAKESPEARE, 1807. Illustrated by *Arthur Rackham*.   8
    (*See also* Biography, Essays.)

Lawrence, David Herbert (1885–1930).
    THE WHITE PEACOCK, 1911.   (*See also* Essays.) 914

Loti, Pierre (1850–1923).
    ICELAND FISHERMAN, 1886. Translated by *W. P. Baines*.   920

Lover, Samuel (1797–1868).
    HANDY ANDY, 1842. Lover was a musician, portrait-painter, song-writer and actor who also wrote four novels of which this is generally accounted the best.   178

Lytton, Edward Bulwer, Baron (1803–73).
    THE LAST DAYS OF POMPEII, 1834. A romance of the first century A.D.   80

Mann, Thomas (1875–1955).
    STORIES AND EPISODES. Introduction by *Prof. Erich Heller*, PH.D.   962

Manzoni, Alessandro (1785–1873).
 THE BETROTHED (*I Promessi Sposi*, 1840, rev. ed.). Translated (1951) from the
 Italian by *Archibald Colquhoun*, who also adds a preface.   999
Marryat, Frederick (1792–1848).
 MR MIDSHIPMAN EASY. New Introduction by *Oliver Warner*.   82
 THE SETTLERS IN CANADA, 1844. Introduction by *Oliver Warner*.   370
Maugham, W. Somerset (*b.* 1874).
 CAKES AND ALE, 1930. The finest novel of the author's inter-war period.   932
Maupassant, Guy de (1850–93).
 SHORT STORIES. Translated by *Marjorie Laurie*. Intro. by *Gerald Gould*. 907
Melville, Herman (1819–91).
 MOBY DICK, 1851. Intro. by *Prof. Sherman Paul*.   179
 TYPEE, 1846; and BILLY BUDD (*published* 1924). South Seas adventures. New
 Introduction by *Milton R. Stern*.   180
Meredith, George (1828–1909).
 THE ORDEAL OF RICHARD FEVEREL, 1859. Introduction by *Robert Sencourt*.   916
Mickiewicz, Adam (1798–1855).
 PAN TADEUSZ, 1834. Translated into English prose, with Introduction, by *Prof.
 G. R. Noyes*. Poland's epic of Napoleonic wars.   842
Modern Short Stories. Selected by *John Hadfield*. Twenty stories.   954
Moore, George (1852–1933).
 ESTHER WATERS, 1894. The story of Esther Waters, the servant girl who 'went
 wrong.' Introduction by *C. D. Medley*.   933
Mulock [Mrs Craik], Maria (1826–87).
 JOHN HALIFAX, GENTLEMAN, 1856. Introduction by *J. Shaylor*.   123
Pater, Walter (1839–94).
 MARIUS THE EPICUREAN, 1885. Introduction by *Osbert Burdett*.   903
Poe, Edgar Allan (1809–49).
 TALES OF MYSTERY AND IMAGINATION. Introduction by *Padraic Colum*.   336
                                                (*See also* Poetry and Drama.)
Priestley, J. B. (*b.* 1894).
 ANGEL PAVEMENT, 1931. A finely conceived novel of London.   938
Quiller-Couch, Sir Arthur (1863–1944).
 HETTY WESLEY, 1903. Introduction by the author.   (*See also* Essays.) 864
Radcliffe, Mrs Ann (1764–1823).
 THE MYSTERIES OF UDOLPHO, 1794. Intro. by *R. A. Freeman*. 2 vols.   865–6
Reade, Charles (1814–84).
 THE CLOISTER AND THE HEARTH, 1861. Introduction by *Swinburne*.   29
Richardson, Samuel (1689–1761).
 PAMELA, 1740. Introduction by *George Saintsbury*. 2 vols.   683–4
 CLARISSA, 1747–8. Introduction by *Prof. W. L. Phelps*. 4 vols.   882–5
Russian Short Stories. Translated, with Introduction, by *Rochelle S. Townsend*. Stories
 by Pushkin, Gogol, Tolstoy, Korolenko, Chehov, Chirikov, Andreyev, Kuprin,
 Gorky, Sologub.   758
Scott, Sir Walter (1771–1832).
 The following Waverley Novels each contain an Introduction, biographical and
 bibliographical, based upon Lockhart's *Life*:
 THE ANTIQUARY, 1816. Introduction by *W. M. Parker*, M.A.   126
 THE BRIDE OF LAMMERMOOR, 1819. A romance of life in East Lothian, 1695. New
 Introduction by *W. M. Parker*, M.A.   129
 GUY MANNERING, 1815. A mystery story of the time of George III. New Intro-
 duction by *W. M. Parker*, M.A.   133
 THE HEART OF MIDLOTHIAN, 1818. Period of the Porteous Riots, 1736. New Intro-
 duction by *W. M. Parker*, M.A.   134
 IVANHOE, 1820. A romance of the days of Richard I.   16
 KENILWORTH, 1821. The tragic story of Amy Robsart, in Elizabeth I's time. New
 Preface and Glossary by *W. M. Parker*, M.A.   135
 OLD MORTALITY, 1817. Battle of Bothwell Bridge, 1679. New Introduction by
 W. M. Parker, M.A.   137
 QUENTIN DURWARD, 1823. A tale of adventures in fifteenth-century France. New
 Introduction by *W. M. Parker*, M.A.   140
 REDGAUNTLET, 1824. A tale of adventure in Cumberland, about 1763. New Intro-
 duction by *W. M. Parker*, M.A.   141
 ROB ROY, 1818. A romance of the Rebellion of 1715.   142
 THE TALISMAN, 1825. Richard Cœur-de-Lion and the Third Crusade, 1191. New
 Preface by *W. M. Parker*, M.A.   (*See also* Biography.) 144
Shchedrin (M. E. Saltykov, 1826–92).
 THE GOLOVLYOV FAMILY. Translated by *Natalie Duddington*. Introduction by
 Edward Garnett.   908
Shelley, Mary Wollstonecraft (1797–1851).
 FRANKENSTEIN, 1818. With Mary Shelley's own Preface.   616
Shorter Novels.
 Vol. I: ELIZABETHAN. Introduction by *George Saintsbury* and Notes by *Philip
 Henderson*. Contains: Deloney's 'Jack of Newberie' and 'Thomas of Reading';
 Nashe's 'The Unfortunate Traveller'; Green's 'Carde of Fancie.'   824

VOL. II: SEVENTEENTH CENTURY. Edited, with Introduction, by *Philip Henderson*.
Contains: Emanuel Ford's 'Ornatus and Artesia'; Aphra Behn's 'Oroonoko';
Neville's 'The Isle of Pines'; Congreve's 'Incognita.'   841
Vol. III: EIGHTEENTH CENTURY. Edited, with Introduction, by *Philip Henderson*.
Contains: Beckford's 'Vathek'; Horace Walpole's 'The Castle of Otranto'; Dr
Johnson' 'Rasselas.'   856

Sienkiewicz, Henryk (1846–1916).
QUO VADIS? 1896. Translated by *C. J. Hogarth*. Intro. by *Monica Gardner*.   970
TALES. Edited, with Introduction, by *Monica Gardner*.   871

Smollett, Tobias (1721–71).
THE EXPEDITION OF HUMPHRY CLINKER, 1771. Introduction by *Howard Mumford
Jones*, and 36 pages of Notes by *Charles Lee*.   975
PEREGRINE PICKLE, 1751. Introduction by *Walter Allen*. 2 vols.   838–9
RODERICK RANDOM, 1742. Introduction by *H. W. Hodges*.   790

Somerville, E. Œ. (1858–1949), and **Ross, Martin** (pseudonym of Violet Florence
Martin, 1862–1915).
EXPERIENCES OF AN IRISH R.M. Contains the authors' two books, *Some Experiences
of an Irish R.M.*, 1897, and *Further Experiences of an Irish R.M.*, 1908.   978

Stendhal (pseudonym of Henri Beyle, 1783–1842).
SCARLET AND BLACK, 1831. Translated by *C. K. Scott Moncrieff*. Introduction by
Prof. F. C. Green, M.A., DR.PHIL. 2 vols.   945–6

Sterne, Laurence (1713–68).
TRISTRAM SHANDY, 1760–7. Intro. by *George Saintsbury*.   (See also Essays.) 617

Stevenson, Robert Louis (1850–94).
DR JEKYLL AND MR HYDE, 1886; THE MERRY MEN, 1887; WILL O' THE MILL,
1878; MARKHEIM, 1886; THRAWN JANET, 1881; OLALLA, 1885; THE TREASURE
OF FRANCHARD. Introduction by *M. R. Ridley*.   767
THE MASTER OF BALLANTRAE, 1889; WEIR OF HERMISTON, 1896. New Introduction
by *M. R. Ridley*.   764
ST IVES, 1898. Completed by Sir Arthur Quiller-Couch. Introduction (1958) by
M. R. Ridley.   904
TREASURE ISLAND, 1883; and KIDNAPPED, 1886. Introduction by *Sir Arthur
Quiller-Couch*.   (See also Essays, Poetry, Travel.) 763
Story Book for Boys and Girls. Edited by *Guy Pocock* (1955).   934

Surtees, Robert Smith (1803–64).
JORROCKS'S JAUNTS AND JOLLITIES, 1838.   817

Swift, Jonathan (1667–1745).
GULLIVER'S TRAVELS, 1726. An unabridged edition; with an Introduction by *Sir
Harold Williams*, F.B.A., F.S.A., M.A.   (See also Biography, Essays.) 60
Tales of Detection. Introduction by *Dorothy L. Sayers*. Nineteen stories, tracing the
development of the genuine detective story during the last hundred years.   928

Thackeray, William Makepeace (1811–63).
HENRY ESMOND, 1852. Introduction by *Walter Jerrold*.   73
THE NEWCOMES, 1853–5. 2 vols. Introduction by *Walter Jerrold*.   465–6
PENDENNIS, 1848–50. 2 vols. Introduction by *M. R. Ridley*, M.A.   425–6
VANITY FAIR, 1847–8. Introduction by *Hon. Whitelaw Reid*.   298
THE VIRGINIANS, 1857–9. 2 vols. Introduction by *Walter Jerrold*.   507–8
(See also Essays and Belles-Lettres.)

Tolstoy, Count Leo (1828–1910).
ANNA KARENINA, 1873–7. Translated by *Rochelle S. Townsend*. With Introduction
by *Nikolay Andreyev*, PH.D., M.A. 2 vols.   612–13
MASTER AND MAN, 1895; and OTHER PARABLES AND TALES. Introduction (1958)
by *Nikolay Andreyev*, PH.D., M.A.   469
WAR AND PEACE, 1864–9. Introduction by *Vicomte de Vogüé*. 3 vols.   525–7

Trollope, Anthony (1815–82).
THE WARDEN, 1855. The first of the 'Chronicles of Barset.' Introduction by
Kathleen Tillotson, M.A., B.LITT.   182
BARCHESTER TOWERS, 1857. The second of the 'Chronicles of Barset.' Introduction
(1956) on Anthony Trollope's 'Clergy' by *Michael Sadleir*.   30
DOCTOR THORNE, 1858. The third of the 'Chronicles of Barset.'   360
FRAMLEY PARSONAGE, 1861. The fourth of the 'Chronicles of Barset.' Introduction
by *Kathleen Tillotson*.   181
THE SMALL HOUSE AT ALLINGTON, 1864. The fifth of the 'Chronicles of Barset.' 361
THE LAST CHRONICLE OF BARSET, 1867. 2 vols.   391–2

Turgenev, Ivan (1818–83).
FATHERS AND SONS, 1862. Translated by *Dr Avril Pyman*.   742
SMOKE, 1867. A new translation, with Introduction, by *Natalie Duddington*.   988
VIRGIN SOIL, 1877. Translated by *Rochelle S. Townsend*.   528

Twain, Mark (pseudonym of Samuel Langhorne Clemens, 1835–1910).
TOM SAWYER, 1876; and HUCKLEBERRY FINN, 1884. Introduction by *Christopher
Morley*.   976

Verne, Jules (1828–1905).
FIVE WEEKS IN A BALLOON, 1862, translated by *Arthur Chambers*; and AROUND
THE WORLD IN EIGHTY DAYS, translated by *P. Desages*.   779
TWENTY THOUSAND LEAGUES UNDER THE SEA, 1869.   319

Voltaire, François Marie Arouet de (1694–1778).
   CANDIDE, AND OTHER TALES. Smollett's translation, edited by *J. C. Thornton.* 936
                                         (*See also* History.)
Walpole, Hugh Seymour (1884–1941).
   MR PERRIN AND MR TRAILL, 1911.   918
Wells, Herbert George (1866–1946).
   ANN VERONICA, 1909. Introduction by *A. J. Hoppé.*   997
   THE WHEELS OF CHANCE, 1896; and THE TIME MACHINE, 1895.   915
Wilde, Oscar.
   THE PICTURE OF DORIAN GRAY, 1891.   (*See* Poetry and Drama.)
Woolf, Virginia (1882–1941).
   TO THE LIGHTHOUSE, 1927. Introduction by *D. M. Hoare,* PH.D.   949
Zola, Émile (1840–1902).
   GERMINAL, 1885. Translated, with an Introduction, by *Havelock Ellis.*   897

HISTORY

Anglo-Saxon Chronicle. Translated and Edited by *G. N. Garmonsway,* F.R.HIST.SOC.
   Foreword by *Prof. Bruce Dickins.*   624
Bede, the Venerable (673–735).
   THE ECCLESIASTICAL HISTORY OF THE ENGLISH NATION. Translated by *John
   Stevens,* revised by *J. A. Giles,* with notes by *L. C. Jane.* Introduction by *Prof.
   David Knowles,* O.S.B., M.A., LITT.D., F.B.A., F.S.A.   479
Carlyle, Thomas (1795–1881).
   THE FRENCH REVOLUTION, 1837. Introduction by *Hilaire Belloc.* 2 vols.   31–2
                          (*See also* Biography, Essays.)
Chesterton, Cecil (1879–1918). A HISTORY OF THE U.S.A., 1917. Edited by *Prof. D. W.
   Brogan,* M.A.   965
Creasy, Sir Edward (1812–78).
   FIFTEEN DECISIVE BATTLES OF THE WORLD, FROM MARATHON TO WATERLOO, 1852.
   With Diagrams and Index. New Introduction by *Audrey Butler,* M.A. (OXON.).   300
Gibbon, Edward (1737–94).
   THE DECLINE AND FALL OF THE ROMAN EMPIRE, 1776–88. Notes by *Oliphant
   Smeaton.* Intro. by *Christopher Dawson.* Complete text in 6 vols.   434–6, 474–6
Green, John Richard (1837–83).
   A SHORT HISTORY OF THE ENGLISH PEOPLE, 1874. Introduction by *L. C. Jane.*
   English history from 607 to 1873. Continued by: 'A Political and Social Survey
   from 1815 to 1915,' by *R. P. Farley,* and revised to 1950.   727–8
Holinshed, Raphael (*d.* 1580 ?).
   HOLINSHED'S CHRONICLE AS USED IN SHAKESPEARE'S PLAYS, 1578. Introduction by
   Prof. Allardyce Nicoll and *Josephine Nicoll.*   800
Joinville, Jean de. *See* Villehardouin.
Lützow, Count Franz von (1849–1916).
   BOHEMIA: AN HISTORICAL SKETCH, 1896. Introduction by *President T. G. Masaryk.*
   H. A. Piehler covers events from 1879 to 1938.   432
Macaulay, Thomas Babington, Baron (1800–59).
   THE HISTORY OF ENGLAND. The complete text in four volumes, which together
   contain 2,450 pages. Introduction by *Douglas Jerrold.*   34–7
                             (*See also* Essays.)
Maine, Sir Henry (1822–88).
   ANCIENT LAW, 1861. Introduction by *Prof. J. H. Morgan.*   734
Mommsen, Theodor (1817–1903).
   HISTORY OF ROME, 1856. Translated by *W. P. Dickson,* LL.D. Introduction by
   Edward A. Freeman. 4 vols. (Vols. III and IV only.)   544–5
Motley, John (1814–77).
   THE RISE OF THE DUTCH REPUBLIC, 1856. Intro. by *V. R. Reynolds.* 3 vols.   86–8
Paston Letters, The, 1418–1506. 2 vols. A selection.   752–3
Prescott, William Hickling (1796–1859).
   HISTORY OF THE CONQUEST OF MEXICO, 1843. 2 vols.   397–8
Stanley, Arthur (1815–81).
   LECTURES ON THE HISTORY OF THE EASTERN CHURCH, 1861. Introduction by *A. J.
   Grieve,* M.A.   251
Thierry, Augustin (1795–1856).
   THE NORMAN CONQUEST, 1825. Introduction by *J. A. Price,* B.A. 2 vols. (*Vol. I
   temporarily out of print.*)   198–9
Villehardouin, Geoffrey de (1160 ?–1213 ?), and **Joinville, Jean, Sire de** (1224–1317).
   MEMOIRS OF THE CRUSADES. Translated, with an Introduction, by *Sir Frank T.
   Marzials.*   333
Voltaire, François Marie Arouet de (1694–1778).
   THE AGE OF LOUIS XIV, 1751. Translation by *Martyn P. Pollack.*
                          (*See also* Fiction.) 780

ORATORY

British Orations. The 1960 edition of this selection of British historical speeches contains selections from four of the most famous of Sir Winston Churchill's World War II speeches. 714

Burke, Edmund (1729–97).
SPEECHES AND LETTERS ON AMERICAN AFFAIRS. New Introduction by the *Very Rev. Canon Peter McKevitt*, PH.D. (*See also* Essays and Belles-Lettres.) 340

Demosthenes (384–322 B.C.).
THE CROWN, AND OTHER ORATIONS. Translated with an Appendix on Athenian economics by *C. Rann Kennedy*. Introduction by *John Warrington*. 546

Lincoln, Abraham (1809–65).
SPEECHES AND LETTERS, 1832–65. A new selection edited with an Introduction by *Paul M. Angle*. Chronology of Lincoln's life and index. 206

POETRY AND DRAMA

Anglo-Saxon Poetry. English poetry between A.D. 650 and 1000, from 'Widsith' and 'Beowulf' to the battle-pieces of 'Brunanburh' and 'Maldon.' Selected and translated by *Prof. R. K. Gordon*, M.A. Reset, and revised by the translator, 1954. 794

Arnold, Matthew (1822–88).
COMPLETE POEMS. Introduction by *R. A. Scott-James*. 334

Ballads, A Book of British. Introduction and Notes by *R. Brimley Johnson*. Ballads from the earliest times to those of Yeats and Kipling. 572

Beaumont, Francis (1584–1616), and Fletcher, John (1579–1625).
SELECT PLAYS. Introduction by *Prof. G. P. Baker*. 'The Knight of the Burning Pestle,' 'The Maid's Tragedy,' 'A King and No King,' 'The Faithful Shepherdess.' 'The Wild Goose Chase,' 'Bonduca,' with a glossary. 506

Blake, William (1757–1827).
POEMS AND PROPHECIES. Edited, with special Introduction, by *Max Plowman*. 792

Brontë, Emily.
POEMS. (*See* Fiction.)

Browning, Robert (1812–89).
POEMS AND PLAYS, 1833–64. With a new Introduction by *John Bryson*, M.A., dealing with the four-volume Everyman Browning set. 2 vols. Volume III, containing *The Ring and the Book*, Browning's long dramatic poem (No. 502), is temporarily out of print. 41–2
POEMS, 1871–90. Introduction by *M. M. Bozman*. 964

Burns, Robert (1759–96).
POEMS AND SONGS. A very full selection and a very accurate text of Burns's copious lyrical output. Edited and introduced by *Prof. James Kinsley*, M.A., PH.D. 94
(*See also* Biography.)

Byron, George Gordon Noel, Lord (1788–1824).
THE POETICAL AND DRAMATIC WORKS. 3 vols. Edited with a Preface by *Guy Pocock*.
(*See also* Biography.) 486–8

Century. A CENTURY OF HUMOROUS VERSE, 1850–1950. Edited by *Roger Lancelyn Green*, M.A., B.LITT. 813

Chaucer, Geoffrey (*c.* 1343–1400).
CANTERBURY TALES. New standard text edited by *A. C. Cawley*, M.A., PH.D., based on the Ellesmere Manuscript, with an ingenious system of glosses, page by page. 307
TROILUS AND CRISEYDE. Prepared by *John Warrington* from the Campsall Manuscript. 992

Coleridge, Samuel Taylor (1772–1834).
THE GOLDEN BOOK. (*See also* Essays, etc.) 43

Cowper, William (1731–1800).
POEMS. Intro. by *Hugh I'Anson Fausset*. (*See also* Biography.) 872

Dante Alighieri (1265–1321).
THE DIVINE COMEDY, first printed 1472. H. F. Cary's Translation, 1805–14. Edited, with Notes and Index, by *Edmund Gardner*. Foreword by *Prof. Mario Praz*. 308

De la Mare, Walter (1873–1956). (*See* Essays.)

Donne, John (1573–1631).
COMPLETE POEMS. Edited, with a revised Intro., by *Hugh I'Anson Fausset*. 867

Dryden, John (1631–1700).
POEMS. Edited by *Bonamy Dobrée*, O.B.E., M.A. 910

Eighteenth-century Plays. Edited by *John Hampden*. Includes Gay's 'Beggar's Opera,' Addison's 'Cato,' Rowe's 'Jane Shore,' Fielding's 'Tragedy of Tragedies; or, Tom Thumb the Great,' Lillo's 'George Barnwell,' Colman and Garrick's 'Clandestine Marriage,' and Cumberland's 'West Indian.' 818

English Galaxy of Shorter Poems, The. Chosen and Edited by *Gerald Bullett*. 959

English Religious Verse. Edited by *G. Lacey May*. An anthology from the Middle Ages to the present day, including some 300 poems by 150 authors. 937

Everyman, and Medieval Miracle Plays. New edition edited by *A. C. Cawley*, M.A., PH.D. Forewords to individual plays. 381

Fitzgerald, Edward (1809–83). *See* 'Persian Poems.'

Fletcher, John (1579–1625). *See* Beaumont.

Ford, John (1586–1639). *See* Webster.

Goethe, Johann Wolfgang von (1749–1832).
FAUST. Both parts of the tragedy which are the core of Goethe's life-work, in the re-edited translation of *Sir Theodore Martin*. (*See also* Biography, Essays.) 335

Golden Book of Modern English Poetry, The. Edited by *Thomas Caldwell* and *Philip Henderson*, containing some 300 poems by 130 poets, from T. E. Brown to Stephen Spender and C. Day Lewis. 921

Golden Treasury of English Songs and Lyrics, The, 1861. Compiled by Francis Turner Palgrave (1824–97). Enlarged edition, containing 88-page supplement. 96

Golden Treasury of Longer Poems, The. Revised edition (1954) with new supplementary poems. An anthology ranging from Chaucer to Walter de la Mare. 746

Goldsmith, Oliver (1728–74).
POEMS AND PLAYS. Edited, with Introduction, by *Austin Dobson*. 415
(*See also* Fiction.)

Gray, Thomas (1716–71).
POEMS: WITH A SELECTION OF LETTERS AND ESSAYS. Introduction by *John Drinkwater*, and biographical notes by *Lewis Gibbs*. 628

Heine, Heinrich (*c.* 1797–1856).
PROSE AND POETRY. With Matthew Arnold's essay on Heine. 911

Ibsen, Henrik (1828–1906).
A DOLL'S HOUSE, 1879; THE WILD DUCK, 1884; and THE LADY FROM THE SEA. 1888. Translated by *R. Farquharson Sharp* and *Elanor Marx-Aveling*. 494
GHOSTS, 1881; THE WARRIORS AT HELGELAND, 1857; and AN ENEMY OF THE PEOPLE, 1882. Translated by *R. Farquharson Sharp*. 552
PEER GYNT, 1867. Translated by *R. Farquharson Sharp*. 747
THE PRETENDERS, 1864; PILLARS OF SOCIETY, 1877; and ROSMERSHOLM, 1887. Translated by *R. Farquharson Sharp*. 659

Ingoldsby Legends, or *Mirth and Marvels*, by 'Thomas Ingoldsby, Esq.' Edited by *D. C. Browning*, M.A., B.LITT. 185

International Modern Plays. August Strindberg's 'Lady Julie,' Gerhard Hauptmann's 'Hannele,' Brothers Čapek's 'The Life of the Insects,' Jean Cocteau's 'The Infernal Machine,' and Luigi Chiarelli's 'The Mask and the Face.' Introduction by *Anthony Dent*. 989

Jonson, Ben (1573–1637).
PLAYS. Introduction by *Prof. F. E. Schelling*. 2 vols. Complete collection. 489–90

Keats, John (1795–1821).
POEMS. Revised, reset edition (1944). Edited by *Gerald Bullett*. 101
(*See also* Biography.)

Kingsley, Charles (1819–75).
POEMS. With Introduction by *Ernest Rhys*. (*See also* Fiction.) 793

La Fontaine, Jean de (1621–95).
FABLES, 1668. Presented complete in the renowned Sir Edward Marsh translation. 991

'Langland, William' (1330?–1400?).
PIERS PLOWMAN, 1362. Translation into modern English by *Donald* and *Rachel Attwater*. 571

Lawrence, David Herbert (1885–1930). (*See* Essays.)

Lessing, Gotthold Ephraim (1729–81).
LAOCOÖN, 1766, AND OTHER WRITINGS. Introduction by *W. A. Steel*. Contents: 'Laocoön'; 'Minna von Barnhelm,' 1767, a comedy in five acts; and 'Nathan the Wise,' 1779, his philosophical drama. 843

Longfellow, Henry Wadsworth (1807–82).
POEMS, 1823–66. 382

Marlowe, Christopher (1564–93).
PLAYS AND POEMS. New edition with an Introduction by *M. R. Ridley*, M.A. 383

Milton, John (1608–74).
POEMS. New edition by *Prof. B. A. Wright*, M.A., based on Milton's editions and manuscripts. With a new Introduction by *Prof. Wright*. (*See also* Essays.) 384

Minor Elizabethan Drama. 2 vols. Vol. I. Tragedy. Norton and Sackville's 'Gorboduc,' Kyd's 'Spanish Tragedy,' Peele's 'David and Bethsabe,' and 'Arden of Feversham.' Vol. II. Comedy. Udall's 'Ralph Roister Doister,' Lyly's 'Endimion,' Peele's 'Old Wives' Tale,' Greene's 'Friar Bacon and Friar Bungay,' etc. Introduction by *Prof. A. Thorndike*. Glossary. 491–2

Minor Poets of the Seventeenth Century. The Poems of Thomas Carew, Sir John Suckling, Lord Herbert, Richard Lovelace. Edited and revised by *R. G. Howarth*, B.A., B.LITT., F.R.S.L. 873

Modern Plays. R. C. Sherriff's 'Journey's End,' W. Somerset Maugham's 'For Services Rendered,' Noel Coward's 'Hay Fever,' A. A. Milne's 'The Dover Road,' Arnold Bennett and Edward Knoblock's 'Milestones.' Introduction by *John Hadfield*. 942.

Molière, Jean Baptiste de (1622–73).
COMEDIES. Introduction by *Prof. F. C. Green*. 2 vols. 830–1

New Golden Treasury, The. Introduction by *Ernest Rhys*. A companion to Palgrave (q.v.), giving earlier lyrics than he did, and also later. 695

Omar Khayyám (*d.* 1123?). (*See under* Persian Poems.)

Palgrave, Francis Turner (1824–97). *See* 'Golden Treasury of English Songs and Lyrics, The.'   96
Persian Poems. Selected and edited by *Prof. A. J. Arberry*, M.A., LITT.D., F.B.A. 996
Poe, Edgar Allan (1809–49).
    POEMS AND ESSAYS. Introduction by *Andrew Lang.*   (*See also* Fiction.) 791
Poems of our Time. An Anthology edited by *Richard Church*, C.B.E., *M. M. Bozman* and *Edith Sitwell*, D.LITT., D.B.E. Nearly 400 poems by about 130 poets.   981
Pope, Alexander (1688–1744).
    COLLECTED POEMS. Edited with Intro. (1956) by *Prof. Bonamy Dobrée*, O.B.E., M.A. 760
Restoration Plays. Introduction by *Edmund Gosse.* Includes Dryden's 'All for Love,' Wycherley's 'The Country Wife,' Congreve's 'The Way of the World,' Otway's 'Venice Preserved,' Farquhar's 'Beaux-Stratagem,' Vanbrugh's 'Provoked Wife.' Etherege's 'Man of Mode.'   604
Rossetti, Dante Gabriel (1828–82).
    POEMS AND TRANSLATIONS. Introduction by *E. G. Gardner.*   627
Shakespeare, William (1564–1616).
    A Complete Edition, based on Clark and Wright's Cambridge text, and edited by *Oliphant Smeaton.* With biographical Introduction, Chronological Tables and full Glossary. 3 vols.
          Comedies, 153; Histories, Poems and Sonnets, 154; Tragedies, 155
Shelley, Percy Bysshe (1792–1822).
    POETICAL WORKS. Introduction by *A. H. Koszul.* 2 vols.   257–8
Sheridan, Richard Brinsley (1751–1816).
    COMPLETE PLAYS. Introduction and notes by *Lewis Gibbs.*   95
Silver Poets of the Sixteenth Century. Edited by *Gerald Bullett.* The works of Sir Thomas Wyatt (1503–42), Henry Howard, Earl of Surrey (1517 ?–47), Sir Philip Sidney (1554–86), Sir Walter Ralegh (1552–1618) and Sir John Davies (1569–1626.)   985
Spenser, Edmund (1552–99).
    THE FAERIE QUEENE. Introduction by *Prof. J. W. Hales*, and Glossary. 2 vols. The reliable Morris text and glossary are used for this edition.   443–4
    THE SHEPHERD'S CALENDAR, 1579; and OTHER POEMS. Introduction by *Philip Henderson.*   879
Stevenson, Robert Louis (1850–94).
    POEMS. A CHILD'S GARDEN OF VERSES, 1885; UNDERWOODS, 1887; SONGS OF TRAVEL, 1896; and BALLADS, 1890, Introduction by *Ernest Rhys.*   768
          (*See also* Essays, Fiction, Travel.)
Swinburne, Algernon Charles (1837–1909).
    POEMS AND PROSE. A selection, edited with an Intro. by *Richard Church.*   961
Synge, J. M. (1871–1909).
    PLAYS, POEMS AND PROSE. Introduction by *Michaél Mac Liammóir.*   968
Tchekhov, Anton (1860–1904).
    PLAYS AND STORIES. 'The Cherry Orchard,' 'The Seagull,' 'The Wood Demon,' 'Tatyana Riepin' and 'On the Harmfulness of Tobacco' are included, as well as 13 of his best stories. The translation is by *S. S. Koteliansky.* Introduction by *David Magarshack.*   941
Tennyson, Alfred, Lord (1809–92).
    POEMS. A comprehensive edition (1950), with an Introduction by *Mildred Bozman.* 2 vols.   44, 626
Twenty-four One-Act Plays. Enlarged edition, new Introduction by *John Hampden.* Contains plays by T. S. Eliot, Sean O'Casey, Laurence Housman, W. B. Yeats, James Bridie, Noel Coward, Lord Dunsany, Wolf Mankowitz and others.   947
Webster, John (1580 ?–1625 ?), and **Ford, John** (1586–1639).
    SELECTED PLAYS. Introduction by *Prof. G. B. Harrison*, M.A., PH.D. In one volume: 'The White Devil,' 'The Duchess of Malfi,' 'The Broken Heart,' ' 'Tis Pity She's a Whore.'   899
Whitman, Walt (1819–92).
    LEAVES OF GRASS, 1855–92. New edition (1947) by *Dr Emory Holloway.*   573
Wilde, Oscar (1854–1900).
    PLAYS, PROSE WRITINGS, AND POEMS. Edited, with Introduction, by *Hesketh Pearson.* Including the two plays, 'The Importance of Being Earnest' and 'Lady Windermer's Fan'; his novel, 'The Picture of Dorian Gray'; the poem, 'The Ballad of Reading Gaol'; the essay, 'The Soul of Man,' etc.   858
Wordsworth, William (1770–1850).
    POEMS. Edited, with Introductory study, notes, bibliography and full index, by *Philip Wayne*, M.A.   203, 311, 998

REFERENCE

Reader's Guide to Everyman's Library. Compiled by *A. J. Hoppé.* This volume is a new compilation and gives in one alphabetical sequence the names of all the authors, titles and subjects in Everyman's Library and its supplementary series, Everyman's Reference Library and the Children's Illustrated Classics.   889
    Many volumes formerly included in Everyman's Library reference section are now included in Everyman's Reference Library and are bound in larger format.

ROMANCE

Aucassin and Nicolette, with other Medieval Romances. Translated, with Introduction, by *Eugene Mason.* 497

Boccaccio, Giovanni (1313–75).
DECAMERON, 1471. Translated by *J. M. Rigg*, 1903. Introduction by *Edward Hutton*, 2 vols. Unabridged. 845–6

Bunyan, John (1628–88).
PILGRIM'S PROGRESS, Parts I and II, 1678–84. Reset edition. Introduction by *Prof. G. B. Harrison*, M.A., PH.D. *(See also* Theology and Philosophy.) 204

Cervantes, Saavedra Miguel de (1547–1616).
DON QUIXOTE DE LA MANCHA. Translated by *P. A. Motteux.* Notes by *J. G. Lockhart.* Introduction and supplementary Notes by *L. B. Walton*, M.A., B.LITT. 2 vols. 385–6

Chrétien de Troyes (fl. 12th cent.).
ARTHURIAN ROMANCES ('Erec et Enide'; 'Cligés'; 'Yvain' and 'Lancelot'). Translated into prose, with Introduction, notes and bibliography, by *William Wistar Comfort.* 698

Kalevala, or The Land of Heroes. Translated from the Finnish by W. F. Kirby. 2 vols. 259–60

Mabinogion, The. Translated with Introduction by *Thomas Jones*, M.A., D.LITT., and *Gwyn Jones*, M.A. 97

Malory, Sir Thomas (fl. 1400?–70).
LE MORTE D'ARTHUR. Introduction by *Sir John Rhys.* 2 vols. 45–6

Marie de France (12th century), LAYS OF, AND OTHER FRENCH LEGENDS. Eight of Marie's 'Lais' and two of the anonymous French love stories of the same period translated with an Introduction by *Eugene Mason.* 557

Njal's Saga. THE STORY OF BURNT NJAL (written about 1280–90). Translated from the Icelandic by *Sir G. W. Dasent* (1861). Introduction (1957) and Index by *Prof. Edward Turville-Petre*, B.LITT., M.A. 558

Rabelais, François (1494?–1553).
THE HEROIC DEEDS OF GARGANTUA AND PANTAGRUEL, 1532–5. Introduction by *D. B. Wyndham Lewis.* 2 vols. A complete unabridged edition of Urquhart and Motteux's translation, 1653–94. 826–7

SCIENCE

Boyle, Robert (1627–91).
THE SCEPTICAL CHYMIST, 1661. Introduction by *M. M. Pattison Muir.* 559

Darwin, Charles (1809–82).
THE ORIGIN OF SPECIES, 1859. The sixth edition embodies Darwin's final additions and revisions. New Introduction (1956) by *W. R. Thompson*, F.R.S. 811
(See also Travel and Topography.)

Eddington, Arthur Stanley (1882–1944).
THE NATURE OF THE PHYSICAL WORLD, 1928. Introduction by *Sir Edmund Whittaker*, F.R.S., O.M. 922

Euclid (fl. *c.* 330–*c.* 275 B.C.).
THE ELEMENTS OF EUCLID. Edited by *Isaac Todhunter*, with Introduction by *Sir Thomas L. Heath*, K.C.B., F.R.S. 891

Faraday, Michael (1791–1867).
EXPERIMENTAL RESEARCHES IN ELECTRICITY, 1839–55. With Plates and Diagrams, and an appreciation by *Prof. John Tyndall.* 576

Harvey, William (1578–1657).
THE CIRCULATION OF THE BLOOD. Introduction by *Ernest Parkyn.* 262

Howard, John (1726?–90).
THE STATE OF THE PRISONS, 1777. Intro. and Notes by *Kenneth Ruck.* 835

Marx, Karl (1818–83).
CAPITAL, 1867. Translated by *Eden* and *Cedar Paul.* 2 vols. Introduction by *Prof. G. D. H. Cole.* 848–9

Mill, John Stuart (1806–73). *See* Wollstonecraft.

Owen, Robert (1771–1858).
A NEW VIEW OF SOCIETY, 1813; and OTHER WRITINGS. Introduction by *G. D. H. Cole.* 799

Pearson, Karl (1857–1936).
THE GRAMMAR OF SCIENCE, 1892. 939

Ricardo, David (1772–1823).
THE PRINCIPLES OF POLITICAL ECONOMY AND TAXATION, 1817. Introduction by *Prof. Michael P. Fogarty*, M.A. 590

Smith, Adam (1723–90).
THE WEALTH OF NATIONS, 1766. Intro. by *Prof. Edwin Seligman.* 2 vols. 412–13

White, Gilbert (1720–93).
A NATURAL HISTORY OF SELBORNE, 1789. New edition (1949). Introduction and Notes by *R. M. Lockley.* 48

Wollstonecraft, Mary (1759–97), THE RIGHTS OF WOMAN, 1792; and **Mill, John Stuart** (1806–73), THE SUBJECTION OF WOMEN, 1869. New Introduction by *Pamela Frankau.* 825

THEOLOGY AND PHILOSOPHY

Ancient Hebrew Literature. Being the Old Testament and Apocrypha, arranged by
R. Bruce Taylor. 4 vols. *Volumes I and IV only in print.* 253, 256

Bacon, Francis (1561–1626).
THE ADVANCEMENT OF LEARNING, 1605. Introduction, Notes, Index and Glossary,
by *G. W. Kitchin.* *(See also Essays.)* 719

Berkeley, George (1685–1753).
A NEW THEORY OF VISION, 1709. Introduction by *A. D. Lindsay*, C.B.E., LL.D. 483

Browne, Sir Thomas (1605–82).
RELIGIO MEDICI, 1642. New Introduction by *Halliday Sutherland*, M.D., F.R.S.L. 92

Bunyan, John (1628–88).
GRACE ABOUNDING, 1666; and THE LIFE AND DEATH OF MR BADMAN, 1658. Introduction by *Prof. G. B. Harrison*, M.A., PH.D. *(See also Romance.)* 815

Chinese Philosophy in Classical Times. Covering the period 1500 B.C.–A.D. 100. Edited
and translated, with Introduction and Notes. 973

Descartes, René (1596–1650).
A DISCOURSE ON METHOD, 1637; MEDITATIONS ON THE FIRST PHILOSOPHY, 1641;
and PRINCIPLES OF PHILOSOPHY, 1644. Translated by *Prof. J. Veitch.* Introduction
by *A. D. Lindsay*, C.B.E., LL.D. 570

Ellis, Havelock (1859–1939).
SELECTED ESSAYS. Sixteen essays, with an Introduction by *J. S. Collis.* 930

Gore, Charles (1853–1932).
THE PHILOSOPHY OF THE GOOD LIFE, 1930. 924

Hindu Scriptures. Edited by *Nicol Macnicol*, M.A., D.LITT., D.D. Foreword by *Rabindranath Tagore.* 944

Hobbes, Thomas (1588–1679).
LEVIATHAN, 1651. Introduction by *A. D. Lindsay*, C.B.E., LL.D. 691

Hooker, Richard (1554–1600).
OF THE LAWS OF ECCLESIASTICAL POLITY, 1597. Introduction by *G. C. Morris*, M.A. 201–2

Hume, David (1711–76).
A TREATISE OF HUMAN NATURE, 1739. Intro. by *A. D. Lindsay*, C.B.E., LL.D. 2 vols. 548–9

James, William (1842–1910).
PAPERS ON PHILOSOPHY. Introduction by *Prof. C. M. Bakewell.* 739

Kant, Immanuel (1724–1804).
CRITIQUE OF PURE REASON, 1781. With an Introduction by *A. D. Lindsay*, C.B.E.,
LL.D. Translated by *J. M. D. Meiklejohn.* 909

King Edward VI (1537–53).
THE FIRST (1549) AND SECOND (1552) PRAYER BOOKS. Introduction by *Bishop
Gibson.* 448

Koran, The. Rodwell's Translation, 1861. Intro. by *Rev. G. Margoliouth*, M.A. 380

Law, William (1686–1761).
A SERIOUS CALL TO A DEVOUT AND HOLY LIFE, 1728. Introduction by *Prof. Norman
Sykes*, F.B.A., M.A., D.PHIL. 91

Leibniz, Gottfried Wilhelm (1646–1716).
PHILOSOPHICAL WRITINGS. Selected and translated by *Mary Morris*, with an
Introduction by *C. R. Morris*, M.A. 905

Locke, John (1632–1704).
TWO TREATISES OF CIVIL GOVERNMENT, 1690. Introduction by *Prof. W. S. Carpenter.* *(See also Essays.)* 751

Malthus, Thomas Robert (1766–1834).
AN ESSAY ON THE PRINCIPLE OF POPULATION, 1798. New Introduction by *Prof.
Michael P. Fogarty*, M.A. 2 vols. 692–3

Mill, John Stuart (1806–73).
UTILITARIANISM, 1863; LIBERTY, 1859; and REPRESENTATIVE GOVERNMENT,
1861. Introduction by *A. D. Lindsay*, C.B.E., LL.D. *(See also Science.)* 482

More, Sir Thomas (1478–1535).
UTOPIA, 1516; and DIALOGUE OF COMFORT AGAINST TRIBULATION, 1553. Introduction by *John Warrington.* Revised edition (1951). 461

New Testament, The. 93

Newman, John Henry, Cardinal (1801–90).
APOLOGIA PRO VITA SUA, 1864. Introduction by *Sir John Shane Leslie.* 636
(See also Essays.)

Nietzsche, Friedrich Wilhelm (1844–1900).
THUS SPAKE ZARATHUSTRA, 1883–91. Translated by *Prof. A. Tille* and revised by
M. M. Bozman. Introduction (1957) by *Prof. Roy Pascal*, M.A., D.LITT. 892

Paine, Thomas (1737–1809).
RIGHTS OF MAN, 1792. Introduction by *Arthur Seldon.* 718

Pascal, Blaise (1623–62).
PENSÉES, 1670. Translated by *John Warrington.* Introduction by *Louis Lafuma.*
This translation is from Lafuma's second edition. 874

Ramayana and Mahabharata. Condensed into English verse by *Romesh Dutt*, C.I.E. 403

Robinson, Wade (1838–76).
THE PHILOSOPHY OF ATONEMENT, AND OTHER SERMONS, 1875. Introduction by
F. B. Meyer.   637
Rousseau, Jean Jacques (1712–78).
THE SOCIAL CONTRACT, 1762; and OTHER ESSAYS. Introduction by *G. D. H. Cole.*
(*See also* Biography, Essays.) 660
Saint Augustine (353–430).
CONFESSIONS. Dr Pusey's Translation, 1838, with Introduction by *A. H. Arm-
strong,* M.A.   200
THE CITY OF GOD. Complete text of John Healey's Elizabethan Translation, 1610.
Edited by *R. V. G. Tasker,* M.A., B.D., with an Introduction by *Sir Ernest Barker.*
2 vols.   982–3
Saint Francis (1182–1226).
THE LITTLE FLOWERS; THE MIRROR OF PERFECTION (by Leo of Assisi); and THE
LIFE OF ST FRANCIS (by St Bonaventura). Introduction by *Thomas Okey.*   485
Spinoza, Benedictus de (1632–77).
ETHICS, 1677; and ON THE CORRECTION OF THE UNDERSTANDING, 1687. Translated
by *Andrew Boyle.* New Introduction by *T. S. Gregory.*   481
Swedenborg, Emanuel (1688–1772).
THE TRUE CHRISTIAN RELIGION, 1771. New and unabridged translation by *F.
Bayley.* Introduction by *Dr Helen Keller.* 960 pages.   893
Thomas à Kempis (1380?–1471).
THE IMITATION OF CHRIST, 1471.   484
Thomas Aquinas (1225–74).
SELECTED WRITINGS. Selected and edited by *Father M. C. D'Arcy.*   953

TRAVEL AND TOPOGRAPHY

Borrow, George (1803–81).
THE BIBLE IN SPAIN, 1842. Introduction by *Edward Thomas.*   151
WILD WALES: the People, Language and Scenery, 1862. Introduction by *David
Jones,* C.B.E., the painter and Borrovian.   (*See also* Fiction.) 49
Boswell, James (1740–95).
JOURNAL OF A TOUR TO THE HEBRIDES WITH SAMUEL JOHNSON, 1786. Edited, with
a new Introduction, by *Lawrence F. Powell,* M.A., HON. D.LITT.   387
Calderón de la Barca, Mme (1804–82).
LIFE IN MEXICO, 1843. Introduction by *Manuel Romero De Terreros.*   664
Cobbett, William (1762–1835).
RURAL RIDES, 1830. Introduction by *Asa Briggs,* M.A., B.SC. 2 vols.   638–9
Cook, James (1728–79).
VOYAGES OF DISCOVERY. Edited by *John Barrow,* F.R.S., F.S.A. Introduction by
Guy Pocock, M.A.   99
Crèvecœur, J. Hector St John de (1735–1813).
LETTERS FROM AN AMERICAN FARMER, 1782. Intro. and Notes by *W. Barton Blake.*
640
Darwin, Charles (1809–82).
THE VOYAGE OF THE 'BEAGLE,' 1839.   (*See also* Science.) 104
Defoe, Daniel (1661?–1731).
A TOUR THROUGH ENGLAND AND WALES, 1724–6. Intro. by *G. D. H. Cole.* 2 vols.
(*See also* Fiction.) 820–1
Kinglake, Alexander (1809–91).
EOTHEN, 1844. Introduction by *Harold Spender.*   337
Lane, Edward William (1801–76).
MANNERS AND CUSTOMS OF THE MODERN EGYPTIANS, 1836. With a new Introduction
by *Moursi Saad el-Din,* of the Egyptian Ministry of Education.   315
Park, Mungo (1771–1806).
TRAVELS. Introduction (1954) by *Prof. Ronald Miller,* M.A., PH.D.   205
Polo, Marco (1254–1324).
TRAVELS. Introduction by *John Masefield.*   306
Portuguese Voyages, 1498–1663. Edited by *Charles David Ley.*   986
Stevenson, Robert Louis (1850–94).
AN INLAND VOYAGE, 1878; TRAVELS WITH A DONKEY, 1879; and THE SILVERADO
SQUATTERS, 1883. New Introduction by *M. R. Ridley,* M.A.   766
(*See also* Essays, Poetry, Fiction.)
Stow, John (1525?–1605).
THE SURVEY OF LONDON. The fullest account of Elizabethan London.   589
Wakefield, Edward Gibbon (1796–1862).
A LETTER FROM SYDNEY, AND OTHER WRITINGS ON COLONIZATION. Introduction
by *Prof. R. C. Mills.*   828
Waterton, Charles (1782–1865).
WANDERINGS IN SOUTH AMERICA, 1825. Introduction by *Edmund Selous.*   772